D1103838

Dig

Dig

SOUND AND MUSIC IN HIP CULTURE

PHIL FORD

OXFORD
UNIVERSITY PRESS

OXFORD
UNIVERSITY PRESS

Oxford University Press is a department of the University of Oxford.
It furthers the University's objective of excellence in research, scholarship,
and education by publishing worldwide.

Oxford   New York
Auckland   Cape Town   Dar es Salaam   Hong Kong   Karachi
Kuala Lumpur   Madrid   Melbourne   Mexico City   Nairobi
New Delhi   Shanghai   Taipei   Toronto

With offices in
Argentina   Austria   Brazil   Chile   Czech Republic   France   Greece
Guatemala   Hungary   Italy   Japan   Poland   Portugal   Singapore
South Korea   Switzerland   Thailand   Turkey   Ukraine   Vietnam

Oxford is a registered trade mark of Oxford University Press
in the UK and certain other countries.

Published in the United States of America by
Oxford University Press
198 Madison Avenue, New York, NY 10016

Library of Congress Cataloging-in-Publication Data
Ford, Phil, 1969–
Dig : sound and music in hip culture / Phil Ford.
pages   cm
Includes bibliographical references and index.
ISBN 978-0-19-993991-6 (hardback : alk. paper)   1. Popular music—
History and criticism.   2. Music—Social aspects.   I. Title.
ML3470.F68   2013
781.64—dc23   2013005947

10 9 8 7 6 5 4 3 2 1

Printed in the United States of America
on acid-free paper

For Clare Ford, my Mum

Acknowledgments

There is an esoteric book somewhere that lists the author as "The Interdependent Universe," and this seems pretty apt to me. The interdependent universe is the real author of every book: no book was ever written without the support of a thousand and one connections, large and small, between its author and everyone he or she encounters in the process of writing. But even though I could just thank the interdependent universe and call it a day, that would be no fun for anyone, since the point of the acknowledgments page is to provide pleasurable suspense to those who might plausibly find their names written therein—a suspense to be resolved either in the satisfaction afforded by seeing one's contribution noted or (more likely) in the disappointment of having been forgotten. To those soon to experience the latter, I am sincerely sorry. The interdependent universe is a big place and I have a poor memory, so it was bound to happen. Whether or not your name appears here, it is nevertheless true that if you have ever so much as suffered one of those hallway-ambush conversations for which I am known, you *deserve* to see your name here, and you have helped me in ways for which I am truly grateful.

Suzanne Ryan, my editor at Oxford, is the Good Fairy Godmother of Hip. From the moment in 2007 when she first listened to my idea for this book and then for the next five years as she waited for me to finish it, her faith and patience have allowed this project to take form and ripen. I am also grateful to her editorial assistant, Adam Cohen, and to the design and production staff at Oxford University Press.

I am especially grateful to my colleagues in the musicology department at the Indiana University Jacobs School of Music. Special thanks go to Peter Burkholder and Massimo Ossi, who as department chairs supported my research and guided me through my first years at IU; to Tina Muxfeldt, for her conversation; to Dan Melamed, for his shrewd advice; and to Michael Long, who read my work with sympathy and understanding. Halina Goldberg, Ayana Smith, and Giovanni Zanovello have all generously put up with the aforementioned hallway ambushes and generally brightened up the place with their good cheer. I would also like to thank Gwyn Richards, the dean of the Jacobs School of Music, whose grant of a semester course release gave me the time I needed when I needed it, and to the Indiana University Office of the Vice Provost for Research for the award of a Summer Research Fellowship.

My students at the Jacobs School have helped me forge and sharpen the ideas in this book. I owe a particular debt of gratitude to the participants of my "Sound, Music, Counterculture" seminar and my course "Process Music" (whatever that is). Dan Bishop, Kerry O'Brien, Jon Yaeger, and Alisa White have been invaluable interlocutors throughout my time at Indiana. Special thanks go to Carolyn Carrier McClimon, who found order in the chaos of Norman Mailer's draft manuscripts for "The White Negro," and to Joanna Helms, who assisted me with many aspects of this book's final formatting and editing.

This book originated in the research I did for my dissertation, whose flaws are entirely my fault and should reflect no discredit on the teachers with whom I was fortunate to work, especially Michael Cherlin, David Grayson, James Hepokoski, and Joel Weinsheimer. But I have always been fortunate in my teachers: the pianists Michel Block and Leonard Hokanson and the Zen teacher and translator Shohaku Okumura have contributed in other, less obvious ways to my development as a musician and a human being.

My first and best teachers, though, were my parents. Jay Ford's deep feeling for the written word and old-school ethic of humanist learning has always stood as a model of scholarly engagement to me. Clare Ford has been the greatest influence on my life. An unassuming person, she has taught me what it is to undertake large works and persevere in them; a gentle person, she has shown me what toughness really is. To her this book is dedicated.

This book owes its largest intellectual debt to art historian and curator Graham Larkin. When we were both fellows at the Stanford Humanities Fellows Program (then under the enlightened stewardship of Seth Lerer), Graham tipped me off to the significance of Marshall McLuhan, and our regular Chinese food truck conversations about McLuhan, media, and mediated presence led me to many of the basic insights of this book. Graham's meticulous and insightful reading of the book during and after its composition contributed many new ideas and saved me from a great many infelicities of prose.

Over the years, many friends have helped me write this book in countless direct and indirect ways. Thanks and warm affection go to Byron Almén, Jonathan Bellman, Elizabeth Bergman, Patrick Boley, Jim Buhler, Tim Dunne, Andy Flory, Heather Hadlock, John Howland, D. D. Jackson, David Brent Johnson, Richard Leppert, Mark and Jill Mazullo, and Albin Zak. I am also indebted to other scholars in the hip biz—Michael Szalay, Melissa Goldsmith, Joel Dinerstein, and especially Lee Konstantinou—who shared their work-in-progress with me.

I owe a special thank-you to Peggy Brooks, whose late husband, John, is the focus of this book's last chapter. She has been tremendously generous with her time, her memories, and her collection of John's scores, recordings, books, and letters. More than that, though, her support and encouragement of my work on John Benson Brooks is one of the greatest gifts I received in the course of writing this book. I also thank Don Heckman and Gunther Schuller for speaking to me about their work and friendship with Brooks, and to the late Robert Lucid for his encouragement of my work on Norman Mailer.

Securing copyright permissions is no one's idea of a good time, but on occasion it did allow me to make contact with the families of artists (and sometimes the artists themselves) whose work has been so meaningful to me over the course of writing this book. I would like especially to thank Gary and Laura Grimshaw, Charna Halpern, Danny Hellman, Mary Hicks, Serena Naeve, and Margo Shustak. Special thanks go to Naz Pantaloni, who contributed invaluable advice on securing copyright permission for the images, poems, song texts, musical examples, and archival materials that appear in this volume.

I would like to thank the librarians and staff at the Institute of Jazz Studies archives at Rutgers University at Newark, the Harry Ransom Center at the University of Texas at Austin, the Stanford University Special Collections, the Hoover Institution Library and Archives, the Lilly Library at Indiana University at Bloomington, the Kent State Special Collections and Archives, the University of Southern California Libraries Special Collections, the Bentley Historical Library at the University of Michigan, the Louis Round Wilson Special Collections Library at the University of North Carolina at Chapel Hill, and Bill Schurk at the Jerome Library at Bowling Green State University.

My wife, Helen Ford, is my best reader and a damn good editor. She is the brains of the outfit, and I cannot begin to do justice to her influence on every word in this book. I am deeply grateful to Helen's parents, Phil and Barbara Shively, and to my sister, Julia, for their constant love and support. Try as I might, I find I cannot avoid acknowledgment-page clichés, and it gets harder the nearer I get to the heart of my heart, my family. "I thank my wife for putting up with me" . . . "this book could never have been written without" . . . "words cannot express" . . . blah blah blah. But it turns out that some clichés are clichés because they are so obviously true. Helen and my children, Nicholas and Alice, did have a certain amount to put up with (absences while traveling for research, boring dinnertime lectures on magical hermeneutics, etc.); I never could have written this book without them; and words cannot express my gratitude and love.

Contents

Dig

DIG (an introduction)

Q: Mr. Geets Romo, how would you define "dig"?

A: Well you know man like when you dig something.

Q: Well yes, but...

A: Well dig, baby. It's like you know when you dig some chick or some cat? You know, when you pick up on something, you dig it, you dig?

Q: To "dig," then, would mean to like, to understand, or to appreciate....

A: Dig. It's like...no it's more like uh, in music, you dig? You know what is a quarter tone? Like you get a note in there between C and C sharp and that's its *own sound*, you know? I mean you can't call it C because it isn't. That's like dig. Dig means, dig. Like you don't dig, and you say "dig," I dig where you're at. Like, I'm the wrong cat, it's the wrong word, dig?

Q: Ladies and gentlemen, now you begin to see one of our problems with the hip language. Each hip word or phrase carries with it an implication of the speaker's background and his involvement with hip society. In other words, the phrase "I dig" not only means "I understand" but "I am a special sort of person who understands in a very special way."

A: Yeah, that is *exactly* what I said!

Q: In other words, I am hip.

A: Dig yourself baby, you got a ways to go.[1]

—Del Close and John Brent

Hipness resists thought. Although hip style is ubiquitous—as is our mingled hunger for and resentment of its prestige—it seems armored against inquiry, defying all attempts to regulate its meanings. Hipness cannot be understood in a distanced and analytical way, Geets Romo tells us, but must be felt and experienced. When Cannonball Adderley complimented his Village Vanguard audience for "being so really hip," he explained, "you get a lot of people who are supposed to be hip, and they act like they're *supposed to be hip*, which makes a big difference....You know, hipness is not a state of mind, it's a fact of life....You don't decide you're hip, it just happens that way."[2] Deciding you're hip is what LeRoi Jones (later Amiri Baraka) called "hipness as such," which means observing canons of hipster behavior, "initialing ideas which had currency in the circles, talking the prevailing talk, or walking the prevailing walk."[3] However, authentic hipness is won only when you engage in an intellectual or spiritual or artistic struggle for yourself, without anyone else to tell you what is hip. If you praise a Charlie Parker solo only because you think you should, your taste is mere social-climbing affectation; digging can only come from a resonance between the sound of the music and the texture of your own life. Parker's well-known line, "if you don't live it, it won't come out of your horn," is both a hip motto and a prescription for hip self-fashioning.[4] Digging isn't just liking, it's about getting involved.

If no one can tell you what is hip, then no one can tell anyone else, either. The obvious objection to any attempt at a study of hipness, then, runs something like this: hipness, by its very nature, resists definition, because it resists authority. Trying to analyze hip culture in order to extract the habits of mind or expressive tropes by which it is constituted is a grotesque violation of what hipness fundamentally is. Hipness is not an idea, style, or habit, but rather a stance toward the square, uptight, unfree world, renegotiated moment by moment as the individual deals with whatever that world might propose. Each individual is challenged to act—or not act—on an understanding of squareness or unfreedom in his or her own way. There are no rules to learn or loyalties to enforce. It is woven into the very fabric of hipness that it not offer itself up to analysis, and if it does somehow find itself analyzed, those items under examination would shrivel, losing whatever hip aura they might have had. There is something Heisenbergian about hip culture: observing it, we change it. This is the working problem of coolhunters, those fashion consultants who infiltrate city neighborhoods in which hip styles evolve in order to discover what the hip kids consider cool.[5] The difficulty coolhunters encounter is that although they can streamline how hip styles are processed into industrial manufacture, they can do nothing about what happens once they are brought to market. The hip kids who develop new styles abandon them once they are widely issued.[6] And so the coolhunter is forever running in circles, following the increasingly rapid cycles by which hip urban youth adopt and discard styles. The ever-escalating speed of obsolescence is a result of the success of modern market research. Hip styles, once they enter into mass awareness, are no longer hip styles.

And yet there are also clearly ways in which hipness is not just some ineffable and spontaneous expression of individual uniqueness. Whatever Cannonball Adderley says, hipness is *both* a way of life and a state of mind. By "state of mind" I mean an aesthetic, or better yet a sensibility; for more than half a century, the hip sensibility has structured self-understanding and self-representation, thought and expression, in various recognizable ways.[7] Certain ideas, images, critiques, and tropes of representation have recurred in hip culture since World War II, persistently shaping how people imagine themselves and their relationship to society. Hipness is not weightless; it leaves footprints. Its traces are made by artists and intellectuals, by the characteristic motions of personalities guided by hip sensibility, on the music and writing of the 1940s to the present. Further, those traces can be understood historically, and their cumulative pattern tells us something about the large motions of postwar American culture.

No sensibility can be reduced to ideas, but the vast constellation of feelings and imaginings that constitute hipness is structured around a central axis of what Thomas Frank calls the "countercultural idea." I define this as the idea that social existence is in a certain way unreal or unfree and is to be resisted by aesthetic creation, either of artworks or of the self. The countercultural idea is underwritten by a conception of the individual's alienation from society—alienation that is due not to any specific political wrong but to something more radical, a clash of consciousness and perception. It is not only that society fails to satisfy human needs; in dulling creativity, self-awareness, and self-expression, it does not even offer the basic conditions by which humans might find satisfaction. On this account, even if individuals think of themselves as free subjects, they are in fact treated as objects within a faceless and objective system, like rats caught in a laboratory maze.[8] The system is cunningly made, so that those inside it do not perceive it as a system at all.[9] And so the system does its work silently and invisibly, foreclosing the ways by which people might experience their true freedom. Those who live forgetfully within the system become assimilated to it, its forms replicating and metastasizing in their minds and souls. The idea of society as a "rat race" was a commonplace of midcentury social criticism; what gave it a hip flavor was the notion that the hipster was armed with a special kind of consciousness that allowed him to understand the maze in a distanced, ironic way.[10] He watched the other rats run after the cheese, which he knew to be an artifact of a constructed system, the prize for a game contrived by some anonymous, impersonal *them*—the Establishment, the System, the Man. Even if the hipster, too, found his own way to get the cheese, he knew it was a game all along. The hipster could represent a kind of evolutionary mutation: while all the other rats scrabbled around the inside of the maze, he was the first to get the idea of standing up and peering over its walls. He could not escape the maze, but he could see it *was* a maze. He was in it, but not of it. This is the fundamental orientation of hip consciousness: it is a binary orientation that maps the world into hip and square, somewhere and nowhere, with the hipster stuck in nowhere but always remapping it within the (imagined) frame of somewhere.

To the hipster, it is by means of culture that the system stamps individuals into a uniform square mold. A 1950s hipster might have named TV quiz shows and *Life* magazine as examples of this kind of co-opting culture; in 2013, it might be Fox News and reality TV. And so it is *culture* that becomes the medium of resistance rather than politics as such. Even though the term "counterculture" was not used until the late 1960s, the countercultural idea is well named, as it underwrites the tendency to construe dissent as the act of creating a culture counter to the mainstream.[11] Making counterculture means aesthetic cultivation, either of the self or of those things from which we might build a self—books, art, and especially music.

Nearly everyone who has ever considered the matter has taken it for granted that music is the royal road to hip: every hip subculture at least tags along with some kind of music, and for many subcultures music is their *raison d'être*. But hipness is wedded to music at an altogether deeper level. In hip culture it is sound itself, and the faculty of hearing by which sound becomes sensible, that is the privileged part of the sensorium. The reasons for this go to the heart of the countercultural idea's special kind of social critique and the particular historical situation of those midcentury intellectuals who transposed that critique into what Scott Saul has called a "new intellectual vernacular."[12]

Above all, postwar American intellectuals mistrusted the mass: mass society, mass culture, and mass movements, along with all the factions, bureaucracies, and ideologies that went with them. Many of them had lived through the Popular Front 1930s and witnessed the European regimes of politicized mass murder only to emerge into a new age of atomic mass death. Their collective mood was one of negation and apostasy: as Seymour Krim put it, in the early 1950s "everybody seemed to be an 'ex' something."[13] They could no longer accept old Socialist orthodoxies—nor yet could they quite accept the new American imperium. Cold War intellectuals announced, bemoaned, or yearned for an "end of ideology," but in any event they could not do without a critical distance from country and culture.[14] Criticism became a fraught enterprise: intellectuals are in the business of making statements and taking positions against whatever is taken for granted in art and politics, and yet it had come to seem as if any position, rigorously formulated and firmly held, would stiffen into the hard, unyielding forms of ideology. Intellectuals who came of age in the 1940s and 1950s sought the vocation of criticism, but not its forms; hipness fascinated them in part because it fulfilled the function of criticism while evading all concrete commitments and positions. And in any event, a commitment to mass culture critique made the hip stance of cultural disaffiliation not only attractive but perhaps even necessary. For young intellectuals in the 1950s, hipness was the right idea at the right time. Most obviously, it traded on the complex symbolic power of African American identity.[15] But it also provided the answer to Daniel Bell's question of whom young leftists were to attack when they no longer had the Popular Front's old roster of enemies:

> If [the democratic-socialist little magazine] *Dissent* has had a single unifying idea...it is its conceptualization of America as a *mass society,* and its attack on the grotesque elements of such a society. And here *Dissent* begins to merge in identity with *Universities and Left Review,* and other new voices of the Left which attack modern society. The concept of the *mass society,* however, has a peculiar amorphousness. Those who used

the older vocabulary of radicalism could attack "the capitalists" or even "the bourgeoisie," but in the *mass society* one simply flails out against "the culture," and it is hard to discover who, or what, is the enemy.[16]

To the younger dissenting intellectuals in the postwar era, it would increasingly seem that the enemy was not simply "the culture," but a mass culture shaped by a fatal abstraction of meaning from human experience.

Among LeRoi Jones's editorial files for *Yugen* and *Floating Bear,* two of the most influential Beat little magazines, there is a note from Gregory Corso congratulating Jones on his appearance in the landmark anthology *The New American Poetry.*[17] But Corso dismisses the "statements on poetics" that appeared in the last section of the book: "Don Allen's anthology a landmark—yr poems great and lovely—but yr statement & everybody's meaningless in that they are for ones-self, stational, and all stational things can be knocked down—once you take a position...All positions must be contradicted, else it's bullshit."[18]

Corso writes that "all stational things can be knocked down," and printed words, clotted into literary and political positions, are stational things. The mere act of asserting something in writing excludes the possibility of asserting something else, unless it follows in due sequence, and sequence in turn imposes a logic of its own. Language imposes fixity, linearity, one-sidedness and one-at-a-timeness on the moving, three-dimensional, multivalent, everything-at-once reality of lived experience. Written words flatten out reality, but sound carries it forth in all its fullness. John Benson Brooks, a jazz composer, autodidact philosopher, and compulsive diarist we will meet in Chapter 6, writes in one of his notebook entries that "a <u>word</u> is a to-some-extent-size collective snapshot of some thing—a <u>sound</u> is but a trace of something, or emission from its behavior."[19] For the intellectuals of postwar hip culture, sound was a medium for the energetic processes of life itself, a stencil from the real.[20] By getting in touch with the sounds of things, the writer could achieve a new kind of literary communication and make literature responsive to life in the concrete—life as it is lived by actual people at particular times and places. This new vocation for literature was justified not only on aesthetic grounds but on political and ethical ones as well. A commitment to sounded immediacies meant commitment to living a certain way of life and being a certain kind of person. By the same token, it meant resisting an abstraction of human experience and personality that lay at the root of a calamitous modernity.

At about the same time Corso wrote his note, Marshall McLuhan was beginning to publish his theories of how writing had displaced oral/aural communication:

The phonetic alphabet and all its derivatives stress a one-thing-at-a-time analytic awareness in perception. This intensity of analysis is achieved at the price of forcing all else in the field of perception into the subliminal. For 2500 years we have lived in what Joyce called "ABCED-mindedness." We win, as a result of this fragmenting of the field of perception and the breaking of movement into static bits, a power of applied knowledge and technology unrivalled in human history. The price we pay is existing personally and socially in a state of almost total subliminal awareness.[21]

By turning audible speech into visible marks on paper, Western culture transformed utterances from sounding events, experienced by real bodies in real spaces at real times, into weightless, placeless, timeless abstractions. All McLuhan's subsequent work was devoted to understanding how this fundamental abstraction from sound to sight, ear to eye, altered the psychodynamics of Western culture.[22] McLuhan suggests that this abstraction allowed Western societies to wield great power over the natural world, but that the Western subject, individualized by the experience of literacy, had lapsed into a vast insensibility. Sunk in his individuality, he was bound to linear thought, his experience starved of tactility and depth. His analytical fixed point of view had made private property, specialization, and bureaucratic management possible, but at the cost of alienation, conformity, nationalism, and militarism. McLuhan explained most of what had gone wrong in the past five hundred years as the result of eye dominance enforced by print. But he believed that "sense-ratios" were changing, that electronic media were beginning to give the West "an ear for an eye" and delivering it back into the tribal state of orality—a "secondary orality" made possible, paradoxically, by advanced literacy.[23]

McLuhan's ideas would later become the main theory by which the mass counterculture of the 1960s understood its historical moment. But his theories grew out of a strain of radical thought from the early postwar years that attacked the same abstraction of cognized meaning from lived experience. This assault was carried out by a broad front of artists and intellectuals working out a number of social and aesthetic problems within various traditions—poets like LeRoi Jones and Gregory Corso, novelists like Norman Mailer and Jack Kerouac, composers like Harry Partch and John Cage, anarchists like Dwight Macdonald and Paul Goodman, radical Freudians like Erich Fromm and Wilhelm Reich, religious intellectuals like D. T. Suzuki and Alan Watts, to say nothing of critics, philosophers, painters, sculptors, dancers, and dramaturges that together made what Daniel Belgrad has called "the culture of spontaneity."[24] Though many of these figures were concerned with abstraction as a problem of individual aesthetic experience, they also asked a larger question: What kind of society resulted from the abstraction and impoverishment of human experience, and how might art transform that society?

The figures we will encounter in this book include musicians—Cab Calloway, Miles Davis, Thelonious Monk, Charlie Parker, Lester Young, Lennie Tristano,

Fred Katz, Bob Dylan, and John Benson Brooks—as well as those who lie at the Venn-circle intersection between an emergent hip culture and the postwar generation of writer-intellectuals. These include Jones, Kerouac, and Mailer, plus others less well known, such as Dan Burley, Anatole Broyard, Seymour Krim, and John Clellon Holmes. The intellectual vernacular that grew out of their work challenged meaning with experience. Here *meaning* denotes that which is cognitive, abstract, placeless, and timeless; *experience,* by contrast, is embodied, concrete, and anchored in place and time.[25] Within the hip intellectual vernacular, music matters because it is made of sound, and sound matters because it is made and felt by bodies—bodies embedded in particular zones of space and time. When Kerouac and Mailer made a cause of the hip stance they saw in the streets and nightclubs they frequented, sound became the vessel of their quarrel with the abstract meanings of written words.[26]

The irony in all this is that no intellectual cohort had ever been more intoxicated by the written word. When Broyard titled one of his essay collections *Aroused by Books*, it was for good reason. When he looked back at his life, he saw books—books read throughout successive careers as a soldier, bookshop owner, freelance hipster intellectual, and reviewer, books read for pleasure and duty, books read in service of intellectual competitiveness and the project of hip self-fashioning in early postwar Greenwich Village:

> I realize that people still read books now and some people actually love them, but in 1946 in the Village our feelings about books—I'm talking about my friends and myself—went beyond love. It was as if we didn't know where we ended and books began. Books were our weather, our environment, our clothing. We didn't simply read books; we became them. We took them into ourselves and made them into our histories. While it would be easy to say that we escaped into books, it would be truer to say that books escaped into us. Books were to us what drugs were to young men in the sixties.[27]

Or perhaps it would be truer to say that books were what rock was to young men in the sixties. In the Allen Ginsberg Papers at Stanford University, there is a note from Carl Solomon responding to Allen Ginsberg's daydream of starting his own avant-garde little magazine. Solomon suggested the name *Effeminacy*: "Boy, how'd you like to walk into the Remo and hear people say, 'That cat's the editor of 'Effeminacy'?'"[28] This note, while undated, was written sometime in the 1950s; a decade later, the same sorts of people would have the same sorts of conversations about the names of the rock bands they dreamed of forming. Avant-garde little magazines like Jones's *Yugen* or Jay Landesman's *Neurotica* were the first institutional homes for the intellectual encounter with the hip sensibility. Their jumbles of poems, stories, essays, letters, manifestos, drawings, translations, satires, pranks, and literary miscellanea were ideal laboratories for the great experiment this book chronicles—that of fusing words and music, or, more broadly, verbalized ideas and a musical sensibility. It is entirely typical that the off-Broadway musical *The Nervous* Set (a satirical revue by, for, and about the Beats) was about a young man starting his own avant-garde literary review:

> Here comes Brad
> Welcome to the scene
> What's shakin', Dad
> With your magazine?[29]

And yet this mad love of words, pushed to its end point, reversed into its opposite, into an impatience and fury with the limitations of writing and a yearning to express what words cannot. McLuhan's idea of advanced literacy reversing into secondary orality seems less a prophecy than a simple observation, one not lost on McLuhan's 1960s counterculture readers, who imagined themselves as "primitives of an unknown culture" and rock music as the catalyst for the reappearance of a tribal society in which they might live.

Conservative intellectuals have always mistrusted hipness, in part because it can seem like an abandonment of the rational mind's responsibilities. Norman Podhoretz called the Beats "the know-nothing Bohemians"; Hilton Kramer mocked Susan Sontag's "strenuous flights of cerebration on behalf of ideas that promised deliverance from the tyranny of cerebration."[30] But Kramer's comment points to a problem that hip culture never overcame, and that scholars writing about it cannot overcome either. Cannonball Adderley wasn't wrong: from one point of view, hipness *is* a way of life—the full living out of a life whose form is identical to its process, which cannot be captured in writing any more than a waterfall can be kept in a bucket. Hipness first emerged in the 1930s as the dandified stance of young men in black urban neighborhoods. They left no records of themselves; while sometimes written about, they did not write. The great exception, *The Autobiography of Malcolm X*, is not a hipster's memoir but something different, a hostile recollection as if of another person entirely.[31] Jazz musicians didn't so much verbalize hipness as embody it: their music seemed to be saying something, but what it might be remained a riddle to the literary intellectuals who happened upon it.[32] In trying to solve that riddle, those intellectuals abstracted hipness, reified it, made it a public cause, and fitted it to those ideas with which it shared a family resemblance—Existentialism, Zen, Abstract Expressionism, Gestalt therapy, or anything else that might promise to liberate experience from merely intellectual understanding. Hipness emerged from subcultural isolation through the intercession of those for whom it was a state of mind they could cultivate and write about. Of course, for intellectuals to succeed in affirming experience against merely intellectual understanding, they needed to express themselves in ideas, couched in words.

In "Hip, Hell, and the Navigator," an interview with Norman Mailer published as a coda to "The White Negro" in *Advertisements for Myself,* Richard Stern immediately spotted the problem with using hipness as a basis for literature:

> The interesting thing about Hip is that Hip shouldn't belong to writers. If you're a genuine hipster you're committed, it seems to me, to a kind of anti-expressionism, Dada, or something like that. You're interested in the quality of the experience itself. If you're a sincere hipster you shouldn't be a writer.[33]

A related problem confronted Bernard Wolfe, a bohemian writer, sometime pornographer, and onetime assistant to Leon Trotsky who co-wrote the first book on hipness, *Really the Blues* (1946).[34] In an afterword to his hipster novel *The Magic of Their Singing* (1961), Wolfe considered the problem of representing hip speech within a crafted literary style:

> Very hip people will object that their brothers have been presented as speaking a broader, richer, more nuanced tongue than they in fact do. That is so. A more phonographic rendition of their somnambulistically flattened and laconic rhetoric would make it quite impossible to write books or, indeed, anything more sustained than a postcard: a novel developed around a vocabulary of twenty or thirty words must be repetitive to the point of schizophrenia.[35]

In a similar vein, the jazz writer and record producer Ross Russell wrote a letter to Harlan Ellison musing on the possibilities of the "jazz novel" and enumerating its many difficulties:

> The fact is a jazz novel is a tough kind of book to write. Evidence: the importance of the music contrasted with the rather large number of unsuccessful jazz novels! The first big problem is to find enough people who combine an understanding of jazz with writing ability. Beyond this, it is damned difficult to write about music, and about musical performance. Also: jazz musicians are inarticulate to the point of being mutes, in most cases (the reason I don't think a musician is ever going to write "the jazz novel")—they express themselves with great virtuosity on their instruments, but not in dialogue. Also: Most of them spoke, and still to a considerable extent speak in their special language with its limited vocabulary which relies importantly on inflection.[36]

When Russell writes that hipster idioms are based on a "limited vocabulary which relies importantly on inflection," he is noting a fundamental problem of hipness for writing. If hipness is oriented to individual experience in particular times and places, its characteristic expression is correspondingly rendered less in the meanings of words than in the performative nuances by which they are uttered. The meaning of a word can be abstracted from the time and place of its utterance—can be written down, copied, paraphrased, and otherwise recorded. The performative nuance, though, is fully comprehensible only in the total situation in which it appears. Charlie Parker's line "if you don't live it, it won't come out of your horn" gives us the syllogism that lies at the core of the Heisenbergian logic of hipness: if you don't live it, it isn't hip; if you write it, you aren't living it; therefore, if you write it, it isn't hip.

We might begin to suspect that the "hip culture" created by Mailer, Russell, and Wolfe, along with the many other intellectuals who crowd these pages, is merely a bookish and mostly white appropriation of an African American vernacular. Since 1946, the year *Really the Blues* gave hipness its literary debut, hip culture has grown out of the racially plural strands of intellectual and vernacular culture to become something that its black progenitors in the 1930s would not have recognized. Even more fundamentally, the hip sensibility's relationship to verbalized meaning (as well as its Heisenbergian logic) suggests that the mere fact we talk about it—the mere fact that this book you are reading exists—is proof that we have missed our mark. It is important to remember, then, that writing the intellectual history of hipness is an inherently contradictory and perhaps impossible act, to be judged largely in terms of its inevitable failure. In writing about the intellectual history of hipness, we are not writing a history of hipsters, or even the history of hip itself. We are necessarily writing the story of how hipness is mediated into intellectual and ultimately mass-cultural awareness—that is, into the very things it tends to oppose. If there is one thing I would ask the reader to keep in mind, then, it would be this: the development of hip culture is a dialectic of the enduring necessity of the printed word against hip culture's conviction that experience can never be captured in printed words. From this tension emerges all the distinctive features of hipness as an intellectual history.

This book does not ask "What is hip?" but rather "What is hipness?"—a distinction that will be more fully explained in the first chapter. For now it suffices to say that this book is not going to tell you what is hip, who is hip, how to be hip, or how hip its author is. The mere existence of a book on hipness seems to demand that its author either demonstrate his own hipness or boast of his lack of it—each being a possible qualification for writing such a book and both perhaps amounting to the same thing. Writing about hipness violates the taboo against unconcealed social climbing. Hipness is a high-denomination currency in the economy of symbolic exchange, something that Sarah Thornton calls subcultural capital. Claiming it for yourself is a *faux pas*, like bragging about how much your boss likes you, and invites your readers to suspect you're fooling yourself. So how hip, or unhip, am I? The question is beside the point. Do we ask someone writing about Romanticism whether he or she is sufficiently Romantic? No, because Romanticism does not dominate the sensibility of present-day intellectuals. It is the peculiar power of a living sensibility to compel its contemporaries to believe there are no options outside of it: one may be for it or against it or ambiguous about it, but it is somehow impossible to imagine discussing it in terms that do not assume its priority. (It is hard enough even to see it as a sensibility and not simply the natural order of things.) Once it is no longer a living sensibility, it no longer defines the range of thinkable positions. With the benefit of historical distance, writers can see it simply as one epoch in cultural history among many. Indeed, this is what I have tried to do in writing an intellectual history of the hip sensibility in its first three decades, from the late 1930s through the late 1960s. If hip culture offers us a good deal of delusion and posturing to go with its great works of imagination, my aim has been to understand a little better, without sentimentality or anger, the roots of its destructive illusions and profitable conceits alike.

But hipness *is* a living sensibility, and its great artifacts and documents—Allen Ginsberg's *Howl*, Bob Dylan's *Highway 61 Revisited*, and Lester Bangs's rock criticism, for example—still shape a contemporary sense of expressive, social, and political possibility. What is at stake in these and similar works is resistance: the sense that there is an alternative to American hypercapitalism, and that those who trade in cultural signs, the artists and intellectuals, can fight a hegemony enforced by propaganda and cultural standardization. Joseph Heath and Andrew Potter rightly assert that in our times "counterculture has almost completely replaced socialism as the basis for radical political thought."[37] The countercultural idea enshrines the hip intellectual as a latter-day version of the philosopher-king—a sort of philosopher-guerrilla. Little wonder that our own hip intellectuals are jealous of their prerogatives and mistrustful of skeptical historians.[38]

To the historian of postwar American culture, hipness represents the same dangers that the French Revolution does to French historians: both are topics burdened with contemporary political interests and the demands of faction. François Furet writes that scholars of the French Revolution, unlike those studying the Merovingian Kings, are "asked at every turn to present their research permits"—to declare their loyalties, so that their arguments may be reduced to mere opinions, concomitant with presumed party affiliation, and so that their work may be thus legitimized or ignored.[39] But such demands betray a mentality that is authoritarian and uncomfortable with real intellectual work. Stuart Hampshire's definition of the intellectual—one that guides my own use of the term throughout this book—suggests that intellectual work is defined by its relative independence from such restraints:

First, an intellectual is someone who takes it for granted that a strenu-
ously developed and articulate intelligence constitutes a claim to be recognized, and an independent status in society, even apart from any
solid achievements in science or scholarship or literature.... Second, an
intellectual is someone who refuses to be confined to one specialized,
or professional, application of his power; he will be ready to inquire into
almost anything that is formulated in sufficiently strict intellectual
terms, and will find delight in the process of inquiry, quite independently of the results.... Third, an intellectual is someone who never
lowers his voice in piety, and who is not prepared to be solemn and
restrained, in deference to anything other than the internal standards
of the intellect and the imagination.[40]

By these terms, Anatole Broyard and John Sinclair, whatever their differences,
can equally claim the mantle of "intellectual." In refusing "deference to anything
other than the internal standards of the intellect and the imagination,"*Partisan
Review* mandarin and LSD anarchist alike claim the same liberty. Granted, none
of us is completely free in this way—even Sinclair had to trim his sails to the
winds of political change—but we might respect the idea of this freedom all the
same.[41]

The continued authority of the countercultural idea means that most of the
writing around this topic is taken up with the supposed transgressions and resistances of zoot-suiters, beboppers, hip-hoppers, beats, hippies, punks, and all the
increasingly fractured subcultures that broadly share the hip sensibility's notion
of the expressive self in opposition to a deadening mainstream culture. Because
such writing tends to assume the same opposition in its own understanding of
American life, it is often uncritical, judging its subjects by the authenticity of
their revolt even as it ruefully acknowledges their occasional folly.[42] Dick
Hebdige's *Subculture: The Meaning of Style,* deservedly the most influential
academic study of hip style, suffers somewhat from this problem, as do the many
studies that follow its lead.[43] My own work follows Frank's *The Conquest of Cool*
and Heath and Potter's *The Rebel Sell* by refusing to take countercultures at their
own valuation, seeking instead to understand hip social critique as a cultivated
stance and an effort of collective imagination located at a specific moment of
history. The latter books are often crude in their analysis, though, and suffer
from an overeagerness to destroy what other writers are too apt to protect.[44] In
any event, unlike Heath, Potter, and Frank, I am interested not in the truth or
effectiveness of countercultural critiques but in their style. Nearly everyone who
has written on hipness and counterculture deals with the politics of aesthetics;
what interests me is the aesthetics of politics.[45]

These arguments will be expanded in Chapter 1. It will suggest that hipness is
a historically situated, contingent entity, arising at some poorly documented

point among urbanized African Americans in the interwar United States. It undergoes transformations as it enters intellectual and mass-cultural awareness; over time, many odd items, from many unexpected quarters, are added to its inventory. The example developed at length in this chapter is Zen Buddhism: though it might seem peculiar that such an austere religion should have recommended itself to the excitable Beats, hipness was an adaptable entity, and in any event Zen fit well within a sensibility that prized spontaneity and mistrusted linguistic abstraction. It is pointless to argue whether Zen or anything else really belongs in the inventory of items assimilated to the hip sensibility. Nothing is essentially hip; things can *become* hip as they enter a branching network of cultural associations, but hipness itself can be defined only as the network itself, not as any privileged node within it. This conception of hipness runs counter to the idea of co-optation, which insists that some objects are more authentic than others and that it is a matter of political urgency that we distinguish which is which. But this idea leads nowhere. In hip culture, what matters is not sociological reality but imagination and make-believe—with the added complication that hip culture is a kind of make-believe that, in order to deliver its aesthetic charge, must in some way be taken as real.

The subsequent chapters assume and build on the conceptual foundation prepared in Chapter 1. Chapter 2 develops a picture of an emergent hip culture in the 1930s and early 1940s, during which hipness established itself as an African American poetics of self and then, in the late 1940s, began its transformation into a wider intellectual vernacular, or (in LeRoi Jones's words) "a *general* alienation in which even white men could be included."[46] From the beginning, hipness was mapped into an imaginative geography: the "nowhere" in which hipsters imagine themselves condemned to live, and a fleeting and provisional "somewhere" they fashion out of their own expressive culture. This somewhere/nowhere binary grew out of the African American hustling ethic of "game ideology" and was diffused throughout the intercultural network by which hip culture came to be constituted. Notably, its traces can be heard in jazz—for example, in Thelonious Monk's rhetoric of ironic disaffiliation.

Chapter 3 continues to trace how the "new intellectual vernacular" of hipness coalesced at the end of the 1940s by focusing on a particular locus of its development, an unpublished cache of the Beats' home recordings from 1949 to 1951, which John Clellon Holmes made on a borrowed acetate cutter. The Holmes acetates capture Holmes, Jack Kerouac, Allen Ginsberg, and their friends experimenting with various combinations of music and their own words. The most curious items on these recordings are the Beats' attempts at vocal jazz improvisation, and in particular a couple of attempts at emulating the early free-jazz experiments of Lennie Tristano. If nothing else, this chapter helps clear up the perennial question of how much musical ability Jack Kerouac possessed; put bluntly, the answer is "not much." But these recordings are significant for other reasons. In this chapter, the problematic of meaning and experience within hip culture moves to the foreground. Chapter 2 deals with the "arrow collar underground," a relatively obscure group of proto-Beat writers who configured the hip sensibility within the cerebral and wordy milieu of the New York Intellectuals. The Beats represent a different tendency from within the same literary culture, more apt to find *somewhere* in the intensities of lived experience. In these early years, the Beats began to map the somewhere/nowhere binary onto a coherent array of paired terms: presence vs. abstraction, sensation vs. cerebration, wholeness vs. separation, the spontaneous present vs. the planned future, and above all, experience vs. meaning. The Beats valued recorded sound because they could map it onto the first term of each of these binaries: presence, sensation, wholeness, the present moment, and experience. Their early experiments in reconciling sounded experience with verbal meaning, though, cannot really bear the weight of this belief, and the Holmes acetates offer an opportunity to consider the current of melancholy running beneath the Beats' impossible project of capturing the evanescent traces of life itself in their imaginative works.

Although jazz has ever been honored as the parent of hipness, it was the Beats, with their demotic and participatory aesthetic, rather than coolly modernist jazz musicians like Monk and Tristano, who set the tone for the hip sensibility as it enjoyed its breakout success in the 1960s. While Chapter 2 considers the early Cold War style of hip intellectualism—ironic, skeptical, literary, disaffiliative, and colored by the era's general dislike of the mass—Chapter 4 describes how it changed within a mass counterculture. Hans Ulrich Gumbrecht's heuristic opposition of "meaning culture" and "presence culture," analogous to my opposition between the concrete meanings of experience and the abstract meanings of words, can usefully frame this historical shift in hip aesthetics and sensibility.[47] The story of hipness is the story of presence culture breaking into meaning culture, and while the earlier generation sought a complicated reconciliation of meaning and presence, the later one sought a purer presence in which meaning might dissolve altogether. This complicated succession of moods within the hip sensibility registers on three exemplary pieces of music, each separated from the others by about a decade: Charlie Parker's "Ornithology" (1946), Ken Nordine's "Sound Museum" (1957), and Bob Dylan's "Ballad of a Thin Man" (1965). Each piece reflects the hipster's strategies of ironic perception, though in a way that reflects the nuances of its positioning within the hip culture of its decade.

In its discussion of Bob Dylan, Chapter 4 develops a distinction between words and Word. Lowercase-w words are what you are reading right now, visible marks on paper that can be reproduced indefinitely and whose meaning is thereby unbound to space and time. Uppercase-W Word is oral utterance, language as a sounding event whose meanings cannot be abstracted from the bodies, spaces, and times by which they are made manifest. The earliest hipsters begat, the Beats signalized, and Dylan apotheosized a hipness of Word. But in "The White Negro" (1957), it was Mailer who gave it a philosophy and a manifesto. The first part of Chapter 5 gives a general history of the idea that underwrites his essay—that sound not only represents but embodies concrete experience, and that it has a unique power to actualize the energetic processes of human life in its listeners. "The White Negro" articulates a strain of postwar radical critique for which it is abstraction from life that has resulted in the totalitarian horrors of the modern age, and it outlines a program of existential liberation in which sound is the medium for the exchange of human energies. Mailer's novel *An American Dream* (1964/65) tells the story of a man who murders his wife and sets out on "that uncharted journey into the rebellious imperatives of the self" that Mailer had first mapped out in "The White Negro." Mailer's protagonist is challenged to free himself by harnessing the energy that flows within and among individuals; music, like sex and violence, is a medium of time and body through which humans can negotiate the ebb and flow of initiative and momentum in each arising moment of existential contention. For Mailer, writing is a quasi-musical project, an attempt to create a literary "sound" that issues from risky endeavors whose outcomes are never known in advance and whose meanings are disclosed only in their unfolding—in other words, to model writing on musical performance.

John Benson Brooks is as obscure as Mailer is well-known, but his career in the 1960s—a long period of public silence punctuated by the release of his strange and instantly forgotten last album, *Avant Slant* (1968)—throws the preceding chapters of this study into new light. The story behind this album gathers up several of the threads that run throughout the history of hip culture, notably the complicated interface between its modernist and postmodernist moods and the question of what an artistic practice of presence would really look like. Pushed to its furthest point, it looks a lot like Frank O'Hara's not-entirely-serious idea of Personism, an art that dissolves into the anonymity of each person's everyday private life.[48] Brooks's life's work is almost entirely private: his relatively few recordings are the iceberglike visible peaks of a vast, submerged, half-century-long project of musical and spiritual illumination that he recorded in a monumental series of notebooks. This concluding chapter revisits the problem of co-optation and suggests that this radical privacy of artistic practice may offer something of the freedom that counterculture ideology has always promised, though at the high price of negating the pleasure that hipness has always afforded—the pleasure of transforming life and personality into a public and consumable work of art.

These chapters are arranged in more or less chronological order, and collectively they narrate the history of a change in how Americans understood themselves from the 1940s through the 1960s. This was a change in the imaginative life of America, the appearance of a new cast of characters in what Mailer called the "dream life of the nation."[49] The dream life is a boundless domain with ever-shifting internal borders. It is a network of affective and conceptual connections across time and subcultural space, arrayed in such a way that understanding the full implications of, say, the magical hermeneutics of John Benson Brooks (Chapter 6) means knowing something about the occult interpretive style implicit in the Harlem hustler's game ideology (Chapter 2), the occult theology underpinning "The White Negro" (Chapter 5), magical thinking in late-1960s Movement politics (Chapter 4), and the idea of the sound recording as magical fetish (Chapter 3). And each of these, in turn, depends on the rest. There is no natural sequence for these connections, no fixed starting point, any more than there is a first neuron in the brain. The form of hip culture is the rhizome, not the root, and as Marshall McLuhan well understood, it is better grasped through pattern recognition than linear logic.[50] I have tried to make this story reasonably linear, but only as a convenience for the reader, whom I should remind (or warn) that the map is not the territory, and that this book could as easily have been ordered any number of other ways, none of which would be anything more than a two-dimensional flattening of a three-dimensional reality. As it is, the material strains against its constraints on the page; ultimately, this is a topic that asks for an act of total, instant, and synoptic comprehension of its many parts, which I can hardly expect, unless, like Arthur Schopenhauer, I demand that one read this book straight through twice.[51] (And that would be asking a lot!) So again, I ask readers to keep in mind that the discourse of hipness has always been constituted in the productive tension between the printed word and impossibility of hip experience—or any experience, really—ever being captured in printed words.

1

Koan

Communities are to be distinguished, not by their falsity/
genuineness, but by the style in which they are imagined.
—Benedict Anderson[1]

... we all thought *experience itself was good. Any experience*....
Consciousness itself was a good. And anything that took us
outside—that gave us the dimensions of the box we were caught
in, an aerial view, as it were—showed us the exact arrangement
of the maze we were walking, was a blessing. A small *satori*.
Because we knew we were caught, knew beyond a doubt that we
were at an impasse: where to next, Uncle Whitehead, Daddy
Camus? But we had yet to take measure, find out all we could
about what held us, kept us "fascinated." In the old sense of
that word. Hypnotized. How to circumvent, bypass, or take on
the monster.
*A recurring dream in my teens: I was, alone or with others, plotting
an escape from some kind of prison. Prison camp, it was all
outdoors. Barbed wire and guards. After many machinations we
escape. We really do. We travel far, through woods, various
landscapes, arrive at a house. Where we are given shelter, only to
find out that the house is part of the prison. We're still on prison
grounds. I usually woke up at that point.*
—Diane di Prima[2]

What Is Hip?

Inevitably, a study of hipness will prompt the question asked in the title of the
familiar song by Tower of Power: "What is hip?"[3] Like a Zen koan, "What is hip?"
is a riddle that at once demands and refuses an answer. It lodges itself like a
splinter in our mind and works its way in deeper as we meditate on it, irritating
and goading us. As we contemplate the riddle, its simple boundaries dissolve; we
find we can't even get the words straight.

What is *hip*? First of all, is it *hip* or *hep*? A glance at the *Oxford English Dictionary*
(with its wonderfully researched citations of early usage) reveals that they are

functionally the same word, though since World War II the latter version has seemed increasingly old-fashioned and has the ring of a square and off-key mis-hearing of "hip." In truth, both words were used interchangeably from the first decade of the twentieth century (the *OED*'s first documented use of *hip* dates from 1904; for *hep*, 1908), although "hep" is actually a bit more common in the first observations of the hipster that appeared in the 1930s black press. ("Hipster" is the preferred term of a slightly later time; social-observation columns such as Dan Burley's "Back Door Stuff" were more likely to identify them as "hepcats.") The earliest print uses of these words make clear their origins in the criminal underworld and the sphere of leisure and entertainment. In other words, they originate from a spoken rather than written milieu—or, to adopt Marshall McLuhan and Walter Ong's terms, they are products of orality rather than literacy. Variant spellings of words in mainly oral usage have to do with ways of rendering the sound of speech rather than etymological differences.

Oral culture poses problems for the lexicographer, not least because usage is only ever recorded after the fact, at a point where origins have become obscure. Thus *hip* has gained many competing and fanciful etymologies. David Maurer, a professor of English who studied the argot of confidence men and other marginal groups, maintained that "hip" is a corruption of "hep," which came from the name of a Chicago saloon keeper, Joe Hep.[4] In his ethnography of Greenwich Village beats, Ned Polsky stated that the word is derived from the opium addict's expression "to be on the hip," meaning to smoke opium from a reclining position.[5] Robert S. Gold favored the explanation that hip "derives by analogy with having one's hip boots on—i.e., the way in which they protect the wearer from bad weather or dangerous currents is analogous to the way in which awareness or sophistication arms one against social perils."[6] Dizzy Gillespie, Greil Marcus, John Leland, and many others have passed along David Dalby's assertion it comes from Wolof, a West African language spoken by many Africans exported as slaves to the United States. On this account, *hip* comes from the verb *hipi* (to open one's eyes) and *hip cat* comes from *hipicat* (the word for a man who is aware).[7] But we do not know for certain what the etymology of "hip" is and doubtless never will. This also goes for other words, like *bebop*, that have emerged from street argot into wide use. The *OED*, with characteristic prudence, tells us simply that the etymology of *hip* is unknown.

What *is* hip? As President Bill Clinton shrewdly remarked in another context, it depends on what the meaning of the word "is" is. Nearly all discussions of hipness are plagued by a fundamental defect of language. My claim is that hipness is an aesthetic and a sensibility, which is to say, it is like an operating system—a code, running largely below the threshold of conscious thought, that constellates habits of mind and patterns of taste; orders our everyday perceptions of what is meaningful, true, and beautiful; and shapes individual acts of artistic creation. In this it is much like modernism, whose postwar American career is tangled with that of hipness. Writing about hipness, then, and groping for definitions, we might wish for a lexical distinction akin to that between "modern" and "modernist," something to mark the difference between hip and an -ism of hip.

In Chapter 4, I discuss Ken Nordine and Fred Katz's album *Word Jazz* and its strong period flavor of midcentury modernism. Imagine it is 1957 and I am writing a review of *Word Jazz*. If I were to say that it is very *modern*, I would be making an aesthetic and historical claim for it: that it is up-to-date, neither derivative nor backward-looking, and that, as a work that takes its place in the present day, it competes with and holds it own against other pieces of music that likewise try to claim our attention with their grasp of the modern moment. And I might point out certain technical features to make my point—Katz's flirtation with bitonality and quasi-Stravinskian rhythms, say, or the use of *musique concrète* episodes. But in making this claim, I would also tacitly accept the aesthetics of the modern. If I say that "Sound Museum" is modern, I also suggest that I think such distinctions hold; that it matters whether or not this piece is up-to-date; that if I could not argue that the piece is modern, it would not have the same claim on our attention. If, on the other hand, I say that "Sound Museum" is *modernist,* I am making a different sort of claim. I do not necessarily endorse modernism but merely note its effects on the music under discussion. Neither do I say that Katz and Nordine claim the modern moment through their use of bitonality and *musique concrète* episodes, but only that these are things someone might have used to stake that claim in 1957. The *ism* marks the difference between a normative evaluation, in which one judges something in the terms of an aesthetic theory that exerts a moral force, and a descriptive evaluation, in which one places something within the terms of an aesthetic theory about whose values one remains agnostic.

Short of creating an ugly neologism (hippism?), we have no words to mark the distinction between hip and an -ism of hip, no term for the artist whose works are in dialogue with those habits of mind that constitute the hip aesthetic. Perhaps *hipness* will have to do. For when we ask, *What is hip?* we are already subtly defining in advance the kind of inquiry on which we are embarking. We set about trying to understand what really *is* hip, rather than the circuitous and unlikely paths by which things gain meaning within a hip sensibility—that is, by which they gain hipness.

This confusion often afflicts academic writing on hipness. In Ingrid Monson's "The Problem with White Hipness," for example, hipness is largely the white projection of a racial and sexual wish-fulfillment fantasy epitomized by Norman Mailer's "The White Negro," with its inadvertently racist mythologization of the black hipster as the sexual psychopath who alone can escape the soft totalitarianism of American life.[8] The "problem with white hipness," then, is that it is a distortion of black social reality. "The White Negro" joins other representations of race and gender in presenting an ideologically loaded picture that sharply contrasts with how black jazz musicians understand themselves and the working realities of their lives. Monson's own response is to pursue ethnographic study of the jazz world in order to arrive at a truer understanding of the complex dynamics of race and gender.

However, to find fault with Mailer's sociology, as nearly all the many critics of "The White Negro'" do, is to assume that what Mailer writes about hipness—indeed, what anyone writes about hipness—ought to make true statements about how people live their lives and can be discounted when it does not. But if hipness is an aesthetic concept comparable to modernism, the expressive texts written from within its influence cannot properly be judged in terms of ethnographic realism. To pursue the analogy with modernism further: we could certainly quarrel with normative modernism if we disagreed with its warrants—its historical teleology, its anxiety over audience, its formalism, and so on—and many have. But when those quarrels are settled, or the disputants have at least agreed to disagree, and all we seek is to ask what modernism was and how its warrants shaped cultural practice, we no longer care much whether modernism paints a true picture of the world, but seek instead to understand what effect it had on those for whom it did paint such a picture. This is how I approach hipness. Like Monson, I do not believe that writers under the spell of the hip aesthetic present a true picture of the world. However, I do not seek a social understanding of the aesthetic, but rather the opposite. When I write of "hipness" or "hip culture," therefore, I use the term in the descriptive rather than normative sense, as a culture bound by certain characteristic tropes of expression and habits of mind.

Indeed, I think it is essential to uncouple hipness from a lingering assumption that it ought to align with social reality, because if we look for instances of hipness only where we feel confident we have found a hipster of the right pedigree, we will forever remain caught in the tail-chasing dynamic of hipness, its eternal and fruitless quest for authenticity, for a stable place free of co-optation—such a place being, by the Heisenbergian logic of hip culture, impossible. In Chapter 4, I discuss the concept of the "generation gap," a notion to which Americans of all ages gave credence in the 1960s but that turned out to have been something of a collective hallucination. However, the social reality (or unreality) of the generation gap is not what is interesting about it; what is interesting is the way it became a constituent element of an aesthetic image of self by which Movement participants could understand their relationship to the rest of the world. (By "Movement" I mean the loose amalgam of counterculture and New Left that is the main actor in the cultural revolution of the late 1960s and early 1970s; I will discuss this entity more fully in Chapter 4.) Movement youth, influenced by McLuhan's theories of secondary orality in the electronic age, thought that the music of Bob Dylan and the Beatles acted as a "tribal drum" that fused their consciousness into a single organism dispersed around the globe, sending and receiving messages instantaneously and simultaneously.[9] The sense of oneself as a cell of this organism, or, to use another McLuhanite metaphor, as a player in a worldwide Happening, defined both a political identity and a dynamic of musical reception.[10] But if some dropped acid on the weekend and went groggily to their office jobs on Monday morning, does it matter? Should we ignore them and look for better objects of study? It mattered to Movement leaders, because they believed their form of life complemented their real commitment to creating a new world. For them, the weekender with a buckskin vest on the hanger next to a business suit was a phony whose commitment went no deeper than style. But Movement true believers were fighting a hopeless battle, demanding political purity in a stance that was always already aesthetic. Hipness was never more than the sum of its representations.

What is hip? We might object that it doesn't matter what we *call* it; it's the thing itself that matters. The word "hip" has only been around for about a century, but the nervy attitude to which the word refers has been around a lot longer. How much longer depends on whom you ask. John Leland writes that "Ralph Waldo Emerson, Henry David Thoreau, Walt Whitman and Herman Melville, in a brief flurry from 1850 to 1855, laid out the formal groundwork for hip," and that "no skater, raver, indie-rocker, thug, Pabst Blue Ribbon drinker or wi-fi slacker today acts without their permission."[11] Greil Marcus draws a line from Jonathan Edwards to Bob Dylan by way of William S. Burroughs and Doc Boggs, suggesting that the American face has always worn the mask of cool— indeed, that coolness lies at the bedrock of American history.[12] And R. U. Sirius (Ken Goffman), a disciple of Timothy Leary, finds the roots of counterculture in the myths of Abraham and Prometheus.[13] At their most expansive, transhistorical understandings of hipness proceed from the belief that hipness isn't made, but just *is*. It is a mode of consciousness that is always available, like a radio station always broadcasting, waiting for someone to tune in.[14]

This is an appealing thought, but it makes hipness a shapeless and near-useless object for historical contemplation. If we believe that skate punks, Herman Melville, and the patriarch Abraham are all hip, we must define *hip* very generally, and in ways that obscure how various subjectivities have been constructed in their respective historical moments.[15] If we take the definition of the word on which all dictionary and conversational uses tend to agree, it is an attitude of keeping one's eyes open and perceiving truths hidden from superficial understanding and therefore denied ordinary people. But such an attitude could describe not only Old Testament patriarchs but practically every philosopher or religious seer in history, and a good many artists as well (to say nothing of numberless cranks and oddballs). Furthermore, the contents of this knowing stance— kinds of truths that ought to be revealed, the nature of the self to be enlightened, and the nature of the enlightenment—are hardly the same at all times. As historians of religion have recently insisted, even enlightenment has a history.[16]

It is not much better to say that hip sets a gnostic attitude in a marginal or oppositional relation to existing sites of social or cultural authority. Was Socrates then a hipster? The Buddha? Igor Stravinsky? L. Ron Hubbard? Conceiving hipness as the expression of a specifically American national character, as Marcus does, is more modest yet not much more easily proved. Marcus, though, is less interested in proving anything than in staging a virtual conversation between American historical figures and listening for the resonances between their voices. The question of who has read whom, and to what effect, is never addressed and for Marcus is perhaps beside the point.[17] In this study, it is the whole point.

Extending the lineage of hipsters back through the centuries before the emergence of a discourse of hipness gives the contemporary vernacular a more distinguished ancestry, of course, and perhaps this is one reason to interpret hipness as a transhistorical phenomenon. But this ennobled bloodline comes at a cost, not only of historical coherence but of social insight. In Chapter 2, I warn against looking too much at hipsters and not enough at hipness. But it makes little sense to treat them as entirely separate phenomena; hipness without hipsters gives us a historical locus without people to inhabit it. When the black press began to chronicle the doings of hipsters in the late 1930s and early 1940s, it was responding to something new on the scene, a new social type: the dandified black operator who negotiates spaces of urban modernity transformed by the Great Migration. Malcolm X's story of arriving in Boston as a rube and finding a way to assert himself in urban space through self-stylization is the paradigmatic country-to-city narrative of the black migrant. The figure who negotiates such spaces is armed with a something like a philosophy and an axis of orientation within an imaginary geography of somewhere and nowhere (see Chapter 2). But this is a "philosophy" articulated by tight cuffs and pointed shoes rather than treatises. Robin Kelley writes, "seeing oneself and others 'dressed up' was enormously important in terms of constructing a collective identity based on something other than wage work, presenting a public challenge to the stereotypes of the black body, and reinforcing a sense of dignity that was perpetually being assaulted."[18] Farah Jasmine Griffin notes that the migration-era city harbored many sites of symbolic self-definition, some of which (the street corner) were places where men's identities could be created and contested, while others (the kitchenette) functioned the same way for women. Racial, regional, gender, and class identities were at stake in every such place of self-invention:

> In the context of the migration narrative, urban spaces—kitchenettes, workplaces, street corners, prisons, and theatres—are some of the sites where migrants, white powerholders, and the Northern black middle class vie for control. All these spaces are created by a sophisticated urban power, yet this very power is engaged in a constant struggle to

maintain control over them. The contest over space is symbolic of the larger contest over black bodies. Within these spaces, a struggle ensues in which the migrant tries to resist efforts to dominate him or her.[19]

Hipness must be understood as originating in an African American project of defining and asserting the self along particular lines and through a certain set of symbols. From around 1948 onward, artists and intellectuals within hip culture would put those symbols in play with others from European and Asian literary and intellectual traditions. The network of coherencies that people have made of those disparate cultural symbols constitutes the historical reality of hipness. But that network is grounded in a specific historical experience.

Though it is slack and self-serving to view hipness as an esoteric higher consciousness available at all times to those sufficiently enlightened, there are two ways we might profitably understand hipness within a more expansive historical frame than the bare century of its discourse. In the first place, we might consider Guthrie Ramsay's notion that bebop represents a strain of Afro-modernism that forms a cultural response to the social conditions of modernity in general and also, more particularly, to conditions that postwar America placed on African Americans.[20] Following Ramsay, we might consider hipness another of the ways modernism accommodates itself to modernity—for people, finding themselves caught in the ceaseless and accelerated flow of change in modern life, to come to understand their relationship to that flow and even to harness its force to their own lives. Ramsay borrows this conception of modernism from Marshall Berman, who writes:

> To be modern . . . is to experience personal and social life as a maelstrom, to find one's world and oneself in perpetual disintegration and renewal, trouble and anguish, ambiguity and contradiction: to be part of a universe in which all that is solid melts into air. To be a modern*ist* is to make oneself somehow at home in the maelstrom, to make its rhythms one's own, to move within its currents in search of the forms of reality, of beauty, of freedom, of justice, that its fervid and perilous flow allows.[21]

This modernism is different from what we might call the period style of American midcentury modernism, which will be discussed at greater length in Chapters 2 and 4. Within Berman's more expansive frame, modernism becomes a genealogy of cultural responses, a repertoire of functionally interconnected ideas and attitudes cultivated in the face of a centuries-old long wave of modernization—a repertoire to which midcentury modernism, bebop, and hipness all belong, and which are inextricably tangled with one another. And these latter entities are in turn linked to others from earlier phases of modernity. Seen from Berman's high vantage point, the hipster becomes a new incarnation of Henri Murger's Bohemians and Walter Benjamin's *flâneurs*.[22]

The second way one might understand hipness within a wider historical context is related to this first. If modernism is a genealogy of cultural responses to centuries of capitalist modernity and hipness occupies a point on its family tree, then hipness itself constitutes a genealogy, a branching system of associations that bear a family resemblance to one another. This genealogical conception of hipness is my best answer to the koan.

The Suzuki Rhythm Boys

To explain what I mean by family resemblance, I will return to the koan, which has changed slightly from *What is hip?* to *What is hipness?* So, what is it? I have defined *hipness* as an aesthetic and sensibility shaped by the countercultural idea, but this does very little to sort out what does and does not belong to that sphere I have called "hip culture." There is the danger of circularity here: hip culture is that which forms out of hip sensibility, and hip sensibility is that which is defined by hip culture. So it is tempting to seek some criterion, some single aspect, that all items of hip culture can be said to possess. But the moment we offer any suggestions a swarm of counterexamples will come immediately to mind. We are in the same situation as Ludwig Wittgenstein, who was similarly unable to find a single common thread that bound together all instances of what are called games. Between board games and card games, schoolyard games and ball games, "we see a complicated network of similarities overlapping and crisscrossing: sometimes overall similarities, sometimes similarities of detail."[23]

To this problem Wittgenstein offered the notion of the "family resemblance," for in studying the genetic attributes (build, eye color, etc.) shared within a family one finds that such attributes braid together in the same way as the attributes of games. Perhaps paradoxically, an entity composed of such resemblances still coheres as something we might intelligibly discuss, even as we discover that there is no one item held in common across all its constituent parts. Wittgenstein uses the metaphor of a corded thread to represent this paradoxical kind of coherence: "the strength of the thread does not reside in the fact that some one fiber runs through its whole length, but in the overlapping of many fibers."[24] What the fibers have in common is their overlapping, which is not a thing but a patterning, a process. In thinking about the family resemblances among items that belong to hip culture, we might call that process *history*.

When considering the general phenomenon of family resemblances within hip culture, we might look at a single attribute—something analogous to blue eyes or brown hair—that is present neither in every member of the family nor only within the family, but whose presence in the genealogy, in combination with other attributes, goes some way toward establishing what makes the family distinctive. Since I have been using the koan as an extended metaphor, I may as well consider the link between hipness and Zen Buddhism. I do not say that Zen is hip; rather, Zen belongs to the –ism of hip. This means that by some historical process Zen has ended up the sort of thing that comes readily to mind when we wish to describe people who seem uncannily calm and cool, or when a company wants to brand a product as cool and a little mysterious.[25] If we cannot say that Zen really *is* cool in some essential way, we can at least point out that it has become a cliché to think that Zen is cool.[26] And so I will attack my koan from another direction and interrogate my own cliché: Why is it that the Zen koan should suggest itself as a metaphor for discussing hipness in the first place?

Earlier I asked rhetorically whether the Buddha was a hipster, and we might give any one of three answers. If we are asking whether the historical figure of Siddhartha Gautama himself participated in the network of intellectual and social filiations by which the historical phenomenon of hipness makes itself available to the historian, then obviously not. If we ask whether he was possessed of the same state of mind as Jack Kerouac or Charlie Parker, then who knows? But if we ask whether Kerouac and Parker might have been seen, by themselves or their followers, reflected in the image of the Buddha, then we must answer yes. Kerouac himself made the connection between Parker and the Buddha explicit in *Mexico City Blues.*

> Charley Parker Looked like Buddha
> Charley Parker, who recently died
> Laughing at a juggler on the TV
> after weeks of strain and sickness,
> was called the Perfect Musician
> And his expression on his face
> Was as calm, beautiful, and profound
> As the image of the Buddha
> Represented in the East, the lidded eyes
> The expression that says "All Is Well"
> —This was what Charley Parker
> Said when he played, All is Well.[27]

Even earlier, in *The Dharma Bums,* this connection was implicit: interestingly, the cover drawing for the first UK edition of Kerouac's novel looks very much like Charlie Parker sitting zazen (Fig. 1.1). Such associations struck some observers as absurd. James Baldwin, skeptical of the Beats' attempted fusion of black culture and Zen, mockingly dubbed the Beats "the Suzuki rhythm boys."[28] Alan Watts, the pre-eminent popularizer of Eastern religion in America, felt that Kerouac's hybrid "Beat Zen," with its strenuous rejection of American society,

Figure 1.1 Cover of the UK edition of *The Dharma Bums* (London: Deutsch, 1958). The Lilly Library, Indiana University, Bloomington.

manifested an effortful spirit alien to true Zen.[29] Kerouac's various writings on Buddhism display the enthusiastic naïveté of an autodidact trying to reconstruct an entire tradition from a handful of secondary sources and bad translations.[30] But however fanciful, "Beat Zen" resulted from the Beats' recognition that their own outlook bore some resemblance to certain Zen tenets.

Below I list seven interdependent points of contact between the Beats' hip sensibility and Zen. Most of my points pertain to features Zen shares with other schools of Buddhism, and more connections between Asian metaphysics and the postwar American artworld could be imagined. However, the connections I list are the ones that outline the emergence of a new register of intellectual life—those artists and intellectuals who, after the failure of the Popular Front, found a new foundation for their oppositional culture in an "emphasis on personal direct experience," as Gary Snyder writes:

> I moved in circles that were acutely critical of the direction of American politics and economics, but were also painfully leaving the hope of an ideal Socialist world behind. We were post-Stalin, and found some inspiration in the relict Syndicalist-Anarchist traditions of the Finnish and Italian workingmen's societies of San Francisco, and the teachings and example of Gandhi. As working poets and artists we were repelled by the neo-conservatism in fashion in the academies then. We got our poetics from William Carlos Williams, Ezra Pound, D. H. Lawrence, Gertrude Stein, Wallace Stevens, William Blake, and folksongs. Most of us were reading the Chinese poetry translations of Arthur Waley, Witter Byner, Florence Asycough, and of course Pound. We were exploring haiku and further Zen through the books of R. H. Blyth. We were people of the Far West, loving our continent for its great wild beauty, feeling no ties to Europe. Our politics and aesthetic were one. Dr. [D. T.] Suzuki's exposition of Zen gave us an idea of a religion and an all-embracing view of nature to augment that of scientific Ecology, which had already begun to instruct us . . . .
>
> For us, in our energy of the fifties, early Buddhism, Laozi, Gandhi, Thoreau, Kropotkin, and Zen were all one teaching. We stood for original human nature and the spontaneous creative spirit. Dr. Suzuki's Zen presentation of the "original life force," the "life-impulse," "the enlivening spirit of the Buddha"—the emphasis on personal direct experience, seemed to lead in the same direction.[31]

1. Zen is concerned with reality as it unfolds in the present moment. Our thoughts about past and future, our reminiscences and planning, our patterns of behavior arising from memory and anticipation—in short, the tissue of

associations and self-definitions that cohere into a sense of an individual self with a life history and direction—are delusions. Jazz, with its improvisatory ethic of creation in the moment; hipsterism, in its pursuit of kicks without regard for social convention or consequence; and the postwar avant-garde, with its existentialist embrace of spontaneous action (for example in Harold Rosenberg's notion of "action painting") together constituted a cultural space receptive to Zen metaphysics.[32]

2. In the Zen tradition, language is seen as an abstraction of reality that permits us to imagine and represent things outside the present moment. Language gives us conventional meanings for things, including our own identities, but those meanings are incapable of capturing the true nature of reality. Reality in itself is empty: no object or process "out there," and no experience "in here," has a self-nature—an enduring, inherent, separate essence. Subject and object are two sides of the same coin, each dependently arisen from the other. So there can be no stable meanings to inhere in objects: things don't *mean* anything, or else their meanings are nothing more or less than themselves, which is what Buddhists call *tathata*—"suchness" or "thusness"—or what in Western philosophy is called haecceity. This resonated with the Beats' conviction that the meaning of reality is to be found in our direct experience of it, outside the abstractions of language. Suchness, the sensed wordless immediacy of things, was above all what they sought to evoke in their writing—"no time for poetry but exactly what is."[33]

3. If Zen phenomenology is concerned above all with (1) experiencing the present moment and (2) experiencing everything that manifests within time as lacking self-identity and permanence, then the world and all the things in it are experienced as the continuous and present unfoldment of processes and actions. Ernest Fenollosa had developed this idea in his theory of the ideogram, which Ezra Pound brought to the world's attention in 1919: "Things are only the terminal points, or rather the meeting points of actions, cross sections cut through actions, snap-shots."[34] Likewise, the individual turns out to be something more like an action than an object: as Buckminster Fuller later wrote, "I seem to be a verb."[35] Although Fenollosa and Pound's ideas influenced many schools of twentieth-century poetry (see Chapter 5), they were particularly relevant to the Beats, who sought above all to evoke action, fluidity, and evanescence in their writing.

4. Buddhist philosophy sees the separate self as a delusion and all things as empty and impermanent; it holds there to be no dualism between subject and object, mind and matter. Since Western philosophy has generally assumed a stable self that apprehends (in some more or less occluded way) an objective reality, Zen seems paradoxical and illogical.[36] The hip fascination with strangeness—things that are *far out* in ways we will come to understand better in Chapter 4—made Zen particularly appealing to the Beats and their fellow

travelers.[37] As Theodore Roszak pointed out in his discussion of the 1960s counterculture, Zen was improbably appealing to hip youth for this same reason: "Zen's commitment to paradox and randomness could be conveniently identified with the intellectual confusion of healthily restless, but still unformed minds."[38]

5. Early popularizations of Rinzai Zen suggested that there is an unsocialized and spontaneous true self that can be recaptured from the conditioned and conventional ego. Zen practice was portrayed as a means for a highly socialized and conditioned people (whether Japanese or Cold War American) to understand their conditioning as such. Stories of Zen masters smacking their students, roaring with unmotivated laughter, and answering serious philosophical questions with Marx-Brothers zaniness had an obvious appeal to Americans caught in the sway of the hip sensibility, for which spontaneity was a supreme value. Again Roszak writes, "Perhaps above all, Zen's antinomianism could serve as a sanction for the adolescent need of freedom, especially for those who possessed a justified discomfort with the competitive exactions and conformities of the technocracy."[39]

6. Zen koans use language against itself, creating unsolvable puzzles often derived from the logical workings of words. In the Rinzai school (which the Beats, influenced by D. T. Suzuki, took for the entire Zen tradition), practitioners use koans to force their minds against the limits that the conventions of language place on their perception of reality. Robert Fink has written that "the experience of Rinzai was ... presented to Westerners as a dangerous existential struggle with the void" in which the practitioner was faced with the stark choice of madness or enlightenment.[40] This appealed to the Romanticism of the Beats, but more importantly it offered a precedent for Beat attempts to use language to get outside of language, to capture in the frozen forms of printed words the flow of experience itself. In trying to make language do what it cannot, koans and Beat writing aim to present consciousness with something it can never break down or assimilate—an anvil to break the hammer of the mind.

7. Inasmuch as Zen offers a critique of society, it follows from its critique of individual human consciousness. Individuals are deluded by their thoughts, believing themselves and others to be real and durable things in an objective world. They come to see the world in terms of self and other, subject and object, and acting on this dualistic scheme of consciousness they treat other beings as mere objects, counters to be moved around in some abstract game. Human beings become mere quanta of labor and the natural world only a fund of resources to serve the self. To Suzuki, this social pathology was particularly characteristic of the West, whose long traditions of dualistic philosophy had ended in the profound unhappiness and anxiety of the modern West.[41] Suzuki's viewpoint was easily conformable to the countercultural idea, with its rat-in-a-

maze picture of social existence. Thus it seemed natural for Snyder and his friends to imagine that "Gandhi, Thoreau, Kropotkin, and Zen were all one teaching." Their point of view was an American extrapolation from Zen thinking rather than one characteristic of Zen institutions in Japan, which tended to accommodate themselves to whatever political authority prevailed at a given time.[42] As Snyder noted early on, Western Buddhism is in part an attempt to marry Buddhism's psychological insight with social activism: "The mercy of the west has been rebellion; the mercy of the east has been insight into the basic self."[43]

What is at stake here is not any one tendency (Zen, anarchism, ecology, etc.) that Snyder and his friends pursued, but rather the connection that they felt lay between them—spontaneous creativity, an orientation toward holism, and "the emphasis on personal direct experience." If Zen could be fitted to Beat literature, it could also be fitted to jazz, Existentialism, Gestalt and Reichian psychotherapy, and certain modernist and avant-garde precincts of European art traditions in literature, painting, and music. And all these things could be fitted independently to one another, too, because their common point of departure was the individual's concrete experience of the present moment.

Some of these connections were obviously superficial. For example, Fred Katz's album *Zen* (1957), a series of compositions for the Chico Hamilton quintet in Katz's Neoclassical modernist style, has only the most casual connection to its title. The title track, the second movement of Katz's *Suite for Horn*, has a few moody woodblock strikes and a delicate *shakuhachi*-like clarinet line in its introduction and coda. It is left to Fran Kelley's windy liner notes to make an explicit connection between jazz and Zen, positing the subconscious mind as the source of both jazz creativity and Zen meditation:

> A glimpse of Zen in method, i.e. absolute concentration on two opposites, black and white (the literal success of which is impossible) frees the subconscious, the gray meditative source, for release. Here, the Zen principle and the one of jazz is shown in relation. The 'gray meditative release' corresponds to the creativity in jazz-improvisation. Zen is defined too briefly in the big Websters. If you are curious to really comprehend its true meaning, extensive study is needed. Jazz in 'definitive' use is as broad as its musically political parent, democracy, which it so communicatively chalices.[44]

This sort of writing feeds the suspicion that Zen became a fad in the late 1950s mostly because it allowed intellectuals to assert their authority without having to make any sense. As for the music itself, Kenneth Rexroth didn't find it impressive even as a piece of exotica, writing to Lawrence Lipton that Katz's "dreadful 'zen' is much inferior to the old blue Columbia 12" Whiteman 'Concert' rendition of 'Japanese Sandman'" and that Katz himself was a "pretentious snob."[45] But the history of hipness, like the history of pop music it closely follows, is a history of imposture. I am borrowing this notion from Jonathan Lethem, and like Lethem I am not saying it as if it's a bad thing.[46] Along with Brian Eno, I believe we should try to find some way in which calling something "pretentious" (i.e., that which is pretended) could be a compliment:

> The common assumption is that there are "real" people and there are others who are pretending to be something they're not. There is also an assumption that there's something morally wrong with pretending. My assumptions about culture as a place where you can take psychological risks without incurring physical penalties make me think that pretending is the most important thing we do. It's the way we make our thought experiments, find out what it would be like to be otherwise.[47]

Veracity is not the point; imagination and play is. What matters is that Americans could find a place for Zen within a constellation of familiar European and American cultural entities, and in so doing create new culture of their own. Buddhism had already come to the United States as early as the late nineteenth century, but to relatively little public effect.[48] Zen's appearance on the postwar intellectual scene was different, because this time it arrived in a cultural landscape that had been prepared for it, and whose categories of thought and feeling allowed it to register as a meaningful variation on an existing model rather than as a mere curiosity. The connections between Zen and hipness were neither causal nor linear. Zen originated some fourteen hundred years before Kerouac and was unknown to the young black men who, on the streets of northern cities in the 1930s, first made a spectacle of spontaneity, living in the moment, subverting language, and being generally far out. But the family resemblance between Zen and hipness allowed the latter to absorb something of the former, with lasting consequences to both.

I do not argue that Zen is the key to understanding hipness, or even that it is especially important to hip culture. I have discussed it at length in order, first, to introduce ideas of presence, holism, spontaneity, and experience that will be more fully developed in later chapters, for even though hipness is not uniquely associated with such ideas, it became the medium by which they were most widely diffused throughout American culture after World War II. Second, I have focused on Zen in order to turn up the magnification on one item of family resemblance and to consider its place within a vast network of cultural associations. In doing so, we might come to realize that hipness *is* that network. It cannot be defined in any other way: as Nietzsche once remarked, "all concepts in which a whole process is summarized in signs escape definition; only that which is without history can be defined."[49] I have already written that hipness was never more than the sum of its representations. Throughout the rest of this book, we see how the figures of representation discussed here ramify through a net of complex filiations and circuitous chains of influence. There is no one attribute of any single point within the net, no aspect of any artist, artwork, style, or idea, that is universally shared by all the others. The only thing shared by all nodes within the network of hip culture is the pattern of historical linkage between them. (This is another way of saying that nothing is hip forever.) To privilege any part of the network as authentically hip, and to identify hipness with those parts so privileged, or to define hipness in their terms, is to collapse its historicity. If I have argued that John Leland's historical definition of hipness is too loose, it seems to me that his fundamentally intercultural understanding of it is just loose enough:

> From a proprietary standpoint, hip is a mess. Ralph Ellison, writing about black bohemianism, threw up his hands in dismissal: wasn't bohemianism a white rip-off of black styles? But this is the way hip travels. It is like a game of telephone. African Americans were copied by white Americans, who were copied by French existentialists, who were copied by white intellectuals, who were copied by black hipsters, who were copied by Jewish rappers, who were copied by Brazilian street kids, who were—well, I think you know where this is taking us. It is taking us to the Jungle Club in Tokyo, where Japanese hipsters wear dreadlocks and emulate the funk musician Bootsy Collins. No one along the way can really take full credit for this evolutionary development, and yet here we are—you, me, and Bootsy.[50]

In Leland's account, a long transnational, transcultural, transtemporal chain of influence—the family tree of hipness—ends up in Japan, which is right where we started, with the Suzuki Rhythm Boys.

The Devil's Staircase

To open ourselves to a truly historical understanding of hipness we must become fearless in the face of bad art. We must accept things that we feel, deep in our heart, are not hip, cannot be hip, have never been hip, are but feeble mockeries of hip—we must accept them not as hip but as outliers in the network of family resemblance that constitutes what hipness is. For if we accept that *The Dharma Bums* is a part of hip culture, whatever James Baldwin might have said, then we also have to accept Rod McKuen's "Haiku Poems" (a track from McKuen's Beatsploitation record *Beatsville*) as a development along the same line; so is

Tony Scott's *Music for Zen Meditation;* so, more distantly, is the New Age music that trades on Zen's exotic image.[51]

But for many readers I am asking too much. They might argue that Rod McKuen was no Beat and *Beatsville* bears the same relationship to authentic Beat life that a Les Baxter exotica album does to the music of Peru. *Beatsville* is a commercial co-optation of a genuine and uncommodified art form and way of life, an attempt to profit from something intended as an alternative to a profit-chasing culture in the first place. And here we stumble on the great problem of hipness: the problem of co-optation.

Gerald Graff once pointed out that humanities scholarship tends to assume that "societies exert control over their subjects not just by imposing constraints on them but by predetermining the ways they attempt to rebel against those constraints, by co-opting their strategies of dissent."[52] This co-optation is not conceived as a benign pattern of influence or the mere adoption of ideas, but as something more sinister, "the defusing and domesticating of ostensibly opposi-tional forms of culture by their tolerant acceptance and commercialization" that Herbert Marcuse first theorized, calling it "repressive desublimation" or "repres-sive tolerance."[53] And if this was true in 1989, when Graff was writing about the effect that the idea of co-optation was having on a then-new culture-studies idiom within the humanities, it is still roughly true now. Co-optation is a habit of mind we cannot shake. If, as Brian Eno says, we assume that there are "real" people and people who are pretending to be something they're not, then like-wise we assume that there is "real" culture and a parasitic culture that counter-feits it. The gap between real and counterfeit is what we call "authenticity."

A flood of recent books and articles has battered the concept of authenticity, or at least its unself-conscious use in pop music studies, beyond hope of redemp-tion.[54] And yet we are at an interesting point in history, where on the one hand intellectuals no longer admit to believing that any kind of music is more "authentic" than another but where they cannot quite do without the concept either. To think of hipness in the critically agnostic way I have suggested, as a descriptive rather than normative concept, is to renounce authenticity and all its works: it is to renounce the vocabulary of transgression, resistance, and co-optation that still marks a great deal of writing on popular music. Even more radically, it is to renounce the entire oppositional vision of culture in a capitalist society that the countercultural idea represents.

Must we learn to love capitalism, then? For most pop-culture intellectuals this is certainly asking too much. Isn't there *something* in America's hypercon-sumerist culture we might still resist? And if there is, by what principle might we still resist it? If counterculture is only a consoling myth and all culture is always already compromised within the capitalist system (as I argue in the next chapter), where's the hope? In the last chapter of this book I will offer my own tentative answer to these questions: in short, yes, I think there are things we might "resist"—or, put in a less self-dramatizing way, there are things we might choose not to accept—and I do think there is something we can do about them. But I am not advocating what most people would think of as "cultural resistance." In fact, I would argue that the very notion of cultural resistance—the idea that culture might save us from political and social ills—is futile. We are looking for love in all the wrong places, asking the cultural commodities we consume that they not have anything to do with commodification or consumption, looking to culture to save us from itself. Somehow, we must find another way to think about culture. For now I will say only that whatever notions of freedom we might entertain, the idea of co-optation gets us nowhere.

In Bernard Wolfe's novel *The Magic of Their Singing,* a group of hipsters on the run from the police hide out in that early stronghold of academic hip, the New School for Social Research. They attend a lecture titled "Beat and the Poetic Muse," delivered by "a small, emaciated man with wisped hair" and a "tight voice that seemed poised for the falsetto":

> As you all know, a clattering new spirit is afoot in the esthetic back-alleys of the land, as in the community's hidden deeps and on its outermost fringes. Everywhere the deliberately raucous young and the voluntarily dispossessed are gathering in odd social and esthetic pockets to thumb their collective nose at the standards and stances of the square ingroups. Their rallying cry is hipness. Their new manna is pot and peyote. Way-outness is their credo. High on their list of enemies, indeed, first among their targets of choice, are work, sobriety, ambition, the gray flannel suit, nine-to-five enterprises, programmatic heterosexuality, congenital optimism, the armored musculature, science, the atom, government, patriotism, manners, the daytime, sunny weather.[55]

Half a century later, the professor is still at it, still thin, still bald, a white guy in a bow tie complacently lecturing his black students about hip-hop (Fig. 1.2).

The would-be hip professor is a comic figure, his wifty presence standing in ironic counterpoint to the raw vitality of the music he teaches. Less obviously, though, he is also a focus of anxiety. Hip-hop and Beat poetry are art forms of rebellion. By talking about them, the professor gives them academic legitimacy and cultural authority. This catches hipsters in a dilemma. The entire point of having a counterculture is to create a space of cultural freedom, and such a space needs to be sustained by a certain kind of authority: poets need journals to publish their poems, musicians need venues to play, and everyone needs an audience. But countercultural art draws power from its resistance to authority. Hipsters resent the intrusion of outsiders, but they also feel alienated from a society that doesn't understand their culture.[56] So although they might jeer at the academics who claim authority over their music and lifestyle, they cannot

Figure 1.2 Danny Hellman, cartoon for "Hip Hop 101," *The Source* (September 2003).

really renounce academic sanction, because they cannot renounce the cultural capital it represents.

This dilemma has been a part of hipness from the beginning. Anatole Broyard's "Portrait of the Hipster" (1948), one of the first and best intellectual treatments of hipness, concludes with a meditation on the paradox of hip authority. Broyard ends by noting how the hipster was fated to perish not from starvation and obscurity but from success. Intellectuals would inevitably seek out his opinions ("Was it *in there?* Was it *gone?* Was it *fine?*"), and here the hipster was undone, because recognition was *somewhere,* while the authority of his stance came from *nowhere,* from the power it defied. Broyard finishes his article by mocking the hipster who has been turned inside-out in this way:

> Jive, which had originally been a critical system, a kind of Surrealism, a personal revision of existing disparities, now grew moribundly self-conscious, smug, encapsulated, isolated from its source, from the sickness which spawned it. It grew more rigid than the institutions it had set out to defy. It became a boring routine. The hipster—once an unregenerate individualist, an underground poet, a guerrilla—had become a pretentious poet laureate. His old subversiveness, his ferocity, was now so manifestly rhetorical as to be obviously harmless. He was bought and placed in the zoo. He was *somewhere* at last—comfortably ensconced in the 52nd Street clip joints, in Carnegie Hall, and *Life.* He was *in there*...he was back in the American womb. And it was just as unhygienic as ever.[57]

Hip culture cannot coherently claim to be both outside and inside, rebel and authority. Every generation of hipsters since Broyard's "Portrait" has tried to solve this dilemma, and none has succeeded. But the dilemma remains, because no one can overlook the obvious and enormous success of the countercultural idea. The later chapters of this book deal with what can truly be called a cultural revolution: the breakout of the hip sensibility into mass awareness in the decade from roughly 1965 to 1975. For a sensibility that saw itself as the permanent outcast of the American mainstream, this stunning success demanded an explanation. In the usual narrative, underwritten by the co-optation theory, the success of hipness in the 1960s is actually a catastrophic failure, a vast flanking operation whereby rebellion was made safe for capitalism. On this account, it was left to lonely bands of authentic dissidents (the punks, in most versions of this story) to create a new, unco-opted rebel culture. Within this narrative, co-optation works to explain away the contradictions of a successful revolt against success, an authoritative position against authority. And if punk now seems as safe and institutionalized as 1960s rock ever was, the co-optation narrative can explain that just as easily. Co-optation is a story that keeps us on the hook, looking for fresher and more appealing kinds of rebellion. A cynic might say that it is a good way to sell more records.

"The professor is making us into a movement, I could puke," snarls one of the hipsters in *The Magic of Their Singing*.[58] From the hipster's point of view, any hip "movement" is a counterfeit that comes to replace the real thing in the minds of the masses who read about it in *Life* magazine or listen to it on a Rod McKuen album. Regardless of their own intentions, the professors or critics or coolhunters who seek to publicize cultures to which they do not belong represent a larger system that co-opts authentic dissent. In the co-optation narrative, the New School professor appears to celebrate Beat values but in fact undermines them. Merely by claiming what does not rightly belong to him, the professor does violence to its meaning. He finds identity in nonidentity, asserting static and replicable meanings for what must remain fluid and unfixed, else it dies; he kills meaning that blooms only in experience. He turns ineffable experience into a program, a cause, a movement, and its reified meanings can then be embodied in commodities, so that squares can go out and buy a Charlie Parker record or a bullfight poster and think that it will confer hipness on them. This is the gist of a poem titled "(to sociologists & publicists of the beat generation)," which appeared in the San Francisco little magazine *Beatitude* in 1959, when Francis Rigney was doing fieldwork on the San Francisco Beat scene for his sociological study *The Real Bohemia*.[59]

> reveal and bastardize
>   the issue of a private search
>   create a sibling vine
>   that croaks the tree
>   and make the most uncommon
>   common knowledge . . .

sorry to say
you miss the point
these things are lived
not sociologized

would you kill everything
before the devastating bloom
appears

boast of humility
try to explain the beat
or utmost: hip
in academic words?[60]

The countercultural idea always condemns those who would explain hipness in academic words and yet always ends up explaining its condemnation in academic words. I was a graduate student in the 1990s, when we all imagined ourselves engaged in "resistance" and "subversion." In our seminars in critical theory, we mapped the dynamic of cultural hegemony and resistance onto the writings of Theodor Adorno, Antonio Gramsci, Michel Foucault, and other cultural theorists whose writings fit our bookishly countercultural temper. (This was around the time Kurt Cobain killed himself; regardless of whether we listened to Nirvana or not, what Cobain killed himself for mattered very much to us then.) In every class we would inevitably end up tracing the theoretical possibilities of an unco-opted radical culture and trying to find little cracks in the formidable armor of the culture industry. In these discussions a certain line of argument would assert itself again and again: that apparently critical forms of mass culture masked a deeper commitment to repression. If one of us argued that *The Simpsons* is both a form of mass culture and an authentic form of mass culture critique, someone else could reply that *The Simpsons* is a part of a system whose overarching effect is to circumscribe dissent from the outset. Once this argumentative move was made (and it always was), every discussion would then be spent in a vain attempt to find forms of expression that somehow managed to avoid becoming a part of the system of mass culture—to find "sites of resistance" that could somehow provide an exception to the totalizations of Frankfurt School mass culture critique. Cultural theory is committed to tracing a utopian course, following Adorno in a search for unadministered cultural spaces. This path is always blocked, though, by the possibility that every promising site of resistance only *seems* to resist. Any apparent exception to hegemony is no exception at all, but simply a deeper manifestation of it, a yet more cunning way to deliver us to its control.

It is depressing to think this way, and also deeply paranoid. Paranoia takes the shape of an infinite spiral stairway—a devil's staircase. Within a paranoid hermeneutics there is a potentially endless supply of explanations, each one of which is like a stair on which the interpreter treads to get to the next. When one explanation fails it is because it has obscured the real truth. (Maybe it is even in on the conspiracy!) The final truth is that step just around the bend—but then *that* step is just the next in an endless series. Paranoia is the point where hermeneutics itself becomes totality, where everything in the world can be explained, but final explanation always lies just out of reach. But when we explain everything, we explain nothing: as Joseph Heath and Andrew Potter point out, the theory of co-optation is a "'total ideology,' a completely closed system of thought, immune to falsification, in which every apparent exception simply confirms the rule."[61]

I cannot claim to have solved the co-optation problem in its own terms. Who could? All I have done is to attack it from a different direction, looking at it as an episode within intellectual and cultural history. If the co-optation thesis condemns us to climb an infinite Devil's Staircase of social-critical paranoia, one escape might lie in giving it a hard stare, breaking its spell, and coming to see it as just another artifact of culture. Which means understanding it in terms of its cultural forms, its aesthetics. The goal of pop culture scholarship has almost always been to find a political understanding of the aesthetic: I wish rather to find an aesthetic understanding of politics.

The Black Spot

Heath and Potter begin their challenge to the co-optation thesis by having some fun at Kalle Lasn's expense, mocking the founder of *Adbusters*, a magazine devoted to Situationist-style subterfuges of advertising, for starting his own line of footwear. Was *Adbusters* selling out? No, Heath and Potter argue, "because there was nothing to sell out in the first place." *Adbusters* was recycling anticonsumerist tropes that had been circulating for decades, and in 2003, just as in 1973, the assumption was that the cure for a toxic, corporate culture was a resistant counterculture. This "counterculture" made and sold products just like the "mainstream" it opposed, but it used a different marketing pitch, and an effective one. It told people that the culture they consumed said something about who they were and what they believed; that marking a cultural distinction between themselves and the "mainstream" was, in fact, a political act, because culture was itself the implement of the subtlest and most pervasive forms of power. Thus Lasn created the Black Spot sneaker to "uncool" Nike, to dethrone the sneaker giant by marshaling the power of hipness against it, and thereby to "set a precedent that will revolutionize capitalism."[62]

But this project did not meet with universal approval from other anticorporate activists. Naomi Klein argued that activists need to preserve spaces free of advertising, not to add their own kind of brand clutter. Lasn responded by calling Klein an "old leftist" who "[hangs] on to an old, 'pure' activism that hasn't had any success for 20 or 30 years," adding "There's a lot of people now who want to jump over the dead body of the old left. We've decided to stop whining about Nike; why not make $10 million and use it to run a media literacy campaign instead? I'm really sick of the whiners."[63] On one side there is Lasn, arguing that capitalism can be turned against itself and reformed into a countercapitalism; on the other is Klein, arguing that capitalism cannot be reformed but can only be contained— excluded from liberated spaces that anticonsumerist activists such as herself must create and maintain. These are the two poles of the co-optation argument, and neither can win. One side can always say that countercapitalism is no different from what it seeks to counter, and the other can always say that pure rejectionism is a recipe for irrelevance and failure. Both sides are right.

So much for the question of whether Lasn's strategy is wise; the argument will continue in other forms, and it can continue without us. What interests me is the aesthetics of the shoe itself, and of the advertising that accompanied it (Fig. 1.3). The ad copy for the Black Spot Unswoosher (the high-top version of original Black Spot) piles on signifiers (hemp, vegetarian, union, "earth-friendly," "pro-grassroots," "kicking corporate ass") that position it within a genealogy of progressive causes, critiques, and verbal idioms going back to the 1960s and earlier.[64] But moving on from verbal markers to those of visual style, we find that these place the ad in the lineage of hip culture just as surely as the ad copy does. Instead of a corporate logo, the Black Spot features a "hand-drawn anti-logo." If corporations use their logos to extend their empires and flaunt their domination, an "anti-logo" suggests the stuff of grassroots insurgency. Other versions of the ad feature an Unswoosher wordmark in the shape of Nike's famous "swoosh," but with a little gout of running ink trailing off at its end, a Brechtian alienation gesture of the sort ubiquitous in radical culture since the 1960s, intended to reveal the made-ness hidden by the glossy surfaces of consumer culture. The heavy, crude-looking stitching on the shoe itself is coded with visual signs of unmediated labor. The typeface is similarly textural, mimicking the rough and uneven application of ink from a worn typewriter or rough stenciling. As David Brooks notes in *Bobos in Paradise,* his satirical account of domesticated countercultural manners, "the educated elites love texture," and rough textures "[connote] authenticity and virtue."[65] Even the single point of color in a monochrome field—the "sweet spot"—and the sans-serif font of the ad copy is in dialogue with advertising codes developed within hip culture: think of similar compositions in Reid Miles's album cover art for Blue Note.[66] Whatever it is that Lasn is "really" doing—whether he is a dupe of capitalism or bringing it down from within—he is doing it within a venerable network of expressive codes.

Figure 1.3 Advertisement for the Black Spot Unswoosher.

In the next chapter I describe one of these codes, the "hipster handshake" (a pointed finger offered in greeting instead of an outstretched hand), which is structured by the same kind of metonymic abstraction Thelonious Monk sometimes deployed in improvisations. Someone once challenged me on this point: How could I compare some lame hipster affectation to Monk's brilliant performances? The difference lies in artistic skill. Thelonious Monk isn't hipper or more authentic than some guy trying to impress girls in a Brooklyn bar, he's a better artist—better at manipulating the same expressive codes, and able, through the force of his art, to introduce new ones. Fran Kelley's pompous liner notes for *Zen* resemble Jack Kerouac's *The Dharma Bums* insofar as both are impostures, but the difference is that Kerouac's was a good imposture, or at least good enough to foster a widespread interest in Asian religion that prompted many to serious religious practice. George Burns is supposed to have said "sincerity is everything—if you can fake that, you've got it made." Substitute "sincerity" with "authenticity" and you have the idea that motivates much of what follows.[67]

Some people feel uneasy with this kind of argument, because it seems to suggest that the political and social attitudes they hold in common with hip culture are just postures. (The lazy hipster baiting that has become routine in the past decade always ends up with this claim. "Hipster" and "poseur" are now practically synonyms.[68]) But it is not so simple. To fake sincerity is not merely to pretend to be sincere while secretly holding other convictions, to talk about "kicking corporate ass" while hypocritically wanting to make money like everyone else. First of all, we tend not to notice the contradictions in the positions we take, even when others kindly point them out for us. We all turn out to be skilled at hiding our inconsistencies from self-awareness.[69] And second, we can reconcile contradictory or absurd beliefs by participating in them: in the moment we act on a belief, we make the belief true.[70] Robert Anton Wilson, a countercultural science-fiction writer and occultist we will meet again in Chapter 6, wrote that "you cannot make three dramatic gestures of rage in a political speech, without beginning to feel some real rage."[71] This fact in turn suggests that the self is not some self-identical entity that persists unchanged through time but is more like a series of events I experience subjectively (and speciously) as a concrete, unitary thing and think of as "who I really am." In other words, our selves are made and remade every minute, whether we know it or not; the hipster simply takes a hand in the creative process.

This view of the *I* as verb rather than noun is what Alfred North Whitehead meant in identifying the self as a "concrescence of prehensions," a constant unfolding process by which the subject is constituted as the meeting point of multiple vectors.[72] Whitehead's understanding of self comes close to the "original human nature and the spontaneous creative spirit" that Gary Snyder found in Zen, and the popularity of Whitehead's ideas among the postwar avant-garde springs from the same fundamental impulse as the Zen fad.[73] A self conceived as a nexus of forces within a field of energy is a self pictured as an integral part of a whole—an overwhelming, concrete, immediate, here-and-now presence within which the hipster tries to live.

This is the *somewhere* that hip culture has tried to grasp and represent for the better part of a century. The new understanding of self this project entails, and the new understanding of art and reality that goes along with it, is what is really at stake in studying hipness. Hipness is about a lot more than recreational drug use, funny haircuts, weird lingo, and the hipster's infuriating attitude of superiority. It is the discourse within which American culture found a new psychological, existential, metaphysical orientation—an orientation that is still with us today, whether we like it or not.

2

Somewhere/Nowhere

In there was, of course, somewhereness. *Nowhere,* the hipster's
favorite pejorative, was an *abracadabra* to make things
disappear. *Solid* connoted the stuff, the reality, of existence; it
meant concreteness in a bewilderingly abstract world. A *drag*
was something which "dragged" implications along with it,
something which was embedded in an inseparable, complex,
ambiguous—and thus, possibly threatening—context.[1]
—Anatole Broyard

Precambrian

For the natural historian, fossils are a bit of luck. It so happens that many living
things have hard parts porous enough for mineral-rich water to seep through
them and so gradually to replace organic material with a detailed mineral replica,
but durable enough not to decay before they have a chance to fossilize. Thanks to
this felicitous balance, we have an amazingly fine-drawn history of life on earth.
However, this history is not complete: organisms with soft tissues only, like
worms and grasses, are seldom preserved. Of the Precambrian era, where no
organisms had hard parts, we know relatively little, but we know that life then
was abundant all the same, regardless of how well it was recorded. It is the same
way with hipness. Around the end of World War II, not only the word "hip" but
hipness itself emerged from the obscurity of an unrecorded oral milieu, but only
once it had a chance to "fossilize"—that is, to be written about and so to enter
the historical record.

Of the late-1950s New York beat scene, Ned Polsky wrote that "the cool world
is an iceberg, mostly underwater."[2] Polsky's uncapitalized beats were not the
same people as the literary Beats who memorialized their way of life:

> Almost all Village beats technically are literate, and some whites have
> even attended college, but at best a sixth are habituated to reading
> (none seem addicted) and far fewer are concerned with writing. Most

square articles on "the beats" go astray because beat writers, being highly visible, get all the attention and thus a small and atypical part is taken for the whole.[3]

What was true for the subjects of Polsky's ethnography is true for hip subcultures generally, and doubly true for the emergent hip culture of the 1930s and early 1940s. Hipsters did not express their views in print, and such third-person accounts of them that we do have are by turns amused, baffled, contemptuous, and clinical, but in every case separated from their subjects by a want of sympathy and common experience. One sociological study from 1945 (whose principle author, Kenneth Clark, was a pioneering African American psychologist) offers an example of the wide gulf between hipsters and their academic interlocutors. What its authors call "the zoot effect" is what I am calling hipness, and their description of a hipster perspective *in* but not *of* society is exactly on point:

> ...this 'zoot effect' may involve...modifications of language (deliberately ungrammatical), high saturation of slang or profane words in ordinary speech, manner and inflection of speech, swagger or exaggeration of some aspect of style of walking, and...style of dress. In short it appears to represent an observable deviation in style of life...of many individuals living within, but not a part of, the larger social and cultural context.[4]

And yet the authors seem unaware of when they are being put on and so fail to understand that much of their informant's account of the 1943 Harlem riots is not to be taken as literally true: "There are many statements of this respondent which cannot be reconciled with the objectively determined facts of this incident," they remark in the po-faced style of sociological research. In later years it would have been clear that their informant spoke in the hipster's trickster idiom that Henry Louis Gates brought to academic attention through his theory of signifyin(g). (I will continue to use this term without Gates's internal parentheses.)

With the exception of a few black journalists and the odd sociologist or linguist, hardly anyone in the 1930s or 1940s thought much about the young black men lounging in the streets or hustling in nightclubs.[5] There was certainly no such thing as a hip novel like *Go* (1952), a hip poem like *Howl* (1956), a hip little magazine like the *Evergreen Review* (founded in 1957), or a hip film like *Shadows* (1957–1959)—the idea of a hip literature or cinema belonged to the 1950s.[6] Of course music was hip, and offhand or dismissive references to jitterbugs and hipsters abounded in the music press.[7] But the hipness of a musician such as Lester Young, however indisputable, went untheorized.[8] Whatever hipness and hip culture may have been (and no one thought to ask), it went publicly unarticulated; what documentation we have of this Precambrian period is just enough to give us an idea of how little we know.

Although almost nothing was written about the hipster in the late 1930s, he cut a familiar enough figure for Cab Calloway to fashion a star image as a zoot-suited hepcat whose songs, seasoned with "Harlemese" slang, tell saucy underworld tales. In such films as *Stormy Weather* (1943), Calloway's image was that of "the sporting man as virtuoso, an amalgam of flash and discipline."[9] In contrast to Young's mien of cool withdrawal, Calloway was "the hipster as extrovert"—a persona that later cooled-out hipsters (Jack Kerouac called them "your bearded laconic sage, or schlerm," in contrast to "hot hipsters" like himself) found a little too frantic.[10] But Calloway also had a tricksterish streak, and as John Leland has pointed out, hipness has always had a trickster element—think of Dizzy Gillespie, Bob Dylan, George Clinton, or the Beastie Boys. When Leland argues that Bugs Bunny is a kind of hipster, you can see his point: "Tricksters advance hip by crossing and recrossing the lines that hem it in. Their tools are not ideals like justice or valor but wit, wile, and self-interest. Nontrickster heroes help societies distinguish between right and wrong; tricksters violate the boundary between the two."[11] None of Calloway's film roles captures this side of him as well as the surviving acetates of his 1941–42 radio program *Quizzicale*.

Quizzicale, one of the first programs by and mostly for African Americans, was "the Harlem idea of what a quiz and music program really ought to be."[12] Each show featured "Harlem experts," ordinary people from the black neighborhood of whatever city Calloway was visiting, answering listener questions for five-dollar prizes. There were also musical numbers from Calloway and his orchestra and hepcat banter between "Doctor Calloway" and his sidekicks "Brother Etcetera Treadway" (Eddie Barefield) and "Brother Sixty-Two Jones" (Milt Hinton). Percival Prattis, later a noted civil rights leader, harrumphed that Calloway was a "Fifth Columnist" working against the interests of the Negro, but if he had little sympathy with *Quizzicale* he at least understood the intention behind it well enough: Calloway was out to "make a mess of all quiz programs."[13] Calloway signified on the standard materials of the quiz show, and signifying is (to borrow a phrase from J. L. Austin) "how to do things with words." "How to do things with words" does not only mean "how to say things"; signifying comprises performative speech acts in which speakers fasten onto the "materiality of the signifier," those sounding qualities that allow the ordered meanings of literacy to go astray.[14] Signifying means making words into sounded and performed actions, rather than letting them lie inert, the dead husks of an administrative meaning. Words are things you do to and with people: in signifying, words are how people get "done," in the sense of the African American idiom that means getting fucked, or fucked up, or fucked with. It goes without saying that *Quizzicale* was heavily larded with Calloway's trademark hip slang. However, his performance and persona are not carried by the meanings of words alone but by the way words are put in motion. *Quizzicale* inverts the conventions of popular quiz shows such as "Kay Kyser's Kollege of Musical Knowledge" and

"Dr. I.Q." The master of ceremonies is not a professorial authority but a jive-talking musician; it is not privileged white people but working-class African Americans who get to show off their knowledge; and knowledge, in this topsy-turvy world, could be the answer to questions like "which would you rather have, money in the bank or a long yellow roadster with the top down, a fur coat on, and a police dog?"[15] To Calloway's middle-class critics, this kind of thing sounded like undignified clowning. Others might have heard a subtle point being made: maybe the Harlem expert knows something you don't. You could have missed the point if you were expecting to hear it conveyed in the meanings of words, though; Calloway's signifying had more to do with the sounds of words.

Given the recent entry of the United States into the war, Calloway had to put up with singing a certain amount of patriotic corn such as "Fightin' Doug MacArthur," but he put some distance between himself and the song by means of what would become a standard hipster dodge, the kind of put-on Jacob Brackman calls "relentless agreement."[16] Calloway concludes the song with a ringing speech, declaiming

> The fight you've made will live forever, General Douglas MacArthur!
> The world will shout with your endeavor, General Douglas MacArthur!
> You've united the people of the Philippines
> The Army, the Navy, and our Marines,
> God bless you, General Douglas MacArthur![17]

in the quavering and stereotypically white tones of a flag-day orator (angled off the stiff rat-a-tat diction of a newsreel reader) and backed by a staccato fanfare from his trumpet section. The upward inflection Calloway uses on every instance of MacArthur's name (something between a question and a command) seems to call history itself to witness the magnificence of MacArthur's achievement—which, in March 1942, mostly consisted of getting run out of the Philippines by the Japanese. Calloway's squarer listeners might have congratulated him on his patriotism, but at least a few of the "Harlem experts" might have had a different idea of what he was up to.

Calloway also signifies on his guests, for example catching onto the educated middle-class R's clearly enunciated by a straight-arrow contestant named Charles Farmer ("I work in the Catholic League and I'm in defense training") and playing them off his own hip drawl:

CALLOWAY: Awright, here's our next contestant. What is your name, brotha?
FARMER: Charles Farmer.
CALLOWAY: Chawles Fawma.
FARMER: Right.
CALLOWAY: Chawles Fawma.

FARMER: Farmer, I . . .

CALLOWAY: Chawles Fawma. I see. No corn I'm havin,' no corn. That's awright.
             Chawles Fawma.[18]

The format of *Quizzicale* allowed Calloway to take on the voices and personalities of straight radio types—for example, the clipped elocutionary manner of an announcer introducing the classical portion of the program. Like the Bugs Bunny short *Long-Haired Hare*, the mock-classical part of *Quizzicale* represents what classical music sounds like to an audience for which it is someone else's culture. From a defamiliarizing distance, operatic singing presents a freakish spectacle of extreme registral shifts, stiffly formal vocalise, notes held to preposterous lengths and at shattering volume, scenery-chewing melodrama, and a range of stagey sobs, sighs, and laughter that correspond to no recognizable human emotion. In *Long-Haired Hare,* Bugs vanquishes an obnoxious tenor by tricking him into singing a single pitch so long and loudly it destroys the auditorium.[19] In his portentous pseudo-operatic introduction to "Nay, Nay," Calloway holds a falsetto high C for twelve seconds (followed by a quiet "whew") after first descending to a croaked D flat three octaves below and climbing his way back up with some vocal exercises ("me-me, you-you, me-me-me-me-me-me-me-meeeee") and a yodel. Throughout this astonishing throwaway bit, Calloway sounds like both the tenor of *Long-Haired Hare* and Bugs Bunny at the same time, his voice careening through musical styles and personae, sounding his signature melismatic wail at one moment and bursting into an unhinged stage laugh ("Pagliacci, a-ha-ha-ha-ha-ha!") in the next. Like Bugs, he is a trickster hero; if, as Leland writes, hip is "being able to play the other guy's game," the trickster plays it by "undermin[ing] all the positions on the board"—or perhaps playing them all at once.[20] This is the rhetorical trope of metalepsis, the "slave's trope" or trope-of-tropes that Henry Louis Gates identifies as the characteristic form of signifying.[21]

The tricksterish dimensions of Calloway's performance and the role of signifying in hipness are clear in hindsight, yet in the 1930s and early 1940s it was not hipness but the hipster that began to show up in the black press, registering as a pest, a pathology, or a joke. Mostly, he was a nuisance: idle, insolent, shady, affected, and unpatriotic, the hipster was an embarrassment to the middle-class columnists who wished their young men might better advertise the progress of the race.[22] (For their part, the hipsters thought middle-class blacks were timid, pretentious fools truckling to white people who despised them anyway.)[23] The great exception was Dan Burley, an entertainment reporter, editor, and part-time jazz pianist whose column "Back Door Stuff" began running in the *Chicago Defender* in 1935 and two years later moved to the *New York Amsterdam News*. A forum for gossip and streetwise social observation, "Back Door Stuff" was the first place where the hipster continuously registered as a presence in black popular culture. Burley was the first to sketch the portrait that other writers would fill out in later years; in his weekly columns, the untheorized stance that Calloway and Young struck in their very different ways began to be put into words.

Burley's first "Back Door Stuff" for the *New York Amsterdam News* announces its goal of observing and documenting Harlem society with an amused and affectionate eye. Burley promises that his column will be

> the true lowdown: all that's smart in modern palavering: the trunk line, the grapevine telegraph: the tom-tom of the gossip tribe, the pulse beat on real life: It's the harbinger of ultra-fashionable trends, the interpreter of the masses: it's swing time on paper, folks: the blustering decrier of the wrongdoer, the lilting lyric herald of progress.[24]

Transcribing the "tom-tom of the gossip tribe" is a straightforward enough goal, but to make a column into "swing time on paper" is to capture lightning in a bottle, freezing in typeset prose the flow and rhythm of life as it is lived. In *Really the Blues,* Mezz Mezzrow and Bernard Wolfe would credit Burley for their understanding that jive is *"the language of action . . .* [which] comes from the bars, the dancehalls, the prisons, honky-tonks, ginmills, etc., wherever people are busy living, loving, fighting, working or conniving to get the better of one another."[25] Giving readers the true lowdown is not simply a matter of transcribing words, but transcribing also the contexts from which words draw their meaning. As those contexts are always in motion, so too are the meanings inscribed in them. Burley was not only the first to note this understanding in print; his writing was also the first to perform it. Every stratum of Harlem society (including the slumming white tourists) registers in "Back Door Stuff" through its verbal idiom. Like a boxer, Burley sticks and moves, signifying on each idiom in turn and weaving his polyphony of voices into an extended jive that is not so much an idiom itself but an idiom of idioms, a metalepsis. Burley's was the first hip literary voice. He was the first writer to set himself up not merely as the observer of the characters on the street corner, but as a literary exponent of their sensibility. Still, he was clearly not one of them: putting "swing time on paper" already implies some distance between the observer and the observed.

In his second column for the *New York Amsterdam News*, Burley gives us a quick pen portrait of the hipster: "Lenox Avenue is his kingdom. Worldly wise, he ekes out an existence in lean times that allows him to keep out of the bread lines, dodge WPA toil and the other distasteful avenues of regular labor. He knows Lenox Avenue and the avenue knows him."[26] Already we can see the hipster's features emerging, like a face in a drying Polaroid picture. Here is someone for whom larger society is subtly inimical, not to be opposed outright but gotten around. He is an operator: what makes him distinctive is not a settled philosophy but a stance that is worked out in the process of living, in the encounter with contingency, in situations that call for a smooth hustle. In 1939, Burley fleshed this portrait out into the zoot-suited hipster we can recognize from Malcolm X's recollections of his early life as a hustler called "Detroit Red." Burley describes the zoot suit and the exaggeratedly aloof posture by which its wearers showed off its billowing lines:

> First, he's togged out in a draped coat that pinches in sharply at the waist and then blossoms about the hips and ends with a sassy flair. His britches start 'way up, almost under his arm-pits and are hitched even higher by gaudy braces over the shoulders. The pants peg down to the top of his shoes, ballooning a bit at the knees. The hat is a Tyrolese version of the damage done to Max Schmeling's face after a smack by Joe Louis, and the brim shades the wearer's features in the best George Raft manner.... He slowly rises on the balls of his feet and luxuriously lowers himself and does it again and again, letting his knees expand...he drops the index finger of one hand stiffly down and then inclines the upper portion of his body into a quarter-stoop and struts stiff-leggedly in a semi-circle.[27]

In this account, the hipster emerges as the "pylon around whose implacability the world obsequiously careered," in the words of Anatole Broyard's later *Partisan Review* essay "Portrait of the Hipster" (1948).

Broyard would end his essay with a cold depiction of the domesticated hipster, now a pet of the intellectuals:

> Ransacking everything for meaning, admiring insurgence, they attributed every heroism to the hipster. He became their 'there but for the grip of my superego go I.' He was received in the Village as an oracle; his language was the *revolution of the word, the personal idiom.* He was the great instinctual man, an ambassador from the Id.[28]

Years earlier, one of Burley's correspondents had similarly suggested that the hip writing of "Back Door Stuff" might be a furtive indulgence for downtown intellectuals:

> Your column's appeal to the Cosmopolite, the Sophisticate, the Bohemian ...and that peculiar new species of homo sapiens, the Hipster, is not to be disputed. Incidentally, I suspect even the alleged Intellectual takes a sneap-peep at the jive every so often. You know the score. He thinks it 'rawthah crude infantile, only for the rabble,' yet all the while looking to see whether or not he rated a mention in the column.[29]

The week after this letter appeared, Burley himself went further, suggesting that hipness is not simply something that intellectuals might co-opt, but a new and alternative kind of intellectualism. The "Back Door Stuff" column for April 24, 1943, "In Which a Hipcat is Studied by Experts," featured a satirical dialogue between Big Educator, a blowhard out to "save the race" ("whether the 'race' wanted to be saved or not"), and Social Worker, who is not light-skinned enough to "pass" and so is stuck in Harlem, trying to make a living from the social pathology of his neighbors. Big Educator is a hip parody of the reactionary black middle class: he asserts, "You know our biggest problem is to let the world know all Negroes are not alike, and in these days of war and turmoil I am convinced we should be as inconspicuous as possible." He blusters cluelessly about the baggy drape and tight cuffs of the zoot suit while Social Worker tries to set him straight, though Social Worker is a bit clueless himself. He knows that hip style has something to do with a mood of social discontent but talks about the zoot suit as if it were a fixed signifier of social meaning: "the tightness of the cuffs is the badge of modernity among our younger generation," he pronounces. If Big Educator is a parody of middle-class community leaders, Social Worker is a parody of those intellectuals who are discovering an urgent and timely message in hipness without understanding that it is not the kind of message they are accustomed to finding in books. Hipness may be as much a philosophy as a style, but it does not consist in fixed and definable positions.

At one point, Big Educator gets confused about what Social Worker means by "hip boots":

SOCIAL WORKER: You don't quite understand. Hip boots do not mean literally that the boots reach the hips. There is no physical phenomena involved. The term is used in a totally different sense. Hip boots indicate a certain degree of mental acumen the wearer has attained. They are the Harlem equivalent of a college degree from the Institution of the Sidewalk.

BIG EDUCATOR: I still do not understand. Hmmmm! Hip boots, college degrees, mental acumen. My good fellow, it doesn't make sense. How can hip boots be confused with a degree from an accredited college! Bah! It is extraordinarily silly for you to tell me that shoes which curl at the ends have something to do with the acquisition of wisdom!

SOCIAL WORKER: My Dear Doctor. You talk as though I were an authority on this matter. I assure, in fact, I hasten to assure you that I am, myself, feeling my way blindly through a jungle of contradictions trying to reach an equitable conclusion. I am only a student of social phenomena, not an authority. I was told that the shoes the young man wears are called hip boots. Beyond that I can venture no farther.[30]

Though brief, this passage outlines a complete theory of hip. It suggests that a style of clothing can say something about the society and historical moment in which its wearers live, and might be worthy of serious intellectual attention for this reason; that those who properly wear the style understand its deeper meaning—in other words, that the style of a commodity says something about the social knowledge ("mental acumen") of its consumer; that even though this knowledge is not the same as a degree from an accredited college, it is perhaps equivalent or even better; and that whatever this knowledge is, squares like Big Educator will never get it, because they remain stuck in the literal meanings of words. And finally, the most important thing about the zoot suit's elusive meaning is that it is elusive. The realm of hipness is closed to outsiders, and while Social Worker is pretty square, he is at least hip enough to know that he can claim no authority over it. Hipness, then, is not only knowledge, but secret knowledge.

Game Ideology

The idea of hip as secret knowledge was one of the most important insights that Mezz Mezzrow and Bernard Wolfe picked up from Burley and developed in *Really the Blues*. In the latter account, hip speech draws on a secret understanding of oppression that binds African Americans into a kind of conspiracy against society:

> [Jive is] a protest, and not so inarticulate at that. That's what makes it entirely unique, a different kind of language from the traditional Southern Negro's, which didn't challenge the white oppressor but only tried to escape from his eagle eye, and those of his watchdogs. Jive does knit together a kind of tight secret society—but it's a society which resents and nourishes its resentment, and is readying to strike back. The hipster's fraternal order isn't just an escape valve, a defense mechanism; it's a kind of drilling academy too, preparing for future battles.[31]

Really the Blues marks the end of the hipster's early obscurity and the beginning of a shift in intellectual focus. Mezzrow and Wolfe still wrote about hipsters, but their attention had widened to encompass hipness. *Really the Blues* was the first sustained piece of writing to consider what underlying principle might make sense of the hipster's funny clothes, weird jargon, and love of jazz. Not coincidentally, it is also the coming-out party for the White Negro. The Mezzrow mythos was a compound of criminality and elective negritude (the ad copy boasted that Mezzrow had "crossed the color line, *backwards*")[32] that needed only the element of bohemian artiness to attain Norman Mailer's later formula for the White Negro: "In such places as Greenwich Village, a ménage-a-trois was completed—the bohemian and the juvenile delinquent came face-to-face with the Negro, and the hipster was a fact in American life."[33] From this point on, hipness no longer develops in subcultural isolation but fully enters the intercultural network I have described in the previous chapter. The driving force of this exchange is the tricky dynamic of "love and theft" that has ever defined the white relationship to black culture in America.[34] LeRoi Jones puts it well:

> The form and content of Negro music in the forties re-created, or reinforced, the social and historical alienation of the Negro in America, but in the Negro's terms. The Negro jazz musician of the forties was *weird*. And the myth of this weirdness, this alienation, was sufficiently important to white America for it to re-create the myth in a term that connoted not merely Negroes as the aliens but a *general* alienation in which even white men could be included.[35]

To be sure, by the late 1940s some whites had already flirted with jazz and jive. Newspapers in the early 1940s carried the odd moral-panic story of young white jitterbugs for whom jazz was a gateway to more illicit thrills, and some of the ubiquitous glossaries suggested that hip jive (or at least one version of it) was a white teenage code.[36] The now-forgotten film musical *Mr. Big* (1943), a variation on the Garland-Rooney story formula of kids putting on a show, treats hip jive as a kind of white teen craze and, in a pattern repeated countless times before and after, tries to carry on as if black people had nothing to do with it. And yet blackness, and white desire for the more expansive possibilities of selfhood that blackness seemed to represent, reads like a guilty secret in this film, a near-return of the repressed, like a secret on the verge of confession.[37] As the kids rehearse for the big show, they try out a blackface number and find it a little corny; when a group of black singers (the Ben Carter choir) happens by and begins to sing along, the missing element is found. In *Mr. Big* as in minstrelsy generally, black people are there to help white people loosen up and express themselves, but that's the only reason they're in this film; they don't get stories of their own.[38] In a scene where the two teen leads black up, the film makes a sight gag out of the fact that they have only blacked up half their faces, so when they turn to face the camera we see that one half of their faces is a negative of the other. This is a startlingly direct metaphor for the relationship between black and white in hip culture—the secret that *Mister Big* cannot quite bring itself to tell (Fig. 2.1).

The big jive number—a Buddy Pepper song called "Hi, Character"—runs a variation on the familiar pitched battle between high culture and jazz.[39] The students have been forced to put on a production of *Antigone*, but the moment the

Figure 2.1 Still from *Mr. Big* (1943).

stuffy society matron who runs the school is tricked into leaving, they go from faux-Greek monotone chanting to a lively choreographed swing number. "Hi, Character" plays off the contrast between jazz and the classics by posing Donald O'Connor as a Hellenic statue that gets down from its pedestal and cuts some rug. This is the *Barber of Seville* routine from *Babes in Arms*, with hip jive thrown in as a novelty gimmick. It's not without its charms, but it does not feel particularly hip. A present-day audience will mostly think it feels safe, and white, as milk. Missing from this film is the sense of a subalterity and transgression where something more consequential is at stake than jitterbugging at a school show.

This is what *Really the Blues* supplies. The first sentence of the book sets the tone of the whole: "Music school? Are you kidding? I learned to play the sax in Pontiac Reformatory."[40] In *Really the Blues* as with later pieces such as "The White Negro," secret knowledge is underworld knowledge. Consequently, though not entirely on purpose, the literature of the White Negro sets up an unspoken and treacherous syllogism: if blacks are hip and hipness is criminal, then blacks must be criminal. (We will return to this problem in Chapter 5.) But the association between hipness and hustling is not simply something a white jazz clarinetist and his ghostwriter worked out between them in 1946. The hipster as trickster, operator, or hustler (which aren't the same things, granted, but aren't easy to tell apart either) is an aspect of the hip stance that *Quizzicale* and "Back Door Stuff" capture, and it was part of the street life that those who were there remember in their autobiographies.[41]

Jack Kerouac once told John Clellon Holmes that the hipster sees himself *in* but not *of* society.[42] This insight is basic to the distinctions that go into fashioning hip culture and the hip self. In *The Autobiography of Malcolm X,* a young Malcolm Little is initiated into his new life as a streetwise operator when a shoeshine man tells him "the main thing you got to remember is that everything in the world is a hustle."[43] This is a statement of what R. Lincoln Keiser calls "game ideology"—a trickster worldview the hustler adopts and by which he sees any given situation in which he is acting as a game.[44] By this cognitive move, the hustler estranges his perception from the taken-for-granted facts of the social world; he is in it but no longer of it. To view everything as a hustle or a game is to revalue social rules and see them not as moral imperatives but simply as strategies, and not necessarily any strategy of your own. The hustler's picture of himself as a player in a game is a picture of the rat caught in a maze, bound by arbitrary rules and stuck in a system others have made for their own ends. Within this view, the people in the game are either duped by it or understand it for what it is, and the latter use their knowledge to gain whatever advantage they can. Such is the dualistic worldview that sociologist Harold Finestone encountered among the heroin-addicted Chicago hipsters he studied in the early 1950s:

> The image of himself as "operator" was projected onto the whole world about him and led to a complete skepticism as to other persons' motives. He could relate to people by outsmarting them, or through open-handed and often ruinous generosity, but his world seemed to preclude any relationship which was not part of a "scheme" or did not lend itself to an "angle." The most difficult puzzle for him to solve was the "square," the honest man. On the one hand the "square" was the hard-working plodder who lived by routine and who took honesty and the other virtues at their face value. As such he constituted the prize victim for the cat. On the other hand the cat harbored the sneaking suspicion that some squares were smarter than he, because they could enjoy all the forbidden pleasures which were his stock in trade and maintain a reputation for respectability in the bargain.[45]

The view of the world as hustle could be reduced to a simple fourfold scheme:

1. There is a prize, and the goal of playing is to win it.
2. There are posted rules for playing.
3. The game is rigged, as the posted rules and the means for winning are not the same.
4. What it really takes to win the prize is to figure out an angle or covert accommodation within the overt structure of the game.

The first two statements (the goal and the rules) pertain to the overt structure of the game; the third and fourth (the fix and the angle) are about the covert and true state of play.[46] Game ideology is a dualistic view, a way of looking at the world divided into false appearance and true-but-unseen reality. In such a schema, knowledge is hidden, occult; truth is esoteric and available only to the initiated, those who have been hipped to it.

Everyone plays the game but only the initiated understand the fix, and the relative states of knowing define social and economic power. In the line Flava Flav and Chuck D knock out between them in "Fight the Power"— "People, people we are the same / no we're not the same 'cause we don't know the game"— the humanistic rhetoric of universality is shown up as another hustle, a way of disavowing the real but covert inequalities of the American economy. Let's call the game "making it in America"; the goal is middle-class prosperity; the posted rules state that success is tied to individual merit, education, and hard work within the law. But the game is fixed, and the fix is race: what it really takes to win is to be white. Stealing is against the rules, as is pimping, drug dealing, and every other kind of black-market hustle, but for black people (so the argument of game ideology goes) what the rules put off-limits are what it takes to win the game. The trick is getting away with breaking the overt rules; a good hustle will end up being in some way a part of the white power structure it subverts:

> The members of the subculture, almost to a man, defined hustling in general terms as a way of "making it" without killing oneself on whitey's jobs. Operationally, this "making it" encompasses a variety of "games" (i.e., hustles) run in a smooth, slick manner. Hustlers were quick to point out that their games do not represent crimes of violence against individuals. Rather, they are tactful circumventions of the law, and in most cases success is facilitated by cooperation from police and judicial officials.[47]

As the heroin dealer in Jack Gelber's *The Connection* says, "I believe that anything that's illegal is illegal because it makes more money for more people that way."[48] Within game ideology, society is divided between an overground and an underground, each deniably dependent on the other: the outcasts are cast out precisely because they provide a service that polite society cannot admit it needs.[49] Thus Robin Kelley writes that Malcolm X's initiation into hustling "illuminated the power of the trickster figure or the signifying monkey, whose success depended not only on cunning and wiles, but on knowing what and how the powerful thought."[50]

And so the operator is given to systemic critique. Success or failure in any enterprise is not the result of individual contingencies; you do not win or lose just because you beat or are beaten by one particular person.[51] The adversary is not an individual but a system, abstract and impersonal, which in black vernacular could be personified as "the Man." Sixties radicals would later say that the fundamental act of radical criticism was to "name the system." By giving this abstract and impersonal system an identity that is at once abstract and absurdly personal, the African American vernacular named the system with a deadpan irony that implied a social critique of some complexity. "The Man" is not a man, but a position of power: as one of *The Connection*'s junkies says, "I'm the Man if you come to me. You're the Man if I come to you."[52]

The hip critique of society as system tends toward an inverted morality. For the operator, conventional morality is just another hustle: it is how the Man keeps you straight, which is to say, playing a game you can never win. The operator's morality is not founded on such qualities as nobility, bravery, justice, or honesty, but being true to himself, to his own perceptions and experience, whatever they may be. The part of "The White Negro" that provoked the most outrage was Mailer's suggestion that the murder of a defenseless storekeeper by a pair of thugs might be considered an act of courage. The criminal may do something objectively bad, runs the argument, but in carrying out the imperatives of an authentic badness, realizing the true badness in himself and fearlessly exploring all its domains and capacities, he is maintaining an integrity that is in a sense more admirable than the morality of someone who is well-behaved simply because he fears or cannot imagine any alternative. In Mailer's essay, we see how a literary hip culture takes over from the hustler's ethic the notion that conventional morality signifies arbitrary and repressive convention, while subversion of morality becomes admirable, even heroic, when it is in service of the authentic self. A conventionally good man may be admired for being honest and sincere: he says what he means and he means what he says. However, authenticity is a different and (as Lionel Trilling puts it) a "more strenuous moral experience": it is not merely bringing feeling and avowal into agreement but discovering what one's real feelings are.[53] Thus, as Charles Taylor writes, the personal project of authenticity drives a wedge between the good and the moral.[54]

Smart Goes Crazy

Hipness as social critique, as the view from the underground, as transgression and crime, as an orientation to present experience, as a kind of secret knowledge—these were the strands that intellectuals in the later 1940s were beginning to gather together into . . . what? A philosophy? A political critique? An aesthetic movement? A spiritual revival? In some sense hipness lay prior to any of these—it was a sensibility and an aesthetic that might have colored or informed a political, philosophical, spiritual, or aesthetic movement, but it could not be limited to any of them. However, this was not immediately clear.

1948 seems to be a historical pivot, a point where a small handful of writers were beginning to think seriously about hipness while the rest were groping for a vocabulary with which to describe it. Perhaps it is something like a college fad? A 1948 *Life* photo essay, in which white fans of Slim Gaillard perform elaborate full-body greetings, portrayed hipsterism in much the same way as *Mr. Big*, as zany but harmless teenage hijinks.[55] Perhaps it is a whim of fashion? For one

1948 *Ebony* article, "eccentricity in everyday living as well as music" meant paste-on beards, horn-rimmed glasses, butterfly bow ties, and meerschaum pipes.[56] Or is it an exotic and sinister political tendency? A 1948 *Time* article about Dizzy Gillespie suggested an affinity between bebop's cult sensibility and socialism, casting bebop attitudes toward Dixieland jazz as a quarrel with "decadent" music, which made beboppers sound like Zhdanovites denouncing the enemies of Socialist Realism.[57] A 1948 cartoon short called *Make Mine Freedom* explained the threat of socialism in the character of "Dr. Utopia," a snake-oil salesman who tries to peddle his medicine of state central planning to credulous Americans. The metaphorical figure of the Communist is rendered as a zoot-suited hipster, complete with oversize bow tie, skinny moustache, drape suit-coat, pegged pants, wide-brimmed flat-top hat, and a sharky grin pulled into a V.[58] The language of these various artifacts, conflating hipness with fashion or socialism, rings false to our ears, but a more adequate vocabulary was not yet widely available. In 1948, it was hard to grasp that hipness is neither style nor ideology, but a stance—a way of styling your clothes, hair, gesture, speech, and music with the aim of creating an aesthetic distinction between you, the discrete observing critical outsider, and the square world you find yourself living in. It is not just fashion, and it is not just politics: it is a stance within which fashion becomes political and politics becomes fashionable.

What made hipness difficult (though all the more tempting) for intellectuals to grasp was that it was a new kind of thing, an attitudinal or existential template that left open spaces into which they could insert the ideologies, philosophies, movements, and traditions they already knew. Hipness was a key that could fit any lock. In 1948, the first hip little magazine appeared: *Neurotica* ran until 1952 and documented the very earliest phase of intellectuals' experiment with understanding their learned preoccupations in terms of hipness. Taking on the Freudian flavor of the times, hip alienation became "neuroticism" and frank talk about sex (under cover of a homebrewed radical Freudianism) became a way to transgress. Dostoyevsky's Underground Man is invoked in *Neurotica*'s opening manifesto, whose formula of alienation plus artistic creation would persist forever afterward in the self-understanding of hip intellectuals and artists: "We are interested in exploring the creativeness of this man who has been forced to live underground, and yet lights an utter darkness with his music, poetry, painting, and writing."[59] In 1948, *Neurotica* published John Clellon Holmes's short story "Tea for Two," probably the first piece of hipster fiction, and this was also the year when Holmes, Kerouac, and Ginsberg began listening to Symphony Sid's all-night radio broadcasts of bebop and casting their musical enthusiasm in terms of subcultural identity, thinking and talking of themselves as a "beat generation."[60] And 1948 was the year that Anatole Broyard published his "Portrait of the Hipster," casting his subject in terms familiar to his *Partisan Review* readers by alluding to Freud, Picasso, Dostoyevsky, Thorstein Veblen, William Empson, the Laocoön, Synthetic Cubism, Pound and Fenollosa's theory of the ideogram, and Kenneth Burke's grammar of rhetorical figures, all in seven pages. At the end of the 1940s, the vocation of the hip intellectual began to take shape: as Allen Ginsberg wrote, it was the moment when "smart went crazy."[61]

This postwar project of reconstituting hipness within European traditions of art and thought had a long prehistory. The project of "glorifying" jazz by finding a European lineage for it (or, conversely, by renewing European art music with the primitive vigor of jazz) was already three decades old by the end of World War II.[62] By the end of the war, many intellectuals felt that jazz and the Western arts traditions shared an underground affinity and that it was the task of the modern critic to bring their kinship to public awareness. Thus *Jazz Forum,* an English little magazine that ran from 1946 to 1949, was founded on the belief that "whoever really appreciates jazz also really appreciates Dante, Hindemith, Paul Klee: because he has the taste of creativeness and some feeling for the direction of our evolution."[63] American intellectuals too believed in the relevance of jazz to the cause of art, even in advance of knowing very much about it. Although Clellon Holmes would later remember himself and his friends as "bop-mad," in 1948 he seemed rather to have been working up to being bop-mad: "I'm still puzzled by [bebop] as music, although I hear plenty of fine things in Dizzy and Parker, and there is no doubt in my mind that it is an authentic response to this post-war (or is it pre-war?) world."[64] Holmes looked to bebop for documentation of the postwar world and auguries of the coming apocalypse, judging the music by how authentically it expresses its social and historical situation. Such was the response of a literary intellectual rather than a typical jazz fan.[65]

In the Ginsberg collection at Stanford University there is a fan club card for Symphony Sid from around this same time:

> Dear Member—
> Thanks for falling into the Symphony Sid Bop Club. It's a kick to know that you're in our groove.
> Enclosed is your charter membership card. Stash it in a cool spot because it'll mean a whole lot of real gone freebees for you.
> Keep diggin' the all-night, all-frantic one over WMCA-570 first on the dial—and I'll hip you to all the things that are jumpin' off.
> Your boy—
> Symphony Sid[66]

This card—a piece of commercial hokum not so different from the Ovaltine Little Orphan Annie Secret Decoder Pin of Jean Shepherd's childhood—is written in a laborious jive style that we can hear Ginsberg, Holmes, and Kerouac trying on in the conversations they recorded on acetates a year later (see Chapter 3).[67] The effect is not quite idiomatic; the Holmes acetates are an auditory mirror in which the Beats strain to catch their reflection, wearing a borrowed and ill-fitting accent like children dressing up in clothes three sizes too large. To put it in Sarah Thornton's Bourdieusian way, the Beats in the late 1940s were finding in jazz a way to enhance their own subcultural capital. This does not mean that they were mere poseurs pretending to acquire tastes in order to enhance their status, though. As Carl Wilson points out, "this isn't a ruse: you just start to see what's *plausible* and *exciting* for you about those tastes."[68] Although hip culture makes authenticity its cardinal virtue, authenticity is never what makes any piece of hip culture fun or interesting or even beautiful; it is the richness of the play and pretending that matters. In the emerging hip intellectual culture of the 1940s, smart may have gone crazy, but it went deliberately, artfully, calculatedly crazy.

I have already said as much in the previous chapter but need to say it again, because if I call people such as Wolfe, Broyard, or Mailer "hip intellectuals," the obvious objection would be that they don't seem all that hip. Norman Mailer in particular always seems to provoke this response. James Baldwin wrote that his jazz musician friends "did not for an instant consider him as being even remotely hip... they thought he was a real sweet ofay cat, but a little frantic."[69] Artists within hip culture fashion their personae as works of art, but with Mailer the effort showed. In Mailer's papers there is a picture of him from around the time he wrote "The White Negro" proudly sporting an ill-advised and short-lived beatnik beard (Fig. 2.2). Mailer was tone-deaf, but when he decided that hipness was the new revolutionary force he had been looking for, he "rented a saxophone in order to 'honk' along with the music of Thelonious Monk."[70] One of Mailer's entrées into hip culture was his maid's boyfriend, and Abbie Hoffman, performing the ritual patricide that one generation of hipsters always performs on the previous, mocked Mailer for having a maid in the first place, and in a demotic idiom intended to help his own readers forget his university degrees from Brandeis and Berkeley.[71] Indeed, the history of hip culture presents an unbroken spectacle of hip intellectuals trying to live down their middle-class origins. Can we trust what Mailer or any other intellectual might have to tell us about hipness? "The White Negro" practically begs us to ask whether Mailer's ethnography is accurate (are there really hipsters such as he describes?) or else to ask more complex questions of personal authenticity and racial identity (is Mailer's idea of a hipster the real thing? is Mailer the real thing? is there even such a thing as a "real thing"?).[72] Either way, the discussion typically focuses on the hipster rather than on hipness, so that hipness is conceived at the outset in terms of its purest embodiment, the hipster as an ideal type.[73]

Consequently, many conceptions of hipness are based on the most extreme and marginal figures, the "lucifugous creatures of the darkness," rather than the less exotic, more commonplace kinds of people for whom hipness was less the point of existence than a happenstance of it.[74] The latter were the sorts of people

Figure 2.2 Photo of Norman Mailer, c. 1957. Harry Ransom Center, the University of Texas at Austin.

who in the 1940s began to play a role in the development of the hip sensibility, because the hip sensibility started to play a role in their lives. Columbia University students, jazz journalists, bookshop owners, advertising men and the like were not so much "hipsters" as people invested with a certain amount of hipness. They had interesting friends, lived in the Village, had a few more sex partners than average, smoked a little reefer, frequented the better bars, took evening classes at the New School, had advanced taste in music and books—but they were not the Dostoyevskian rebels that Mailer and the Beats mythologized.[75]

Most of the literary intellectuals who formed the circle Broyard inhabited in the late 1940s were hipsters in this limited sense. Chandler Brossard called the type the "Arrow Collar underground man" in his novel *Who Walk in Darkness,* a thinly fictionalized representation of the circle to which he and Broyard belonged.[76] Brossard later wrote that this group was not the same as the mythic Beat generation. "In point of historical fact [the Beats] got their act together several years after a far less romantic, perhaps less huggable, and certainly less publicized group of pioneers" that included Broyard, Brossard, Seymour Krim, the poets Milton Klonsky and Delmore Schwartz, and *Neurotica* editor Jay Landesman, among others.[77]

To be sure, New York's many bohemian and artistic circles interlocked in complex ways, and these two groups were not mutually exclusive. Holmes remembers Landesman hosting parties that drew the people-with-hipness on the scene, and he sketches a heterogeneous group that did not yet think of itself in terms of a "Beat generation" or any other exclusive subcultural identity.

> Five o'clock inevitably brought people: Anatole Broyard with that week's facsimile of the Broyard Girl—blonde, tooled, wordless—changing as little, version to version, as Anatole changed from year to year; Robert Lowry as big and bearish in his corduroys as a grizzly with the face of a panda; Marshall McLuhan (when he was in town) improvising ideas like a combination Spengler, Picasso, and Mort Sahl; little, zany William Poster with his clear, darting eye for subtle values; Chandler Brossard as difficult to crack as a horse chestnut and just as tart when you did; Paul Mazursky doing his funny Brando imitations while Stanley Radulovich did his serious ones; Carl Solomon yoinking around so frenziedly on a pogo stick that one night he put the end of it right through the floor into the restaurant below—and all their girls, and their friends' girls, and their friends' friends, and even nameless others who may have just heard the hubbub and walked in the door.[78]

In this vignette we see Beat (Holmes, Solomon) and sort-of-but-not-exactly Beat writers (Broyard, Brossard, Lowry, Poster) partying together, along with an actor (Mazursky), a painter (Radulovich), and even McLuhan, who long before he became a 1960s guru had written an early piece of mass-culture critique in *Neurotica*.[79] But for all this intergroup flux, the membership and cultural values of Broyard's circle gravitated towards the "New York Intellectuals" clustered around *Dissent, Commentary,* and above all *Partisan Review,* the main institution of intellectual opinion in the early Cold War.[80] *Partisan Review* was founded in defiance of Stalinist orthodoxy and was henceforth guided by a bedrock allegiance to the free individual intelligence against all forms of ideological standardization and coercion.[81] The New York Intellectuals' sovereign virtue was intellect: they aspired to critical omniscience, monumental synthesis, great works, genius, and they wielded their hyperarticulate intelligences like dueling swords, both in the pages of little magazines and in tense, competitive parties of the sort John Cassavetes amusingly depicted in *Shadows.* They treasured political apostasy, fallings out over points of aesthetic principle, and all the drama of lives lived for the sake of ideas.[82]

As Burley had predicted, intellectuals found in hipness an alternative intellectualism, and the younger members of the *Partisan Review* circle used it to customize an existing stance. Hipness could represent a yet subtler and more elusive principle of elite knowingness; its mood of disaffiliation could outfit a principled refusal to align with any particular ideology; an orientation toward intense experience might make for great literature. And its African American origins gave it an allure that the "primitive" had always held in the modernist imagination. George Lewis writes that for intellectuals in the postwar United States, African American culture ever appears "as consumable exotica, always and already available to the 'mainstream.'"[83] However, the attitude of the arrow collar underground was ambivalent. Their fundamental orientation was toward thought, and their embrace of experience was always bracketed by thought and thereby distanced, abstracted, and qualified. In his memoirs, Broyard wrote, "I wanted to be an intellectual . . . to see life from a great height, yet I didn't want to give up my sense of connection, my intimacy with things. When I read a book, I always kept one eye on the world, like someone watching the clock."[84] But the opposite was true as well: in the midst of the world, the hip intellectuals of the early Cold War always kept one eye on the book.

Seymour Krim began as an aspiring younger member of the *Partisan Review* crowd but by the end of the 1950s threw his lot in with the Beats. In "What's *This Cat's Story?*" he looked back on himself and his *PR*-emulating cohort, alienated from their own lives, seduced by visions of critical-theoretical omnipotence, and seeking to reconstruct the world of human experience in the abstract terms of ideas—"I wanted to swallow the entire fucking world and spit it out again not merely as an artist but as some kind of literary-human-intellectual God."[85] For Krim, the Beats had stormed to freedom, unintimidated by the condescending scorn of the New York Intellectuals and able finally to write from their experience in a way that the older group could never allow themselves: "it is the concrete vision of life which gives sex appeal, or 'it', to writing: and from the colorless versions of reality which our domesticated older writers were cautiously offering, like reformed alcoholics clutching their cokes, the beats have taken over like stomping Texas cowboys . . . ."[86] But if Beat hipness was more strongly marked by an aesthetic of presence than that of the arrow collar underground, it was not so distant from the 1950s intellectual scene as Krim would have us believe, either; it was a matter of emphasis within a literary culture that sought to balance its vernacular influences with the European art traditions in which it was grounded.

Irony

Broyard recognized that those who gravitated toward Greenwich Village had discarded identities granted by their social origins and inhabited new, self-invented personae. "Nobody in the Village had a family," Broyard would write; "we were all sprung from our own brows, spontaneously generated the way flies were once thought to have originated."[87] Broyard himself was involved in an especially pro-longed and elaborate kind of identity creation: the light-skinned son of a Creole family that had moved from New Orleans to New York during the Great Migration, he chose to "pass for white" as he began his literary career and kept his racial identity hidden for the rest of his life.[88] Perhaps unsurprisingly, he was particularly sensitive to the artistry that goes into making a self. Broyard tended to read social phenomena from a stylistic rather than sociological point of view, and his originality lay in reading the assumed personae of his bohemian acquain-tances as social fictions rather than as social facts, in terms of their artifice rather than the social conditions that may have created them. For Broyard, the ele-ments of hipster style—irony, surprise, "second-removism"—amounted to something like a language, and as Wolfe noted in his account of wartime Greenwich Village, this language was one of gesture:

> The first thing the Village insisted on was that nobody be defined in terms of where he came from, or of what he did. . . . All the same, you did get to be known as this rather than that. You took on an identity from the stride you showed as you walked down the main drags, the laxness with which you occupied a space on a Washington Square bench, the angle at which you tipped your beer mug, the frankness or sneakiness with which you eyed passing girls. You were . . . what you added up to in your day-to-day stances and gestures, your style at a bar, your bearing on the streetcorner, sum total, in short, of your impacts on eyes and ears. . . .[89]

Like Mailer's essay, Broyard's "Portrait of the Hipster" is a character study that casts hipness in terms of an ideal-typical hipster.[90] But whereas Mailer was most interested in hipsters as revolutionaries, Broyard was interested in hipsters insofar as he could read them as texts. Consequently, his "Portrait" is hermeneu-tical in a way that "The White Negro" is not. Broyard's chronicles of Greenwich Village life represent his ambition to write from an "intimacy with things," to record minute and closely observed details of bohemian experience and extract the meanings they enclosed.[91] One such detail is what might be termed the hip greeting: "brushing palms for handshaking, extending an index finger, without raising the arm, as a form of greeting."[92] As trivial a form of expression as this may seem, Broyard takes it seriously as a sign with both an internal form and a social meaning. Its form is metonymic, in Kenneth Burke's terms, substituting a single part or aspect of the gesture for the whole and reducing a complex gestalt to a concrete signifier. Michael Cherlin writes that metonymy's "basic strategy is to understand something incorporeal or intangible in terms corporeal or tan-gible."[93] Here what is intangible is less the formal gesture of the square handshake itself than the implications in which it is embedded—what it says about the one who extends a hand and the other who extends a hand in return, about their relations, their relative status, the unspoken social compacts that govern their behavior, the society that is structured by these and countless other governing rules, and the time within which it all unfolds. What a drag: as Broyard writes, "A *drag* was something which 'dragged' implications along with it, something which was embedded in an inseparable, complex, ambiguous—and thus, possibly threatening—context."[94] So the hip handshake is a "jive definition" that cuts the world down to manageable size, a reductive abstraction from the social field into a single, crystallized, bluntly tangible sign.[95]

However, we might find other ways to understand the same gesture in Burke's fourfold typology of rhetorical tropes. The hipster handshake's reduction of whole to part recalls synecdoche, and in any event both synecdoche and metonymy can serve irony, whose cognitive signature is its "perspective of perspectives."[96] The hip greeting signals awareness of the perspective reflected in the unironic gesture *as* a perspective and only one of many possible ways of looking at the total situation. The hip deformation of the ordinary handshake takes place through the action of a rhetorical trope that reduces an unironic whole (hands extended, firmly grasped, and shaken) to an ironic abstraction (the single aspect of touching palms abstracted and made the whole of the gesture).[97] As the gesture is abstracted, the perspective communicated by the original gesture is bracketed and revealed as an artifact of consciousness, or an *objet trouvé* of some distant, alien civilization. Seen in the *sub specie aeternitatis* light of irony, the perspective becomes estranged, unreal, absurd; the hipster is in it but not of it. The hip perspective, as Mezzrow and Wolfe noted, is a consciousness of the "fraud of language."[98]

Broyard uses Eurological terms to describe a complex relationship to language that could just as easily be understood in terms of African American signifying practice, a fact that was not lost on him.[99] He alludes to signifying in a cutting aside ("the use of the sexual metaphor was also a form of irony, like certain primitive peoples' habit of parodying civilized modes of intercourse") that banishes it to the realm of anthropology. Burke was a more legible context for Broyard's analysis: irony was the spirit of the age, the groundtone of literary-intellectual life in the early Cold War. In "Irony as a Principle of Structure" (1949), Cleanth Brooks identified irony as a potential inherent to all poems, a function of their capacity to generate new meanings as they appear in different contexts. He also saw this irony as a weapon the modern poet could wield in order to show up the falseness of a middlebrow, commercial culture.[100] Brooks and Burke, a veteran of the Popular Front who had developed a rhetorical theory that was also a theory of action, gave intellectuals in the Cold War a way of being politically engaged without compromising their aesthetic autonomy.[101] For Broyard's milieu, then, irony was at once the essence of literature, a literary device, an ethical stance, and a means of social action demanded of the writer by the modern world. And it was not only Broyard who saw new possibilities for understanding African American vernaculars in terms of Burke's rhetorical theory. As Lee Konstantinou writes, Ralph Ellison (who otherwise disliked Broyard's "Portrait") sought to deploy Burke's notions of ironic perception as a "form of symbolic warfare, undermining stereotypes, disrupting fixed categories, unveiling the very dynamic of symbolic action in the form of fiction."[102] Ellison wrote that the "one stable thing I have in this sea of uncertainty is the raft of [Burke's] concepts on which I lie as I paddle my way towards the shore." To Konstantinou, it was Burkean irony, not Marxist class politics, that offered Ellison a new way to oppose racism after World War II, and it was Rinehart, the figure of the hipster that appears in Ellison's *Invisible Man,* who embodied it.[103] Irony was the anchor of an emerging Afrological discourse that fought stereotype images by denaturing and derealizing them.

Whether considered in the light of signifying or Burkean irony, the hip greeting subtracts or withdraws socially sanctioned meaning—the meaning that the ordinary handshake gathers through the function it serves in its social context. Something as unremarkable as a handshake becomes a test that one can pass only through prior understanding of one's interlocutor. Such an understanding falls outside the shared and consensual meanings of ordinary social intercourse. When Broyard considers the social meaning of a reductive deformation of referent, then, he suggests that it communicates "a priorism," the "indefinable authority" that issues from the hipster's "knowing the score."[104] But if knowingness is the fundamental mode of hipness, the object of knowledge is always-already known. The ironic reduction of a gesture—in this case, a handshake—communicates "prior understanding, there is no need to elaborate, I dig you, man, etc."[105] Herbert Gold alludes to something similar in an essay on Beat hipness. The Beat, like the 1940s hipster, "wears music, art, and religion as a kind of secret handshake...he now says 'you dig the Bird? Proust? Zen?' 'I'm hip,' says his friend. This phrase means: No need to talk. No more discussion. I'm with you. I got you. Cool. In. Bye-bye."[106]

The hip greeting is a shortcut to meaning, a sign of secret and shared understanding. I will return to the question of what that understanding might be, but first I wish to note an enabling assumption of both Broyard's arguments and my own, that the rhetorical forms of hip gestures survive being transplanted from one cultural context to another. On this account, the meanings of hip culture are not the property of any one subculture, medium, or historical moment; they circulate continuously through a network that sends its rhizomes throughout time and subcultural space. The hip greeting is not just a Village mannerism limited to the late 1940s, but a gesture whose form of metonymic or synecdochic reduction appears, for example, in jazz and hipster slang—*to blow,* from *to blow smoke,* meaning to smoke marijuana; *to give* or *slip some skin,* meaning to greet someone by shaking hands or slapping palms; *face* for an anonymous (usually white) stranger.[107] Much more recently, the "finger guns" version of the hip greeting is so familiar it has become a joke. Some years ago I went to a lounge exotica show at a Minneapolis club and saw a local music-industry mogul execute a revised version of the metonymic reduction of gesture, applauding each piece by snapping his fingers rather than clapping hands. While the meanings of this gestural form have changed over sixty-odd years, it continues to reappear in ever newer guises, trailing fresh implications along with it at each appearance.

Miles and Monk

Jazz, too, bears the traces of this form, but before considering how the rhetorical form of ironic reduction may be found in jazz, we might consider how such a gestural trope may be found in music at all. One aspect of gestural communication is its deformational quality—how the hip reduction of gesture, for example, takes an interlocutor's "horizon of expectations" as its cognitive starting point.[108] The handshake is a gestural form hallowed by convention. Within a community that shares an understanding of what the gesture means, there are also governing expectations of what it should look like, and these are deliberately undermined when a finger is presented in greeting instead of a hand. But the hip gesture is not simply an entirely new invention substituted at random for something expected; it is still in some ways a recognizable version of the original thing. This is a deformation of gesture: its expressive effect is dependent on a shared understanding of a normative gesture and its distance from the altered version.

American popular music depends heavily on a small number of well-worn phrase forms: the twelve-bar blues, the parallel period (typically a thirty-two-measure form that may be diagrammed *abab* or *abac*), and, most common of all, the lyric binary (*aaba*).[109] The lyric binary form typically consists of an initial phrase (*a*) that is immediately repeated with little variation and is then followed by a contrasting phrase (*b*). This *b* phrase is often harmonically mobile, passing through several nontonic harmonic areas, usually by sequence, before settling on a tonic half-cadence. This half-cadence serves as the dominant preparation for the last phrase, a final repetition of *a* that resolves the harmonic tension introduced in the *b* phrase and that gives the form a sense of thematic closure. The form follows a narrative arc Graham Wood calls "recognition, repetition, and resolution" through the three *a* limbs, but it is the *b* limb that throws the surrounding pattern of repetitions into relief.[110] Jazz musicians have several names for the *b* limb: the inside, the channel, the middle eight, the bridge. These names all express something fundamental to the expectations listeners bring to their understanding of any given instance of the form—that something will cut a channel between blocks of similar material, ending a repetition on the one hand and arranging a resolution on the other. Thus a sense of closure, even affirmation, emerges from this pattern of repetition all the more strongly and is further enhanced by hypermetric symmetry, as each of the four limbs in a lyric binary form is typically eight measures long.

Some forms are buried mechanisms that regulate foreground events while remaining hidden to all but the most sophisticated ears, but the lyric binary is not one of them. Ears accustomed to jazz or Tin Pan Alley numbers will take the turns through the form's four parts with the same haptic and unconscious assurance as one might use in walking from the bedroom to the kitchen. Throughout its long history—a history that extends back through Tin Pan Alley to operetta, and yet further back to *bel canto* opera and eighteenth-century Austrian popular music—the lyric binary form's intuitive and easily audible shape has constituted a horizon of expectations against which composers have played games of misdirection, substitution, and gratification.[111] For example, Herbie Nichols repeatedly explodes the lyric binary form's feeling of symmetry and closure by expanding one or more of its limbs past the expected eight-measure duration—for example in *Step Tempest*, which expands the final *a* limb from eight to fourteen measures, or in *Chit Chatting*, which expands the *b* limb to twelve measures and outfits the final *a* with an eight-measure coda that reappears, largely unchanged, as a kind of refrain between subsequent choruses.[112] Miles Davis's "So What" is likewise a deformation of the lyric binary form, but it employs a strategy opposite to Nichols's.[113] Instead of expanding the form, Davis's lyric binary pares away all but the most minimally differentiating musical information. Here the "tune" is scarcely a tune at all, but only a bass riff answered by a harmonized two-note motive. And the *b* limb is barely differentiated from the *a*. All that changes is the modal center: it is D in the *a* limbs and moves up a semitone, to E flat, in the *b* limb. The form is not articulated through thematic contrast; the only thing that sketches the formal boundaries of lyric binary form is the travel between modes. And it is the shortest possible trip, up only one semitone.

In short, "So What" is a hip deformation of the hoary *aaba* phrase form. The apparatus of formal differentiation that popular song composers used to dramatize their forms—thematic contrast, contrast in rhythmic profile, and the carefully calibrated sequence of half and authentic cadences—is gone. Like the hipster's greeting, Davis's deformation of a well-worn pattern presents an abstraction, a form reduced to a single aspect—lyric binary reduced to the contrast provided by its *b* limb, and the contrast of a *b* limb reduced to a change in mode. And this is not hard to hear: Davis poses his reduction of the lyric binary form against his listeners' prior understanding. The rhetorical abridgments of this piece are essential to the mood of refined cool that has made it "an instant signifier of hip," repeatedly covered and sampled by musicians and used in films as a token of hip enlightenment.[114] Davis's styled minimalism depends on the deployment of a trope—rendering something hip by reducing its formal outlines to a sketch or, even further, a suggestion. "So What" does not state, it implies, and so it seems to embody the nonchalant authority of Davis, attired in an Italian silk suit, back turned to his audience.

Thelonious Monk's 1948 Blue Note recording of "Misterioso" with Milt Jackson works this trope of ironic reduction in a different though similarly audible way.[115] Here it is not the phrase structure that is reduced, but the contours of the melody, a zigzag pattern of broken sixths (see the vibraphone line in Fig. 2.4) that ends on the flat-seventh scale degree (A flat), which hangs suspended like an unanswered question at the conclusion of the head. The main take of the 1948 recording consists of a head over blues changes, a chorus from Jackson, one from Monk, and an out-chorus. After Monk and Jackson play the head together, Jackson begins his solo, and Monk accompanies by taking the fundamental contour of the ascending sixth and bending it into a minor seventh, the interval implied by the hovering A flat at the end of the head and the cycling-back to the B flat tonic at the beginning of Jackson's chorus. Throughout this chorus, Monk bluntly repeats this ascending-seventh figure, in registral augmentation, at signal points in the blues phrase structure (Fig. 2.3). Monk's comping is not chordal, but linear, and as such it is an abstraction of the tune's melodic line. Like the hipster's greeting, this abstraction is metonymic, with the ascending-seventh contour standing in for the whole tune and compressing into a single brute sign its complex unfolding in time. The original tune is maximally (if abstractly) implied even as it is rendered minimally present. Heard against Jackson's florid improvisation, Monk's comping sounds doubly compressed, laconic almost to the point of disappearing entirely.

Although Monk evidently took some care to plan this gesture (it appears in the alternate take as well), it does not remain a local effect. Traces of this reduction of tune to gesture pervade Monk's solo and, most notably, the out-

Figure 2.3 Thelonious Monk, "Misterioso" (1948), Milt Jackson's solo with Monk accompanying (mm. 1–4).

Figure 2.4 Thelonious Monk, "Misterioso" (1948), out-chorus with Milt Jackson (mm. 1–8).

chorus. At this point Jackson plays the tune straight as Monk abandons it for a series of metrically displaced gestures based again on the ascending-seventh contour (Fig. 2.4). The effect here is similar to that of Monk's comping during Jackson's solo. Monk is in the texture but not of it. He holds aloof from the proceedings, alluding to the tune but leaving it unstated until the last four bars.

In June 1957, Monk recorded a septet that included John Coltrane and Coleman Hawkins for Orrin Keepnews's Riverside label. Two recordings from that session, "Well, You Needn't" and the fourth take of "Off Minor," show Monk working out the rhetoric of hip reduction differently.[116] Both tunes are lyric binary forms, and in both recordings Monk plays a two-chorus solo. (In the solo on "Off Minor," Art Blakey plays a drum break in the *b* limb of Monk's second chorus.) In these recordings, Monk subjects his tunes to a process of decomposition during the three consecutive appearances of *a* that result from the sequence of two lyric binary choruses (*aaba**aaba***). Both solos begin in linear fashion: in "Off Minor," Monk propels a line of continuous eighth-note motion across a harmonic steeplechase in the hornlike manner of the bebop pianists, albeit in Monk's parsimonious style (Fig. 2.5, mm. 1–8). But the second *a* (Fig. 2.5, mm. 9–16) begins to arrest the continuous motion of the solo, retracting into a gnarled paraphrase of the tune.

This rhythmic decomposition is arrested in the final *a* of Monk's first chorus but becomes pronounced again in the first *a* of the second chorus (Fig. 2.6, mm. 33–40). After measure 36, the sense of a line continuously engaging the harmonic form of the tune falls away. But as the horizontal dimension of the work dwindles, the vertical dimension gains strength. What remains is a series of high-register chords whose harmonic identity is blurred by a haze of dissonance and whose relationship to the tune's rhythmic profile is erased by rhythmic displacements. The final *a* of Monk's solo before the drum break continues this erasure to a disorienting point (Fig. 2.6, mm. 41–48).

Figure 2.5 Thelonious Monk, "Off Minor" (1957), Monk's solo (mm. 1–15).

Figure 2.6 Thelonious Monk, "Off Minor" (1957), Monk's solo (mm. 32–48).

If Monk subjects standards to an "acid bath," as Andre Hodeir once wrote, this limb of Monk's solo presents a tune fully immersed, its features eaten away, leaving only a bare and corroded skeleton.[117] But even as the solo's linear complexities disappear, they are telescoped into the increasingly fearsome harmonic complexities that bristle in the few chords now standing in for the tune. The effect is of a complicated tune reduced to an outline, but with its original complications preserved and bunched into another musical dimension.

Monk is not simply taking away elements of the tune's structure and replacing them with noise; he is reducing those elements into abstractions that preserve

Figure 2.7 "Off Minor" chords in root position, mm. 38–47.

something of their original complexity. It is easy to hear the final measures of this solo as a heedless physical assault on the piano, but analysis of its clusters suggests a degree of calculation. The chords in measures 41–43, however oddly voiced, are easily read as versions of the chords prescribed for each measure. The chords of measures 38–39 and 44–47, by contrast, do not at first glance appear to have much to do with the changes. But if one assumes that these chords, like those of measures 41–43, are conceived along a tonal axis—if, for example, one assumes that the root of the chord in measure 38 is a B-flat—then something striking emerges. The clusters of measures 38, 39, 44, 46, and 47 all have substantially the same intervallic content (Fig. 2.7).[118]

These are not impulsive fistfuls of notes, but elaborate substitutions on the changes. All the same, this is very hard to hear, even on repeated listenings. One is aware of the harmonic density of this passage, and perhaps even that the chords one hears are somehow related to the chords of the tune. But clearly the listener's horizon of expectations is stretched to its limits here. The passage of measures 32–47 does not refer back to the tune in the same way the earlier part of the solo does. It presents only an aspect of the tune, much disguised, standing in for the whole.

Monk's solo in "Well You Needn't" follows a similar course, from continuous linear engagement with the tune's form to a discontinuous chordal reduction of it. Like many of Monk's compositions, "Well, You Needn't" is stitched together from the varied repetition of simple motives. In this case, there are really only two: a "white key" arpeggiation through a tonic chord (marked *x* in Fig. 2.8), and a two-note retort on black keys (marked *y* in Fig. 2.8). This is a reductive kind of hearing, though, and it is easier not to hear it like this: the line's rhythmic impulse pulls the two motives together, gathering up momentarily at the top of the *x* motive's ascent and then releasing itself, ricocheting off the subsequent *y* motive.

The excerpts from "Misterioso" and "Off Minor" demonstrate Monk's "acid bath" techniques—the ways he subjects the tunes he plays to various kinds of reduction. In a sense, these reductive processes are acts of perception: Monk's improvisations submit compositions to a leveling, reductive gaze that burns through perceptual habits and makes abstract distinctions. In "Well You Needn't," the distinction made is between its component white-key and black-key motives. As Monk's improvisation moves toward the beginning of his second chorus (Fig. 2.9, mm. 31–32), continuous linear variation gives way to a discontinuous series of high-register chords, just as it does at the analogous point in "Off Minor." The precise pitch content and voicing of these chords change in measures 31–48,

Figure 2.8 Thelonious Monk, "Well, You Needn't" (1957), x and y motives.

Figure 2.9 Thelonious Monk, "Well, You Needn't" (1957), Monk's solo (mm. 24–47).

but not very significantly. What matters is their pattern: irregularly spaced chords and minimal riffs alternate between black-note and white-note pitch collections. Here Monk again reduces a tune to a single aspect—the division of a generative musical idea into white-note and black-note motives—which he articulates with blunt comic ferocity. If we think of improvisation as a process of perception, we might say that Monk fixes his tune with a hard stare that bores through its familiar contours and defamiliarizes it, revealing an alien musical landscape bathed in the peculiar light of Monkian irony.

All the examples so far show Monk applying his reductive abstractions retrospectively, presenting a tune straight and then deforming it in the subsequent improvisatory sections. In his 1948 Blue Note recording of "I Should Care," his strategy is the opposite, prolepsis rather than analepsis.[119] Here, instead of reducing a head tune to an abstract essence in subsequent improvisations, Monk applies a complex series of abstractions to the tune's climax (the two chords that accompany the words "as lovely as you" in mm. 27–28) to generate a cryptic two-chord introduction that leads equivocally to the tune's opening Em^7 chord (Fig. 2.10).[120] But even though this operation differs from those of "Misterioso," "Off Minor," and "Well You Needn't," all reduce a complicated process to a concrete, tangible sign into which the original complications are compressed.

Figure 2.10a Thelonious Monk, Monk's introduction (mm. 1–3), "I Should Care" (1948).

Figure 2.10b "I Should Care" (1948), mm. 27–29.

Monk's two-chord introduction to "I Should Care" is a gesture of ambiguous motion and uncertain direction, but at the same time it is weirdly emphatic and deliberate. One critic likens this introduction's bundling of contradictory qualities to a Buster Keaton routine on a high diving board:

> The diver's natural movement (like that of the pianist introducing the tune) is to launch his body (the music) in a progressive and continuous thrust. But Keaton, reaching the end of the board, suddenly terrorized by the height, breaks his fluid motion down into a dozen contradictory and almost simultaneous movements.[121]

The expected sense of goal-directed movement is undercut because the generic harmonic function of the introduction (setting up the first chord of the tune) has eroded. Monk respected the principle of surprise—something else that Broyard considered inherent to the rhetoric of hip—and liked to lead his listeners and musicians to unexpected places.[122] So his introduction to "I Should Care" immediately veers out of harmonic orbit. The first chord of the introduction is a small surprise in itself. Formed by a close-voiced fusion of measure 27's Bm⁷ chord with the vocal line's cross-relational A sharp, it is an unexpectedly dissonant chord blurted out of the silence of the recording's in-spiral groove. But this chord is at least retrospectively recognizable within the harmonic orbit of the subsequent performance, as an applied dominant of the tune's opening Em^7 chord. The second chord of the introduction, by contrast, bears no clear functional relationship to either the preceding chord or the subsequent one and thus obscures the listener's temporary sense of tonal orientation. Indeed, this chord does not arise from a relationship to its surroundings, but from a relationship to a chord that will not be played for another two minutes. It is a transposition of the substitute chord Monk uses in measure 28—an A sharp half-diminished seventh chord minus the third—up a whole tone, to C. (The root motion in mm. 27–28 is B to A sharp; in the introduction, it is B to C.) And in his introduction Monk subjects the chord sequence of measures 27–28 to further misdirections: he blurs the sonority of the second chord with a nonchord tone (the A) and creates a nondirectional inner line by holding certain tones from within the chords past the initial attack.

The likelihood that anyone could hear all these operations is close to nil. Listeners end up asking of Monk the question that modernist composers such as Arnold Schoenberg have made them ask throughout the last century: Are we supposed to hear these things? The idea that suprasensible meanings might lie hidden in a piece of music—indeed, that such "inner" meanings might constitute the music's truest significance and value—suggests that the music exists to be analyzed rather than listened to. It might, however, suggest something less obvious: that those hidden devices are not there to be heard, but simply to *be,* and that hidden meaning is not for an audience but for the artist, not for the schooled but for the illuminated. Such is the signification of magic: as Marshall McLuhan remarked, a magical symbol "does not refer, it is."[123] Magical thinking appears in passing throughout this study, and in the last chapter I will explain magical hermeneutics more thoroughly to understand the work of John Benson Brooks, a jazz composer who was also a dedicated student of Marc Edmund Jones, an astrologer and occult philosopher.[124] Monk was no occultist, but by its nature the hip sensibility tends toward the habits of occult interpretation. In the vision of the world furnished by game ideology—the apparent is the false, the hidden is the true— hip knowledge is vouchsafed as a kind of hidden, literally occult knowledge, and the hipster becomes (as Broyard styled him) "keeper of enigmas, ironical pedagogue, a self-appointed exegete."[125] The hipster's communication is not the straightforward exchange that we expect in ordinary social intercourse, where messages are meant to be understood and meanings, where unclear, can be learned. Hip utterances are riddles whose meanings are not to be learned or decoded but are (as we have seen) always-already known. The hipster's response to the puzzled square—if you have to ask, you'll never know—is likewise the reply of the esoteric sage.[126] A hip utterance, then, might be calculated to convey little more than its mystery. In "I Should Care," for instance, the introduction has an exoteric meaning: it is the part of the form that inducts the listener into the tonal and affective world of the standard that is to be played. We know it is supposed to mean *something,* but on first hearing we know just as surely that we do not know what. Like the hip greeting, the introduction ostentatiously places a hurdle to our understanding, and in both cases the hurdle involves the abstraction of a gesture from the perspective warranted by its functional context. What results is paradoxical, gestures that are simultaneously voluble and cryptic, inviting and withholding.

Somewhere/Nowhere

And now to revisit a question left unresolved in an earlier part of this chapter: What is the secret, shared, and *a priori* understanding that lies behind the hip greeting? In a word, it is *somewhereness*. The crux of Broyard's "Portrait" is his understanding of the basic orientation of the hipster's philosophy, a binary distinction the hipster applies to everything he encounters: hip and square, the real world and the bird world (as LeRoi Jones put it), or somewhere and nowhere.[127] The hipster, Broyard writes, is really nowhere; his inner existence is oriented by his drive to get somewhere. Failing this, he is like a beetle on its back, in an absurd and deadly situation, a victim of contingency. The world is a drag, so he gets his revenge on it by re-editing it, cutting it down to size by casting it in reductive "jive definitions." These definitions are applied in the hipster's speech, gesture, dress, and music. They are meant to place the hipster outside of contingency, beyond the humiliating confinements of society. They are tokens of the hip "philosophy of somewhereness," announcing that the hipster knows the score—the nowhereness of a wider society to which he is a conscientious objector. Two hipsters who greet one another in the style of ironic reduction perform their awareness. They turn a social gesture into an ironic abstraction, plucking it out of the common run of taken-for-granted meanings. In estranging it from function and consensual meaning, they make it an esoteric sign, something like a secret handshake; they communicate behind society's back. They're hip, and the main thing they're hipped to is the basic alienation of the individual from society.

The somewhere/nowhere binary maps onto the picture of the world as game—false appearance and hidden knowledge. From the first, to see society divided into somewhere and nowhere was to have participated in a particular historical experience, that of urbanized African Americans in the era of the Great Migration. Above all, it was white racism that was nowhere. In Dizzy Gillespie's recollections, racism was the bottom line of hipness: "a really hip guy wouldn't have any racial prejudice."[128] In his social analysis, though, Broyard kept things abstract. He did not say much about what oppressed the hipster; for that matter, he would not have wanted to suggest that the hipster really *was* oppressed. It was enough for him to note how the hipster feels himself alienated from the mainstream, however that mainstream might be understood. And at this point Broyard's analysis ceases to be uniquely his own. As he describes this geometry of somewhere and nowhere, of an individual permanently at odds with society, he is joined by almost every subsequent account of hipness. The individual is unfree; the hipster makes an issue out of it. His very being offends the proprieties of American society. He dresses outlandishly, he listens to nonconformist music, he lives in the moment, he gets his kicks where he can find them. The sources of the individual's unfreedom are variously described in countless later portraits of the hipster at odds with his surroundings. Broyard, with characteristic abstraction, called it "contingency"; Mailer referred to "the totalitarian tissues of American society"; for Abbie Hoffman, it was America spelled with a "k." What all these writers share is the sense of a hip image of self fashioned by what Thomas Frank calls the "countercultural idea."[129]

The countercultural idea relies above all on the image of an inauthentic existence that demands resistance and subversion, either by an individual's attitude of rebellion or by artistic creation. It is a political idea insofar as it renders a specific critique of society, particularly American society, but among political ideas it is unique in the specifically cultural remedy it proposes. The remedy may lie in cultivating a certain style of music or a certain style of self, but regardless, the countercultural idea is an ethic of aesthetic cultivation. Its exponent is the person who "has been forced to live underground, and yet lights an utter darkness with his music, poetry, painting, and writing"—or even just a cool haircut.[130] This aesthetic, the countercultural notion of the beautiful, is hipness, which is equally an aesthetic of music and the self.

I prefer thinking in terms of the countercultural idea instead of the more traditional "bohemia" for two reasons. First, the term *bohemia*, as used by writers from Henry Murger onward, refers primarily to the social forms of the countercultural life and only secondarily to the antinomian ideas that underwrite them.[131] Second, I want to differentiate between an older, European image of cultural opposition and its postwar American variant. Our homegrown bohemia is predicated on a specific image of America that has emerged largely since World War II. Frank sketches this image in a few deft strokes:

> Call it, for convenience, the "countercultural idea." It holds that the paramount ailment of our society is conformity, a malady that has variously been described as over-organization, bureaucracy, homogeneity, hierarchy, logocentrism, technocracy, the Combine, the Apollonian. We all know what it is and what it does. It transforms humanity into "organization man," into "the man in the gray flannel suit." It is "Moloch whose mind is pure machinery," the "incomprehensible prison" that consumes "brains and imagination." It is artifice, starched shirts, tailfins, carefully mowed lawns, and always, always, the consciousness of impending nuclear destruction. It is a stiff, militaristic order that seeks to suppress instinct, to forbid sex and pleasure, to deny basic human

impulses and individuality, to enforce through a rigid uniformity a meaningless plastic consumerism.[132]

In Mailer's version, it is the "collective condition . . . to live with the instant death by atomic war . . . or with a slow death by conformity with every creative and rebellious instinct stifled" that forces everyone either to surrender or to resist— and the hipster, of course, resists.[133] In the postwar discourse marked by the countercultural idea, the hipster is a figure on a ground, negatively defined by the totalizing system that Frank and Mailer describe. From the hustler's game ideology, the countercultural idea inherited an understanding of the world as a rigged game and a belief that the sources of unfreedom lie in systems rather than any malign individual. But if the countercultural idea grew out of a picture of black alienation within a white system, in consequence hipness became (as LeRoi Jones put it) "a general alienation in which even white men could be included."[134] African Americans were most likely to focus on the system of white racism as the motive for hip disaffiliation, but the intercultural discursive network through which hipness developed in the late 1940s made this picture more abstract, conceiving of society as an infernal machine for the manipulation of human will, action, and awareness. (This image is allegorized in a cover for the anarchist-pacifist little magazine *The Needle;* see Fig. 2.11.) The specifically African American critique was of a white society that had rigged the game so black people could not win; the countercultural idea pictured society as a game rigged so that *nobody* could win. As Michael Szalay writes, hip came to "provide an image designed to pass over and go beyond difference."[135]

Once the "nowhere" side of the binary—the system against which the hipster rebels—was generalized in this way, it could do more and different kinds of cultural work. No longer conceived only in terms of white racism, the system could also be imagined in class and gender terms, as an oppressive system of capitalism, matriarchy, or both. Mailer was the first major writer to link hipness with Marxist critique, and so doing he anticipated the main development of the following decade.[136] In the 1940s and 1950s, though, hip anticapitalism registered more often as an ambient gender resentment. Barbara Ehrenreich has argued that hip dissent in the early Cold War was directed less against conformism than feminization. If women demanded financial support to keep house and raise children, they forced their husbands to submit to the drudgery of work and tied them to an emasculating domesticity. In this view, capitalism was a secret collusion between business and women; it was a system that was not only enslaving but feminizing as well. And so the hipster's flight from square society was also a flight from the obligations of family, and "somewhere" was conceived as a zone of sexual free play, where hipsters could "[get] their sex free, with no more financial foreplay than perhaps a bottle of California red wine, and even this could, with any luck, be left to the woman."[137]

Figure 2.11 Lowell Naeve, "Our Ultimate Aim Is a Decentralized Society," front cover illustration for *The Needle* 1, no. 3 (1956). The Lilly Library, Indiana University, Bloomington.

The terms by which the system was most often defined were drawn from a highbrow literature of social critique, much of it in the pages of the intellectual little magazines, whose contributors were often disabused ex-Marxists or refugees from totalitarian societies. These writers sought to understand the relationship between totalitarian politics and culture—how totalitarian social systems could invade the individual life of the mind and debase the complexity and ambiguity of thought they saw enshrined in modernist art and literature. In placing their analyses within the American context, they attacked conformism, consumerism, and above all the mass society and mass culture. These social forces were publicized for a much wider audience in a number of accessible, highly influential studies, which in turn were publicized in mass publications such as *Readers Digest* and *Harper's Bazaar*.[138] In 1957, the president of IBM, Thomas J. Watson (nobody's idea of a hipster), appropriated William Whyte's famous expression in complaining that "the organization man [is] as depersonalized as a jellyfish wrapped in cellophane."[139] As Jacques Maritain has written, nothing succeeds in America like vigorous self-criticism, and Cold War mass culture critique was successful indeed.[140] Krim might not have liked to admit it, but the success of hipness in postwar intellectual and cultural history is bound up with the social criticism that appeared in the pages of *Partisan Review*. To Mailer's "ménage a trois" of the delinquent, bohemian, and Negro, we might add an unlikely fourth: the tweedy and bespectacled Cold War intellectual. As Scott Saul writes:

> The hipster was born, we might say, at the crossroads—at the place where the civil rights movement met these works of social criticism. He seemed to have some crucial, if puzzling, answers for those seeking to understand the newest forms of political dissent and to translate cultural critique into subcultural practice. For leftist intellectuals who prized cultural engagement, the hipster was a paragon of improvisatory existential action—someone who lived by his wits and not by cultural convention, and who took inspiration from an art form (jazz) that was populist but not popular. At the same time, for those looking to criticize the Cold War domestic ideal, the hipster offered a model of tough urban manhood and gave a powerful counterimage to the suburban dad minding his barbecue and commuting dutifully to work. It was no coincidence that *Playboy* magazine was founded just as the hipster was breaking through to the culture at large, nor was it surprising that the magazine became a key sponsor of jazz, building a nationwide circuit of music festivals starting in this period.[141]

In Chapter 4, we will see how during the later 1960s and early 1970s the reach of the hip sensibility widened past the boundaries of a few small (albeit increasingly well-publicized) bohemian enclaves to the consciousness of a mass audience. The countercultural idea spread from serious social analysis to mass culture as it diffused into almost every field of cultural endeavor: literature, advertising, journalism, film, the visual arts, humanities scholarship, fashion, standup comedy, and so on. This cultural shift—and a feeling of dismay at seeing a formerly elite idea democratized—is described everywhere in the autobiographical writings of those, like Milton Klonsky, who survived to see their notions of hipness rendered obsolete by the new cultural forms that erupted in the 1960s and 1970s:

> The nonconformist and dissenting spirit of the Village, in art, literature, manners & morals, has by its very success . . . resulted in the establishment

of a new kind of disestablishmentarian Establishment.... The life-style of the Village since World War II, the Hip, has undergone the same sort of transmogrification.... The tourists of yesteryear, who used to come down to the Village with their maps and guidebooks, cameras dangling from their necks, and nudge each other whenever they spotted a typical beatnik or maybe a boheme. They've all gone Hip.... For with the advent of the Hip as a mass evangelical movement, heralded by all the media, what has emerged is not, as sometimes claimed, a sub- or counter-, but part of the boss, culture, right now the most booming and successful stand on the American midway.... So Rome in its time must have been taken over by romanized Goths, Greece by hellenized Romans.[142]

The countercultural idea leaves its fingerprints on contemporary discourse in exhausted words now applied to ordinary things: revolutionary, transgressive, subaltern, subversive, edgy, raw, underground, resistant, oppositional, heterodox, counterhegemonic, outlaw, rebel, marginal, iconoclastic, radical, insurgent, etc., etc. Frank rejects the familiar notion that this ubiquitous antinomianism represents a "co-optation" by capitalist interests. He argues rather that capitalism is essentially antinomian: the countercultural idea is always already co-opted.[143] But this is hardly a new idea.[144] Joseph Schumpeter, for example, wrote of capitalism's "creative destruction"—a notion on which he based his "terrible observation that there is a clandestine alliance between the avant-garde and the bourgeoisie."[145] Schumpeter's idea of "creative destruction" in turn was adumbrated in a famous passage of *The Communist Manifesto*:

> The bourgeoisie cannot exist without constantly revolutionizing the instruments of production, and thereby the relations of production, and with them the whole relations of society.... All fixed, fast-frozen relations, with their train of ancient and venerable prejudices and opinions are swept away, all new-formed ones become antiquated before they can ossify. All that is solid melts into air, all that is holy is profaned...."[146]

Whatever their differences, Schumpeter and Marx agree that capitalism's relentless drive to competition and innovation imprints itself on those who orient themselves to the future and not the past, who seek always to liberate themselves from tradition, and who respect no authority save that of their own leveling intelligence. In this view, the opposition between bourgeois and bohemian is less a battle between two entirely different and irreconcilable groups than the contradictory expressions of a single (though hardly homogeneous) culture. These are what Daniel Bell has called the cultural contradictions of capitalism, which George Orwell dispatches in a vinegary aside: "nine times out of ten a revolutionary is merely a climber with a bomb in his pocket."[147]

This is not to say that dissent is merely a symptom of the capitalist dynamic of creative destruction. (Or, more crudely, that protesters are only spoiled, slumming trust fund kids, using Daddy's money to protest what Daddy did to earn it—a cherished and indispensible myth of conservative punditry.[148]) Social movements are brought into being by real injustices that demand real resistance. But in hip culture, "resistance" becomes an aesthetic as well as political matter, and it manifests everywhere, far from the front lines of actual conflict. It becomes something that gives shape to our perceptions; it gives us an image of the authentic self; it becomes a way to persuade. For each of these modalities, we can call to mind a corresponding image: the academic explaining the subversiveness of some piece of pop culture, the rock star performing a nonconformist persona, and the television commercial proclaiming the edgy iconoclasm of some brand of car. All are reenacting a shared and cherished image in the public sphere, and for the most part that is where the image stays. The point of ritual enactment, after all, is to make an experience perennially available yet safely sublimated. Kurt Cobain died for our sins: he rebelled for us, so that we may with easy conscience pay our bills, worry about our children, and tip our mail carrier at Christmas. If there is something puzzling about Cobain, who died a wealthy man, wearing a t-shirt reading "corporate magazines still suck" on the cover of *Rolling Stone,* we might resort to the tired language of co-optation to explain it—or, if we wish to preserve our idealized image of rock as rebellion, simply not think about it too much.[149] So when I try to understand what it means when the rhetorical trope that shapes a certain hipster gesture appears also in the music of Thelonious Monk, I do not wish to offer a version of the hackneyed interpretive strategy by which any quirk or formal innovation is read as the artist's symbolic transgression of a hegemonic order. To do so would be to remain blind and deaf to the complicated tensions between collective representation and lived experience.

We all know the story in which America, cowed by McCarthy and the atomic bomb and coerced by empty affluence, hardens into orthodoxy and conformity in the 1950s, only to enjoy a cultural renaissance as its sexual, psychological, and cultural energies are liberated in the 1960s. (This is what Rick Perlstein has called the declension hypothesis.[150]) The relationship between these decades is sometimes explained in terms of a botanical metaphor: the 1950s were a "seedbed" of later radicalism, and the extravagant political and cultural growths of the 1960s push through the stony soil in which their seeds were planted during an earlier time of drought.[151] But we could use the same metaphor to express a different historical relationship. Many of those seeds did not flourish in the 1960s and 1970s; they grew best in their own soil and were to be choked by the hardier plants that flourished later. The hip culture of the early Cold War defined itself in opposition to mainstream American society, but it shared many of those features that have come to seem paradigmatic of the repressive 1950s of our historical narratives. Cold War hipness was above all ironic, valuing disaffiliation over activism, individualism over populism, skepticism over enthusiasm, and seeking a complicated reconciliation of intellectualism with spontaneous and immediate experience. This was a sensibility not in opposition to its culture, but of a piece with it.

The immediate present of experience, without cerebration, theory, ideological overlay, or even representation—an object of mingled longing and anxiety for Broyard's cohort—gives another meaning to *somewhere,* which I will begin exploring in the next chapter. This chapter has described how the countercultural idea gelled as an all-purpose, infinitely recombinant intellectual orientation sometime around 1948. The next chapter zooms in on a single episode in this emerging intellectual hip culture: the Beat scene in a year-and-a-half period from late 1949 to early 1951, as captured on a series of home recordings made at John Clellon Holmes's Lexington Avenue apartment. In this small virtual world we can hear a group of literary intellectuals groping their way toward a new project whereby the *somewhere* of presence in the moment would somehow be rendered in the abstraction of writing—a thoroughly and unavoidably musical project.

3

Sound Become Holy (the Beats)

Cody. You're not gonna get hardly any of this recorded you know
Jack. Well, that's the sadness of it all[1]
—Jack Kerouac

The magic of the cave image lies in its being, not its being seen.
The symbolic does not refer, it is.[2]
—Marshall McLuhan

Sound Become Holy

Ross Russell was the proprietor of Dial Records and had a hand in some of Charlie Parker's greatest recordings. But he's probably most often remembered for a bitter line in Miles Davis's autobiography: Davis called him "a jive motherfucker who I never did get along with because he was nothing but a leech, who didn't never do nothing but suck off Bird like he was a vampire."[3] The whole story is more complicated, though. Russell was a main operator in the early West Coast bebop scene and later wrote a novel (*The Sound*, 1961) that drew on his experiences in the 1940s.[4] He was also a jazz scholar, biographer, pulp novelist, golf pro, ladies' man, reporter, adventurer, and intellectual scenester-at-large who knew an astonishing range of midcentury artistic figures.[5] To a historian, he is the rarest of birds: a consummate insider of the earliest musical hip subculture who wrote well and self-reflectively of his experiences at the time they happened. In his letters and diaries from the 1930s and 1940s, Russell matter-of-factly records experiences in the innermost sanctum of emergent hip culture that the callow and unpublished Beats, then in their Columbia University days, were only dreaming about. If we disregard all my previous warnings against trying to find a single, privileged point of origin for all hip culture, we might be tempted to imagine the Ross Russell Papers at the Harry Ransom Center as a kind of hip Rosetta Stone, allowing latter-day historians to see plainly what hipness was really all about in its earliest, undocumented, and untheorized period.

And yet the curious thing about Russell's unpublished writings from these early years is that, though he writes about hip people, he never pauses to consider them in terms of hipness. He certainly did later, in *The Sound* and his Parker biography *Bird Lives!* (1973). But by then there were many novels about hipsters, to say nothing of essays, films, sociological studies, and so on, and like everyone else Russell had learned to make sense of their various eccentricities by patterning them within a motivating philosophy and characteristic lifestyle. By 1961, he had arrived at the consensus view that hipsters and jazz musicians launched a revolutionary new movement in American culture. More interestingly, though not untypically, he also believed that sound itself, not any particular musical style or arrangement of pitches, was the motive force behind it: "Jazz & hip postwar rep[resents] a crusade—cf. possession by religious fervor—levelers, crusaders, camp followers. The Sound Become Holy."[6] In *The Sound*, Russell uses Zaida, a central-casting Beat chick, to voice this understanding. Initiating a naïve college-trained pianist into the hip underground, she responds to his schooled patter on diminished ninth chords and whatnot by telling him what's really important. "It's the sound…Like, nobody can sound like anybody else": the sound matters because it is the trace of a unique human presence.[7] If hipness was a crusade, it was one on behalf of raw human subjectivity experienced directly and without the inhibiting artifices of society; sound was the vector of energy on which that subjectivity was borne.

But such philosophical nuances are absent from Russell's unpublished 1949 character sketch of Lee, a girlfriend on whom the character of Zaida appears to have been modeled. As a novelist in 1961, Russell wants to understand the idea that makes sense of the girl, but as a diarist in 1949, Russell wants to understand the girl:

> She is, and was, hopelessly Bohemian, the "gonest" and wildest of hip chicks. She loved sex for itself and was precociously promiscuous. She was daily guilty of violations of the Harrison Act. She spoke a language that perhaps less than 1000 citizens of America could understand. She wore weird and often corny clothes. She could be rude to the point of outrageous insolence. She couldn't hold a job, lived off her family and men, was undisciplined even in her rotten pathetic musical ambitions. She had not a portion of Lydia's [Russell's ex-wife] intelligence, musicianship, or even talent. Even her common sense was questionable. But she was wonderful! Absolutely wonderful!
>
> What was this quality of being wonderful?
>
> It was something ingénue and girlish. Something very very feminine. A joy of living. A constant state of ecstasy over life within the boundaries of the hip jazz world. More it had a truly American quality—of the girl who could be a pal as readily as a loner, who spoke with salty American wit, who was manifestly "don't-give-a-damn," who would buy you a drink or loan you a buck or ask you for a fifty. Who got her kicks in a thousand ways,

some innocent, others decadent. Who could be inspired almost to an orgasm by an auto ride on a spring night, or by going to bed with 6 men.[8]

Russell runs down a checklist of recognizable hipster affectations: sexual license and incomprehensible slang, "weird and corny clothes," inability to hold down a job, and vague creativity without accomplishment in any actual artistic medium. But though Zaida is a narrative contrivance that makes a coherent shape out of these various attributes—in other words, her presence serves to make hipness manifest—Lee is an American girl whose Bohemian mannerisms fail to explain her special *esprit*. There is nothing here to suggest that her personality manifests the vast tidal pull of a new sensibility—a notion common to Beat writings and *The Sound*. In this passage, to be hip has nothing to do with any "crusade" within which sound becomes holy; this would only really occur to Russell later, after the Beats had taught him to see it that way. Indeed, for Russell in the 1940s, hipness as such does not really exist, just the behavioral tics of the hip jazz world.

Obviously, Russell's 1949 characterization of Lee differs from his 1961 portrait of Zaida because novelists generally try to imagine their characters as parts of some larger context. The Beats certainly did, and the context they imagined for their private rebellions shaped the self-understanding of the next generation of hip intellectuals: if the 1960s Movement understood itself a form of advanced consciousness peculiar to a generation and manifest in its chosen music (see Chapter 4), it inherited this idea from Beat novels and poems. The first Beat novel, John Clellon Holmes's *Go* (1952), has a fictionalized version of Kerouac saying "You know, everyone I know is kind of furtive, kind of beat. They all go along the street like they were guilty of something, but didn't believe in guilt. I can spot them immediately! And it's happening all over the country, to everyone; a sort of revolution of the soul."[9] This idea that a shared historical experience had given birth to a shared psychological and spiritual orientation was always a standard part of Beat self-understanding. Allen Ginsberg viewed the Beat "revolution of the soul" as a message carried on an occult wavelength, from various cultural transmitters, to a cohort coming of age in the late 1940s:

A number of subtle revolutions had begun at that time: a change in national music to variable rhythmic base called Bop, a corresponding change in poetic Prosody (W. C. Williams' Variable American Foot), hip styles of diction & posture & hand-gesture signaling revolution of consciousness from Harlem & 52nd Street jazz meccas, breakthroughs of cosmic consciousness (or planetary consciousness if the latter phrase is more acceptable to city-minded critics) occurring to Whitmanic isolatos in myriad cities of these States, drug-induced ecstasies & hallucinations passing from Black and Red subcultural hands into the heads of scholarly whites, changes in body-awareness & recognition of sexual tendernesses heretofore acknowledged by Sherwood Anderson in the same provincial American ken as prophet Walt Whitman.[10]

Russell reserves such grandiose framing of autobiographical incident for his novel; the Beats, in their letters, journals, and home recordings, show that this was how they understood their own experience even as it was happening to them, and how they talked among themselves. When Neal Cassady writes Kerouac about George Shearing, for example, it is not enough to recall fondly their shared experience of hearing the man play, or even to turn him into an archetype; he has to make Shearing an archetype within a cosmic drama featuring Cassady and Kerouac themselves: "God, just heard that great George Shearing, remember God Shearing, Jack? God Shearing and Devil Gaillard. That's us Jack, a mixture of George and Slim. The images we struck of George, a sightless God; of Slim, an all-seeing being."[11] This is what Ernest Van den Haag means when he accuses the Beats of "conspicuous consumption of the self": they cultivate a way of approaching their experience with lip-smacking delectation and a style of writing that advertises its intensity.[12] To Van den Haag, Kerouac's writing is phatic, saying only that it is saying something, and the experiences toward which it grandly gestures turn out to be negligible: "There are relentless mutual invitations to 'go, man, go,' to have experiences and to make you experience them—to feel something—but all it ever comes to is verbal flatulence and the most extreme banality of experience, articulation and thought."[13]

This is unfair, but it lies close to a valuable truth. Kerouac's mode of writing is not so much phatic as deictic: rather than assert meaningful propositions about experience that can be tested or refuted, he simply points, with great praise and enthusiasm, at an experience that must always remain partially undefined. His writing is meant to point toward experiences that, remaining ineffable in themselves, lie always outside the moments of writing and reading. As the focus of Kerouac's deixis, the experience-in-itself remains a vanishing point on the horizon to which the reader's attention is drawn, its stubborn presence encouraging an openness to sensation in the reader parallel to Kerouac's own. Experience takes place in a specific and concrete time and space that writing, by its nature, does not occupy. Beat writing makes immediacy in time and space its great theme and performs the impossibilistic gesture of moving beyond its own inherent abstraction from that immediacy. It attempts an alchemical transmutation of pure experience into words and words back into experience. It does not matter if, as Van den Haag charges, the experiences so celebrated are themselves nothing special. As Diane di Prima wrote, "we all thought *experience itself was good. Any experience.*"[14]

Beat writing is about experience as such. In fact, it is not quite right to say it is "about" experience. It aims at participating in experience, in the sense of "participation" developed by the anthropologist Lucien Lévy-Bruhl—it is consubstantial with experience, made from the same stuff.[15] One odd little document of this kind of participation is a poem titled "To James Clay" that Sherry Riley, an aspiring Beat poet, once sent to the editors of *Down Beat*.[16] The poem was typed on a torn scrap of paper, with a note at the bottom—"written while listening to the band play this tune at the Club Interlude":

> "Gone with the Wind"
> Yes, I am gone
> Gone with your wind
> Low in your sax
> And high in your flute
> A wailing wind
> James Clay's band!

The poem's theme is the characteristically Beat urge to merge with and participate in sound. Even more, the document itself embodies a rhetoric of participation, its torn edges and explanatory note vouching for its authenticity as the trace of a lived encounter, like a drip in a Jackson Pollock painting. The poem raises a claim, not merely of representing Riley's experience of hearing James Clay, but of being part of it.

Russell's way of narrating incidents from his own life is much more prosaic. Of a visit to Bud Powell sometime in 1949, Russell writes:

> Allan and I had a swim at the 145 Street Municipal pool, ate dinner at Eddie's on St. Nicholas, and stopped by to see Bud Powell who played his newest composition Dance of the Infidels. Arresting and sinister. He seemed lively, social and rational. Terrible pad. Dressed in slippers and an old, battered coffee-colored satin dressing robe with rear seam split. A group of admirers in attendance. We sent out for a bottle of chilled port and discussed a record date.[17]

Russell writes about his experience the way we might describe our own visit to someone with whom we are on friendly though not intimate terms. The details he notices (shabby dressing gown and slippers, chilled port, and hangers-on in a dingy apartment) could easily be woven easily into a story of *la vie de bohème* like those in *The Sound*, or for that matter the story of Powell's own life, darkened by squalor and mental illness. But insofar as Russell acknowledges Powell's psychological problems, it is indirectly and in passing, and in any case Russell's point is not to experience something extraordinary or to use these observed details in service of some dramatically satisfying story (imagine what Kerouac would have done with it!) but only to check in on a colorful associate and maybe do a little business.

Russell knew that Powell was an important artist, the kind of person about whom people would tell stories for years after his death, and he could have imagined this incident as an as-yet-untold anecdote, framed and lit as if for a movie, with larger significances laid on each word and action. For that matter, it is always possible for any of us to do this. French philosopher Roger-Pol Droit suggests that we "practice make-believe everywhere" as one of his experiments in *philosophie quotidienne*:

> This morning, for instance, you are not going to the baker's and then the post office merely to buy, respectively, bread and stamps. Start off by playing the triumphant customer, entering the bakery. Pay attention to how you thrust open the door (movement of the arm, full of energy, but not too brusque). Regulate your voice correctly, and sing out "good morning," the greeting worthy of a customer who comes in to buy a triumphant loaf. Ask, pay, and collect your change, triumphant still, say good-bye and thank you, watching your every movement, from the confident step toward the door, to the little complicit smile addressed to the lady just coming in to buy—inevitably—her sliced white bread and bar of chocolate.[18]

It is an effort to keep this up, though, and our friends are likely to find it tiresome to be around someone who acts as if his life is a movie, he is the star, and everyone else is a walk-on player. At any rate, Russell never thought to frame things in this way. The mythic dimension of his life became apparent to him only later, when his days as a jazz impresario were behind him and he decided to mine them for a novel. Like almost all of us, it seemed to him that whatever happened to him on a given day, at the time it happened, was just another day.

The Beats made an effort not to see things this way, and this, above all, sets their work apart from their peers. Like children, they entered their own experience in a spirit of make-believe. Little wonder that critics like Van den Haag sniffed out something pretentious in the Beats' public stances: after all, they were pretending, acting out a chosen belief that they were living epochal lives.[19] They did so by stepping outside of the quotidian temporality in which almost everyone lives—a distracted present, half-lost between anxious recall and anticipation—and into a more expansive temporal frame, transmuting the dross of ordinary life into a sweeping story arc and writing themselves into the story. The Beats narrated their own lives within a mythic time in which each moment assumes an ideal relationship to a larger totality of incident.

The Sadness of It All

There is a kind of paradox here, though. Beat writing, grounded in the transient flux of experience, is underwritten by an ideal now-time or constant becoming, the time of improvisation and jazz, and such a temporality is at odds with the dramatic time of Beat self-narration. Perhaps it is for this reason that Alan Watts wrote that Kerouac "is always a shade too self-conscious, too subjective, and too strident to have the flavor of Zen."[20] As I have mentioned in Chapter 1, Zen appealed to the Beats in part because it insisted that only the present and ever-changing moment is real, and that the way most people conceive the present—as something sandwiched between a real past and a real but not-yet-realized future—is delusion. The introductory verse of the Zen koan "Ruiyan's Constant Principle" puts the matter squarely: "Even as you call it 'thus,' it's already changed. Where knowledge doesn't reach, avoid speaking of it. Here, is there any investigating or not?"[21] In the universe conceived as constant flux through a single eternal moment, nothing holds still for inspection; merely to name some part of it is to grasp at and abstract it from the total flow. To name, then, is to falsify; to think, talk, or write about something is already to have lost its true reality—that reality only disclosed at the moment of a vividly felt experience. The temporality represented by "Ruiyan's Constant Principle" cancels the possi-bility that one might ever arrest an experience or permit events to gel into a stable narrative structure. This left the Beats in an impossible position, grasping the moment and at once watching it slip through their fingers.

Such a collision between incommensurable temporalities produces an experi-ence of loss and a kind of nostalgia. For Svetlana Boym, the nostalgiac "desires to obliterate history and turn it into private or collective mythology, to revisit time like space, refusing to surrender to the irreversibility of time that plagues the human condition."[22] Jack Kerouac, who called himself "the Great Rememberer redeeming life from darkness," was that kind of nostalgiac.[23] His novel *Visions of Cody* especially represents an attempt to create something like a memory palace, a storehouse of fugitive things captured and preserved from devouring time and forgetfulness. This passage from the novel's first large section is one in a series of prose sketches of remembered scenes rendered in minute poetic detail:

> A SAD PARK OF AUTUMN, late Saturday afternoon—leaves by now so dry they make a general rattle all over and a little girl in a green knit cap is squashing leaves against the wire fence and then trying to climb over them—also mothers in the waning light, sitting their kiddies in swing seats of gray iron and pushing them with grave and dutiful playful-ness—A little boy in red woodsman shirt stoops to drink water at the dry concrete fountain—a flag whips through the bare bleak branches—salmon is the color of parts of the sky—the children in the swings kick their feet in air, mothers say *Wheee*—a trash wirebasket is half full of dry, dry leaves—a pool of last night's rain lies in the gravel; tonight it will be cold, clear, winter coming and who will haunt the deserted park then?[24]

This passage issues a stream of visual fragments ending in the double-exposure image of the life of the park and the lifeless park, glimpsed together in an instant. The passage of time; the mystery of passing time and the seasons; the sadness of all the tiny beautiful things that are lost to time—all telescoped into a single crisp line set off by a semicolon. That last line works both sides of the Beat temporal paradox, capturing time and at once losing it, in its final vision of a dry cold landscape of mute objects carrying on without us. It is a complicated, melancholy emotion close to that of Mahler's *Das Lied von der Erde*, whose first movement reminds us of a world that remains indifferent to all our attempts to possess something of it:

> The firmament stays forever blue and the earth
> Will long stand firm and bloom in spring
> But then you, Man, how long will you live?
> Not a hundred years can you delight
> In all the rotten trinkets of this earth![25]

Kerouac's compulsive remembering was his way of stanching the flow of time—a fool's errand, like trying to hold back the tide. But Kerouac's foolishness is Pierrot-like, made poignant both by the impossibility of its aims and by his awareness of their impossibility. The "nostalgia for the present" that saturates his writing flows from the knowledge that to remember is to forget; to record is to erase; to grasp is to lose.[26]

A recent experiment in memory conducted by a neuroscientist named Karim Nader bears out this intuition on a deeper level. Nader injected into rats a drug that suppressed memory formation, so as to prevent the rats from associating a given sound with an electric shock. Later, he administered the drug to a rat that had already been thoroughly conditioned to associate the sound with pain. At the moment the rat heard the sound and flinched in anticipation of the shock, Nader injected the drug, and astonishingly the rat not only forgot the ensuing shock, but that it had ever associated the sound and the shock in the first place. Erasing a single instance of recollection erased the memory itself. We are accustomed to imagining that whenever something happens to us it makes an original memory that can be filed away in some mental drawer and then retrieved at any later point we wish to recall it; Nader's experiment suggested, however, that we remake the memory anew every time we remember.[27] And as Jonah Lehrer writes, this in turn suggests that every recollection of a memory dulls its edges; the more we remember, the more the real object of memory fades away and is replaced by our own simulacrum of it:

> The Nader experiment . . . reveals memory as a ceaseless process, not a
> repository of inert information. It shows us that every time we

remember anything, the neuronal structure of the memory is delicately transformed, a process called reconsolidation... The memory is altered in the absence of the original stimulus, becoming less about what you remember and more about you. So the purely objective memory, the one "true" to the taste of the madeleine, is the one memory you will never know. The moment you remember the cookie's taste is the same moment you forget what it really tasted like.[28]

Ever since Ginsberg dubbed Kerouac's writing "spontaneous bop prose," it has been a commonplace to suggest that his art aspires to the condition of music.[29] I would rather say that his writing, trying to grasp the time-borne flow of human energies, aspires to the condition of sound. The idea that sound embodies such energies runs throughout the twentieth-century avant-garde (see Chapter 5). It makes sense, then, that Kerouac should have decided to make the long central section of *Visions of Cody* an apparently unedited transcript of tape-recorded conversations between Kerouac, Cassady, and their friends. Ginsberg's elegiac essay on *Visions of Cody* considers why Kerouac would abandon textual composition for the faithful reproduction of a stoned conversation with all its "halts, switches, emptiness, quixotic chatters, disconnections, meaninglessness, occasional summary piths."[30] Ginsberg justifies Kerouac's procedure by comparing it to similar experiments in painting (abstract expressionist "action painting") and poetry (Robert Olson's projective verse), arts of a recorded action whose charge "lies in the consciousness of doing the thing, in the attention to the happening, in the sacramentalization of everyday reality, the God-worship in the present conversation, no matter what."[31] Experience is not the same as its repetition, its re-presentation, in knowledge, and it is the former rather than the latter that the Beats held holy.

> Thus the tape may be read not as hung up & boring which it sometimes is, but as a spontaneous Ritual performed once & never repeated, in full consciousness that every yawn & syllable uttered would be eternal— and here it is immortalized after all by the Great Rememberer and his Cast of Characters remembering themselves while still alive.[32]

Recorded sound, then, is sound become holy: it captures pure experience—the raw granular texture of reality—and bears forth a pure remembering. Kerouac's expedient of taping his conversations allows the experience and its repetition in memory to arrive at the same time and remain forever fixed in his artwork. Thus Kerouac and his friends, "remembering themselves while still alive," might solve the koan, living in the moment while the tape releases their exploits into narrative and history. The gap between experience and its mediation vanishes, or so the Beats believed, at least some of the time.[33] Yet it should be obvious that recording is just another kind of representation and repetition, and transcription in prose is yet another.

There is something about recording that makes us believe we have encountered an unmediated reality, though, and lets us forget the medium that permits the illusion. Maybe we want the illusion, anyway. As Ginsberg writes, the "Frisco Tape" section matters "if you love or know these characters & want their reality," which describes most of those who have ever written about the Beats.[34] To "want their reality" is to unfold the two-dimensional world-in-print of the Frisco Tape section into a virtual three-dimensional space, to imagine (and so to inhabit) the rooms in which these events have been recorded. John Shapcott imagines the Cassady living room as a "democratic location for storytelling" charged with sonorized, boplike energies.[35] Preston Whaley, gesturing at the ambivalent reality of such a virtual space, calls it a "simulacrum."[36] Such simulacra are always ready to be projected, like a 3D hologram, from the flat disc of the record. Greil Marcus, writing about Bob Dylan's unedited and unreleased basement tapes, permits himself to unfold such a holographic space and enfold himself within it:

> The sound, as it is on the original tapes of the best-known basement songs, is clear and intimate, full of air, the shape of every note plain—a sound that makes you feel you're in the room, that places the room around you as you listen. It's a room, as it reappears in sound, you can almost picture: low ceiling, dim corners to hide in. A room to fool around in; a place where anything can happen, but where nothing happening would make as much sense as anything else.[37]

The subtitle of Marcus's *Old Weird America* is "The World of Bob Dylan's Basement Tapes," and "the world" is an apt figure for what tapes always seem to promise. But the promise can never be kept, and Kerouac knew it: as he said to Cassady, that's the sadness of it all.

Digging What They Dig

In late 1949, John Clellon Holmes's brother-in-law left an acetate recorder—a machine that cuts sound grooves into blank shellac disks—in Holmes's Lexington Avenue apartment. Like Jay Landesman, Holmes hosted parties fed by a steady stream of figures from New York's emerging hip intellectual scene, and the recordings Holmes made during these parties preserve a little more than five hours of Holmes and his friends (including Kerouac, Ginsberg, and Kerouac's friend Seymour Wyse) goofing around, reading their work, listening to music, and trying out their own version of vocal jazz improvisation.[38] As Holmes remembered it, "All of us, then, were bop-mad, indefatigable, stone-broke, and full (we imagined) of ravishing jazz-ideas."[39] Recorded between October 20, 1949, and March 30, 1951, two dates for which there is firm evidence, the Holmes acetates document the Beats before they had become the Beats, when they were only just beginning to publish their work and Holmes had yet to write his *New York Times* birth announcement of the "Beat Generation."[40]

If you wished to find a moment perfectly suspended between the Beats' experience and the fame they won for their experience, you could not choose better than this interval of a year and a half.[41] In October 1949 Ginsberg was in a mental institution, trying to "cure" his homosexuality and at the same time befriending Carl Solomon, one of those "best minds of my generation" who would inspire the most famous line in twentieth-century poetry.[42] Also in October 1949, Kerouac had just returned from a road trip with Neal Cassady that would form the basis for *On The Road*. March 1951 is the month in which Holmes completed *Go*, and just a few days after March 30 Kerouac would begin writing a draft of *On The Road* on a single long spool of typewriter paper—the legendary scroll that has become a hipster saint's relic, not just a document of Kerouac's "spontaneous bop prose" but the embodiment of it.[43] Forever torn between its desire for cultural authority and its fear of co-optation, the hip sensibility prizes obscure and uncorrupted beginnings and forever seeks the Edenic point at which a dissenting hip culture has not yet been corrupted by its success. Recorded by the Beats before Beatnik faddism and media ballyhoo could complicate the purity of their revolt, the Holmes acetates seem to offer just such an Eden—a utopia soundscape that in some inarticulate way we might imagine we could visit. The Holmes acetates offer themselves up as historical fetishes, promising a return to true origins. Again, though, this is a promise that cannot be kept.

If the Holmes acetates are a soundscape, they are what R. Murray Schafer called a lo-fi soundscape:

> In the ultimate lo-fi soundscape the signal to noise ratio is 1 to 1 and it no longer possible to knew what, if anything, is to be listened to. . . . Everything is close-miked. There is cross-talk on all the channels, and in order for the most ordinary sounds to be heard they have to be monstrously amplified.[44]

Listening to the Holmes acetates, our ears strain to capture words and music swallowed up by surface noise; music played on a distant radio or voices at a party hover on the edge of hearing, and they are broken off by smears and breaks where the machine has been started and stopped. Acetate cutters were clumsy devices, and acetate recordings are fragile and rare. As they could only be made singly, acetates are usually unique records, and their shellac can crack, grow mold, or peel away from the metal backing. For sound archivists, discovering a cache of acetates is a mixed blessing: an acetate holds out the possibility of res-cuing a lost sonic past from the traceless era before tape, but its grooves deteri-orate every time it is played. Like human memory, to play acetates is to participate in their decay; their promise recedes from our touch. Even in the form of a digi-tized preservation copy, the sounds of these objects' decay seem the embodi-ment of faded memory. We could try to clean them up, of course, enhancing their signal, suppressing their noise, and stripping the patina of age from them. But then that act of memory, even as it aims at perfection, would be just another reconsolidation, another subtle transformation of the original memory into whatever it is we want from it—whatever it is we are—now. And if we keep the noise and dive into it, treating it as the trace of these object's private history and the fetish of a history in which we might try to participate, we are drawn into a hide-and-seek game of memory in which what we seek recedes forever in front of us.

These records were in private hands until Kent State University accessioned them in the mid-1990s. And yet, aside from a sound clip of Ginsberg reading "A Mad Gleam," none of them appears to have been made public.[45] Maybe this is because it is hard to know what to do with them: they are ambiguous as history and doubtful as aesthetic objects. They are documents of lives but do not tell a tale, and we cannot easily approach them as a source for unpublished poetical and musical works.

Well, we can, sort of. Ginsberg's reading of "Fie My Fum," for example, is an interesting alternate version of the one published in the *Collected Poems*.[46] We might think of it as a recovered work, an alternate take to be presented side-by-side with the familiar version the way multiple takes appear in CD reis-sues of jazz albums. The poem, if not exactly jazzy, has an ad-man's vernacular ring that prompted Holmes and Ginsberg to call it a "cosmic juke-box ditty" and "a great archetypal jingle."[47] Ginsberg's reshuffling of the poem's Burma-Shave cadences in this reading, with Dizzy Gillespie's "Shaw 'Nuff" playing in the background, might suggest the improvisational strategies of a jazz musician. But Ginsberg warns against making too much of the music playing in the background; this was no jazz-and-poetry piece, but something else:

> [Holmes] made a few recordings of Kerouac and myself during parties or after.... Symphony Sid was background in Holmes' early recordings—an all-night radio show that played advanced bebop. The radio was on when he turned on his tape machine. It wasn't a deliberate attempt to put poetry and jazz together. Jazz was all around anyway, it was part of the ambient sound.[48]

At the beginning of his recitation, Ginsberg introduces himself ("these are the images of Allen Ginsberg") and rattles through his poems one after the other in a subdued near-monotone, beginning and ending each one without any attempt to cue them to the bebop tunes playing on the radio. The music and voices of unidentified partygoers go their own way in the background, but if there was no attempt to read poetry with jazz, there was also no attempt to filter out ambient sounds either. The recording is not of a reading in which the sounds of poetry are privileged over the contingent noise of social space; Ginsberg does not treat the read poem as the performance of a "work" that maintains its integrity by setting boundaries against non-poetical, non-intentional noise. Neither is Ginsberg trying to create some new kind of work fused from words and music, as it appears Holmes was trying to do in reading the unpublished "Fragment of Attila" to Sergei Rachmaninoff's "Vocalise."[49] The way Holmes begins the poem at the first main cadence of the "Vocalise" and ends it at the music's final cadence; the rough parity of words and music in sonic space; the reedy urgency of Holmes's voice; the way he paces himself to the slow tempo of the Vocalise and mimics the music's long swells and plaintive caesurae—all suggest a more old-fashioned *Gesamtkunstwerk* ambition. Ginsberg's reading, on the other hand, manifests the avant-garde goal of marrying art and life, which the Beats pursued in a vernacular register, the marriage consummated at last, they thought, with jazz. Here art is what happens off in the corner while life, the radio and party chatter, goes on in the apartment. The read poem is art unfolding from life, just as life is meant to be what unfolds from art.

When Jack Kerouac reads a selection from his first novel *The Town and the City,* his reading voice is different from Ginsberg's: it is wry and ironic, kidding the nostalgia already beginning to trickle into his own prose.[50] But like Ginsberg, Kerouac conceives his performed text not as a work, but as a dialectic of art and life. He lays bare the artifices of writing, carefully enunciating the punctuation of a long sentence for the benefit of his audience, one of whom cheers him on with a (rather deliberate) cry of "Go!" Kerouac is clearly trying to harness the dialogic and performative character of jazz to his own prose; as Shapcott writes of the Frisco Tape, we encounter an "intersubjective dynamic in which the individual speaker and the surrounding community empower one another along bebop's antiphonal structural lines."[51] As with Ginsberg's reading, music is playing in the background, and when Kerouac comes to the end, literary performance trails off into music as he hums a riff along with the radio, leaning away from the microphone to switch off the machine. What we hear is not a literary work; it is an occurrence in the lives of these people, decades ago. It is not an object, but an event.

In a sense, the Holmes acetates tell us how to listen to them. Ginsberg's and Kerouac's readings suggest we hear them not as works that need to be rescued from the chaos of noise, but as elements wedded to the chaos and shading imperceptibly into it. So heard, our own hearing becomes implicated in these recordings, too, as it is drawn outward from intentional sounds to contingent noises.

Such also is the style of hearing cultivated in the loose body of scholarship called "sound studies" or "auditory culture studies": to reverse background and foreground and make noise into sound.[52] We take a sound formerly discarded as noise, as the unwanted and unintentional byproduct of whatever activity (musical or otherwise) is held to be the proper object of perception, and move that noise to the foreground of our attention, so transmuting it back into sound. The study of auditory culture is often a study of the avant-garde, but it also does the avant-garde's cultural work. It carries out John Cage's ambition to project hearing away from discrete and intentional sounds and out into the totality of auditory space, asking us to perceive perception, to hear listening, or (as Kerouac put it) to dig what we're digging.

ALLEN GINSBERG: The center of art is always an interest in personality, and in the way people are using people . . .

JACK KEROUAC: And in the way people dig what they're digging

AG: . . . not the ideas themselves but the way they learn to dig what they're digging

JK: . . . Is it not, is it not

AG: It's the aesthetic site of the drama of the way they're working, in the emotions of that, and the motions of emotions about that, not the ideas themselves

Unidentified off-mike speaker (Holmes?): What do you say, Mr. Kerouac?

JK: It's the way people are digging what they dig.

AG: But what about what they dig? What's the final . . .

JK: Well now we won't bother with that now, but on a later record

AG: OK

[break in recording]

AG: Yeah, that's right, and also, that what happens is that what you get, you get immortality cut-rate you said (yeah) you get immortality but you get a corporeal immortality, see, rather than just floating on through time without your body, 'cause your voice, which is part of your body and completely physical thing, remains. (yeah) Y'know?[53]

It is impossible to tell how long the break in recording lasted, and what degree of continuity can be presumed in the two segments that lie on either side of it. But read together, these two segments hint at the Beats' emerging idea of hip poetics and its relationship to recorded sound. Kerouac and Ginsberg suggest two ideas here: first, art is best understood not in terms of any definable idea but as what emerges from a field of emotional energies within which artists create their work; second, by preserving sound, the recording also preserves the reading body and the corporeal presence of the read poem. The conjunction of these two ideas suggests that recordings preserve something better than ideas and something more than artworks—they might preserve "not the ideas themselves but the way they learn to dig what they're digging," the energy field as well as the artworks that are constituted there. Too bad Kerouac didn't try to answer Ginsberg's question about what they dig, the final and indisputable *fons et origo* of all hipness. If anyone could have answered this question, at any point in history, it should have been these two, at this exact moment. (It would be nice to imagine that they did when they turned off the machine.) Either way, the ultimate point of origin again turns out to be a vanishing point, moving away from the interpreter as steadily as the interpreter moves toward it.

When Kerouac and Ginsberg heard their own recorded voices (an experience much rarer in 1949 than now), they reflected on how recordings can release the voices of the dead from their bodies. The same thought had always occurred to those first hearing their voices coming from the phonograph's horn, as Jonathan Sterne and Friedrich Kittler have noted.[54] And this might also be our experience of listening to these voices now, long after Holmes, Ginsberg, and Kerouac are gone. We sense the gap between us and them, even as the grain of auditory detail makes them seem, at times, almost close enough to touch. The acetates allow us the voyeuristic feeling that we are eavesdropping on those legendary, long-ago parties. Holmes recorded Stan Getz's "Running Water" off the radio: listening to it, at a certain point, we realize that it isn't just another broadcast transcription, but that we are listening to someone listening to music—an oddly intimate experience.[55] After the pianist (Hank Jones) and bassist (Curley Russell) take their solos, Getz and the drummer (Max Roach) begin trading fours and the clicks of surface noise resolve indeterminately into another sound, a listener's (Kerouac's?) excited tabletop drumming. A voice off-mike exclaims "blow Stan Getz, blow!"

Can we listen still closer? Listening to listening, can we hear how they heard? It is tempting to think so. For one thing, it could solve a durable problem in Kerouac scholarship: whether and to what degree his writing really reflects the influence of jazz. Kerouac's critics always try to read his prose as a kind of jazz, but such interpretations are ultimately elusive; set down on the page, they are missing a last degree of detail. Admirers tend to take Kerouac at his word, sometimes repeating his admonition to "tap from yourself the song of yourself, blow!—now!" without saying much more about how the jazz forms in Kerouac's ear found specific analogues in his prose.[56] As Jon Panish has pointed out, scholars such as Regina Weinreich and W. T. Lhamon "discuss his spontaneous method and practice more specifically but are still fuzzy when it comes to explaining *how* his prose imitates jazz."[57] And something of this fuzziness was enacted when Kerouac himself tried to blow actual, unmetaphorical jazz. Writes Panish, "Kerouac's overarching depiction of the process of creation in jazz is one that requires almost no training, skill, or education: just pick up a horn, tap into your emotions, and 'blow.'"[58] And when Kerouac, with little in the way of skill or training, tried to do something that required both—singing jazz choruses over a repeating pattern of chord changes—the results are disappointing.

But the acetates give us an insight into how sharp (or fuzzy) was Kerouac's knowledge of jazz. Kerouac's duet with Seymour Wyse on Dizzy Gillespie's "Hot House" demonstrates a basic scaffolding of jazz form and texture unmoored from prescribed harmonic content.[59] The performance is divided into two choruses, each one roughly charting the thirty-two-bar *aa¹ba* form of the tune. A couple of added beats notwithstanding, Kerouac and Wyse do manage to track the eight-measure divisions of the tune, with Kerouac singing a bass line against Wyse's solo. In their first chorus Kerouac sings the same line for each of the three *a* limbs of the *aa¹ba* form. (The middle eight is rather muddled and undersung). The line's harmonic rhythm is far too slow for the bebop idiom: its first three notes are each held for two bars, which gives the performance a sound oddly like early Medieval organum. But its notes (B flat–A flat–G–E–F–G), although not quite idiomatic, at least fit the tune in a minimal way. Kerouac likely figured this line out ahead of time, rehearsing and fitting it to repeated hearings of the record. In the second chorus Kerouac switches to a four-in-a-bar walking bass pattern, although now the notes are sung somewhat at random and do not appear to bear any harmonic relationship to the tune. Halfway through the second limb of the second chorus, Wyse does a double-time lick which has the same compressed, explosive logic within the overall rhythmic flow of the "solo" as Charlie Parker's solos did, and in the same place (the halfway point of a phrase) a jazz musician might have put it. But there is hardly any pitch content to Wyse's lick. The gesture is broadly right but narrowly wrong; its grammar is OK, but its words are gibberish.

We can deduce a few things about Kerouac's jazz knowledge from this performance. First, and most basically, Kerouac knew that jazz improvisation takes place over a pattern of repeated chord changes grounded in a bass line. He further knew the four-part lyric binary form that structures most jazz tunes, and could either count or feel his way to the breaks between the four limbs of the form well enough to remain oriented within it. His ear was good enough to fit a simplified countermelody to the *a* limbs of a complicated bebop tune, though not good enough to devise one for the trickier *b* limb, and not good enough to find appropriate pitches for the tune once he stopped holding notes for two measures and attempted to sing four in a bar. He and Wyse know enough about jazz texture to mimic aspects of it (the double-time break, four-in-a-bar walking bass), but not enough to outfit their texture with appropriate pitches. In sum, Kerouac's musical knowledge is fuzzy. He heard the way jazz arranges musical ideas, but not the logic of the ideas themselves. His understanding of jazz was broad and conceptual, which is to say, he had thoughts about jazz, not jazz thoughts.[60]

Astounding and Prophetic

October 1949 was the high point of Kerouac's and Holmes's enthusiasm for Lennie Tristano. Holmes's tastes ran to modernist compositions such as Stravinsky's *L'Oiseau de feu* (a broadcast of which Holmes recorded onto acetate 12), and Tristano's modernism was a familiar point of reference in an unfamiliar music he was learning to appreciate.[61] The most unusual acetate recordings are a pair of *a cappella* vocal improvisations (titled "Logic" and "The Absolute") that Holmes, Kerouac, and Wyse did in imitation of Tristano's "Intuition" and "Digression."[62] The latter were the first recorded attempts at collective jazz improvisation without agreed-on chord changes, key, or time signatures. Although unreleased until 1956, the Beats had heard them on Symphony Sid's overnight bebop show.[63] Holmes describes the party at which "Logic" was recorded:

> One night, Seymour [Wyse] brought to a party of mine several demon-stration discs, only one side of which had been used, and, pleasantly mulled on beer, which in those days we always bought in enormous quart bottles, and never more than four at a time, after which someone was delegated to go down to the deli below and purchase more. Soon I got Jack to read the two slight selections from *Town and City* (both of which were considerably thinned in the published version), after which our exuberance quickly outran any such "literary" projects, and we got down to making records of ourselves, riffing over recorded solos. One of our passions just then was the work of pianist Lennie Tristano, who was, perhaps, the most avant-garde of the younger jazzmen of that year, and who, just a month before, had recorded, the first attempt at total, freeform, atonal improvisation, a record called "Intuition," not yet released, but played occasionally by Symphony Sid on his all-night radio show. We decided to attempt a similar thing, and the "Three Tools" were born, flourished briefly, and passed away.[64]

Kerouac wrote about this recording session in a journal entry dated October 20, 1949: "Went into town to school and signed at all the classes without attending. On Thurs. night Holmes and Seymour and I made some astounding 'prophetic' voice-music recordings that sound like Tristano's 'Intuition.' I did a few boyishly sad Hamlet soliloquies."[65] Against the ineptitude of these performances—I have never played "Logic" in public without the audience laughing—Kerouac calling them "astounding" and "prophetic" might seem like a bit of wry self-mockery. But a letter he had written to Ginsberg the previous year suggests otherwise. Writing about a different party where he made "mad jazz records all night" (of which sadly no trace remains), he boasts that "some of it is actually great jazz":

> During the course of the night I discovered a new mode of singing that is greater than Sarah Vaughan, although I haven't got the voice or technique to carry it through—however I'm sure that this mode of singing is the singing of the future. I really am tremendously prophetic about jazz, Tom [Livornese] realizes this. This mode of singing combines Tristano with Vaughan.[66]

It's not great jazz. Except for a mysterious woman named "Lee," who sings an affecting version of "While You Are Gone," no one on any of these early recordings can carry a tune.[67] In "Logic," Holmes bah-boos his way through an atonal Bing Crosby imitation, while Kerouac, singing as "out" as he can, hops up and down through a randomly angular line like a hyperactive kid jumping on a bed. Heard against the Tristano recordings, "Logic" demonstrates a lack of swing, of intonation, of even a local sense of key, of the ability to share and pursue ideas the way jazz musicians do. Simon Frith, musing on the unanswerable question of what constitutes bad music, suggests that whether it is the result of incompetent musicians, incongruous emotions, or unlikely cross-genre excursions, bad music "means essentially *ridiculous* music, and the sense of the ridiculous lies in the gap between what performers/producers think they are doing and what they actually achieve."[68] The reason people laugh at "Logic," I suppose, is the gap it manifests between Kerouac's claims to visionary musical greatness and what we hear. It is the same gap that lies between what the child sees as a fort and what Mom sees as a pile of sofa cushions when she walks into the living room.

But for this reason our laughter might be more affectionate than mocking. As I have said before, the Beats participated in their own experience the way children participate in theirs, and this was their great gift. As Sasha Frere-Jones writes, it is arrant stupidity to insist that artists must be in life exactly what they claim to be in their artistic personae.[69] Who cares if Kerouac couldn't really sing jazz? He wasn't a jazz musician; he was a writer who made his readers think of jazz musicians, and his persona as a naïve jazz savant was part of the literary performance.

Besides, even if it's not a real fort, a sofa-cushion fort tells you something about the person who made it. I'm not saying that Kerouac was merely pretending to feel something in "Logic"; I suspect he really did feel something. (Or maybe there is less of a difference between pretending to feel something and "really" feeling it than we might like to think.) We might find a clue to what it was in his later "Belief and Technique for Modern Prose." "Struggle to sketch the flow that already exists intact in mind," Kerouac wrote; it is a good epigram for "Logic," and suggests what Tristano's free improvisation might have meant to him.[70] Flow is not the same as the expression that might be found for it. Flow is a moving thing, something borne along by the movements of life, or in fact is not a thing at all but a direct realization of the life movement itself. The moment it is captured in thought and fixed in representation, it is no longer flow. This was the basic, perhaps insoluble aesthetic problem of spontaneous prose: to find a way to let flow congeal into a fixed textual object without falsifying it, without flow becoming merely another *thing*. This suggests why jazz was so important to the Beats. It seemed to them that moving forms—"tonally moving forms," in Eduard Hanslick's useful phrase—might best "sketch the flow that already exists intact in mind."[71] Furthermore, although Tristano and his musicians were improvising, they weren't improvising on *things*. They had boiled away all the impedimenta of thought, the time and key signatures and Tin Pan Alley standards that bind musicians together and to their audience, and the residue left when all else had evaporated was pure and ineffable flow, the forms and movements of jazz improvisation without the accretions of replicable thought and meaning. This, at least, is how Tristano's free improvisation would have appeared to the Beats. In his exchange with Kerouac, Ginsberg said that the center of their art was "the aesthetic site of the drama of the way they're working, in the emotions of that, and the motions of emotions about that, not the ideas themselves." The live experience of blowing jazz constitutes such an aesthetic site; the recording captures the "motions of emotions" about and through that site.

Kerouac and his friends, then, might have experienced "Intuition" as something like an x-ray of the inner structures of improvisation and so too of the mind. Theodor Adorno had made a similar claim for Schoenberg's expressionist monodrama *Erwartung;* as Daniel Albright writes, he argued that although

> all previous composers present only representations of passion, flimsy symbolic equivalents to passion... Schoenberg has managed to write music that embodies the brain's physiological responses to shock and trauma. It is as if the score to Schoenberg's *Erwartung* were a sound generator hooked up to an electroencephalograph: Schoenberg descended beneath all codes and conventions to discover what the nervous system actually sounds like.[72]

Replace "nervous system" with "imagination": the Beat aesthetic, if parallel to an earlier expressionism, placed it in a vernacular register, within a hip aesthetic still enmeshed with European modernism. What Schoenberg's expressionism had in common with the emergent Beat ethic of spontaneity is the idea that there is an inner realm to which music can give access—but only music that "descend[s] beneath all codes and conventions." This is the Absolute: music and poetic revelation allow hip consciousness access to what Kerouac called the "unspeakable visions of the individual."[73]

In an exchange of letters between Holmes and Ginsberg the summer before these recordings were made, Ginsberg writes about life in the mental institution to which he had just been committed and tries to explain the imagery of "Pull My Daisy," the better-known version of "Fie My Fum." "'All my doors are open' because I am aware of two worlds of being; one of thought in which I dwell, one of feeling in which I am being driven by Time to enter," he writes, marking the boundary between speakable and unspeakable realms of experience that his own poetry would try to cross and recross throughout his life.[74] Ginsberg notes that he's not there yet: "'All my doors are open' is more of a boast than an actuality for me." But if he cannot yet render that ineffable realm in writing, he can at least point towards it. The focal image of Ginsberg's deixis is the rose, which is common to both "Fie My Fum" and "Pull My Daisy." Ginsberg writes that he understands the rose "to be feeling (or moments of feeling, epiphanies, illuminations, that open up like roses and are complete & sufficient unto themselves & undefinable by thought."[75] How to define in writing what is indefinable in thought: this is the Beat literary project in a nutshell. Jazz is to Kerouac what the rose is to Ginsberg: it is where the ineffable opens into time and blooms in experience.

What is astonishing and prophetic about "Logic" is the experience Kerouac, Wyse, and Holmes had in recording it. They felt for themselves an artwork that moved beneath them in the same time as life, the deep structures of human consciousness palpable in their movement from person to person, in mysterious convergences and spontaneous inspirations. Singing "Logic" is not the same as hearing it. To sing it would have been to experience moments where individual minds could come together in the same uncanny way as they do in a jazz performance—to experience what Kerouac called "the IT," the "big moment of rapport all around."[76]

At times you can hear—or think you can hear—outward traces of this inner experience. About a minute into "Logic," the different voices pull away from one another and then reach a point where their centrifugal motion is suddenly checked and reversed. At this point the three voices wheel around and land together like a flock of birds, a spontaneous order apparently realized without planning or even conscious intent. There is an analogous moment beginning about 2:20 into Tristano's "Digression," where a somewhat orderly collective eighth-note flow breaks, scatters, and regroups into a kind of spontaneous cadence.[77] Contemplating a recorded moment of strange synchronization between Charlie Christian and Kenny Clarke, Scott DeVeaux writes that "this kind of telepathic empathy happens more often than one might think in jam sessions."[78] For a group of musical neophytes to experience this for themselves must have seemed a kind of magic—truly astounding, possibly prophetic.

Stenciled off the Real

I hear this moment, and I can convince myself that I have penetrated the veil of mediation that surrounds all historical moments and have arrived at last at the center of history. I strip away the artifices of Beat autobiographical fictions and become privy to a mythic moment that is not yet myth, where the IT reveals itself, where jazz consummates the marriage of art and life, where an early, premonitory shudder of a new sensibility might have been felt somewhere in the collective spirit of America. My hearing of this recording is unavoidably colored by the distance between its own moment, when the Beats were beginning to imagine a jazz-inflected hip sensibility and trying to live within it, and mine, when that sensibility has become a "permanent American style."[79] The acetates seem to bridge the gap between moments. Their sepia soundscape, with all its crackles and smears and dull unresonating sounds of things happening too far from the microphone, becomes a little world in which I find myself at home. I might imagine myself a visitor at Holmes's parties; the auditory presence of these mythic figures stands in for the dream of living in their company. But within the auditory geography of the Holmes acetates I feel something I don't in the Beats' more crafted autobiographical fictions: boredom. Like a guest at one of Holmes's parties, I sit listening to the other guests chatting and cutting up, singing along with their records, drumming their fingers in time to the music. I'm bored, though, because I'm not really there. Whatever moving vector of social energy that is galvanizing their attention as it passes from one to the other, misses me. I can hear the intimate details of their interactions, but I can't touch or move anything. I'm a ghost. Sterne and Kittler have written of how often people have heard recordings and imagined themselves in the company of the dead, but here it's just as easy to feel that I'm the one who's died.

Recordings, like photographs, are mass-reproduced traces of presence, pieces of sound and space broken off from the world and handed around, fetishized, and taken as surrogates of the real thing. In this way, Susan Sontag writes, photographs usurp reality:

> ...a photograph is not only an image (as a painting is an image), an interpretation of the real; it is also a trace, something stenciled off the real, like a footprint or a death mask. While a painting, even one that meets photographic standards of resemblance, is never more than the stating of an interpretation, a photograph is never less than the registering of an emanation (light waves reflected by objects)—a material

vestige of its subject in a way that no painting can be. Between two fantasy alternatives, that Holbein the Younger had lived long enough to have painted Shakespeare or that a prototype of the camera had been invented early enough to have photographed him, most Bardolators would choose the photograph. This is not just because it would presumably show what Shakespeare really looked like, for even if the hypothetical photograph were faded, barely legible, a brownish shadow, we would probably still prefer it to another glorious Holbein. Having a photograph of Shakespeare would be like having a nail from the True Cross.[80]

We think photos are dispassionate witnesses and look to them for confirmation of facts. They are, or seem to be, the instruments of history. Yet this is not what charges them with significance and power. The hypothetical photo of Shakespeare does not fascinate because it shows us what he really looked like, but because it is an emanation from his real presence in a way that a painting is not. It is like a piece of the True Cross because, like a saint's relic, it is something the man touched; it participates, takes part, in his presence. As we will see in the last chapter, participation is the basis for magical consciousness; thus a photo or recording can become a magical object, made potent through its consubstantiality with what it represents.[81] The tape section from *Visions of Cody* is then a talisman intended not merely to represent the "motions of emotions" in the place of their evolutions, but invoke them bodily, as a séance invokes a dead spirit.[82] Listening to the Holmes acetates' mediated soundscape in this way, we might find ourselves not merely listening to recordings but experiencing them as a place where we make ourselves at home.

But this is a belief on which we must act, a part we must play, in order for the magic to work; dragged into the cold light of rational scrutiny, it does not hold up. Listening critically, we become aware of a gap between the Three Tools' musical experience and our own. Recordings always seem to suggest that here, in the surplus of their auditory detail, is the fine grain of history our imagination has always promised. But it's a cheat; history shrinks from our grasp. And from this exudes a melancholy that clings to old records as surely as their musty smell. Wayne Koestenbaum writes of his fascination for old opera 78s, which is pulled along by the promise that each recording might map the origins of musical or sexual desire. Koestenbaum compares himself to Nipper, the HMV dog who, looking for his absent master in the hole at the center of the gramophone horn, "is an image of a mass-produced replication (a record) seeking its original." "We, listening to opera records, occupy the dog's seat. We are trying to enter a hole backwards, trying to go back in time, through the looking glass, to find a phantom."[83] Koestenbaum begins to ponder holes:

I've always been fascinated by the spindle hole. Everything on the record's face conspires to highlight it: the price circles it; the label and the round window in the protective paper envelope echo its shape. Remove a vintage Melba record from its sleeve and you see, printed on the inside of the envelope, a photograph of the diva, as if the round center of the envelope were a window onto a retreating, hermetic world.[84]

The hole, Koestenbaum continues, "has always spoken to me of the emptiness at the center of a recorded voice and the emptiness at the center of a listener's life." The Holmes acetates open up another hole that we might enter to pursue a "retreating, hermetic world," but as that world keeps retreating, so, like all recordings, do they offer as their final reward only a new emptiness at the heart of their sonic plenitude. The Holmes acetates most easily lend themselves to a nostalgia for an imagined historical moment, but they are also occasions for contemplating the melancholy of recorded sound itself. Recordings constitute a kind of memory, and like human memory they inspire false confidence. The recording, betraying its limits, becomes a kind of *memento mori*. To remember is to forget; to record is to erase; to grasp is to lose.

The poem that became "Pull My Daisy" has been a leitmotif in this chapter, and here it makes one last appearance, in the 1959 film *Pull My Daisy*, a half-hour film that Robert Frank and Alfred Leslie made with Kerouac, Ginsberg, Gregory Corso, Peter Orlovsky, the composer David Amram, and the painter Larry Rivers. The jaunty title song to which Amram sets the poem nails the signature Beat mixture of melancholy and giddy exhilaration, but even more it is the film's odd diegesis that places it in the register of memory and loss—of nostalgia.

It was widely believed that this film was created spontaneously, like John Cassavetes's *Shadows*, whose ending proclaimed "the film you have just seen was an improvisation." As always seems to be the case with Beat fictions, this was "more of a boast than an actuality."[85] After a chaotic period of shooting and a pair of recording sessions for which Kerouac turned in a drunk, incoherent monologue, Frank and Leslie edited their raw stock into a tightly organized but spontaneous-feeling film in which there is no synchronized, diegetic sound, but rather a kind of paradiegesis in Kerouac's voice-over narration and Amram's intermittent scoring.[86] The dialogue and music we hear is parallel but not identical to what we see the characters say and do. In the party with the Bishop, for instance, a fast bebop piece starts up on the soundtrack and we see the characters playing instruments, but it is clearly not the same music. There is an unseen and unaccounted-for rhythm section, and the characters' playing gestures are so conspicuously unaligned with the music that it is clear this is no error of synchronization but something else—the substitution of an inside-the-film diegesis with one outside the film, a story told by the narrator rather than by the characters themselves. It is never clear whether the dialogue Kerouac puts in the mouths of the characters tells us what they are saying, what they are thinking, or what Kerouac imagines them saying. What he remembers them saying, maybe. (This feels most true: not for nothing was Kerouac called "the Great Rememberer.") But if so, then this film memory is no more reliable than any other kind. We see but don't hear the characters; their sounds are supplied by a third party who is not present with them. In the Holmes acetates, it is the other way around: we hear people but don't see them. In *Pull My Daisy*, Kerouac reconstructs auditory space for us; in the Holmes acetates, we reconstruct visual space in our minds' eye. In neither case, though, are we really there. *Pull My Daisy* and the Holmes acetates stand in an inverted relation to one another, but in both it is the amputation of a sense that locates the narrative in memory. Memory is revealed to be inherently, irremediably broken and partial, an amputated sensorium in which the lost sense, like a phantom limb, still aches.

The music and narration of *Pull My Daisy* were intended to conjure the Beat scene circa 1959, but the film was also a loving glance back at the kind of leisurely and unforced sociality, captured on the Holmes acetates, that Kerouac and his friends had enjoyed a decade earlier and could enjoy no longer. It is a commonplace to say that the success of *On The Road* ruined Kerouac's life; for one thing, it kept him from living the kind of life that had been the very source of his art. Permanently drunk, under siege from fans, immured in his mother's house, and increasingly isolated from all his old friends, memory was all he had left at the end. A sad 1961 letter to Carolyn Cassady shows that the life *Pull My Daisy* pictured was the life Kerouac felt had already slipped away from him:

> The other business about how I've turned into an orating drunken 'author' is all true—But I'm fighting against it, *now*, it has been forced on me really by thousands of interrupting maniacs from here to Sweden—
> (if you only knew how it's managed)—
> It's managed blindly & with no real ill-intent by numberless interlopers who, for instance, would not let you and & I sit talking religion by the fireplace for a minute, it's smelled out somehow, or could I have an oldtime day alone with Neal? No—Eugene Burdick was right saying 'the circle is closing in' on me, Allen, Neal etc.[87]

Throughout the 1960s, Kerouac resented his own fans ("my only clientele are kids who steal my books in bookstores") and ended up detesting the hippies who claimed him as their inspiration.[88] No other figure in hip culture registers more clearly the dialectical play of continuity and change in the hip sensibility as it moves from the 1950s to the mass counterculture of the late 1960s and early 1970s. The next chapter will suggest that it was the Beats rather than modernist jazz musicians like Tristano who set the tone and agenda of the later counterculture. At the same time, Kerouac was a writer of skill and refinement who came to loathe the counterculture's principled inarticulacy and proud ignorance of literary tradition.[89] He is that paradigmatically modern figure, the revolutionary swept away by his own revolution. The next chapter will trace the development of hip aesthetics away from the skeptical, ironic, individualistic, and high-modernist modes of the early Cold War culture and toward the utopian, demotic, communitarian, and anti-elitist modes of the 1960s and 1970s counterculture. In this new variation on the hip sensibility, the tense equilibrium between presence and meaning maintained in the hip intellectual culture of the Cold War would be broken, and rock, not jazz, would most plausibly manifest the possibilities of a radicalized and electrified culture of presence.

4

Hip Sensibility in an Age of Mass Counterculture

> You ask me what's a square
> I'll tell you what's a square
> He has a certain air
> A square is unaware that he's a square
> That's a square.[1]
> —Milt Gabler and John Benson Brooks

> Without an anti-environment, all environments are invisible.
> The role of the artist is to create anti-environments as a means
> of perception and adjustment.[2]
> —Marshall McLuhan

Right On, Mr. Horowitz

In Stanford University's Archive for Recorded Sound, I once found a pile of discarded paper envelopes of the sort used to hold LP records in place inside their cardboard sleeves. Many of them had been used to advertise a record company's other releases, and some of the advertisements for CBS records took the form of an ersatz newspaper column called "The Inner Sleeve." One, whose bulbous graphical style and labored rockcrit prose placed it in the early-to-mid-1970s, featured a sidebar piece on Vladimir Horowitz, then a CBS artist:

> Vladimir Horowitz is hung up on Chopin. Listen to the way he gets into the mood of the music, highlights the nuances. No one could get as much out of a composer's creativity if he didn't understand every note, every chord. And also have the talent to play it. Horowitz has his own thoughts on what it was that Chopin was saying. He spells them out at some length in notes on the album. For excerpts of what it is that gets to him read the following....[3]

What follows are program notes in the platitudinous style usual to Horowitz's public utterances on music. The last of Horowitz's comments, for Chopin's Polonaise in A Flat Major ("it is indeed a Polonaise for all seasons and all oppressed lands, a Polonaise for the millions of men and women who still hold dear the human spirit") is end-punctuated by the editor's enthusiastic "Right on!" as if Horowitz were talking about Kent State or Attica. What is most striking about this bit of ephemera is that at some point it seemed like a good idea to the management of CBS Records that Vladimir Horowitz, of all people, be marketed in a vaguely countercultural way, with now-dated youth slang being used to give the maestro's ruminations a flavor of hip defiance and rebellion. A decade earlier this way of picturing Horowitz would have looked like a joke, but now it had come to seem natural to claim hip cachet for everything under the sun.

This is one tiny example of the vast cultural shift whose story Thomas Frank tells in his study of postwar business culture, *The Conquest of Cool*. It is usually assumed that advertisers co-opted hip style; Frank's contribution is to show that it is just as true to say that advertising *drove* hip style. In an appendix to *The Conquest of Cool*, Frank finds an ingenious way to quantify the increasing concentration of ambient hipness in American life by tracking how often elements of hip style appear in American magazine advertising between 1955 and 1972. Frank's list of stylistic elements is a simple but dead-on collection of hip markers, not only in advertising but across hip culture generally: minimalist graphics with sans-serif typefaces; self-reflexivity and irreverence toward the product; implications of mass-culture critique; specifically countercultural imagery; and the language of "'escape,' defiance, resisting crowds, rebellion, or nonconformity."[4] Frank's graphs show hipness simmering for the first few years of the 1960s and exploding from 1965 onward. In their own reductive way, these graphs track the changing look and feel of American culture.

We take for granted the stance of cultural opposition whose fortunes Frank traces, and it takes some imagination to grasp how alien and hard to explain it was to most people in the early years of the Cold War. One way to register the omnipresence of hipness in contemporary life is to feel its absence when we look into the near past. To page through the 1950s magazines and newspapers that Frank used in his study is to visit the Land Before Hipness—an America that resembles the one in which we live, though a little off, tonally, maybe just a bit too normal, blithely unaware of the cultural tsunami about to hit.[5] Before 1957, it was unclear what kind of thing hipness might be, and however picturesque and appealing (or threatening) its isolated manifestations were, it had not yet seeped into everyday vernacular experience. There were jazz clubs and a couple of legendary New York hangouts such as the White Horse Tavern and the San Remo Bar, but there were none of the hipster bars, restaurants, and boutiques common to gentrifying city neighborhoods nowadays. There were no free alterna-weeklies to guide hip consumers or filter local art and politics through a lens of hip snark; for that matter, there was no hip snark, *Mad* magazine aside, or at least nothing nearly so pervasive as the attitude of sarcastic, pop-savvy knowingness that shows like *The Simpsons* and *Family Guy* have lately made inevitable in blog comment threads and Facebook status updates.

Before the mid-1960s, the traces of hip culture in American popular discourse were like the raisins in a pudding. After 1957, the year of Kerouac's breakout success with *On the Road,* there were suddenly a lot more raisins. The *Village Voice* and a few little magazines such as *Evergreen Review* and *Kulchur* began to float a sustained discourse of hipness. At the same time, hipsters became picturesque features of news stories, novelty records, TV detective shows, exploitation movies, and pulp novels, and tourists flocked to bohemian communities in San Francisco and Greenwich Village to take pictures of the urban primitives living in the midst of American modernity.[6] But after 1965, the raisins *were* the pudding. In the mid-1960s hipness abruptly moved from the margins to the center of American life. It was no longer the colorful affectation of artists, loafers, delinquents, and kids, but a lifestyle that anyone might choose. The underground press, rock magazines such as *Creem, Crawdaddy!,* and *Rolling Stone,* radical political publications such as *Ramparts* and *Liberation,* countercultural films, hippie sci-fi novels, a steady stream of articles in mainstream newspapers and magazines trying to understand "what the young are trying to tell us"—to say nothing of hip clinics, hip schools, hip churches, and every kind of hip business—all burst forth in astonishing profusion. The "Inner Sleeve" Horowitz ad bears witness to how the hip sensibility began to dominate in places formerly alien to it and the degree to which hipness had gained a sustained, institutional presence in American life. The mid-1960s witnessed the birth of that now-familiar oxymoron, the mass counterculture.

And yet the hip sensibility above all defines the individual in opposition to the mass. Hip culture's problematic of cooptation and the Heisenbergian relation of hip style to mass awareness assume this opposition. Understanding how the hip sensibility changed in the 1960s means understanding how it came to terms with the contradictions inherent in its development. These contradictions were reconciled (temporarily) through a new notion of consciousness. The countercultural idea had always placed special emphasis on consciousness; after all, its founding mythology was the hipster's awareness of unfreedom and the distance between this awareness and everyone else's. As Diane di Prima wrote, "consciousness itself was a good. And anything that took us *outside*—that gave us the dimensions of the box we were caught in, an aerial view, as it were—showed us the exact arrangement of the maze we were walking, was a blessing."[7] In the later 1960s, though, the focus shifted from individual to collective consciousness. The idea that a shift in mass youth consciousness could precipitate revolution—an escape from the maze—not in some distant and hoped-for future time but right now, suggested how tensions between hip sensibility and a new era of mass counterculture could be resolved. What remained consistent from the 1940s through the 1960s was a schema of asymmetrical consciousness: in the game ideology I discussed in Chapter 2, the hipster sees through the square but not vice versa; one side takes the higher ground. What changed, though, was a vaster sense of agency. In the late 1960s, it no longer seemed enough for hip individuals to remake their own little worlds; suddenly, it seemed possible that a global, collective hip consciousness could remake the world entirely. This change is reflected in how the square's encounters with hipness were framed in imaginative representation. In the 1940s and 1950s, he is baffled and bested by the hip individuals he meets on his jaunts underground; in the populist 1960s variant of the hip sensibility, the square is confronted by the youthful avatars of an enlightened mass consciousness.

New ideologies played out in new aesthetics. The hip culture of the 1960s may have grown out of the 1950s, but it was voluntaristic rather than disaffiliative, populist rather than individualist, and temperamentally opposed to the self-conscious intellectualism of the early Cold War's modernist dialect of hipness. 1960 counterculture had inherited one of the meanings of *somewhere* from an earlier hip culture—*somewhere* as "presence culture," the world of intense experience disclosed in the moment and unadulterated by secondary reflection and representation.[8] But although 1950s intellectuals were ambivalent about pure presence and concerned above all with the problem of mediating it into literature, 1960s culture radicalized presence and developed new art forms to encompass its widened scope. Writing about one of the 1960s' characteristic cultural forms—the "fluxkits" of the avant-garde Fluxus group—Hannah Higgins considers how this kind of art is oriented to unmediated presence and a holistic fusion of art and its audience:

> ...the stuff in the Fluxkit makes an experience for the handler that *is* the sensation contained in it; the Fluxkit is not *about* sensation. The operative word *about,* like the word *of,* insists on the distance between object and user: "That is a painting about pain" or "of a pipe." In the Fluxkits, actual stuff is present—"That is a pom-pom"; it is not *about* a pom-pom unless a particular user proceeds down that path of association. Removing *of* and *about* represents two challenges to entrenched patterns of thought: first, if a piece is not *about* things but actually *is* them, then the signifying chain often applied to visual art in semiotic analyses needs to be modified to make physical or actual experiences central to the process of signification; second, and more important for my purposes, these works problematize the Western metaphysics since Plato and Aristotle, which insists on dividing primary experience (the feel or scent of the pom-pom) from secondary experience (mental concepts about it).[9]

This orientation toward primary experience—holism, immediacy, presence, participation, and embodied sensation—overlapped with the broader radical culture in the 1960s. The rock counterculture added a dash of millenarian populism to this stew of notions to create a cultural mood we think of as "the sixties"—a pseudo-periodizing term that is really a convenient shorthand for a vast tectonic shift in American taste and ideology.

The effects of this shift were manifest not only in the aesthetics but also in the institutional fortunes of jazz and rock. Rock siphoned off jazz's traditional audience of hip youth at an alarming rate; as Eric Hobsbawm wrote, "the young, without whom jazz cannot exist—hardly any jazz fan has been converted after the age of twenty—abandoned it, and with spectacular suddenness."[10] To be sure, jazz musicians could still find work in large cities, and recording companies still produced jazz records. But by the mid-1980s it was clear that jazz's continued health as an art form was dependent on the support of charitable foundations and nonprofit arts organizations.[11] Young jazz musicians now had to write grant proposals and compete with string quartets and puppet theaters. In the last thirty years, jazz musicians could choose to live lives as bohemian as their predecessors, but jazz as a profession became simply another arts endeavor. In 1962, Philip Larkin could write that jazz had replaced painting as *"la vie de bohème* in the popular imagination," painting having become rather more respectable: "To desert business or government for the traditional arts nowadays is merely to exchange one kind of establishment for another."[12] But ten years later, tales of *la vie de bohème* would not feature protagonists overthrowing convention to become jazz musicians. If it is true that at midcentury painters had become almost as respectable as professors, in more recent times the same could be said of jazz. In the 1960s, jazz came to occupy a different space in the hip imaginary as the ideas with which it was bound up in its postwar development—modernism and the critique of mass culture in particular—took on new meanings.

The cleft between earlier and later phases of hip culture occurred in the mid-1960s, and the period during which hip culture moves from the periphery to the center of the nation's consciousness ran for about a decade into the mid-1970s. There ought to be a name for the historical actor responsible for this shift, and it is imprecise to call it "the counterculture," for the spread of the hip sensibility was made possible only by an alliance of hip subcultures and political youth movements. I prefer to call this historical actor "the Movement," complete with the ostentatious capitalization its advocates favored at the height of its arc. In the late 1960s and early 1970s, there were many movements, but only one Movement: there were libertarian, anarchist, Maoist, Marxist-Leninist, feminist, American Indian, Chicano, Black nationalist, gay, hippy, ecologist, high-school, collegiate, proletarian, pacifist, and militant movements, but against their factionalizing tendencies they sought a common denominator in youth and their opposition to the Vietnam War. As a Movement, they formed a loose and unstable coalition distinguished by its utopian ambitions, its dreams of revolution, and its tendency to marry political activism to a specifically cultural critique of political and social life.

The agent of the countercultural idea's eventual success in public life was not the New Left, exactly—the more purely political elements of the New Left never overcame their objections to the counterculture's specifically cultural style of resistance.[13] Political leftists, caught up in the co-optation thesis, endlessly debated the wisdom of allying themselves with countercultural leftists. Even the most radical rock groups, such as the MC5, could get signed by a major record company and take their "underground" to the stage, and this fact led to the entirely justified suspicion that cultural styles of rebellion were as much outgrowths of capitalist society as protests against it. One anonymous polemicist wrote that

> while the "hip" bourgeoisie chants Hare Krishna, Imperialism napalms kids in Vietnam and shoots black teenagers in the back for "suspicious behavior." Let the hippies and teenyboppers put up barricades in the streets, burn the banks, and wage guerrilla war on the police, and then, maybe, they will have the right to talk about "liberation."[14]

For their part, the culture radicals could be just as suspicious of political organizers trying to co-opt *their* scene.[15] Ed Sanders's quasi-pornographic Beat/anarchist samizdat *Fuck You: A Magazine of the Arts* memorably took aim at the orthodox Left: "authoritarian assholes, bureaucratic bumfucks, Marxist mothers, we're going to have a revolution in spite of you triplicated, mimeoed, left-of-center Jesuits, so help me Kropotkin!"[16]

At the same time, it is also not quite right to say that the counterculture effected the movement of hip sensibility from the margins to the center of American life by itself. What did the trick was an alliance between cultural and political Lefts:

> a grand geodesic dome fitted together from pieces of Marx, Freud, Zen, Artaud, Kesey, Lenin, Leary, Ginsberg, Che, Gandhi, Marcuse, Laing, Fidel and Lao Tzu, strung with the black banners of anarchy to which the sayings of Chairman Mao have been neatly embroidered, and with a 40-watt rock amplifier strapped to the top—a gaudy, mindblowing spectacle and an impossible intellectual synthesis.[17]

Despite their mutual suspicion, the cultural and political Lefts influenced one another. Hippies went to marches and read Mao; political organizers smoked pot and quoted Dylan. By the end of the 1960s, both sides were theorizing a revolution just around the corner, with each Movement groupuscule mixing notions of political and cultural agency in various proportions. Like hipness itself, the Movement was a loose, syncretic entity, and for all its addiction to manifestos and multipoint programs, it rejected straightforward definitions.

Among the arrow collar underground and to some extent the Beats, hipness had been attractive precisely because it was not really a political idea. In the 1940s and 1950s, hip intellectuals could have their cake and eat it, maintaining their critical vocation and marking their distance from the American mainstream without having to submit to party discipline. In his novel *Who Walk in Darkness* (1952), Chandler Brossard sounds like his *Partisan Review* elders as he contemptuously dismisses Washington Square folkies as communists "singing Stalinized American ballads to a guitar."[18] Greenwich Village hipsters and folkies tended to keep their distance from one another; members of the latter group shared a nostalgia for the Popular Front ethos of the organized social movement, and as Ned Polsky noted, "each of the three words 'organized social movement' sounds obscene to the beat's ears."[19] Polsky did not even call his interview subjects anarchists, since they did not want to promote any kind of -ism. Many of the early articles on the Beats disapproved of their attitude of total resignation; as one writer for the *Village Voice* noted, "almost all articles about the Beat implicitly ask you to make up your mind; stop shilly-shallying and **do** something. Which is the hallmark of the political activist, and frequently these are the people who are writing about this minority."[20] In the 1950s, activists and hipsters were not the same. In the 1960s, they very often were.

It is on this point that hipness in the 1960s most vividly and obviously differs from hipness in the 1950s. For the Movement, the boundary between culture and politics was never clear. The slogan "All power to the imagination!" which appeared on Movement pamphlets and fliers at almost the same time it appeared in the streets of Paris in May 1968, is a statement of the fusion between political and aesthetic horizons.[21] And as Hobsbawm noted, this was perhaps the crucial difference between the newer and older Lefts: "Older observers . . . used to keeping music and revolution apart in principle and to judging each by its own criteria, were apt to be perplexed by the apocalyptic rhetoric which could surround rock at the peak of the global youth rebellion."[22] In the writings of John Sinclair, the founder of the White Panther Party and a tireless organizer of the Midwest countercultural scene, revolution was explicitly theorized as an organic fusion of political, economic, and cultural realms.[23] Sinclair arrived at an anarcho-Marxism in which culture is a force equal to rather than dependent on the political economy. This understanding of the connections between culture and politics—music and the revolution—was fundamental to the philosophy of the White Panther Party, and was rendered in the form of a logo representing a pipe, a guitar, and a rifle (Fig. 4.1), which Sinclair interpreted in this way:

Figure 4.1 Gary Grimshaw, "We Are a People!" book illustration with White Panther Party logo (lower right), from John Sinclair, *Guitar Army* (1972).

> In this drawing the two cross-sticks represent a rifle (on the left) and a guitar (on the right), with a peace pipe full of the righteous sacrament [marijuana] crossing them and bringing those two elements together. We can't have the guitar without the gun or we won't survive, we can't have the gun without the guitar or else we'd just be more of the same old shit we are trying to do away with; and without the sacrament that gives us our vision neither the guitar nor the gun would amount to anything worthwhile.[24]

Few Movement factions conceived themselves in quite the same way as the White Panthers, but many shared the idea of the cultural realm as a space equal to and perhaps coterminous with the political. The "Berkeley Liberation Program," a manifesto that arose from the clash between Berkeley radicals and police over People's Park in the summer of 1969, outlines a thirteen-point program whose tone veers between revolutionary communism (point 1: "We will make Telegraph Avenue and the south campus a strategic free territory for revolution") and counterculture utopianism (point 2: "We will create our revolutionary culture everywhere"), a call for a "soulful socialism" wrapped up with the contradictory slogan, "all power to the imagination, all power to the people." This document, a compromise between different radical constituencies, allegorizes its ideological pluralism with a quotation from Mao and the heraldry of marijuana surmounted by a corona of Mao heads (see Fig. 4.2).[25]

Figure 4.2 Berkeley Liberation Program, inside front cover illustration. Hardin B. Jones Archive, Hoover Institution Library and Archives, Stanford University.

If we could permit ourselves to believe in the notion of a zeitgeist, this flier would surely embody it. It could have existed in its context—seriously offered, and in some quarters seriously believed, as a blueprint of the revolution—only at this particular cultural moment, at the very end of the 1960s. Ten years earlier, the Beats would have approved its idea of a pot-laced "soulful socialism" but been puzzled by its flavor of revolutionary third-world Marxism and indifferent to its call for mass action. Ten years later, this flier would be the sad relic of a future that never arrived. But at the moment it was printed, it seemed nothing more or less than what the times called for.

There was a fantastic universal sense that whatever we were doing was *right*, that we were winning....And that, I think, was the handle—that sense of inevitable victory over the forces of Old and Evil. Not in any mean or military sense; we didn't need that. Our energy would simply *prevail*. There was no point in fighting—on our side or theirs. We had all the momentum; we were riding the crest of a high and beautiful wave.[26]

But as Hunter Thomson wrote in this famous passage, it would not last: "with the right kind of eyes you can almost *see* the high-water mark—that place where the wave finally broke and rolled back."[27] Sinclair's manifesto, the Berkeley Liberation Program, and the other documents of this high-utopian historical moment were carried on the crest of that wave.

The Square

The square is a figure of song and story, an image in the world's collective library of memory. He is one half of an unbreakable dyad in the contemporary imagination, the hipster and the square, figures whose reciprocal roles define a schema of perception that has had an incalculable influence on American culture throughout the past half-century and more. Norman Mailer's "The White Negro" frames a contest between the "frontiersman in the Wild West of American night life" and the "square cell, trapped in the totalitarian tissues of American society."[28] The terms of that contest are laid out in "The Hip and the Square," a list that appeared in *Advertisements for Myself*. If some of the list's oppositions are particular to Mailer's own tastes, others have held their place in the popular imagination for sixty-odd years: wild/practical; instinct/logic; Negro/white; spontaneous/orderly; perverse/pious; nihilistic/authoritarian; body/mind. (Also, Thelonious Monk/Dave Brubeck.)[29] These abstract distinctions coalesce into the perpetually recycled image of an uptight white guy who lives in a bare anonymous suburban tract cluttered with the shiny, candy-colored junk of an empty materialistic civilization. He spends his day at a boring job, chasing promotions without stopping to question whether money and status is a worthy end. He ends each day numbed in the blue glow of the TV, distractedly eating dinner off a little metal tray. He has learned to love the authorities that control him—his boss, his church, his political party, his wife, his friends and neighbors—and now wants nothing more than to control others. He is a joiner and backslapper who hardly spends a moment alone but is alienated from the men whose company he compulsively seeks. Indeed, he is alienated from himself. Whatever he thinks and feels is only a simulacrum of personality left after his authentic consciousness has been scooped out and replaced. What it has been replaced with is something manufactured by an objective, impersonal system he did not make and does not even perceive. Such a man does not understand the emptiness of his life; he does not see the ugliness of the things with which he surrounds himself; he does not know his own family; he does not know himself; he does not even know that he does not know. He has absorbed the American ethic of conformity, authority, and consumerism so thoroughly that he can no longer function without being told what to do, what to like, and what to believe. The system is happy to tell him.

While the square is away at work, his wife tends the home. Like her husband, she has internalized an ideology that requires her to accept an artificial and tightly circumscribed role. She is a great believer in "togetherness," which she has read about in her magazines. She waits on her husband and tends to her children without asking whether she might not be wasting her life living for others as a virtual domestic slave. Maybe she suspects that something is amiss, that on some level she is not really as happy as the good wives whose rigid smiles reproach her from every advertisement. She consoles herself with shopping binges and rebels against her captivity by keeping a watchful eye on the neighbors and punishing transgressions of neighborhood standards with her malicious, gossiping tongue. Some vital part of her has died: the repression of her instincts, the channeling of her creativity and love into meaningless acquisition and enforced togetherness, finds expression in sexual and emotional frigidity. "She appears as a creature of legend, the snow queen—tall, beautiful, appallingly splendid, all cleanliness and whiteness, living in her empty, silent, frigid palace," wrote Elizabeth Hardwick.[30] The image of the inauthentic American woman, like that of the square, is more archetype than realistic anthropology, as Hardwick notes. In 1951 the American "snow queen" was already a trope of European representations of America, "a folk belief, a native wonder of the world, exported along with the cowboys and gangsters to other countries." Central to this image was the idea of a woman entombed in a "solar emptiness warmed occasionally by the dim sounds of the soap opera," where, "bored and idle, she may play bridge in the afternoon." For all her social routines, the American snow queen is always alone. The bridge game "is only a pantomime, a wordless ballet simulating sociability, for she has no true friendship or communication with other women"—or even with her own family.

An analysis of the square and his snow queen wife can only remain on a level unavailable to them, because the essence of their condition is their obliviousness to it. Were they to understand it, they would not be the same sort of people. The dominant trait of "Mr. Jones" in Bob Dylan's "Ballad of a Thin Man"—the ur-square of Movement myth—is a limited awareness that we, the audience, do not share. The song lyrics do not take his part; the narrator's voice establishes him as a mere object of spectacle, unable to see in himself what we see clearly in him. As Greil Marcus writes, "you're set up to imagine him as whoever you're not."[31] Insofar as Mr. Jones exists as a character within a narrative, his only marked attribute is that he does not understand what is clear to the narrator, whose voice sketches a series of bizarre encounters, each one capped by the jeering refrain, "Because something is happening here, but you don't know what it is, do you, Mr. Jones?"[32] In every strophe of the song, Mr. Jones is in over his head: try as he might, he does not and cannot understand the one-eyed midgets, sword-swallowers, and geeks that confront him. Dylan's Delphic lyrics provoked endless interpretation by those who saw him as a Movement oracle, and Dylan, always one to guard his mysteries carefully, never gave anything away. But it is clear that however one interprets this song, its images dramatize how Mr. Jones inhabits a plane of consciousness that does not intersect with those around him. If we decide the song is about drugs, we might imagine that everyone but Mr. Jones is turned on.[33] Huey Newton thought the song was about racism: Mr. Jones is the white racist who has been treating black people as if they were freaks provided for his amusement but now realizes that all along *he* was the freak.[34] Nat Hentoff thought the song was about the "generation gap" and argued that the young are privileged with a holistic understanding denied their elders.[35] From this point of view, Mr. Jones has encountered the "New Consciousness" that has begun to sprout like a genetic mutation among the members of the young generation, and he no more understands it than a pig can read a newspaper. Whichever interpretation one chooses, each furnishes its own way of making the same distinction between an observer's level of consciousness and another, lower one, which is observed.[36]

The 1960s feels like the rightful home of a perspectival stance in which one stands outside a frame of reference shared by "the Establishment," "the System," or "the Man." As a trope of cultural representation, though, its roots run both back to the 1940s and forward to the present day. One of the main incidents of the novel *Who Walk in Darkness* (1952) involves a well-heeled advertising agent who falls in with a circle of underground men at a Greenwich Village bar. The advertising agent is the type of square for whom a trip to the Village is a sort of urban safari, an opportunity to indulge in exotic, forbidden pleasures. This kind of character was not simply an invention of Brossard's. Young men from good colleges would travel from their jobs Uptown to mingle with the artistic types and the liberated girls who were supposed to have read Wilhelm Reich. One letter writer to the *Village Voice* (signed "Yale '54") describes visiting the Village

> in the manner in which sailors come into a foreign town: for an evening of excitement and color, a romp among the natives (and native women), and then off, back to duty, back to the ship and the sea and home, perhaps never to return, or even think again, of the (I must admit) languorous, exotic port left behind.[37]

Brossard's depiction of how the square is humbled by his new hip "friends" offers the satisfaction of revenge. The square is left grinning foolishly as the literary wit of the Village natives lays his pretensions bare. Max, the Jewish hipster modeled on Milton Klonsky, makes a series of correct guesses about the way the square lives, each one an indictment of the man's middlebrow, climbing ways, thrown into high relief by the real intellectual attainments of the "underground men" he has unwisely chosen as his companions. The square reads *The New Yorker,* they read avant-garde little magazines; he listens to WQXR (a classical music station), they listen to bop. He goes to modern art galleries, sees French films, and looks forward to going to Paris, mostly in hopes that some of its intellectual glamor might rub off on him. He is willing to pay for intellectual distinction, which is why he is buying everybody drinks. But he's *square,* aware enough to know he is being made a fool of, but not aware enough to get inside the banter of put-ons and put-downs that might as well be a foreign language to him. All he can do is register each new expression—"I get that one. It's a jive expression. Right?"—as a tourist might hunt down an idiomatic expression in a guide book.[38] Anatole Broyard, who as "Henry Porter" in Brossard's *roman à clef* joins in tormenting the square, elsewhere defined hipness as being "superiorly aware."[39] Hip consciousness not only sees, it sees through; the square only sees things as they appear.

Asymmetrical Consciousness

The hip talk that eludes Brossard's advertising agent is a kind of signifying, a double language that challenges interlocutors to remain cognitively limber enough to jump into the meanings between words instead of being caught flat-footed on top of them. Irony is the rhetorical mode by which the asymmetry between hip and square consciousness is instantiated in conversation. In Chapter 2 I suggested that irony is (in Kenneth Burke's words) a "perspective of perspectives"—that is, the awareness of perspective *as* perspective.[40] Ironic consciousness opens up an interpretive double vision. Every utterance comes to signify one thing within the perspective intended and another within a bracketing metaperspective.

Ironic distance from a square utterance might simply arise from a speaker's attitude or tone of voice. If someone mocks political cant by speaking of, say, "Biblical values" with flat pseudo-seriousness (imagine someone like Aubrey Plaza's character from the TV series *Parks and Recreation*), her listeners are aware both of the perspective ordinarily communicated by the phrase itself and the perspective within which it appears as the ritual utterance of politicians and their followers. But ironic distance is also carved out by the rhetorical forms of hip communication, which drive the necessary wedge between perspective and perspective-of-perspectives through the abstraction of a referent. The "hip hand-shake" described in Chapter 2—the substitution of a finger for a hand in greeting—is a metonymic abstraction of an unironic gesture. Confronted with the reductive hip greeting, one sees both its referent (the full hand extended) and an abstraction (the raised finger) within which the contours of the original may be discerned. The referent remains in mind, but the abstraction undermines its authority. The hipster is at a second remove from language—*in* it but not *of* it, as Jack Kerouac said of the hipster's relationship to his environment.[41] It is the hipster's complex relationship to language and meaning, his awareness of the interplay between referent and its abstraction, that challenges the square's mental flexibility. This is the challenge Brossard's advertising agent fails. Anatole Broyard called this ritual humiliation "capping the squares." As an "ironical ped-agogue" and "self-appointed exegete," the hipster demonstrates multilevel meaning to his square interlocutors and so establishes his mastery over them.[42] And this ironic doubleness of perspective is coded in the forms of hip culture—for example in Charlie Parker's solo on "Ornithology" (see Fig. 4.3), a record that Broyard might well have consulted in writing his "Portrait of the Hipster."[43]

"Ornithology" is a justly famous solo. The mid-century French jazz critic André Hodeir praised this solo's elegance and "classical purity of construction," and with good reason.[44] The improvisation achieves equilibrium between the centripetal force of periodic repetition and the centrifugal force of asymmetry and surprise. Note, for example, the assonance between the ending of the first phrase (m. 3) and the second (m. 7), a formal symmetry from which springs the next, longer phrase (mm. 9–13). The first two phrases glide to a cadence in their third measure, followed by a measure's rest, and the third phrase begins much as the earlier ones do—but then this symmetry is broken when the C that pops into measure 12 opens out into a cadential extension (mm. 12–13), and this phrase spills into the next measure. But it is what happens in the next phrase

Figure 4.3 Charlie Parker, "Ornithology" (1946), Parker's solo (mm. 1–23).

that is most remarkable. The phrase structure of "Ornithology" is AA¹, with the two A phrases each comprising sixteen measures. The fourth phrase of Parker's solo begins by alternating arpeggiated chords with chromatic neighbor motion; the descending C major arpeggio of measure 15 connects to the descending A minor seventh arpeggio of measure 16 by means of a little winding chromatic figure. But it is the descending arpeggio that captures Parker's interest. In the latter half of measure 16, he returns to the G that begins the first half and descends from it again, altering the arpeggio in accordance with the chord changes. He foreshortens the rhythm here, arriving a hair early at the F sharp that continues the implied melodic line started by the preceding G. The descending arpeggiation through the foreshortened sixteenth-note rhythm, begun in measure 16, continues in measures 17–20, as Parker unfolds a series of variations on the unimposing little cell that first appeared in measure 15. And yet, while all this developing variation has been going on, our attention is drawn away from the line that divides the two sixteen-measure strophes of the tune. That line has been elided; Parker began to grow his complicated rhythmic variation from its seed in measure 15 and continued its development through the bar line. The improvised line establishes its own teleology, which cuts against the expected points of arrival and departure implied by the tune's cycling structure. The internal development of Parker's improvised line rubs against the imposed divisions of the tune. In the words of Jay-Z (who writes about an analogous kind of friction that can arise between a rapper's flow and the beat, or cycling rhythmic groove, of a hip-hop track), Parker "hangs a drunken leg over the last bap and keeps going, sneaks out of that bitch."[45]

It is also worth noting the rhythmic shifting that goes on in this passage. A lyrical strain—the notes in measures 16–20 marked with asterisks—coalesces out of the onrushing arpeggios and neighbor motions. But the appearance of rhythmic diminution in measure 16 tugs this lyrical strain away from the strong parts of the measure (with the exception of the down beat F natural in measure 19, which provides a fleeting anchor that the ensuing rhythmic complications pull against). The feel of this passage is definite and sharp-edged, with each note so well chosen it might be the product of minute retrospective calculation, and yet none of it feels four-square. Parker wages a two-front war on four-squareness, with an inner direction for his improvisation that wrong-foots the listener attuned to the tune's formal divisions, and with his rhythmic shifts within the line. (Actually, there is another front, which Hodeir notes: the avoidance of sounding the tonic of a given chord in strong parts of the measure.) This solo has a sense of being in its song structure without quite being of it. It signals awareness of its song structure, of course—the intricate games improvisers play have no meaning without reference to it—but the tendency of the bebop improvisation is to pull away from its orbit, to take an alternate path, to tell a different story: to *go out*. The pleasure it gives the listener is one of mental friction between what is heard in the moment and what remains as a mental background. That background—chord changes and the phrase shapes they define—is the referent to which bebop stands in an abstracted relationship. The outlines of the referent are recognized in the abstraction, and it is the tension between the two—the friction between what is heard in the moment and what is held in the mind—that constitutes its irony. Bebop, Broyard wrote, is the point reached in jazz at which the relationship between performance and its referent is most strained:

> Surprise, "second-removism," and extended virtuosity were the chief characteristics of the bebopper's style. He often achieved surprise by using a tried and true tactic of his favorite comic strip heroes:
>
> The "enemy" is waiting in a room with a drawn gun. The hero kicks open the door and bursts in—*not upright, in the line of fire*—but cleverly lying on the floor, from which position he triumphantly blasts away, while the enemy still aims, ineffectually, at his own expectation.
>
> Borrowing this stratagem, the bebop soloist often entered at an unexpected altitude, came in on an unexpected note, thereby catching the listener off guard and conquering him before he recovered from his surprise.... That which you heard in bebop was always *something else,* not the thing you expected; it was always negatively derived, abstraction *from,* not *to.*[46]

The square who doesn't dig bebop is like Broyard's enemy gunman, who can aim only at his own expectations. Digging bebop's moments of surprise means that the listener assimilates them into his horizon of expectations, in such a way that those expectations themselves become relative, foregrounded as mere conventions, ripe for subversion. When Parker's solo in "Ornithology" begins to follow its own inner course and assert its own "perspective" against that of the phrase form, we are treated to two perspectives simultaneously, Parker's and the song's. The two perspectives diverge, and for a moment the listener is privileged with a musical double vision, an awareness of the multiplicity of perspective. The jazz musician steps into the cracks between those moments of time that congeal out of perceptual habit—and if they are hip, the listeners will follow.[47] The bop phrase, like the hip gesture, is at a second remove to an established language. The bebopper is aware of language for itself; it is no longer the ground beneath his feet, but a thing he can pick up and observe.

This play of abstraction and referent, the substitution of the unfamiliar for the expected, is a fundamental aspect of musical expression—indeed, all artistic expression. But hipness, like the midcentury modernism that nourished it, brought such substitutions to the center of its aesthetic practices. And what was new in hip culture was the particular social significance attached to the abstraction of generic norms. Something like Parker's solo in "Ornithology" could imply a trip out of the consensus consciousness enforced by the industrial machinery of mass culture and into a space of liberation in which the self could be fashioned anew. As Diane di Prima wrote, the hip were looking for whatever took them *outside.*

The geometry of outside and inside is another way of mapping somewhere and nowhere. Inside is the unestranged view, the square view; when we go outside, we see the system that manufactured the square view. In the 1960s, McLuhan would make this distinction in terms of "environment" and "anti-environment." Hip intellectuals valued jazz in part because it made this trajectory so much a part of its musical substance. Ross Russell, the record producer who recorded and released "Ornithology," mused that the jazz musician (of which Parker was the ideal embodiment) has "always been here and gone. That is he is always on the move physically or musically. He is gone also in the old argot hip sense of gone—levitated, out of this world."[48] The verbal idioms of jazz musicians and their fans are full of inside-outside metaphors. Jazz musicians talk of going out (out of the changes, out of the consensus style) or "playing outside." Russell's friend Louis Gottlieb considered Lester Young's skill at moving in and out of a song's metrical structure to have been his most distinctive stylistic feature; pointing to the metrical shifting in the bridge of "I Never Knew" (a moment of rhythmic/motivic displacement similar to that in "Ornithology"), he wrote "should any philologist of the twenty-first century seek a definition of the expression 'gone!' or 'gone again!' this bridge would do quite well."[49] Fans used similar expressions to describe their own experiences of transcendence, as one critic explained:

> The power of musicians of skill to transport is verbalized in *send me* and "He sends me off the sleep." Over the years caressing effects have been vocalized in 'bye, bye baby" lullabies, and millions have lifted in day dreams to Seventh Heaven. Dancers, threading on air, drift and dream, whirl and swirl in the clouds to nine. It is little wonder that swing devotees, on the basis of such experience, and on the general observations of music as "heavenly" and "melody of the spheres," proclaimed they were sent—propelled by that centrifugal force *out of the world.* In the 1940s *far out* and *away out* became integral to bop and cool. Reinforced by Peggy Lee's 1950 swinging "Show Me the Way to Get Out of This World (Because That's Where Everyone Is)," a psychological set for space travel developed years before attainment.[50]

In the last part of this chapter, we will consider some of the ways music can get outside. The basic orientation of somewhere and nowhere, inside and outside, remains consistent in the music considered in this chapter—Parker's

"Ornithology," Ken Nordine's "Sound Museum," and Dylan's "Ballad of a Thin Man"—but the changes wrought in the hip sensibility as it passes through times and social situations are expressed in the different ways the music finds to signify that orientation.

Elitism

Confusingly, hipster argot in the 1950s found another meaning for *inside*. *Gone, far out, out of this world* could also be *in there*. In one sense, inside was exactly where the jazz fan wanted to be. Jazz, the art form in which a hip sensibility was first cultivated, has always seen itself, and been seen by others, as an insider's art. The mythology of jazz idealizes its dedicated listeners as members of "a nearly closed society of voyagers" drifting from one late-night club to another.[51] Furthermore, social distinction was coded in jazz's musical substance, in its widening of the gap between the referent and its abstraction, or (put differently) in raising the distance and tension between inside and outside, environment and anti-environment. For jazz musicians at midcentury, hipness had something to do with heightening this tension, and, for listeners, in following what the musicians were doing. The increasingly complex improvised lines and chordal substitutions of bebop placed a new strain on listeners' power to detect traces of the standard on which a given performance might be based, and contrafacts such as "Ornithology" (built on the changes to "How High the Moon") demanded that they listen for the relationship between an improvisation and a tune that had not even been stated. In Thomas Pynchon's short story "Entropy," a group of hipsters takes this process of abstraction to its logical endpoint. Musing on the thought that one is supposed to think, not hear, the chords in the Mulligan-Baker "pianoless" quartet, they decide to think everything else as well, playing music by "going through the motions of a group having a session, only without instruments."[52]

In his eponymous 1956 Atlantic recording, Lennie Tristano found new ways to increase the tension between referent and abstraction, raising the stakes in the listener's game. He did this with an arsenal of compositional and technological operations, some of which are enumerated in a letter from John Mehegan, a jazz pianist and teacher, to the editors of *Down Beat:*

> First, to clear up any mystery concerning this record: *Line Up* is *All of Me* in A flat; *East 32nd Street* I was not able to identify; however, I would guess it to be a standard major tune played on the harmonic minor scale, which is a favorite device with Lennie.
>
> What was done on *Line Up* and *East 32nd Street* is as follows: Peter Ind and Jeff Morton were taped at normal, playing a rhythm section

accompaniment of these tunes. Lennie then played a line with his right hand in the bass section of the piano at a slower tempo and in a lower key (probably a perfect 5th down). This tape was then speeded up until it matched the tape containing the rhythmic accompaniment.

There seems to be some confusion in some circles as to whether anything was tampered with, and if so, what. There is plenty of tampering here, but it is not with the tapes containing the rhythmic accompaniment—they are normal. The tampering has occurred on the piano tapes; they have been increased, I would say, some 200 vibrations a second....

The point is that Lennie no longer enjoys an avant-garde position in the art form. The west coast movement and recent trends apparent here in the east have little or nothing to do with the philosophy or the music of Lennie Tristano. Actually, jazz has bypassed Lennie and is ranging far and wide with a healthy vigor which has nothing to do with quiz tunes or multiple tapes.[53]

This letter bears witness to the one-upmanship that has filled jazz magazine letter pages from the beginning. Mehegan's letter is a show of mastery in which he demonstrates his ability to solve Tristano's "quiz tunes" by revealing not only the identities of the tunes but how the album's source tapes were manipulated. Indeed, though the flourish of hi-fi erudition in the third paragraph claims scientific authority, Mehegan ends up claiming the even higher authority of jazz history. Tristano is no longer in the avant-garde, Mehegan writes; history has passed him by. There is here a whiff of the second-hand Hegelianism common to the rhetorical habits of modernism. History is like a train, pulling out of the station at an appointed time with those smart enough to hop on, leaving the rest staring at their schedules.

Mehegan's letter may have been slighting and competitive, but Tristano was competing too, playing from the other side of the board. Mehegan was right to call "Line Up" a quiz-tune: it is a piece of music that challenges listeners to follow a path from their own prior notion of "All of Me" to Tristano's elaborately abstracted instance of it. Where bebop musicians explored the conceptual dissonance between mental horizon and the moment by equipping standards with new tunes and chromatic substitutions on changes, Tristano goes further, stretching the bond between "All of Me" and his version of it to its breaking point with multitracking and tape manipulation. In doing so, he challenges his listeners to a competitive game of connoisseurship that serves to mark the hip from the square. Mehegan is hip to it all—hip to the tunes, hip to the game— and says as much.

Miles Davis played a similar version of the same game by refusing to announce the names of tunes, and listeners who didn't want to play along found themselves scorned as squares. When one letter writer complained in the pages of *Down Beat,* another responded, "why don't those fellows pay more attention to what the musician is playing and forget about titles? If you are familiar with the man's work, he needn't announce the title of a tune. If you aren't hip, well, that's your red wagon."[54] Charlie Parker's inner circle of fans played another game around the bootleg recordings that Dean Benedetti made of Parker's live appearances. Benedetti recorded Parker's solos and then switched off his equipment when other musicians took over. Ross Russell noted that Benedetti's rough editing stripped Parker's solos of contextual clues and added pleasurable complications to "the difficult guessing game aimed at getting the correct answer to the chord sequence of the composition being played."[55] Assuming that Russell is right in saying that one had to have been part of Bird's immediate circle even to hear Benedetti's bootlegs (at least before 1958, when some of them were released on the *Bird on 52nd Street* LP), this was a game for which social as well as musical distinction was the prize.[56] To be among those for whom "auditioning the Benedetti spools became an indoor sport" was to be the hippest of the hip.[57] As Sarah Thornton and others have noted, hipness is a way of marking distinction and bestowing power—the power to define the terms by which people are included and excluded from an inner sanctum. Games of hip connoisseurship articulate hip subcultures into something like a series of concentric rings: the musicians are at the bulls-eye; the square record-buying public, whose relationship to jazz is entirely mediated, is at the outer ring; and the hipsters are fighting to get as close to the bulls-eye as they can. Russell represented this social structure in *The Sound*, particularly in an episode that thinly fictionalizes Benedetti's hoarding of Parker's live performances. When someone suggests that Royo (a stand-in for Benedetti) release his bootlegs of Red (Parker) through a record company, Royo refuses, because his standing in the social circle around Red depends on his exclusive control of them. Having Red's unissued recordings is the closest anyone in his group of hipster hangers-on can get to being Red himself:

> "No friggin' record company!" Royo exclaimed angrily. "I don't dig them people at all, and Red don't either. Red don't put nothin' down when he cuts a commercial record, not his real soul. And these spools ain't for no squares, they're just for us to hear, for the people that really dig, you know!"
>
> And so the spools spun on, drawing the faithful to 117 Grover Whalen Square in increasing numbers. The hipsters rode the shrieking A train, or came from out of town by jalopy or bus, mounted the loose treads, up the stairs strewn with the butts of tailor-mades, or occasionally an emptied wallet flung down in discard by some heist artist. The word had been passed. That stand in Motor City had topped everything

else: the first week, cool, fat, solid; but after that, clear out of this world, gone, the wildest! Donizetti cut to ribbons. Verdi bopped. Man, if you hadn't heard those spools of Royo Dehn's you were not with it at all, were as square as John Home from Rome, really nowhere. And Royo basked in his finest hour, in the cold frowzy-curtained apartment.[58]

Not everyone thought these hip games were good for jazz, which even in the 1950s struggled to be taken seriously by the wider circle of American culture that hipsters were trying to exclude.[59] A month before Mehegan's letter appeared, Tristano declared himself unnerved by how far this kind of game-playing had gone:

> One of the surprising things prevalent in music today [is] the element of competition. It's true of musicians and non-musicians. They can't just listen to the music. They have to compete with it. If it's not in terms of speed—whether they can play as fast as the record—then it's in terms of finding out what the tune is. It's ridiculous. You can't hear music if you're not able to sit back and listen a few times, just listen.[60]

But this is a bit disingenuous, because musicians shared this game with their listeners, and both sides were necessary for it to be played out. The ethic of exclusion, of trials and secret knowledge—in short, an ethic of elitism—is not simply a delusion projected by the fans onto their favorite musicians. It is an ethic cultivated by the musicians as well.

A number of studies from the 1950s, most notably Howard Becker's "The Professional Dance Musician and His Audience," offered various sociological explanations for jazz musicians' elitism.[61] Social behavior is not exclusively the consequence of social forces, though, but may also be a function of attitudes that owe their existence to more immaterial reasons of aesthetics and sensibility. The hip sensibility is a larger entity within which jazz is an originating, constituent, but by no means definitive element; it is the Cold War hip sensibility that is elitist, not just jazz. The "sick joke," for example, is another component of the 1950s hip sensibility, and it shares some of the same formal and aesthetic elements with jazz. As a general phenomenon, "sick humor" is a strain of what Stephen Kercher calls "bawdy, anti-sentimental, aggressively masculine parody and satire" that flourished after the war in *Mad* magazine, Jules Feiffer's *Village Voice* cartoons, and the standup comedy of Lenny Bruce and Mort Sahl.[62] Their new style of humor took stage against the background social phenomenon of the sick joke—a form of humor that consisted in the detonation of a gruesome image within a minimal schoolyard form.[63] (One example, in the vein of 1950s psychiatric humor: Q: Mommy, mommy, what's the Oedipus complex? A: Shut up and kiss me.) Jonathan Miller, writing in *Partisan Review* about the "sick white negro"—that is, the sick joker as hipster—argued that the sick joke is a trial the hipster stages to test an interlocutor's nerve.[64] The sick joke is "a ritual contest of wits" that establishes the social pecking order of the hipster, who is able to affirm liberal sentiments even as he brutally subverts them, and the square, who either misses the irony or else is left muttering in shocked tones that some things are simply not to be joked about. Benjamin DeMott also viewed sick humor as an instrument of social hierarchy, but one that works the same way as the banter that flies about over the head of Brossard's advertising agent.[65] The "sick" conversational mode is one in which every statement is pitched simultaneously at the level of flat literality and on an ironic level that undermines literal meaning. Demott's and Miller's competing understandings of the sick joke have in common the idea that it is a test, either of stomach or cognitive flexibility, that separates the hip from the square. Either way, it is a mechanism of elite socialization.

I have argued that the hip perspective is marked by its assumption of a meta-perspective unavailable to the square interlocutor. This was as true in the 1960s and 1970s as it was in the 1950s. Elitism seems to be inevitable in hip cultures; the perspectival quality of hipness—the way it draws its strength from the positioning of its vantage point outside a common frame of reference—is indispensible. There has never been a truly non-elitist hipness, but though early Cold War hip culture made a point of its elitism, the later hip culture of the 1960s and 1970s was marked by a paradoxical co-existence of its underlying elitism and a new populist ideology. The Movement glossed over this contradiction through the rhetoric of mass political action, though, and framed its own mass movement in terms of a generation gap. As it turns out, the generation gap was something of a Movement myth, but it was a useful one.[66] Capping a square would not be the act of an individual marking distance between himself and someone generically square—that is, someone lacking in hip insight but whose age, class, gender, and race were incidental to his squareness. Rather, it would be a member of the young generation capping a member of the older generation. Conflicts of this sort could also be couched in race or gender terms, but youth was a category that cut across all others and lent the Movement a vision of coherence it otherwise lacked. Square capping would be the deed of someone acting as the avatar of a mass movement against an outsider conceived likewise as the representative of a class. Like the "sick humor" of the 1940s and 1950s, the "put-on" humor of the 1960s and 1970s reflects something of its era's nuances of social positioning. It was a kind of conversational jujitsu: hip rebels could wield their inferior social position as a weapon and turn the weight of Establishment social authority against itself. Jacob Brackman identified two characteristic modes of put-on:

(1) Relentless agreement: the perpetrator beats his victim to every low cliché the latter might possibly mouth.

(2) Actualization of the stereotype: the perpetrator *personifies* every cliché about his group, realizes his adversary's every negative expectation. He becomes a grotesque rendition of his presumed identity, faking heated emotion.[67]

Brackman gives examples of each mode being wielded by a rebellious youth against a well-intentioned square adult in a conversation about (and across) the generation gap:

(1) "Ah, I don't know...Kids today—they're always running. But who knows where they're going? Crazy clothes, loud music—if you wanna call it music—fast cars, drinking, smoking, drugs. The next thing you know, they'll be going out with girls."

(2) "Why don't you go play with your mutual funds or something? Why don't you get off my back? I just want to bug out on your nowhere scene, nowhere man. Excuse me, I gotta go dig some groovy sounds and sniff a pot of airplane glue. Lemme peel out on my boss Harley; that mother takes off like a big-assed bird."[68]

Although the social situation ends up with the hip interlocutor using this rhetorical jujitsu to flip his opponent, the implication is not that the winner of the contest belongs to an elect of superior minds, but to a mass of superior minds. His superiority is not his possession as an individual, but the function of a new consciousness that is practically a genetic quirk, a trait running through an entire generation and radically separating it from what has come before. As Leslie Fiedler pointed out, there was a way of writing about the "New Consciousness" of the 1960s that treated hip awareness in an almost science-fictional way, as a mutation that erupts from within the children of a whole society, giving them strange new gifts that frighten and alienate their elders.[69] It was a way of asserting superiority of consciousness without implying an elite.

But this subtlety was as yet undreamed-of in the 1940s and 1950s. It was not needed: hip intellectuals such as Brossard and Broyard did not want to claim membership in a mass movement, and it never occurred to artists such as Parker and Tristano that they might lead one. The warrant of their authority was not youth but the sovereignty of the individual intellect. The intellect was a weapon of unmasking that let the lone critical outsider see through the fatuity of mass culture.[70] And this, perhaps, is the crux of how the hip sensibility underwent historical change from the 1930s through the 1960s. The early Cold War hip sensibility had much in common with the culture it outwardly opposed, particularly the era's near obsession with the ills of mass culture and mass society. The Movement sensibility, on the other hand, retained the habits of mass-culture critique (scorn for the "phony" and the "plastic," for example) while adapting to its new place in mass culture.[71]

Mass Culture Critique

When hipsters pictured the square as a dupe unknowingly embedded in a vast system for structuring and controlling consciousness, they were working a variation on a more general picture of the mass man and mass culture that prevailed at midcentury. As we saw in Chapter 2, Brossard and Broyard were among the first to set out on the intellectual project of finding likenesses between the hip styles of their urban environment and various items from European traditions of arts and ideas. Chief among the latter was the critique of mass culture and mass society, which especially occupied the New York Intellectuals clustered around literary/political little magazines such as *Dissent* and *Partisan Review.* Irving Howe's 1959 *Partisan Review* essay "Mass Society and Post-Modern Fiction" is exemplary of this discourse:

> By the mass society we mean a relatively comfortable, half welfare and half garrison state in which the population grows passive, indifferent and atomized; in which traditional loyalties, ties and associations become lax or dissolve entirely; in which coherent publics based on definite interests and opinions gradually fall apart; and in which man becomes a consumer, himself mass-produced like the products, diversions and values that he absorbs.[72]

This is the image of social modernity that forms the backdrop for the picture of the square. To the academic reader, it is probably most familiar as the Frankfurt School's notion of the "culture industry," whose currency in popular music studies is partly owed to its fit with the hip sensibility. (Herbert Marcuse's popularity among student radicals in the 1960s marked an early point in the process by which a vernacular mood of rebellion has merged with academic critical theory.[73]) In Howe's thumbnail sketch of mass society, the consumer has replaced the citizen, and indeed has become a kind of standardized product. The false paradise of the consumerist "affluent society" has replaced the citizen's community webbed with ties of voluntary association and grounded in informed and articulated opinion. Accumulating meretricious consumer products has substituted for pursuing individual interests and realizing individual potentialities. And as the massified populace sinks into its overfed torpor, it cedes its power to the militarized and corporatized state. Culture becomes the primary target of this kind of critique, for it is culture that effects this shift from citizen to consumer, public to mass, individuality to conformism, self-awareness to false consciousness. Mass culture is a narcotic that makes the mass docile and ready for manipulation.

However disillusioned they may have been with the Marxism of their youth, midcentury intellectuals tended to retain the Marxist premise that capital is an ever-metastasizing dynamic, progressively replicating its logic within every sphere of human existence. They saw modernist high art, the most uncompromising affirmation of the autonomous individual intellect, as a bulwark against capital and its rationalizations of human expression. And so they believed that high culture and capitalism were in constant conflict, and that high culture was always in danger of being negated by a parasitical mass culture formed in imitation of it. Mass culture theory offered Cold War intellectuals a kind of agnostic Marxism, a way to pursue a Marxist style of critique without having to associate themselves with communists. (The next generation of intellectuals would not be as fastidious about the company they kept.)[74]

Mass culture critique was one thing *Partisan Review* intellectuals, hip literati, and those immersed in the jazz life had in common. Books and jazz alike represented a high art that resisted a degraded mass culture and the mass society that spawned it. It was not enough to listen to jazz indiscriminately; it was important to know that Thelonious Monk was hipper (or, in the terms of modernist historicism, more "necessary") than Dave Brubeck, just as it was important to know that Franz Kafka mattered more than Herman Wouk, and it was important to know why. And in jazz and literary little magazines the "why" was couched in the high-art terms of technical innovation within a tradition. The critical discourse of jazz rehearsed the familiar temporal paradox of modernism, in which the true artwork takes its place in a historical tradition only as it expresses its evanescent historical moment, and it does so only by discovering techniques that obsolesce previous ones and are fated to become obsolete in their turn.[75] The little magazine *Jazz Review*, attempting to do for jazz what *Partisan Review* did for literature, argued for its subjects' place in jazz history by means of notated transcriptions and styles of analysis derived from Eurological traditions of composition.[76] *Jazz Review* was more highbrow than most jazz publications and ran for just three years, but it epitomized the modernist critical mood that pervaded jazz magazines, books, liner notes, and broadcasts at midcentury.[77] This discourse was united in its contempt for mass taste and its self-definition by contrast with mass culture; its plentiful quarrels over who remained freest of mass influence took place on the familiar ground of co-optation.

For the Movement, the question was how a mass counterculture could avoid acting like mass culture more generally. Put another way, counterculture intellectuals had to figure out how they could hold on to the terms of hip critique while exempting themselves from it. One answer lay in the Movement's utopian idea of revolution—a singularity in the intellectual history of hipness, never anticipated in the early Cold War and never reprised since. In the midcentury view, mass society was degraded through the action of mass culture. For the utopians of the 1960s, mass culture could be redemptive if mass society was likewise redeemed. The vision of youth as a new class bound together by hip consciousness permitted a belief in a new society that could remake itself in light of that consciousness.

Countercultural utopianism differed from competing Marxist notions of utopia by insisting that it could be willed into existence here and now. For Theodor Adorno, whose writings on the "culture industry" mark a dystopic intensification of mass culture critique, utopia is radically impossible, but its actual attainment is less important than the space of critique opened when its shadowy image is projected into the administered world.[78] But Movement conceptions of utopia were marked by a sense of its nearness, of the imminence of sudden, total, and irreversible change. The concept of "revolution here and now" distanced the late-1960s New Left from other readings of Marx. As Leszek Kolakowski noted, the New Left maintained that "the concept of a society's 'ripeness' for revolution is a bourgeois deceit."[79] Those in the Movement who favored a cultural rather than political conception of revolutionary action argued that the adjustments to the economic realm Marx thought would come as a consequence of revolution had already secretly happened. They were living in a "post-scarcity" economy that would free people to live however they chose, without jobs, competition, or private property, and without any of the social ills endemic to capitalism.[80] Only the sclerotic outer forms of the old capitalist system remained, and these would crumble away once the mass could see through them. What makes this formulation different from orthodox Marxism is its cross-fertilization with the hip sensibility. If Marxism makes overcoming false consciousness the precondition of revolutionary action, here hip consciousness becomes revolutionary action in itself. The post-scarcity argument concluded that every newly enlightened soul would walk away from the old system, until none were left to prop it up. Thus revolution would arise spontaneously, and people would live by plucking the low-hanging fruit of a post-scarcity economy that was hiding in plain sight. The Revolution is already here: you just have to see it. In 1969 Yoko Ono and John Lennon posted signs on bulletin boards and in newspapers around the world reading "WAR IS OVER! (if you want it)." This was a call for Americans to make a choice against supporting the Vietnam War, though phrased in a way unique to its time, suggesting that the war might end simply through an act of consciousness, when we experience its ending.[81] The notion that imagination and reality might come together, that wishing might make it so after all, is a kind of magical thinking, and as we will see at the end of this book magic began to play a serious role in the hip culture of the 1960s. And music, too, was deeply involved in this intellectual history. The shift in thought about mass culture and society from the 1950s through the 1960s saw a complementary aesthetic shift, and rock was uncoupled from the modernism in which jazz had been embedded.

The Decline of Midcentury Modernism and the Birth of Postmodernism

In midcentury hip culture, the cause of advanced art possessed something like a moral force: the progress of art stood for the progress of man. Julian Beck, the director of Greenwich Village's avant-garde Living Theater, admitted that like other forward-looking artists in the Village at midcentury he once felt proud of New York's great modernist buildings: "at last, we believed, the principles of art were regaining dominion in architecture after a century of domination by the taste of the philistines."[82] "You've got to be modernistic" was an imperative (echoing the title of a 1920s James P. Johnson composition) borne out in such period curiosities as a 1947 *Down Beat* cover story on six arrangers of the "new school," "shining knights of discord and atonality" who pose stiffly around works by Henry Moore and Picasso at the Museum of Modern Art (Fig. 4.4).[83] The first issue of *Neurotica* was decorated with illustrations styled after Salvador Dalí's soft forms (Fig. 4.5); the same sort of imagery also graced the cover of the stridently "out" *Innovations by Boyd Raeburn* (Fig. 4.6) and the Warner Brothers' cartoon short "Dough for the Do-Do" (1949), whose Dalí-esque "wackyland" jumps to a jazz beat.[84]

This was the look of swinging modernity in the late 1940s. In *Blues People* (1963), LeRoi Jones would poke fun at Raeburn's "imitation 'surrealistic' covers, with explanations of the 'symbols' on the back of the jackets," but Jones's mockery extended only to the middlebrow aping of modernist style and not to

Figure 4.4 William Gottlieb, photos of Ralph Burns, Neal Hefti, George Handy, Eddie Finckel, Johnny Richards, and Eddie Sauter at the Museum of Modern Art (1947).

Figure 4.5 Untitled vignette, *Neurotica* 1 (1948).

Figure 4.6 Phyllis Pinkney, album cover art for *Innovations by Boyd Raeburn*, 1945. Music Library and Sound Recordings Archives, William T. Jerome Library, Bowling Green State University.

the modernist mission.[85] For him, truly modern jazz (Charlie Parker, Charles Mingus, Archie Shepp, Cecil Taylor) had not merely imitated European stylistic models but independently worked through parallel problems and, so doing, participated in its own distinct historical moment. Throughout *Blues People,* Jones suggested that the social conditions of African Americans were integral to the state of the musical material in jazz, and that changes in one registered in the other.[86] Real modern jazz was that which participated in the postwar historical experience of African Americans, an experience that had given birth to a sensibility no longer willing to accommodate white racism and no longer satisfied with the "shoddy cornucopia of American popular culture."[87] For Jones, then, rock's abandonment of jazz's musical progress was regressive not only aesthetically but racially as well.[88]

The cultural differences between the 1950s and 1960s were understood by the players involved to be a confrontation between a self-conscious modernism and an equally self-conscious post- (or even anti-) modernism. The modernism exemplified equally by *Partisan Review* and *Jazz Review* championed advanced art against mass culture and an ethic of aesthetic and intellectual autonomy against the demands of mass politics. To the Movement, such priorities came to seem elitist, pleasure-denying, and politically quiescent. American midcentury modernism seemed of a piece with the early Cold War's strain of authoritarian scientism; like atomic physics, it appeared to be the product of uptight white men in lab coats, crew cuts, and horn-rimmed glasses. In Movement thought, modernism epitomized the Western, technocratic style of reason that exalted mind over body, male over female, power over pleasure, bureaucratized meaning over tactile experience. Architectural modernism especially seemed to embody the arrogance of a system indifferent to the lives it encloses. After his early infatuation with New York's modernist edifices, Beck came to see in the "inflexible, rampant, the tall straight rigid buildings" the "straight proud men, the ramrod spines, not bent by labor, the polite voices, everything designed to cut the heart out."[89] In music, too, modernism wore out its welcome. Morton Feldman's 1963 review of one of Gunther Schuller's concerts sounds an early note of what would become a chorus of mockery: Feldman riffs on a fantasy motif of a bourgeois family outing to the countryside; Schuller (with his "third stream nonsense") is imagined as their pastry chef.[90] This review, appearing as it does in *Kulchur,* a little magazine that connected the Beats to the universe of oppositional culture in the 1960s, marks the point where midcentury modernism comes to seem conventional, inhibited, pompous, bourgeois—in a word, square.[91] Four short years later, this kind of criticism would take on a militant edge. "Bourgeois culture is the enemy as is the bourgeois system itself," Ben Morea writes in 1967; "not only Rembrandts and Goethes but the modernists also will find themselves on the scrapheap of western culture."[92]

Hilton Kramer, an art critic and conservative defender of midcentury high modernism, later remarked that "it wasn't the works of James Joyce or Thomas Mann or Ernest Hemingway or Gertrude Stein which were carried in the rucksacks of the antiwar marchers, and it wasn't to the music of Stravinsky or Schoenberg that they marched."[93] This was something on which Kramer and his ideological opponents could agree. Thomas Albright, another art critic who wrote for *Rolling Stone* in its early days, argued that the modernist hip culture at midcentury, unlike the later counterculture, substituted an old bohemian worship of art for the values it had torn down. Consequently, Beat writing and jazz were imperfectly separated from the establishment they ostensibly opposed; Albright suggests that such "traditional artistic concepts as exclusiveness, monumentalism and immortality lingered in sometimes weird ways."[94] Improvisation in music and in Kerouac's "spontaneous bop prosody" freed art from hard distinctions between creation and act, and yet the innovations of jazz and Beat poetry were drawn from European models. Jazz musicians brought music into the streets but still craved the respect of the institutions they had left behind. In contrast, Albright writes, the new counterculture does not have these elitist, Western hang-ups. Everyone is an artist, whether "he draws, paints flowers on his car or plays guitar." If even these media are too traditional, then maybe he just does his thing, "like wearing bells, or being beautiful."[95] Ronald Sukenick, describing the shift of aesthetic values from the 1950s to the 1960s avant-gardes, paraphrases this line of thought:

> Down with the "painterly" qualities in art, with the aesthetic purity of artists. Down with the "tyranny of jazz," in Danny Fields's phrase, as the standard for pop music, and up with extramusical values like noise, volume, performance, dance, politics, sex. No more neat, well-made narrative in film and fiction. Out with sentimental notions about sex.[96]

The times called for new art forms, like the Happening or the Fluxus event score, that might do justice to radical presence. But one could do away with the very idea of an art form and still maintain the basic orientation of 1960s aesthetics: art does not represent, it *is*. If your art is wearing bells and being beautiful, you are engaged in a creative act, but what you create is not *about* anything. You are just wearing bells and being beautiful.

There was never a complete consensus on what kinds of music, aside from the post-Cage avant-garde, might best embody the new post- (or anti-) modernist aesthetic. It is easy to forget that the *Berkeley Barb,* one of the most radical and uncompromising of the underground newspapers, had a good classical music section. Not all of the leading creative figures associated with the counterculture were rock fans: Philip K. Dick preferred classical music, while R. Crumb listened to American roots music and early jazz. Though he later managed the MC5, John Sinclair began his writing career as a jazz critic, and in the same way that John Clellon Holmes acquired a taste for bebop some twenty years earlier, he adopted rock when he decided it uniquely embodied the sociocultural zeitgeist.[97]

In this he was taking a cue from the swelling majority of counterculture intellectuals and rock fans. The dominant narrative of rock in the late 1960s held that the young shared a consciousness radically different from that of their parents, and rock gave voice to it. This consciousness was, above all, radically oriented to the present moment. In an early and important essay, Greil Marcus contrasts how Berkeley professors understood a student uprising (Marx's line about the great events of history happening twice, as tragedy and then as farce) and how young people understood it (Dylan's "Memphis Blues Again"). Marcus writes that "one seeks an academic and intellectual conclusion, a truth that will last the ages; the other tries to establish and confirm the present moment, and in doing so, to save one from it."[98] The old world of art and ideas inherited from Europe was not adequate to the experience of the new generation. Preoccupied with monuments and permanence, with authoritative scriptable meanings that could be handed down through a tradition, it did nothing to honor the ineffable sensation of this moment. Rock suggested a new kind of intellectualism, conceived along entirely different principles.

But did Movement aesthetics suggest a true alternative to modernism, or was it only an attempt to imagine a cultural space outside of modernism from a position within it?[99] Thinkers have offered a number of theses on rock's modernism: rock is the late expression of a century-and-a-half-long dynamic of cultural antinomianism; rock is a new reaction to the old sources of modernist rage and alienation; rock strikes the blow for liberation that modernism had promised but failed to deliver.[100] But if rock is normatively modern in some unself-conscious way (and the jury is still out on that), at the very least it did not participate in anything like the self-consciously modernist project of midcentury jazz. Jazz-critical writing was historicist, arguing for or against a given recording with appeals to the necessity of its historical development. If Movement intellectuals thought of rock historically, they did so in different terms, as something manifesting the next step in the development of consciousness, not as the next step in the stylistic development of an artistic tradition. It was modernism's orientation to both teleology and tradition that the Movement opposed, ignored, or recontextualized into its own mosaic of cultural associations. Rock sometimes recycled modernist icons—Bob Dylan's echo of James Joyce in his stream-of-consciousness lyrics or Frank Zappa's Stravinskyisms in *Uncle Meat*—but only as elements of a larger collection of musical and cultural references. Under such circumstances, Joyce and Stravinsky no longer functioned as a cultural dominant; the art tradition for which they stood as emblems was consigned to being just another voice in a worldwide babel. This condition was allegorized by the cover of *Sgt. Pepper's Lonely Hearts Club Band,* in which Karlheinz Stockhausen rubs shoulders with W. C. Fields, Bob Dylan, and Aleister Crowley. In the era of recordable tape, Evan Ziporyn writes, "all music is available to all people, all the time"; Stockhausen made use of this fact in *Telemusik* (1966), "a musique concrète piece for which the source material is traditional music from dozens of cultures, all of whom, the composer asserts, 'wanted to participate in *Telemusik*...not "my" music, but music of the whole world, of all countries and all races.'"[101] Midcentury modernism lost its privilege in this universal *agora*;

perhaps the simplest good understanding of postmodernism is that it is the historical moment when all cultural dominants are relativized in this way.

As Theodore Gracyk has noted, by around 1965 "rock" came to mean not only rock and roll, a style of music rooted in country and R&B, but a principle of organizing all possible recorded sounds into a rock and roll framework.[102] Even more, though, rock came to mean an aesthetic and a culture that could absorb all cultural influences into itself and thereby embody a new consciousness. Chester Anderson, a science-fiction writer and Beat-turned-hippie intellectual, wrote in the *San Francisco Oracle* that "rock is an intensely synthesizing art, an art of amazing relationships (collage is rock & roll) able to absorb (maybe) all of society into itself as an organizing force, transmuting and reintegrating what it absorbs."[103] Seen this way, rock was an example of what McLuhan called "mosaic" awareness.

Starting with *The Gutenberg Galaxy,* McLuhan designed his own books to be mosaics: shunning linear exposition, he created a collage of epigrammatic and often obscure jottings ("probes"), each of which was a kind of thought-experiment intended to stimulate further reflection on the part of the reader. A probe might be intended to be taken straight, or it might just be an experiment; to a hostile critic, McLuhan once responded, "you don't like that idea? I've got others."[104] McLuhan did not intend a lossless transmission of ideas from his mind to those of his readers but wanted instead to create open spaces in his texts that readers would fill themselves. He called this participatory style "cool"; by contrast, "hot" texts repel interaction. Cool means the seminar, not the lecture; the jam session, not the concert. Cool texts have no fixed point of view: the vanishing-point perspective that implies a single viewer, McLuhan theorized, was a product of Renaissance and print-era consciousness. The latter perspective was isolated and individualistic, analytical rather than tactile. It did not grasp a scene whole but sliced it into distinct and specialized pieces, the better to apply its labeling, quantifying, and classifying habits of mind. Linear perspective took things in one at a time; mosaic perspective grasped gestalts instantaneously and simultaneously. McLuhan's main goal was to understand how media shape our perspective, and he theorized that electronic media were changing the "sense ratios" of the generation that had grown up with television, the ultimate cool medium. As the media landscape "cooled down," it bred a generation of people who were able to take in their environment all at once, to synthesize radically disparate pieces of cultural information, to soak themselves in torrents of media information and not drown. To counterculture intellectuals such as Anderson, this new kind of person needed a new kind of art, and rock had evolved to meet the demands of their new consciousness.

McLuhan was the most important influence on countercultural intellectuals in the late 1960s; as Anderson noted, he gave shape to their intuitions. "Synthesis and synaesthesia; non-typographic, non-linear, basically mosaic and mythical modes of perception; involvement of the whole sensorium; roles instead of jobs; participation in depth; extended awareness; preoccupation with textures, with tactility, with multisensory experiences—put 'em all together & you have a weekend on Haight Street."[105] Now, I do not wish to suggest that McLuhan's theories really explain rock just as 1960s intellectuals thought they did.[106] Cultural theory is often best read as if it were a kind of speculative fiction, and McLuhan was at least honest enough to encourage people to read him this way. This does not deny McLuhan's often valuable insights, which can be surprisingly apt for things that did not yet exist when McLuhan was writing. However, McLuhan owed his freakish popularity to the resonance between his ideas and the hip sensibility in the 1960s, and he paid for it with the sudden and near-total eclipse of his reputation as erstwhile Movement people found other cultural theorists, like Michel Foucault, who better captured the post-1960s mood.[107]

Like Foucault, McLuhan was an early theorist of the postmodern, and his oppositions between the cultures of typographic and electronic media map onto the modern-postmodern antinomies of work-text, purpose-play, design-chance, form-antiform, hierarchy-anarchy, mastery-silence, art object–performance, distance-participation.[108] Albright tacitly relies on these oppositions to draw distinctions between the 1960s counterculture and an earlier jazz modernism, and Anderson develops a kindred set of oppositions (mind-body, linear-mosaic, individual-collective) to write about rock. He writes that rock appeals to the intelligence "with no interference from the intellect," which is to say, to an intelligence seated in the body rather than the mind.[109] Anderson considers the body as the site of new consciousness by speculating on the possibilities of a future rock aesthetics in which bodily sensation might become an element of composition, with rock musicians learning to "play a listener's body like a soft guitar."[110] To Anderson, such ideas are incomprehensible to "typeheads"—those stuck on the other side of the generational divide and trapped in the old, linear, literate way of thinking. Television had begun to transform consciousness by teaching American youth a mosaic style of integrative perception; rock made this transformation total, opening a generational rift between those whose minds were fused in tribal collectivity and those who remained locked in their individualism. Rock seeded American society with a mass asymmetry of consciousness. If the Movement theorized hip consciousness as the mechanism for revolution, then rock was the mechanism for that hip consciousness, calling into being a new social order in which individuals merge into a collective and higher mind. The new social forms of the rock band and commune foreshadow a worldwide social revolution demanding "group participation, total experience, complete involvement."[111]

When the later counterculture honored jazz as its spiritual ancestor, it stressed heat, intensity, community, and bodily transport, not its dialectic of referent and abstraction. In this respect, the 1960s Movement owes much more to the Beats, who saw in jazz a way of distancing themselves from the 1950s aesthetic of irony and paradox, not embracing it. Lawrence Lipton's celebration of the West Coast Beat scene, *The Holy Barbarians* (1958), is typical in its conception of jazz as the main element of a Dionysian ritual that unblocks mental inhibitions. Squares, fascinated by jazz but fearing anything wired so directly into the body, seek relief from their sexual neuroses in psychoanalysis, which will explain everything to them in the rational terms to which their comprehension is limited. (Norman Mailer said much the same thing in his print debate with Ned Polsky over "The White Negro."[112]) Lipton looks at jazz as a form of protest and an alternative, bodily way of knowing, just as the activist intellectuals of the 1960s looked at rock:

> [The Beats] see [jazz] pitting its spontaneous, improvised, happy-sad, angry-loving, ecstatic on-the-spot creativity against the sterile antiseptic delivery room workmanship of the concert hall that squares take for musical culture. And they whisper—coolly, quietly but intensely, "Say it, Satch!" "Tell 'em, Gerry!" "Blow a great big hole in the walls they have thrown up to keep man from man." They know that what the Bird is putting down in those one-two punches on the horn is shock treatment with love as fierce as anger and better than insulin or metrazol.[113]

As silly as this might now seem—his Beats sound like characters in a John Waters movie—Lipton's understanding of jazz was reasonably representative of the literary Beat movement.[114] Allen Ginsberg's occasional early jottings on jazz reveal something of the same conception of it as exotica music of the swinging underworld. "Dope vice & bop go together. Ask anyone in the know," Ginsberg quotes Walter Winchell in a 1952 notebook entry; by way of a gloss, he adds, "there is something ugly going on in my soul again. This last month—preoccupation with queerness, dope, vice & pop, apocalypse of subterraneans, dispersal of attention to practical affairs, call of Amazon voyage."[115] Jazz musicians and fans could not entirely deny the association of dope and vice with bebop, but all the same they resented literary hipsters for whom jazz was the "call of Amazon voyage" just as Brossard's circle resented the Uptowners on their urban safaris. Jazz critics rejected Beat adulation as the uncool intrusion of a tag-along band of poseurs, but in academic discourse the Beat interpretation has prevailed.[116] General studies of the 1950s' new antinomian culture typically have little to say about jazz except to affirm the solidarity between musicians and Beats, invoke the alienation and anger of the African American musician, and associate the quick, nervous energy of bebop with the intensities of action painting and Beat poetry.[117]

However, it is risky to assume that jazz musicians ever shared the same sense of rebellion as the Beats and hipsters who thronged their performances. As Scott DeVeaux writes, "the usual attempt to cast [jazz musicians] as self-conscious revolutionaries or anarchistic hipsters fails to take into account the unique privilege and distinctive ethos of their profession."[118] Bebop musicians may have shared a fear of the police billy club with the hipsters, DeVeaux notes, but what animated the daily practice of their art was something else: a sense of competitiveness, a respect for craft, and a hunger for the learning required to make the technical progress by which they judged one another. Lipton might have heard "shock treatment with love as fierce as anger" in Parker's music, but Parker's fellow musicians—and the fans who wanted to cultivate a musician's professional sensitivity to nuances of improvisational style—heard harmonic, rhythmic, and developmental innovations that built on the accomplishment of older figures and that contributed to the development of the art form. You can hear one of Parker's collaborators in the studio cheering him on at the exact moment he has gone out in his solo on "Ornithology"—a "yeah!" sounding in the rest at measure 20. And jazz listeners, hearing the "yeah!" emerge from the grooves of a newly bought 78 rpm record in 1946, might have felt themselves urged on as well to hear a moment of surpassing excellence the way these musicians once heard it in a Hollywood studio, following Parker on his trip out, feeling perspective pull away from the hardened lines of song form and alight on another shape that has somehow emerged within them, and glimpsing new possibilities of meaning in the doubled musical image. Elizabeth Von Vogt, the sister of John Clellon Holmes, recalls listening to "Ornithology" with her brother around 1948–49, at first baffled by its fluid abstractions and then listening harder as John cued the record back to the beginning. "He hummed loud with the coda— Bird and Miles, and John humming 'How High the Moon' along with them. They angled into and out of each other, meeting at the right places—the melodies echoing sweetly and ending on the same note—and the world came together. It began."[119]

Sound Museum

It is natural for a historian to care more about Charlie Parker's own aesthetics than later misinterpretations of it, and it is likewise tempting to privilege the bebop musician's kind of hipness over Beat and Movement sensibilities. Charlie Parker came first, after all, and the later White Negroes who flocked to the banner of hip were only taking on a role that he and other black musicians had first modeled for them. But as Ralph Ellison pointed out, Parker in his turn modeled himself on other roles—roles with long and tangled histories of their own.[120] There is no firm bedrock of a true, originating, and all-begetting hipness: it is representations, not turtles, all the way down. I have already noted that hipness was never more than the sum of its representations; for Michael Szalay, hip is "an imitative fantasy for which there is, finally, no definitive locus or referent."[121] In hip culture, origin is not essence. There *is* no essence to hipness beyond its history, and that history is an impossibly tangled series of transactions among jazz, rock, folk, hip-hop, classical (etc.) musicians, as well as artists, fans, novelists, filmmakers, comedians, literary intellectuals, academics, activists, coolhunters, and everyone else in whom hip culture has cultivated a sense of humor that laughs at self-repression, a sense of justice that quickens to the spectacle of rebellion, and an assumption that the culture we consume says something about our politics.

The arrangement of hip images over time is not set by the random drift of fashion.[122] Zoot-suited hepcat, bebop musician, arrow-collar underground man, square, snow queen, Beat, beatnik, rock troubadour, or (in John Sinclair's case) "minister of information" for a tribe of rock revolutionaries—the gaudy procession of characters arranges itself into a narrative shape, in which older notions of hip are pushed aside by their riotous offspring. Yet this anthropomorphized story is too crude, because the young did not simply succeed the old. At all points in the development of hip culture, old and new interact in unpredictable and complex ways. Kenneth Burke asks us to imagine a dialectical history, in which strains mingle over time, like voices in a motet, at varying strengths and in myriad combinations:

> But where one considers different historical characters from the standpoint of a total development, one could encourage each character to comment upon the others without thereby sacrificing a perspective upon the lot. This could be got particularly, I think, if historical characters themselves (i.e. periods or cultures treated as "individual persons") were considered never to begin or end, but rather to change in intensity or poignancy. History, in this sense, would be a dialectic of characters in which, for instance, we should never expect to see "feudalism" overthrown by "capitalism" and "capitalism" succeeded by some manner of national or international or non-national or neo-national or postnational socialism—but rather should note elements of all such positions (or "voices") existing always, but attaining greater clarity of expression or imperiousness of proportion of one period than another.[123]

In this spirit, I end the chapter by triangulating Parker's "Ornithology" (1946) with Ken Nordine's "Sound Museum" (1957) and Bob Dylan's "Ballad of a Thin Man" (1965)—three pieces linked by sensibility and differentiated by the contingencies introduced in the period of roughly a decade that lies between each pair.

"Sound Museum" is the longest track on *Word Jazz*, an album of verbal skits and prose poems spoken by Ken Nordine, a Chicago radio announcer, and accompanied by the personnel of the Chico Hamilton Quintet performing Fred Katz's jazz compositions.[124] The conceit of "Sound Museum" is that Nordine is introducing us to the works of art on display in a "very abstract museum in which they show sound paintings." The "sound paintings" are *musique concrète* interludes by Nordine's friend Jim Cunningham, some of which are aggressively noisy, while others sound like ambient music from forty years later. The Sound Museum could be a metaphor for hip culture itself—an archive of images, made of sound or imagined in sound or somehow borrowing from sound its magic potency. Nordine's Word Jazz bears an ironic or signifying relationship to utterance that might recall Cab Calloway's performance as a quiz show MC in the 1940s or foreshadow Bob Dylan's put-ons and provocations.[125] Everything Nordine says is in quotation marks; his Word Jazz is not an utterance in an idiom so much as an utterance of idioms, a metalepsis. In "Sound Museum," Nordine introduces one "sound painting" after the other in the tones of a museum docent, with Katz's background music changing for every introduction. At one point Nordine wrong-foots the listener when he announces (in sinister tones, with an underscore of spooky groans from Katz's cello) that he has taken the listener to a black door, warns that he cannot open it for long ("I think you'll understand why"), and, when he "opens" it, discloses eleven seconds of silence. ("See what I mean?" he asks in a knowing *basso profundo*.) Like the hip discourse of which "Ornithology" is a musical trace, "Sound Museum" head-fakes the listener by warping established conceptual categories.

"Sound Museum" is tightly woven into the cultural history of 1950s hipness I have outlined. As "word jazz," it belongs to a midcentury project to place words and jazz in the same space, and, more generally, to continue the project begun by such hip intellectuals as Mailer, Brossard, and Lipton to draw verbal meanings out of a wordless existential stance they found in jazz. In his docent persona, Nordine introduces another sound painting "that is indicative of the neurotic feeling of our time," and after showing it he concludes, in embarrassment:

> I—I [stammering] think you see my point, uh, now the artist that did this fortunately is, uh, under sedatives at the moment and, uh, we expect that his later work will be much *calmer* and *quieter*, and [trails off]…[in a brighter tone] but we do like to give these young neurotic artists a *chance*. And so I'm glad that the museum has been big about the whole thing, as it were.

He fumbles about for a way out of an embarrassing truth he has admitted, somewhat despite himself, and in his discomfort spackles clichés ("I'm glad that the museum has been big about the whole thing, as it were") into a pleasant façade.

His tone of voice and banal words, however, betray a darker underlying truth, such truths being the usual fruit of the hip sensibility's dualistic hermeneutics. When he speaks of giving "these young neurotic artists a *chance,*" with an unctuous dip in inflection at the end, he wields the patronizing tone of the technocratic liberal who wants to encourage artists' self-expression, even if it means he will have to lock them up for their own good. And this suggestion of therapeutic tyranny is a perfect example of midcentury "sick humor" in its whimsical callousness, its suggestion of what Marcuse would soon call "repressive tolerance," and its vein of psychotherapeutic humor.

Word Jazz lies at the nexus of hip culture and midcentury modernism. Fred Katz's liner-note recollection of his first meeting with Nordine ("I dig this cat!") offers a roll call of high-culture names designed to place their album within the traditions of midcentury vernacular modernism: "A few hours and 37 cups of coffee later we were still discussing 'Word Jazz,' Spinoza, Buddha, Charlie Parker, Freud and 'Word Jazz' again."[126] And the musical style of Katz's compositions also places this album in this cultural register. The track begins with a duet between Katz's *pizzicato* cello and Buddy Collette on flute. In this passage, the cello's unswung ostinato lines, with an internal pattern of stresses meant to pull against the flute's 4/4 line, splay wide over the cello's range, suggesting the knees-and-elbows angularity of early bebop tunes like Parker's "Scrapple from the Apple." Only this music is in the modernist style of midcentury progressive jazz, built from triads, fourths, and fifths mortised together at odd intervals apart. The flute, when it comes in, suggests a different, white-note tonality that, along with its rhythmic disjunction from the cello, articulates a musical texture of nonintersecting strata oddly joined, like forms in a cubist painting (Fig. 4.7).

If they noticed it at all, jazz critics dismissed Nordine's Word Jazz as the result of a record company's opportunism or the work of a jazz pretender with ambitions above his station.[127] And although Nordine has acquired a cult following among latter-day hipsters, many jazz fans would still find it perverse to mention "Sound Museum" and "Ornithology" in the same breath. And to use "Sound Museum" and "Ornithology" to lead off a discussion of "Ballad of a Thin Man" might seem even stranger, not least because of basic ontological differences between the genres of music they represent.

When one builds an analysis on a transcription of a jazz improvisation, as I have for "Ornithology," the reader naturally understands that much of what

Figure 4.7 Fred Katz and Buddy Collette, opening of "Sound Museum" (1957).

makes the performance meaningful will be lost. But jazz criticism has long been carried out in the confidence that notation can convey some large part of a musician's conception. When it comes to analyzing a rock song, though, one immediately becomes tangled in threshold questions of analysis. What to analyze? Is it enough to interpret the words? If one analyzes the music, then which parts, and how? Transcriptions of rock music seldom seem to capture anything more than bare formulas; perhaps progressive rock was so disproportionately represented in the first wave of music-analytical rock writing because it is a genre that repays analysis of notatable musical structures.[128] A song like "Ballad of a Thin Man" leaves the transcriber grasping a handful of air. It is an accumulation of half-minute stanzas cycling through the same handful of chords over the same slow, descending bass line. Nowhere are there chromatic alterations of the chord, motivic fragmentation and development, or any of the other things that have traditionally been taken to signify a jazz performance's place on the evolutionary scale. This is what Lester Bangs meant when he made a distinction between avant-garde jazz as a complex music and rock, by contrast, as "almost idiotically simple."[129]

And Bangs was not calling rock "idiotically simple" as if that were a bad thing. What makes rock valuable is not what might make it smart; rock's aesthetic richness has nothing to do with midcentury intellectual notions of cognitive challenges met and mastered. As Chester Anderson wrote, rock represented an intellectualism of the body and not the mind. Rock's complexity embodied a complexity of experience unprocessed and delivered raw. What Dave Hickey calls "the delicacy of rock-and-roll" is the sound that results when contingency and stress fuzz the simple outlines of the song into an "infinitely complicated, fractal filigree of delicate distinctions."[130] The rock audience understands that it is the stress of performance, of life, or, as Hickey writes, of "contingent community" that fractures a song's plain sonic surface. In the 1960s, rock's challenges were supposed to be existential rather than intellectual; they had to do with how you lived your life, not how you represented it. This meant that the privileged vector of rock's aesthetics was *voice,* the direct embodied trace of life's contingencies.[131] What rock conveyed was the voice amplified and broadcast, and the word released from the captivity of print and made flesh, as it had been in the preliterate and tribal era, which the Movement (following McLuhan) believed was returning in the postliterate electronic age. "We are primitives of an unknown culture," they claimed.[132] Rock songs were not simply messages made of words, but messages of the Word. Mere words are entities whose meanings are replicable across a multitude of print contexts; the Word is the meaning that flows from the individual human larynx articulating words in a unique context.[133] As Simon Frith points out, the relationship of words to music in rock is not simply the setting of words to appropriate music, but the fusion of words and vocal gestures into musical signs that alloy both indissolubly:

Song words work as speech and speech acts, bearing meaning not just semantically, but also as structures of sound that are direct signs of emotion and marks of character. Singers use non-verbal as well as verbal devices to make their points—emphases, sighs, hesitations, changes of tone; lyrics involve pleas, sneers and commands as well as statements and messages and stories (which is why some singers, such as the Beatles and Bob Dylan in Europe in the sixties, can have profound significance for listeners who do not understand a word they are singing).[134]

When, at the beginning of "Ballad of a Thin Man," Dylan sings "you walk into the room," the contour of Dylan's "room," the sour nasal vowel bowed into a little arch, means *this* particular room, the room the square walks into, in *this* particular utterance of *this* story that *this* singer is telling *you*, right now, and telling millions of others like you at the same time. The meaning of this utterance is not given by its musical contour, which is at once too minimal to be worth notating and too complicated to notate adequately, nor simply by the word "room," but the alloy of word and vocal gesture that makes a sign unique to the performative occasion captured on record. When Dylan tells the square, "you try so hard but you just don't understand," all the weight of Dylan's mediated presence is loaded onto that word, and *try* is no longer the word "try." Listening to it again and again, speaking from the grooves of the record, we keep cueing back to the beginning, the word becomes the Word, splitting open and blooming into its ineffable singularity: "try so hard," with a catch of laughter in the throat; "tra-hay," the word "try" split by the laugh; "tra-hay" now sounding like two notes; "tra-hay so hahd" now sounding almost like an arpeggiation through the measure's chord. I can say "try" any way I want in any context it fits, but Dylan's "try" is a unique sign that means, try—from the bottomless depths of squareness—to understand the freaks you meet; try, though all your attempts are doomed by the limits of your understanding; try, though the futility of your actions makes you ridiculous; try, though you will never even know why you fail, because you don't know what you don't know. All that in a single word, *try*, sung just so.

Dylan's phrase making was unerringly resonant. In the underground press, words and lines from his songs punctuated arguments and turned into headlines the way biblical phrases had in the political speeches of the previous century. Todd Gitlin wrote that he and his friends "would fish Dylan's torrent of images, confirming our own revolts and hungers," their traded quotations hypostatizing the meaning of Dylan's sung phrases.[135] When Dylan laughs his way through *try*, it is the laugh heard around the world, the worldwide youth tribe's judgment of the square. Dylan's music allegorized the Movement idea of community: listeners understood Dylan as a voice added to the worldwide chorus, simultaneously and instantaneously heard. The record, a "machined fusion of literacy and orality," fixes the oral meaning that blooms anew within words and makes it replicable, just as printing replicates writing.[136] The record permits the industrial reproduction and diffusion of tribal orality as a new social imaginary. Eric Havelock, like McLuhan, was fascinated by the thought that, with radio, "a single voice addressing a single audience on a single occasion could at least theoretically address the entire population of the earth."[137] A worldwide population dispersed in space could be unified at a single point in time; simultaneously, instantaneously, the young of the world could hear or utter the Word and join a global village. When protestors at the 1968 Democratic National Convention chanted "the whole world is watching" to the TV cameras, it meant that Chicago's police violence was indicted in the eyes of the world, but it also meant something about the protestors themselves.[138] They could feel themselves in the eyes of the world, playing a role in a drama where the world was almost literally a stage and the audience both intimately present and unimaginably huge. In the new tribal world, the voices of rock stars, political leaders, and countercultural gurus bounce from one youth enclave to another, setting up a "world-wide electronically amplified network of the young," as Timothy Leary conceived it, a worldwide jam session of ideas and experience:

> Mario Savio starts a beat in Berkeley. Jerry Rubin brings it up the river to Chicago. Mark Rudd moves it along at Columbia. Hey listen to Red Rudi in Berlin. Now Cohn-Bendit moves on to do a set in Paris. The Shakespearean put-on at San Francisco State. The BEATLES sing it for the ROLLING STONES. The terrestrial conspiracy of [DNA]. The plot of earth. The love-freedom network.[139]

Throughout the postwar 1940s and 1950s, jazz had appealed to young intellectuals whose sensibility was formed within American midcentury modernism: they could understand bebop's dialogue with listeners in modernist terms, as a conversation between individuals whose alienation from mass culture was worn as a badge of honor, and as a cognitive challenge that could be met only within that state of alienation. In the 1960s, rock became the focus of the countercultural imagination for nearly opposite reasons: its appeal lay in its claim to speak for a worldwide youth brigade, joining hands across race and class to take action against an unjust world.[140] In an age of mass counterculture, the hip individual is part of a collective, a vanguard of worldwide change. John Benson Brooks didn't think much of Dylan as a musician ("Bob Dylan, a plebian poet and bullshitting existentialist. He can't play harmonica, guitar, or sing worth a damn but he is a current symptom & famous freak") but was shrewd enough to understand that musicianship as such was not the whole point. The real point was "*The sound of a voice* in continuity of entrances/exits/ in simultaneity of concatenation...the motion of voices with respect to each other."[141] The social image to which Dylan's music gave form was of worldwide commitment and collective experience contained metonymically in the lone singer raising his voice against hegemony.

This was a powerful and seductive image, and though it grew from the same structures of thought and sentiment that "Ornithology" and "Sound Museum" did, Dylan and his audience drew radically different aesthetic conclusions from them. Each of these three pieces proceeded from the stance of asymmetrical consciousness; each assumed the schema of mass culture and tacitly assigned itself a role within it; each applies a kind of perspectival irony on the figure of the square. Of course, the musician's default definition of the square is anyone who doesn't dig his record, and so in each case the music challenges the listener to dig, to follow it on its trip out. The trip out—the irony—in "Ornithology" lies in its musical syntax, in the centrifugal motion of improvisation pulling against the centripetal force of song structure and, more distantly, a shared sense of tradition. In "Sound Museum," Nordine challenges the cognitive flexibility of his listeners with conceptual gags drawn from a repertory of notions peculiar to his wordy, high-modern historical moment. What is *outside* is the conceit of the sound museum, and each *musique concrète* "sound painting" is its own little moon shot of sonic weirdness within an estranging, Barthelme-like conceptual framework. And in "Ballad of a Thin Man," *outside* is the hip mass consciousness embodied in Dylan's mediated performative presence and uncoiling from the elliptical loops of verbal wit, the very utterance of which outlines a new relationship to shared meaning. Each piece is ideologically, aesthetically, and historically separated from the others, and yet they cannot really be understood without understanding their common sensibility, which above all seeks to make *inside* visible and revoke the power that comes of its invisibility. The hip sensibility is at once irreducible multiple and historically coherent, its aspects of plurality and unity dynamically engaged with one another in every piece of hip culture.

5

Mailer's Sound

There are times when I like to think I still have my card in the intellectual's guild, but I seem to be joining company with that horde of the mediocre and the mad who listen to popular songs and act upon coincidence.[1]
—Norman Mailer

"The sound is the thing, man"

When Ross Russell jotted "The Sound Become Holy" as a shorthand for the special quality of Beat life and art, he was following a line of thought that had long considered sound and music uniquely able to participate in human and cosmic reality. Such thinking goes back to antiquity. Allen Ginsberg's paraphrase of a line from Plato's *Republic*—"when the mode of the music changes, the walls of the city shake"—endorsed his own sounding poetics of participation.[2] This line was soon ubiquitous in the underground press and used to connote the apocalyptic political significance attributed to rock in the late 1960s.[3] It is not my purpose to trace the full dimensions of this idea in ancient philosophy or its centuries-long hold on Neoplatonic music theory. One vivid example of the latter seems relevant here, though: a passage from the third book of Marsilio Ficino's *De vita libri tres* (1489), a treatise on magic whose notion of using music to mediate the influence of the cosmos into human life would be shared by John Benson Brooks (see Chapter 6). For Ficino, music is not a representation of mind, but an energetic formation of it:

> But remember that song is a most powerful imitator of all things. It imitates the intentions and passions of the soul as well as words; it represents also people's physical gestures, motions, and actions as well as their characters and imitates all these and acts them out so forcibly that it immediately provokes both the singer and the audience to imitate and act out the same things. By the same power, when it imitates the celestials, it also wonderfully arouses our spirit upwards to the celestial

influence and the celestial influence downwards to our spirit. Now the very matter of song, indeed, is altogether purer and more similar to the heavens than is the matter of medicine. For this too is air, hot or warm, still breathing and somehow living; like an animal, it is composed of certain parts and limbs of its own and not only possesses motion and displays passion but even carries meaning like a mind, so that it can be said to be a kind of airy and rational animal.[4]

Similar ideas appeared again in the nineteenth century, when Arthur Schopenhauer argued that music does not represent the Will but rather embodies it. Richard Wagner promulgated his own very influential version of Schopenhauer's aesthetics, which in turn had much to do with Arnold Schoenberg's expressionist ideal of a music that bypasses the rational and mediating mind and directly embodies the roiling flux of a human soul (see Chapter 3). But the idea of music and sound as embodiment of experience and mind has no single line of transmission, least of all in the twentieth century, when such notions were rediscovered or reinvented several times and in various, often unrelated contexts in and outside of music.[5]

In the 1930s, Antonin Artaud conceived his "theatre of cruelty," a spectacle whose effects would be transmitted to an audience in the same way that the vibrations from the snake-charmer's flute thrum in the belly of a snake. Like Ficino, Artaud believed that each gesture of his ideal art "incites the organism and, through it, the entire individuality, to take attitudes in harmony with the gesture."[6] The point of the "theatre of cruelty," then, is not to represent something to an audience, but to actualize it in them. The audience does not cognize an idea, but feels living processes; the site of its encounter with art is not the mind, but the body. And in conveying this notion, it seems natural for Artaud to reach for an auditory metaphor, and to begin his sketch for a theater of sensation with an account of its sounds:

> If music affects snakes, it is not on account of the spiritual notions it offers them, but because snakes are long and coil their length upon the earth, because their bodies touch the earth at almost every point; and because the musical vibrations which are communicated to the earth affect them like a very subtle, very long massage; and I propose to treat the spectators like the snakecharmer's subjects and conduct them *by means of their organisms* to an apprehension of the subtlest notions.
>
> At first by crude means, which will gradually be refined. These immediate crude means will hold their attention at the start.
>
> That is why in the "theatre of cruelty" the spectator is in the center and the spectacle surrounds him.

In this spectacle the sonorization is constant: sounds, noises, cries are chosen first for their vibratory quality, then for what they represent.[7]

At about the same time, several thinkers were proceeding along parallel tracks, considering how language might variously capture the energetic trace of living process that sound most clearly models. At the beginning of the century, Ernest Fenollosa mused that the Chinese written character, "[speaking] at once with the vividness of painting and the mobility of sounds," was uniquely able to capture the energetic flow of life. His unpublished notes were collected and edited by Ezra Pound for the 1919 essay *The Chinese Written Character as a Medium for Poetry*, the subsequent influence of which (for example, on Charles Olson's energy-field poetics) was huge.[8] Milman Perry's doctoral dissertation (1928) also proved influential in proposing a new way of understanding Homer's poetry as the product of an oral culture for which sound and human presence are intimately connected.[9] And in *Art As Experience* (1934), John Dewey gave an emerging discourse of aesthetic presence its decisive philosophical formulation.

Dewey considered how the characteristics of each art grew from the particular sense it privileged and how a given art form's corresponding sense organ transduced a particular form of energy. For Dewey, the tangle of contending forces cannot really be separated, and the universe is finally to be understood as a single field containing the sum of all energies, which play on human beings and which human beings transform into new impulses—some of them called artworks—that circulate back into the total energy field.[10] This energy field as such lies beyond ordinary human perception, but in phenomenal existence human senses sort its energies into separate channels. The eye gives us the scene, a wide and stable perceptual ground; within that scene there is always change, the dynamic interplay of forces, which registers on the ear. "Sounds are always effects; effects of the clash, the impact and resistance, of the forces of nature," Dewey wrote.[11] We perceive ourselves as discrete bodies within the visual field, in it and yet slightly apart from it; the auditory field, on the other hand, is immersive, permitting us no distance from it. Sound is not a representation of events but an emanation of them, and consequently hearing is a sense that compels immediate and urgent emotion. "Generically speaking, what is *seen* stirs emotion indirectly, through interpretation and allied idea. Sound agitates directly, as a commotion of the organism itself."[12]

Building on Perry's theories of orality in *Orality and Literacy* (1982), Walter Ong later wrote, "Sound cannot be sounding without the use of power. A hunter can see a buffalo, smell, taste, and touch a buffalo when the buffalo is completely inert, even dead, but if he hears a buffalo, he had better watch out: something is going on."[13] For Ong, this intimacy of sound and action, obscured and forgotten in a literate culture for which words are seen and not heard, is the distinguishing mark of orality:

> Fully literate persons can only with great difficulty imagine what a primary oral culture is like, that is, a culture with no knowledge whatsoever of writing or even of the possibility of writing. Try to imagine a culture where no one has ever 'looked up' anything. In a primary oral culture, the expression 'to look up something' is an empty phrase: it would have no conceivable meaning. Without writing, words as such have no visual presence, even when the objects they represent are visual. They are sounds. You might 'call' them back—'recall' them. But there is nowhere to 'look' for them. They have no focus and no trace (a visual metaphor, showing dependency on writing), not even a trajectory. They are occurrences, events.[14]

To reunite word and sound; to turn words back into sound, and thus into actions or events, or contrarily to turn sounds into words, making human actions intimately available through writing; in short, to heal the sundered Word, restoring poetry to the flow of life—this was the great task that writers in hip culture set themselves. When Lawrence Lipton set out to produce a Beat jazz-and-poetry album (*Jazz Canto*, 1958), he wanted neither music accompanied by words nor words set to music, but a radical integration of both, the Word, a new thing (or perhaps something very old) that demanded a new name: he called it Jazz Canto.[15] Struggling to articulate his vision of Jazz Canto in his preparatory drafts for the album's liner notes, he jotted "'Book culture' as a reading exercise for classroom explication. Here poetry is restored to its proper function as a social act, the sound of the word wedded once more to the sound of the music."[16] In later drafts and in *The Holy Barbarians*, the most influential nonfiction book on the hip sensibility since *Really the Blues*, he expanded on the thought, asserting that poetry is fundamentally a vocal art, "silenced by the printing press" and reduced to the role of communicating abstract ideas. What Lipton was after was not merely poems *about* feelings, but poems that realize or embody feelings and penetrate the listener with their force. For that he needed music.

Seymour Krim agreed with Lipton's notions of orality but went further:

> One fascinating point that Lipton raises...is his conception of beat writing as being much closer to oral expression than to the written word. I tend to agree with him; but there are more crucial hints for the future involved here than he follows up. The major breakthrough of beat writing has not been so much in the use of the spoken word for the written, and the typical "open, free-swinging" (Lipton) quality of the style, but rather in the intuitive knowledge that experience must be

converted into immediacy if justice is to be done to the enormous amount we take in daily.[17]

As we saw in Chapter 3, the "intuitive knowledge that experience must be converted into immediacy" fueled the Beats' encounter with jazz. Another Beat poet, Stuart Z. Perkoff, wrote a kind of jazz-and-poetry cantata called *Round About Midnight*, whose Greek chorus of hipsters reminds its poet protagonist that "the sound is the thing, man."[18] In postwar radical culture, sound is always the thing.

The Black Mountain poets as well as the Beats pursued the notion that poetry can project energetic, sonorized impulses to its readers. Charles Olson's essay "Projective Verse" (1950) saw poetry as a vector of action, with the author registering the forces of his environment and transmitting them in turn to the reader through the percussive force of syllable and line. These acoustic elements are in turn impelled by the poet's breath,

> from the breathing of the man who writes, at the moment that he writes, and thus is, it is here that, the daily work, the WORK, gets in, for only he, the man who writes, can declare, at every moment, the line its metric and its ending—where its breathing, shall come to, termination.[19]

Olson's is a near-mystical vision of the poet as a nodal point within the energy field, small in himself and yet vast in his reach, connecting to everything as he draws breath and energy into himself and projects it outward again as poetry.

The poem, then, bears the same relationship to experience as a sound does to an action: it is the physical emanation from experience and not its abstract representation. The poem is no longer the vessel for a certain meaning, and meaning cannot be abstracted from the lived experience within which it appears. There is no distance between form and content, or, as Olson writes in "Against Wisdom as Such," between a poet's wisdom and the poet himself:

> I take it wisdom, like style, is the man—that it is not extricable in any sort of a statement of itself; even though—and here is the catch—there be "wisdom," that it must be sought, and that "truths" can be come on. . . . But they are, in no wise, or at the gravest loss, verbally separated. They stay the man. As his skin is. As his life. And to be parted with only as that is.[20]

When LeRoi Jones wrote his *Kulchur* essay "Against 'Hipness' as Such," it made the same point as the piece from which it took its title: hipness is the very shape your life takes, not just some idea you can add to your store of knowledge. The fascination with what Gilles Deleuze later called "the plane of immanence," along with a complementary critique of all forms of alienation and abstraction from immanence, connected midcentury writers such as Olson and Jones (along with the rest of the Beats) with earlier modernists such as Ezra Pound and later counterculture intellectuals such as John Sinclair, who wrote that Olson's "Projective Verse" essay "had completely blown our minds, and we took it quite seriously as our single dogma to one degree or another."[21]

Such ideas seemed to be in the air during the early years after the war. I have already discussed how Zen Buddhism fit easily into a cultural space receptive to its notion that lived experience is prior to verbal meaning (Chapter 1). Existentialism played this idea out in its own terms—Sartre's "existence precedes essence"—and likewise enjoyed a hip intellectual fad.[22] Writes Daniel Belgrad:

> Existentialism and the aesthetic of spontaneity were most similar in their shared condemnation of the way fixed conceptual structures truncated and falsified reality. Existentialism insisted that human experience exists prior to conceptualizations about it, and in fact cannot be wholly encompassed by such concepts. "Existence," then, refers to the capacity to have experience that exceeds such mental projections. Existentialists struggled to live "authentically," open to the possibilities of existence, and to avoid enslavement to the dictates of conceptual structures and social norms.[23]

In 1952 (the same year as *Visions of Cody*), Harold Rosenberg wrote an influential essay that reconceived abstract expressionism in Existentialist terms and renamed it "action painting." For Rosenberg, the canvas had become "an arena in which to act—rather than as a space in which to reproduce, re-design, analyze or 'express' an object, actual or imagined. What was to go on the canvas was not a picture but an event."[24] In the same year, David Tudor first performed John Cage's Zen-influenced 4'33"—a radical reconceptualization of music as "an arena in which to act" and probably the most influential single piece of avant-garde music ever composed.[25] A translation of Artaud's *Theatre and Its Double* was published by Grove Press in 1958, and its theories of a "theatre of cruelty" composed of the raw stuff of life made an immediate and lasting impression on the Living Theatre, which put its theories into action in its notorious production of Jack Gelber's hipster "anti-play" *The Connection*.[26] In the early 1960s, a spate of new books dealing with various aspects of orality suddenly appeared, most notably McLuhan's *The Gutenberg Galaxy* (1962) and Eric Havelock's *Preface to Plato* (1963).[27] Around the same time, accounts of psychedelic trips began to appear in hip intellectual little magazines like *Evergreen Review*, and for the same reason as articles on Zen and Vedanta: meditation and drugs alike seemed to be technologies of immanence.[28]

This list of connected cultural forms could be multiplied indefinitely. Daniel Belgrad's excellent *The Culture of Spontaneity* fills out the network of artists and intellectuals who seemed to have discovered some new principle of apprehending the world. But "spontaneity"—Belgrad's preferred term for what it was they found—is only one partial way of characterizing that principle; likewise Linda Sargent Wood, viewing the same postwar history from the vantage point of "holism," has hit upon another.[29] Spontaneity, holism, orality, energy-field poetics, the "theatre of cruelty," and hipness itself were all ways of apprehending something both elusive and very basic: an orientation to life lived in all its immediacy and without abstraction.

Abstraction

There is a story (probably apocryphal) of Robert Schumann playing a difficult composition and, on being asked what it meant, playing it again.[30] The point of the story is to say that the only real "meaning" of art is the artwork itself, not anything we might say about it. Meaning, on this account, is like the Map of the Empire in Jorge Luis Borges's tiny story "On Exactitude in Science," a parable of an empire whose passion for cartography led it to create a map exactly as large and detailed as itself.[31] What gives this story its Borgesian strangeness is our awareness that a one-to-one relationship between map and territory is precisely not what we want from maps in the first place, or from any kind of writing. The point of writing is to record a thought and abstract it from the person who thought it and the time and place it was thought—to reify thought and make it portable, so that it might be compared to other thoughts and so added to or subtracted from them and entered into some total equation of stored and crystallized knowledge. In short, writing (of maps, words, or music) takes meaning from the individual's lived engagement with it and places it in a realm outside of time, space, and body. But as Alfred Korzybski famously stated (and as later philosophers of process such as Gregory Bateson never tired of repeating), the map is not the territory.[32] The abstraction against which hip culture was united was not only the fundamental abstraction of meaning from experience, but the literate habit of mistaking the one for the other—confusing the map for the territory—as well as the sometimes disastrous consequences of that confusion.

To understand better the social implications of such abstractions, imagine witnessing a car crash while walking to work. Whatever meaning is assigned to your experience will be determined largely by its place in a certain administrative context, dictated by the laws and customs of society. Your family might want to know how you felt, but the authorities only want to know who was at fault, and their demands will shape the details you recount from your experience. The experience itself goes by in a flash of screeching tires and crumpled metal, a sudden intensification within a flow of experience that in itself has no sharp edges or definite shape. Some time later, a police officer takes your report and you try to unfold this moment into a linear and causal narrative girded with relevant detail (the red compact was turning left when the blue SUV ran the light, etc.). Your report is an abstraction insofar as it "consists in…attending to some aspect of a continuous situation in such a way that a quality or pattern stands out as distinguished from other patterns or aspects of the situation."[33]

Your experience is thus transmuted into a piece of writing typed up for the purposes of a judicial proceeding and eventually filed away in some bureaucratic archive. Now, what relationship does that report have to your experience? It recounts what you remember happening, but it doesn't get at what you felt—the screech of the tires, the percussion of a collision heard and felt deep in the body, the smell of smoke and hot metal, the adrenal burst of fear and excitement. Indeed, individual experience as such becomes an embarrassing fact to be hidden away. What the police and lawyers want is something objective, what "really happened," and the fact that whatever you say is situated in your own experience is only a problem they can either exploit or defend. Something has been abstracted: meaning (or rather the meaning of an incident within the administrative authority that handles the case) has been drawn out of a richer and broader substrate, a blurred rush of sound and sight and tactility.

This rather ordinary abridgement of human meaning within administration grew sinister after World War II. One of the most nightmarish aspects of the Holocaust was the spectacle of a bureaucracy, of the bland, dull sort recognizable everywhere, put to ghastly ends—a vast and meticulous state apparatus of record keeping that allowed the Third Reich to identify, imprison, transport, murder, and dispose of six million Jews. The fact that the implements of destruction here were ledgers and train schedules somehow made it worse; not for nothing did Hannah Arendt write of the "banality of evil."[34] In the first issue of the Beat Anarcho-Buddhist little magazine *Journal for the Protection of All Beings*, Thomas Merton's poem "Chant to be Used in Processions Around a Site with Furnaces" makes a black joke of the dull bureaucratic language enlisted in the service of total barbarism:

> How I commanded and made soap 12 lbs fat 10
> quarts water 8 oz to a lb of caustic soda but it was
> hard to find any fat…

> "For transporting the customers we suggest using
> light carts on wheels a drawing is submitted"

> "We acknowledge four steady furnaces and an
> emergency guarantee…"

Their love was fully stopped by our perfected ovens
but the love rings were salvaged...

All the while I had obeyed perfectly

And yet there is a barbarism to which even a concentration-camp commander
will not lower himself:

Do not think yourself better because you burn up
friends and enemies with long-range missiles without
ever seeing what you have done[35]

To the circle of Anarcho-Socialists around Dwight Macdonald's short-lived but influential little magazine *politics,* the new atomic age promised only technical refinements on the administered mass death of World War II. Macdonald saw the blank cruelty of the Nazi camps and the atomic bombings alike as a consequence of "bureaucratic collectivism," a technocratic and totalizing mode of social organization ascendant in both the West and the East by the end of World War II. Calculative abstraction lay at the root of mass society.[36] Bureaucratic collectivism transforms citizens into the mass by abstracting the individual human identity into a unit of production; it "reduces man to an entity, a certain minute quantity, which is bought, sold, transferred, aided, or crushed by vast, amoral collectives over which he has no control and of whose functions he is completely ignorant."[37] C. Wright Mills wrote that in such a regime, "there are powerful men who do not themselves suffer the violent results of their own decisions," which were judged within narrowly technical limits and entirely at a remove from the human beings they affected.[38] Macdonald marveled that few of the American technicians who helped build the Bomb knew what they were making, and only three of the plane crew that dropped it knew what would happen. "What real content, in such a case, can be assigned to notions like 'democracy' and 'government of, by and for the people'?" Macdonald asked.[39] The idea of individual agency or consent withered in an age when a hypertrophied scientific rationality, bursting its natural boundaries and set to the organization of society, could separate all the links in a chain of action and assign them to separate individuals, each insulated from the actions of the others and thereby from the moral consequences of the whole. The pilots would never witness the deaths of those they bombed; the scientists and technicians who designed and built the bombs would never know the pilots or the dead, or even one another; the managers would only ever talk to other managers; and the American people, in whose name this killing was carried out, would read about it in the papers.

Slaughter on a scale undreamt of by Genghis Khan would thus be a function of tidy accounting and rational planning. Surveying the postwar scene, Erich

Fromm wrote that "man has followed rationalism to the point where rationalism has transformed itself to utter irrationality."[40] What the Holocaust and Hiroshima portended was reason pushed to its furthest extent and reversed on itself; the light of reason become the light of the Bomb.[41] And this madness of reason came of abstraction run riot, the habit of taking the ledger figure for the human being, the map for the territory, the horrifying symbol of which was constituted in those human beings, gassed and burned, who had become nothing more than teeth and hair to be quantified, recorded in a ledger, and stored in a warehouse.

When intellectuals emerged, stunned and blinking, into the postwar age, they felt powerless to do anything about the nightmare they could see so clearly.[42] They could understand the crisis of modernity but could imagine no honorable principle of collective action by which they could confront it. They refused to enlist in any general system of political ideas, for such systems had themselves spawned the deadly abstractions of the modern age. In *Politics and the Novel* (1957), Irving Howe wrote that Americans had always mistrusted ideology, but in terms that seem to paint a generational self-portrait:

> Ideology reflects a hardening of commitment, the freezing of opinion into system. It speaks of a society in which men feel themselves becoming functions of large impersonal forces over which they can claim little control. It represents an effort to employ abstract ideas as a means of overcoming the abstractness of social life.[43]

And yet the intellectuals of Howe's circle—those who read and wrote for *Dissent*, the little magazine that Howe helped found and for which Norman Mailer would write "The White Negro"—still kept watch for some new, hitherto overlooked revolutionary principle.

In the fragile peace of the Cold War these intellectuals sensed the same abstraction everywhere in the offices and ranch houses of the new prosperity. Railing against conformity and consumerism, they pursued the problem of abstraction in the register of mass-culture critique. The managers of the new bureaucratic collectivism, hidden in their distant offices, could plan not only death but dreams for the masses. Every cultural commodity they could contrive would be the abstraction of some experience—a record the abstraction of a night at a jazz club, a bullfight poster the abstraction of *la vie de bohème*—which the passive consumer would accept as a substitute for the real thing. Above all, what troubled hip intellectuals was a pervading and elusive feeling of *unreality*, a sense that in peacetime some part of the war had remained to drain vitality from life.[44]

Or, as Mailer put it:

> PROBABLY, WE WILL never be able to determine the psychic havoc of the concentration camps and the atom bomb upon the unconscious

mind of almost everyone alive in these years. For the first time in civilized history, perhaps for the first time in all of history, we have been forced to live with the suppressed knowledge that the smallest facets of our personality or the most minor projection of our ideas, or indeed the absence of ideas and the absence of personality could mean equally well that we might still be doomed to die as a cipher in some vast statistical operation in which our teeth would be counted, and our hair would be saved, but our death itself would be unknown, unhonored, and unremarked, a death which could not follow with dignity as a possible consequence to serious actions we had chosen, but rather a death by deus ex machina in a gas chamber or a radioactive city; and so if in the midst of civilization—that civilization founded upon the Faustian urge to dominate nature by mastering time, mastering the links of social cause and effect—in the middle of an economic civilization founded upon the confidence that time could indeed he subjected to our will, our psyche was subjected itself to the intolerable anxiety that death being causeless, life was causeless as well, and time deprived of cause and effect had come to a stop.[45]

Whiteness

That is the first paragraph of "The White Negro" (1957). It comprises two sentences, the second of which is 208 words long and reads like the preamble to some hipster Declaration of Independence, which is basically what it was. Like nothing before it, "The White Negro" was a hip manifesto, voicing its era's critique of abstraction and making hipness the principle by which abstraction might be opposed. Mailer conceived of postwar America as a planned and gridded space, mapped out by the same monstrous rationality that had underwritten the great totalitarianisms, within which all human possibilities might be controlled and foreclosed. It would be a softer, American totalitarianism, hygienic and well-lit, compulsorily cheerful, dedicated to the efficient management of human energies in the service of industry—a version of bureaucratic collectivism Belgrad calls "corporate liberalism"—but it would be totalitarian all the same. At a time when intellectuals were stuck in a holding pattern, scanning the horizon for a new radicalism while distrusting any ideology that might motivate it, distrusting indeed the very notion of ideology, Mailer proposed a revolution founded not in ideology at all but in the moment-to-moment movements of the expressive self.[46] It was a vision of revolution as jazz, drugs, and orgasm; the new revolutionary society mapped by the free exchange of human energies; the hipster as the revolution's New Man.

To be sure, Mailer was not the first writer to suggest that hipsters oppose their commitment to the here-and-now to the abstractions of corporate liberalism. Ten years earlier, Broyard's schema of somewhere and nowhere had assumed a similar opposition. Mailer's understanding of how black speech expresses the outsider's encounter with corporate liberalism was not really new, either. *Really the Blues* suggested, as Mailer would later, that jive can "add action metaphors to abstractions, put movement into static phrases, throw warmth into frozen logical categories" because black hipsters have been excluded from the canons of white literacy and because, as outsiders, they can see just how little action, movement, and warmth there is in white speech.[47] The originality and influence of "The White Negro" lay rather in Mailer's notion of hipness as a revolutionary principle without principles, in a literary style made not merely to describe but to enact his revolution, and in his willingness to push the implications of his ideas far past the point of discomfort.

"The White Negro" was both unignorable and intolerable: like an obnoxious dinner guest, Mailer aggravated a lurking unease everyone else tolerated for the sake of good manners. Mailer styled himself a radical, which in "The White Negro" meant an unstable and improvised compound of Reichian psychoanalysis, Anarchism, Marxism, Existentialism, with a bit of the radical reactionary thrown in as well. This was the cocktail of ideas to be served throughout the 1960s, albeit in differing proportions and strengths and with substitute ingredients always at hand. For Mailer, as for the *soi-disant* revolutionaries of the latter decade, "radical" was less a specific place on a continuum of political positions than a general commitment to giving offense. Mailer had no use for racists, but the last thing he wanted was to be another well-behaved and herbivorous liberal. "The White Negro," then, suggested that black men are criminals, psychopaths, and sex gangsters, and differed from a White Citizens' Council tract in supposing this to be a good thing:

> It is quite likely that the reactionary sees the reality more closely than the liberal when he argues that the deeper issue is not desegregation but miscegenation. (As a radical I am of course facing in the opposite direction from the White Citizens' Councils—obviously I believe it is the absolute human right of the Negro to mate with the White, and matings there will undoubtedly be, for there will be Negro high school boys brave enough to chance their lives.)[48]

It has been easy for Mailer's many critics to see that though he may have faced away from the White Citizens' Councils, he stood near the same spot: either way, black men became figures of wild sexual potency and desire. But in "The White Negro," Mailer set a trap for his liberal critics by raising the question of what black men do desire. Eldridge Cleaver would later take Mailer's side against

James Baldwin in part because he didn't want black male sexuality to seem safe and reasonable.[49] A black man fulfilling the paranoid fantasy of the White Citizens' Councils felt like a subversion of white supremacy, while the opposite—bourgeois marriage to suit mainstream ideals of domesticity—felt like capitulation. More recently, Cornel West has confronted this dilemma and asked, "Is there a way out of this Catch-22 situation in which black sexuality either liberates black people from white control in order to imprison them in racist myths or confines blacks to white 'respectability' while they make their own sexuality a taboo subject?"[50] Mailer's essay landed so hard on the first horn of the dilemma that it left its readers feeling they could go nowhere else but the second, and the second was no better than the first.

"The White Negro" runs on the logic of what Roland Barthes called "exnomination."[51] The racial identity of the authorial voice is not marked, though blackness is; whiteness is "normal," the default mode of humanity, while blackness, however celebrated, ends up defined as a figure on a blank ground. Whiteness defines the universal subject; blackness defines a particular one. Thus it is "we" who "suffer from a collective failure of nerve"; the hipster is an abstract and authorial "one" who "exists in the present, in that enormous present which is without past or future, memory or planned intention"; he is "the man who knows the most about how to find his energy and how not to lose it"; but it is "the Negro" who teaches him how. Whiteness constitutes an abstract subject (we, one, man) without qualities. Richard Dyer, following David Lloyd, writes that the centuries-long development of whiteness as a discursive patterning has meant the "attainment of a position of disinterest—abstraction, distance, separation, objectivity."[52] The paradox is that even as the discursive figure of whiteness sustains white privilege by remaining invisible, it finds itself threatened by its very abstraction and insubstantiality and therefore needs to define itself against ethnic particularity in order to avoid vanishing altogether. Blackness serves, then, to delimit whiteness; celebration of blackness becomes just another way to decorate and affirm a white identity.[53]

But "The White Negro" is a complex and dialectical text, and it cannot be explained away too quickly. If, as Dyer argues, "there is something especially white in this non-located and disembodied position of knowledge," Mailer was early in making this connection explicit. "The White Negro" was constructed on a pattern of dualisms that Mailer clarified in "The Hip and the Square," a list of people, things, and qualities grouped into these two categories. "Negro" is hip and "white" is square; following this binary logic, blackness is associated with spontaneity and the embodied experience of the individual, while whiteness is associated with the planned, sequential, abstract, rectilinear logic of authoritarian society. What Mailer takes with one hand he gives with the other: if his essay characterizes blackness as sex and spontaneity while leaving his own position

unmarked, in doing so he characterizes whiteness after all, as something bureaucratic, totalitarian, sexless, cancerous. In "The White Negro," whiteness is the
specter of death evoked in the last lines of Leonard Bernstein's *Neurotica* poem
"Life Is Juicy": it is "the spermless, the painless, the classic, the lean / The dry,
dry dust."[54]

Dyer writes that in films like *Alien* and *Falling Down* there is an excessive or
extreme whiteness, a figure of death and nonbeing, that becomes another Other
against which normative whiteness might define itself. In "The White Negro"
this kind of deathly whiteness is the "non-located and disembodied position" of
totalitarian political control, whose power emanates from everywhere and
nowhere. Its characteristic expression is systematic and abstract violence, as
opposed to the impulsive murderousness of the hoodlum who (in Mailer's notorious example) kills a candy-store owner. For Mailer, killing in hot blood is not
"good" in any conventional sense, but it is more admirable than procedural and
corporate murder by the state. Mailer's open letter to Fidel Castro understands
the difference between their two countries in these terms: "In Cuba hatred runs
over into the love of blood; in America all too few blows are struck into flesh. We
kill the spirit here, we are experts at that. We use psychic bullets and kill each
other cell by cell."[55]

For Mailer, whiteness is linked to the corporate state, and if we ask by what
principle he supposes the state might be resisted, the answer is right there in the
title: white people (or just "people," by the logic of exnomination) are to divest
themselves of their cancerous whiteness and become White Negroes. But if we
ask what principle underlies this notion of blackness as resistance, it is not
enough to say (as has almost every commentator on "The White Negro") that it
is simply sex and psychopathy. There is something that lies prior even to that,
and to understand it we must turn again to "The Hip and the Square" and read
the last pair of opposed terms in Mailer's list: "to listen for the meaning of the
words and obey no other meaning" is square, while "to listen to the sound of the
voice and take one's meaning from there" is hip.[56]

What this opposition implies is, first, is a commitment to what Hannah
Higgins calls "primary experience," the encounter with meanings embedded in
lived situations, and against abstract verbal meaning. But beyond this, Mailer
conceives of primary experience in Wilhelm Reich's terms, as the giving and
receiving of bio-electric energies, a constant and moving flow of impulses in an
energy field.[57] Mailer's emphasis on the sound of the voice suggests that for him,
as for Dewey, Artaud, Olson, and the Beats, experience comes in through the ear.
The tympanum of the ear is the membrane that mediates between individual
human organisms and the wider energy field within which they interact; the ear
is the mechanism by which energies are transduced. Later, in Mailer's *An American
Dream* (1964–65), music becomes both medium and metaphor of those energies.
As Dewey had written thirty years earlier,

Music, having sound as its medium, thus necessarily expresses in a concentrated way the shocks and instabilities, the conflicts and resolutions, that are the dramatic changes enacted upon the more enduring background of nature and human life. The tension and the struggle has its gatherings of energy, its discharges, its attacks and defenses, its mighty warrings and its peaceful meetings, its resistances and resolutions, and out of these things music weaves its web.[58]

Later in life, Mailer identified his collection *Advertisements for Myself* (for which "The White Negro" was the centerpiece) as the point where he found his own style, the discovery of which hinged on moving "from the hegemony of the word to the resonance of the rhythm."[59] Once again, the sound was the thing.

Mailer's Sound

Mailer's biographer Carl Rollyson writes that the most dangerous thing about "The White Negro" was that it proposed "the abandonment of stationary values."[60] As Gregory Corso wrote to LeRoi Jones in 1960, "all stational [sic.] things can be knocked down—once you take a position…All positions must be contradicted, else it's bullshit."[61] For Mailer as for the Beats, the fluid rather than the stationary, energetic process rather than any fixed and atemporal pattern of logical relations, grants new forms of expression, politics, and life. The philosophical crux of "The White Negro" is Mailer's belief that we live in an energy field, and that "its gatherings of energy, its discharges, its attacks and defenses, its mighty warrings and its peaceful meetings, its resistances and resolutions" are the stuff of our lives. Each human transaction is a transfer of energy from which one emerges with either more or less than one started with. "The language of Hip is a language of energy, how it is found, how it is lost," Mailer writes: the hipster has created a new language that tracks the discharges and dissipations of energy and the triumphs and defeats that accompany them.[62] Though it is unclear whether Mailer ever developed a real feeling for jazz, he took it for granted that hip speech verbalized the same relationship to life that jazz wordlessly embodies.[63] In the unpublished first draft version of "The White Negro," Mailer writes:

[Hipster idioms] serve a variety of purposes, being the sensitive expression of inarticulate people, and the nuance of the voice uses the nuance of the situation to convey the meaning—if the words began with jazz musicians as is probably the case, they exist by now (as I have written somewhere else) almost as a new kind of Basic English equipped to describe the subjective states of a man on his daily search.[64]

The final, shorter version of this sentence substitutes "subtle contextual difference" for "meaning," which reflects Mailer's developing awareness that hipness is not exactly about *meaning,* at least in the literary sense. Rather, he writes, its expression lies in

> a pictorial language, but pictorial like non-objective art, imbued with the dialectic of small but intense change, a language for the microcosm, in this case, man, for it takes the immediate experiences of any passing man and magnifies the dynamic of his movements, not specifically but abstractly so that he is seen more as a vector in a network of forces than as a static character in a crystallized field.[65]

The idiom that especially captured the moving and relational aspect of hip was the verb *to swing.* Privileged with awareness of the ceaseless flux in which his own actions take place, the hipster must swing, must keep in step with the moving current of life: "to swing is to communicate, is to convey the rhythms of one's own being to a lover, a friend, or an audience, and—equally necessary—be able to feel the rhythms of their response."[66] It is not only that one feels the flow of one's own energies, but that one finds a way to exchange energies with others. Hipness consists in a kind of oral communication, embedded in the performed and embodied nuances of speech rather than in the fixed and replicable abstractions of type. By way of example, Mailer tells the story of a black hipster, illiterate but with "an extraordinary ear and a fine sense of mimicry," who engages an intellectual young woman in conversation. He doesn't know what she's talking about but swings with her all the same, because he is attuned not to what she says but how she says it—not her standard-issue Riesmanesque ideas but the nuances of a singular personality carried along on the nuances of voice.[67]

Sound is a fluid medium for the exchange of social energy and a metaphor for the "existential errands" of Mailer's own prose—existential, in Mailer's terms, because writing, like sound, is an errand that begins with an impulse and traces a curve of becoming without an end in view.[68] Mailer once defined "existential"—a word he used often and indiscriminately—as the negotiation of situations "where we cannot foretell the end."[69] The writer is challenged to act without ever knowing at the outset what the consequences of his actions might be, and this demands the kind of courage that the corporate-liberal regime systematically drains away. Finding this courage, the writer is free, even if he is doomed or damned. He can win a quantum of new energy in his every encounter with life; he can *make it.* The squarer idea of *making it* has to do with striving for worldly success: getting ahead, getting noticed, and arriving at one's long-planned, long dreamed-of destination in life.[70] The hipster idiom suggests success of a different kind of winning for which the prize is freedom in the moment of intense experience. In a letter to Lipton, Philip Whalen wrote that *making it* means

To be Here, Now, & Live (rhymes with dive, &c) & that you DIG (that is that you like it this way, you like seeing the people you are with are also liking it, are alive, are understanding that you are there & live (same rhyme with drive) & that you are liking them liking the scene & each other, and IT IS HERE AND NOW, not later, not in the Glorious Future, Comrade, not the three-day work-week with retirement at 35 in VistaVision, but now, with the band (GINSBERG: "reincarnate in the ghostly clothes of jazz in the goldhorn//shadow of the band...") or with a woman or with a poem...preferably another person PERSON, which is...or like Miles or Bird, with a horn.[71]

Making it means free, spontaneous action, and for Mailer this not only is what is missing from modern life but is a tonic for it. As Robert Solotaroff writes, Mailer's core idea was that "an individual can become better than his society and grow by bringing courage to a situation for which the result is in doubt."[72]

Mailer saw writers, like hipsters, as "self makers on a quest into the unknown," notes Morris Dickstein: "In line with this faith in self-discovery, Mailer evolved a prose of Carlylean complexity, a cumulative, periodic style designed to convey a sense of risk, the sense of a mind in motion as it examines the world from every angle."[73] Mailer's prose style in "The White Negro" tries not only to represent but to perform its subject—the existential heroism of the writer/hipster who doesn't know how the next line is going to turn out. The 208-word second sentence of the opening sets loose a thought that snakes around and bites its own tail, beginning with the modern subject's repressed knowledge of his powerlessness within the grid of modernity and ending up with subject trapped in a grid reconceived in terms of time rather than space. As the sentence uncoils, it gathers momentum through its long internal parentheses, careening through the horrors of the gas chambers and the Bomb and gasping to its concluding realization that what we are really talking about here is the sense of purpose amputated from our lives by our abiding awareness of stopped time. Does this make sense? Not completely, perhaps, but the meaning is not the thing. The sentence does not try to represent an idea, a product of thought, so much as the action of thought, the becoming of an idea. It is as if the sentence on the page registers, like a field of fresh snow, the clash and struggle of the writer against the grid. What is represented is less the writer's idea than the writer's action—fighting clear of a fog of cowardice and stupidity to arrive at revelation.

I have already suggested that sound is the model for such motions of individual subjectivity; and sound, in its material form as the groove of the phonographic record ("the universe now being glimpsed as a series of ever-extending radii from the center"), also suggests a metaphor for the phonographic registering of the unfolding energies of history.[74] Steve Shoemaker writes that the contortions of the essay's epic second sentence "reflect the struggle to capture the besieged spirit of a crisis-ridden age, to register seismographically, as it were, the effects, large and subtle, of the tragic events of world history on human conscious-ness."[75] The energetic motions of the writing, registered as a seismic (or phono-graphic) trace on the surface of the page, picture the writer as a figure in the total energy field of society, whose baleful impulses penetrate him and which he absorbs, transforms, and redirects outward again in the force of his sentences.[76]

The essay's second sentence, then, is musical. I do not mean this in a commonplace way, saying that it is *about* music (which it isn't) or that its cadence and phrasing is euphonious (which it isn't really either). Rather it tries to *do something musical*—to record, though a phonographic trace of moving thought, something around which the words and ideas circle but to which they are not quite identical. In *Armies of the Night*, Mailer suggests that the writer's skill lies in being able to find the right word while reaching for another, the right word disclosing itself only in the instant of grasping at another thought fractionally off to the side:

> Consider that a good half of writing consists of being sufficiently sensitive to the moment to reach for the next promise which is usually hidden in some word or phrase just a shift to the side of one's conscious intent. (Consciousness, that blunt tool, bucks in the general direction of the truth; instinct plucks the feather. Cheers!)[77]

In the first chapter, I paraphrased George Burns's quip "Sincerity—if you can fake that, you've got it made"—replacing "sincerity" with "authenticity" and suggesting that hip style comprises a rhetoric of authenticity whose value is measured not in its social reality but in its aesthetic force. In "The White Negro," Mailer developed a new rhetoric of authenticity, his "cumulative, periodic style," in part through hearing a false note in his own political writing: "every time I sat down to do an article, I seemed to thicken in the throat as I worded my sentences and my rhetoric felt shaped by the bad political prose of our years."[78] The early drafts of "The White Negro" show a progression of the essay from its origins as a more conventional piece of political/cultural analysis, hemmed in by its author's desire for a formidable and totalizing intellectual system, to the disinhibited final version. In the first manuscript draft of what would become the sprawling final sentence of "The White Negro," one can almost feel the prose thickening in Mailer's throat as he reaches for a valedictorian tone, imagining the present from the point of view of the future ("Some day when the history of human energy is written") and wondering if *Das Kapital* "will not find its place" in some future work. The tone is pompous and—surprisingly for Mailer—pulls its punches:

Some day when the history of human energy is written, and the knowledge of its increments and dissipations, its creators, its efficiencies and tragic wastes, have become relatively subjected to reasonable analysis, I wonder then if the body of Marxist thought, and particularly the epic grandeur of Das Kapital, will not find its place in some even more God-like view of human justice and injustice, in some more excruciating vision of those individual personal and social processes of our lives which lead to our growth or our death. Marx was perhaps the first major philosopher to approach the human condition so simply and precisely as this: we are a body of humans whose life energy is wasted, displaced, and invariably procedurally stolen as it passes from one of us to another.[79]

In the published version, this same passage opens with a phrase that posits no future but instead leaves the sublime immensity of the present alive and uncontained in the reader's mind:

It is almost beyond the imagination to conceive of a work in which the drama of human energy is engaged, and a theory of its social currents and dissipations, its imprisonments, expressions, and tragic wastes are fitted into some gigantic synthesis of human action where the body of *Das Kapital* (that first of the major *psychologies* to approach the mystery of social cruelty so simply and practically as to say that we are a collective body of humans whose life-energy is wasted, displaced, and procedurally stolen as it passes from one of us to another)—where particularly the epic grandeur of *Das Kapital* would find its place in some even more God-like view of human justice and injustice, in some more excruciating vision of those intimate and institutional processes which lead to our creations and disasters, our growth, our attrition, and our rebellion.[80]

The first draft version has a term-paper quality, moving from proposition to proposition in a dull and orderly way; the final version has dash and style. In the first version, the idea Mailer proposes is to be "subjected to reasonable analysis"; in the final version, it is to be "fitted into some gigantic synthesis of human action." In the first version, the thought of the passage is parsed out between two longish sentences; in the final version, Mailer takes the entire second sentence of this passage, sticks it between parentheses, and jams it into the middle of the first sentence at the mention of *Das Kapital*, the effect of which is no ordinary parenthetic aside but a rhapsodic flight ending suddenly with a dash and the speaker recalled to his purpose, with *Das Kapital* named again, the sentence reading now as a single torrential flow of ideas associated in the mind of an individual speaking out of an existential situation, a situation whose end becomes clear only the moment it appears. The first sentence of the first version ventures out for a considerable span of ninety words, but they are buttoned up in an orderly and coordinated series of clauses. The final version is 143 words long: Mailer dares a wider span, long enough to threaten collapse, and rather than coordinate its many parts he builds a kind of cumulative force, in which each successive clause impels the next and then drops away from awareness like a spent rocket booster, leaving only the momentum of the present verbal image, the reader's attention traveling with the moving wave of energy as it pulses from beginning to end. In sum, the revision history of this sentence shows Mailer daring himself to go out, to venture outside the sound of the "Max Lernerish liberal junk" clogging his ears and risk an improvisational, "Existential" prose.[81] But even though Mailer's writing leaves the impression of improvisation, it does so through a carefully calculated and painstakingly crafted rhetoric of spontaneity.[82]

The final draft concludes with this 143-word sentence, whose idea seems almost an afterthought, or perhaps a gesture toward expansion from the narrower aims of the essay to a vaster and more speculative future project. But in the first draft it was intended to open and set the agenda of the entire essay, which at that point was called "Dialectic of the American Existentialist," a title that hinted at its vaulting ambition to marry Sartre, Marx, and Freud (angled off Wilhelm Reich and with an assist from the Marquis De Sade). By the time he finished "The White Negro," much of that specifically intellectual ambition had been pushed aside by Mailer's deeper understanding of what kind of thing hipness is and what it demands. Hipness was no longer the instrument of an intellectual argument but something in itself.

At the beginning of the writing process, he jotted down a list of potential topics:

> The hipster article.
> Could begin with the problem of what has happened to the revolutionary
>   consciousness of the past, where are the rebels
> ~~the Cold W~~
> the unconscious terror of the concentration camp
> the political impotence
> the rise in homosexuality
> and finally as the doubtful answer, the hipster
> their sole relation to Marxism—they are dialecticians[83]

Surprisingly, none of this has to do with blackness, miscegenation, or sexual psychopathy; Mailer's first thoughts run toward political conditions and the problem of the intellectual in the Cold War. As I have noted, the mood of intellectuals in this time is one of apostasy and dispirited watchfulness, a simultaneous wariness of and longing for political principle: in "Dialectic of the American Existentialist," Mailer characterizes the 1950s as an "ignoble time" in which "authorities were desired with anguish and yet no authority could be believed." For Mailer, the hipster breaks the impasse, but in his first draft he is still unable to imagine a way of expressing this idea without a heavy overlay of Marxian analysis. By the final draft of "The White Negro," Mailer had purged almost all traces of his forced attempt to make the hipster out as a "dialectician" and cut the opening eight pages (nearly a third of the total) of the second-draft typescript. The concluding paragraph of the final version is all that remains of Mailer's initial ambition to create a "neo-Marxian calculus aimed at comprehending every circuit and process of society from ukase to kiss as the communications of human energy."[84] Mailer's idea of "translating the economic relations of man into his psychological relations and then back again"—thereby uniting the competing monisms of Freud and Marx into a synthesis more profound than either—was underwritten by his idea of the energy field, which continued to inform the final draft, though it is never explicitly or systematically argued. Mailer clearly found that it is less dramatically effective to explain a theory than show us its results, and in the margin of the third draft next to the paragraph that most succinctly outlined his energy-field theory, he wrote "words are blah":

> Is it not as tenable then to assume that society is more than a concept, more than a mystical reality (which is the suppressed hypothesis Marx finally employed—to his rigorous discomfort) but that indeed society is a biochemical existence which lives in every one of us, directs a large part of our nervous system and grows and changes as we grow and change in that world which is forever changing, sometimes diminished, and of course is always affected by the communications we have with everyone alive.[85]

Ontology recapitulates phylogeny: the postwar intellectual history recounted in Chapter 2, in which intellectuals came to terms with hipness not as a philosophy but as something more basic and elusive, plays out in the growth of "The White Negro" from "Dialectic of the American Existentialist." Mailer starts out with the notion of the hipster as philosopher-in-the-rough and then discards it for a more radical suggestion: what the hipster represents is beyond philosophy, beyond Marx, beyond Freud, beyond all the assumptions and hang-ups of Mailer's own Harvard education, beyond the gamesmanship of the New York Intellectuals, beyond knowing or caring what any of this means. The hipster does not care about the meanings of things, but only their reality, here and now. This, then, is the answer to the riddle of how intellectuals were to find a purpose and a principle without ruling ideology or program: Dig. Swing. Make it.

Enantiodromia

The ideas Mailer worked out in "The White Negro" would influence everything he wrote afterward, especially his novel *An American Dream*. This novel narrates a long day in the life of Stephen Rojack, a decorated war hero, former congressman, TV celebrity, and "professor of existential psychology." As the story begins he is at low ebb—failing, in public, to fulfill the promise of his precocious beginnings, and miserable in his failing marriage to a cruel and violent woman whom he helplessly loves and by whom he is continually defeated. The parallels between Rojack and Mailer's idealized view of himself, and between the crisis in Rojack's life and that in Mailer's in the mid-1950s, are obvious and generally noted. So too is *An American Dream*'s grotesque misogyny, which I will not try to explain or excuse.[86] Most relevant here, though, is that the principle of liberation that Rojack discovers is the one Mailer found in "The White Negro": make it. Victory is life, even if it is a stupid or cruel victory, and all contests are zero-sum: for one to win, another must lose.

> Life is a contest between people in which the victor generally recuperates quickly and the loser takes long to mend, a perpetual competition of colliding explorers in which one must grow or else pay more for remaining the same, (pay in sickness, or depression, or anguish for the lost opportunity) but pay or grow."[87]

In Mailer's world, courage is the sovereign virtue and every failure leads a step closer to death. Victory enriches the individual's being and therefore the totality of Being; it is a mark entered on God's side of the ledger against the Devil, the lord of death who rules over the sterile, rational, planned, gridded domain of corporate-liberal America. Underlying *An American Dream* is an occult cosmology in which God and the Devil are equal combatants locked in a struggle whose outcome is doubtful and intimately related to our own struggles.[88] Mailer's cosmology suggests the Hermetic axiom *as above, so below*: in "Dialectic of the American Existentialist," the energetic circuits of society constitute a nervous system that is imprinted in miniature on our own; in "The White Negro," the hipster creates a new nervous system for himself and so may exert a kind of sympathetic magic on society; in *An American Dream*, the cosmic war between God and the Devil plays out in Rojack's battle to win back lost energy.

This battle begins in an act of murder. Rojack's wife, Deborah, is a powerful adversary in the energy field, willing to brawl though more apt to wound through the tinkling malice of her voice. After a quarrel turns violent, Rojack gets her in a choke hold, and when she signals her submission he continues to bear down until she dies. By daring more and going deeper into the moment of contention, he reclaims the upper hand, and in killing her he wins not only this particular encounter but the initiative she has taken from him. After this liberating act of will, Rojack feels out his new powers as he moves from one enormity to another: he sodomizes Deborah's maid, faces down Mafiosi and cops, beds a nightclub singer, and brutally beats her ex-lover, a black singer and pimp modeled on Miles Davis, Mailer's real-life sexual competitor.[89] In the end Rojack triumphs even over Deborah's Mephistophelean father and the hidden political powers he represents. And he gets away with it all: critics were outraged by Rojack's crimes and impunity, which was probably what Mailer intended—like Rojack, Mailer was willing himself to dare more, and in real time.[90] Because *An American Dream* was originally serialized in *Esquire* and written under inflexible deadlines, Mailer was forcing himself to throw provocations out to his public without a second thought. In a letter to Francis (Fig) Gwaltney, he wrote

> It's a little like playing ten-second chess. You have to take the bold choice each time, because you know you can depend on getting something out of the bold effects—the subtler choices may prove too subtle and fail to come to life with the speed with which you have to write.[91]

On a quick first read, *An American Dream* seems like a weird and overwritten *roman noir,* full of smoky bars, *femmes fatales,* hepcat Negros, powerful men brooding in penthouses, and cops and gangsters who are hard to tell apart. However, understood as an attempt "to dramatize the workings of that architectonic science of expanding energies which reaches down to lend meaning to all human activities," the novel represents a more interesting ambition: to record a moment-by-moment calculus of energies gained and lost.[92] This play of energies pulses under the surface of the overt actions in the story, and it is the former rather than the latter that constitutes the novel's real causality. These energies register on every surface and sensation, on a drink swirling in a glass or in the smell of a cop's breath. Most often, they manifest in acts of sex and violence, which for Mailer would always remain the privileged sites for the contention of human wills, screwing and fighting both being energetic performances in the medium of time and the human body. So too is musical performance, though, and in *An American Dream* music embodies the flow of energy from one person to the other and the ebb and flow of initiative and momentum in every moment of contention.

After a police interrogation, Rojack goes to hear a nightclub singer, Cherry, who is no virtuoso but all the same has mastered the art the capturing the dynamic flux of every passing moment in the nuance of her singing. Music, an art of time, allows both performer and listener to remain poised, as if perched atop the little bouncing ball in a TV sing-along show, in a single moment moving through time, dealing with everything as it comes.[93] Cherry's singing bears the traces of all the unfolding actions in the nightclub, and *vice versa*: the life of the room balances on the fine details of her singing. The whole room swings, cause and effect zinging back and forth through the medium of music. Every person can claim the larger part of this transference of energy, but only Rojack does, and the music becomes the vehicle for his will. He takes in the energies of the room and projects them back outward, gaining the small victories whose accumulated energy will win him the great prize of Cherry herself.

When Cherry's courage fails—this increment of lost energy registered in the cracking of a high note—a "tart" laughs. Cherry 0, Tart 1. Rojack then steals this increment of gained energy by firing a psychic projectile:

> Exhibit: The first tart with the judge giggled hysterically each time Cherry tried to hit the G below high C. Cherry's voice was not particularly ready. One strand of her sound curled up to the pitch. The rest of her fell away. But the attempt was brave. So I called one of those magic bullets I maintained in orbit swinging through the room above the solar center of my head. I instructed it, "next time she giggles, take a fling through her head, ear to ear, score her good." Which the pellet promptly did. Like a bullet going through a ten-inch plank, my pellet sizzled a new streak of emptiness through the core of that tart's thoughts; her dear head quivered as the bullet went through; when she giggled again, the sound was hollow, the empty dopey giggle of a sweet-faced tart.[94]

The girl's hollow laugh registers a minute loss of energy: Tart 0, Rojack 1. Then, during his minute inspection of Cherry's body, Rojack is displeased by her prosaic fat toes and maliciously shoots her with a series of mental arrows, first into her feet and then (prodded by the Devil to an act of black magic) into her womb. Again, the loss of energy registers itself in sound:

> I felt it go in. I felt some damage lodge itself there. She almost lost her song. One note broke, the tempo shuddered, and she went on, turned to look at me then, a sickness came off her, something broken and dead from the liver, stale, used-up, it drifted in a pestilence of mood toward my table, sickened me as it settled in.[95]

To discharge himself of the evil of this deed, Rojack runs to the toilet and vomits out its malignant energy, along with "cruds, violations, the rot and gas of compromise, the stink of old fears, mildew of discipline, all the biles of habit and the horrors of pretense."[96]

And so on and so forth. The entire novel is like this, the record of a man hurtling through a world in which the moon demands his suicide and a woman's life can be won by walking around a high-rise building ledge twice. Such a world, humming with secret communications and ordered by synchronicities and sympathetic links, is the world transformed beyond recognition from the everyday domain of causality to one of magic. For those who have absorbed the assumptions of a scientistic age, in which magic is demoted either to prestidigitation or to a metaphor ("the magic of the movies"), it is easy to assume that the strangeness of this novel must be the result of some subtle writerly ploy. But Mailer isn't being subtle at all. This novel is, in the most literal sense, magical realism: a blunt, you-are-these account of a magical world Mailer experienced as fully real. In an oft-cited interview, Laura Adams assumed that Mailer's accounts of psychic combat were metaphorical, but Mailer insisted otherwise: he was depicting things that had happened to him. "To me, it was a realistic book, but a realistic book at a place where extraordinary things are happening. I believe the experience of extraordinary people in extraordinary situations is not like our ordinary realistic experience at all."[97]

There is a certain paradox here: the closer the writer comes to concreteness, the more abstract his expression. "The White Negro" and *An American Dream* articulate Mailer's version of the midcentury critique of abstraction, but in practice this meant creating a byzantine prose style—the new sound of "The White Negro" updated to the post-Kennedy 1960s—comparable, perhaps, to Coltrane's mid-1960s sound: plangent, prolix, and alienating to a lot of old fans. The same contradiction emerges in an episode of Kerouac's *The Dharma Bums,* in which Japhy Ryder (Kerouac's pen name for Gary Snyder) is trying to explain to Ray Smith (Kerouac) the difficulties of translating Han Shan's poem "Cold Mountain." Ryder reads his translation out loud:

> "Climbing up Cold Mountain path, Cold Mountain path goes on and on, long gorge choked with scree and boulders, wide creek and mist-blurred grass, moss is slippery though there's been no rain, pine sings but there's no wind, who can leap the world's ties and sit with me among white clouds?"

Jack Kerouac, The Dharma Bums (New York: Viking, 1958; repr. New York: Penguin, 1976), 20–21.

He then explains that the original contains five Chinese characters for each line and that he has had to stitch them together with "prepositions and articles and such" to turn a series of disconnected images into a sentence. Smith asks why he doesn't just translate the signs as they are, with nothing added:

> "Why don't you just translate it as it is, five signs, five words? What's those first five signs?"

"Sign for climbing, sign for up, sign for cold, sign for mountain, sign for path"

"Well then, translate it 'Climbing up Cold Mountain path'."

"Yeah, but what do you do with the sign for long, sign for gorge, sign for choke, sign for avalanche, sign for boulders?"

"Where's that?"

"That's the third line, would have to read 'Long gorge choke avalanche boulders'."

"Well that's even better!"

The basic problem of Beat writing was how to capture action without reifying it in typographic abstraction. This passage in *The Dharma Bums* suggests that one could make the English language work the way Ezra Pound supposed that Chinese does, with action taking place as the words crash into one another on the page.[98] However, an unprepared (or unhip) reader happening on this sentence would be mystified, or at least challenged, by "long gorge choke avalanche boulders" and its lack of verbal connective tissue. Again, the result of this raid on linguistic abstraction is itself pretty abstract.

Careful readers will have already noted this paradox in Chapter 2. Thelonious Monk's hidden devices of abstraction and estrangement can be reconstructed only through repeated playback and patient analysis outside the moment of listening—in other words, in abstraction from experience. In Monk's music too we find an apparent contradiction between the abstraction of his expression and the aims of the hip culture to which he belongs. This is not simple contradiction, though, but reversal. Modernism in general, and the dialect of modernism called hipness in particular, have always treated its parent condition, modernity, as a kind of sickness, and its art as a tonic: as *Neurotica* announced in 1948, the hip modern "has been forced to live underground, and yet lights an utter darkness with his music, poetry, painting, and writing."[99] If modern art was a tonic, it treated the sickness of modernity with a homeopathic dose of abstraction. Belgrad writes that this was the strategy also of the action painters—expressionists who were called "abstract" but were in fact the least abstract of artists. Belgrad writes that the "insistent materiality" of their painting "was intended as a radical counterstatement to the 'abstract' quality of the scientific method."[100] Likewise, the abstractions of Monk's music, like the abstractions of modernist art generally, both imitate the fractured condition of modernity and transform it somehow into the very thing modernity lacks. Through Monk's abstractions—his hammered ascending-seventh figures in "Misterioso," for example—one comes to face-to-face with haecceities, musical objects in their mute immovable blunt there-ness. When Monk carries abstraction to its endpoint, what is left is the bare musical object standing forth once again in puzzling freshness: in Viktor Shklovsky's words, the stone is made stony.[101] The other side of abstraction is the world here and now.

The principle here is enantiodromia, which is the idea that a thing or process, in the full exercise of its own qualities and potentialities, will reverse into its opposite. Enantiodromia is a new word for a very old idea, present alike in the *Tao Te Ching* and *I Ching* and in the fragments of Heraclitus.[102] It lies at the heart of Marshall McLuhan's theories of advanced literacy reversing into neotribal orality, and in Erich Fromm's notion of rationalism at its far limit reversing into a destroying madness; we have seen it, too, as the hyperliterate hip culture of the 1940s and 1950s reversed into the presence culture of the 1960s Movement. And we will see it again in the next chapter, in the creative work of John Benson Brooks, whose severe and intellectual Cold War modernism reversed into the proto-postmodernism of his strange album *Avant Slant* (1968). Hipness itself seems to run on the principle of enantiodromia: as the Tower of Power song goes, "sometimes hipness is what it ain't."[103]

Enantiodromia is the sort of idea that (as Frederic Jameson said in another context) "is not a proposition one proves; rather, one seeks...to demonstrate the interest of presupposing it."[104] Which is to say, it is a theory that runs on verification, not falsification, and is justified by the interesting stories it allows us to tell. This was Mailer's rationale for his occult theology, and it is the hallmark of magical theories generally.[105] A materialist such as Jameson would doubtless disapprove the connection, but magical thinking pervades our everyday mental processes more than we might like to admit. Historians sometimes give a passing mention to the place of magic in counterculture, but seldom as anything more than escapism or just another *outré* fascination for those already drawn to exotic novelties. But magic and the hip sensibility are related at an altogether deeper level, in their shared orientation to experience in "that enormous present which is without past or future, memory or planned intention." In the next chapter, we will see that the great archival work of John Benson Brooks—a Great Work in more than one sense—is a site where the latent connections between magic and hipness become manifest. This final chapter gathers up the threads of the preceding ones, especially Lucien Lévy-Bruhl's notion of "participation," the relationship between a hip vernacular and the avant-garde, the tensions between modernist and postmodernist hip sensibilities, and the problem of co-optation. And a number of the figures who have graced the stage of this history—LeRoi Jones, Marshall McLuhan, John Clellon Holmes, Seymour Krim, Kenneth Burke's "perspective of perspectives," Zen—will come back to take one final turn.

6

"Let's say that we're new, every minute" (John Benson Brooks)

Good lord, Pierce thought, snapping shut the book and reinserting it in its row. Star temples and ley-lines, UFOs and landscape giants, couldn't they see that what was really, permanently astonishing was the human ability to keep finding these things? Let anyone looking for them be given a map of Pennsylvania or New Jersey or the Faraways, and he will find "ley-lines"; let human beings look up long enough on starry nights and they will see faces looking down at them. *That*'s the interesting thing, *that*'s the subject: not why there are ley-lines, but why people find them; not what plan the aliens had for us, but why we think there must, somehow, always have been a plan.[1]

—John Crowley

A lady from Texas said: I live in Texas.
We have no music in Texas. The reason they've no
music in Texas is because they have recordings
in Texas. Remove the records from Texas
and someone will learn to sing.
Everybody has a song
which is no song at all:
it is a process of singing,
and when you sing,
you are where you are.
All I know about method is that when I am not
working I sometimes
think I know something, but when I am working, it is quite
clear that I know nothing.[2]

—John Cage

Off-Minor

You have probably never heard of John Benson Brooks (1917–1999), and if you have, you know that he's obscure. Maybe it is perverse to have written a book on hipness, arguing that it is the most influential aesthetic idea of the past half-century, only to end with a careful inspection of a failed and forgotten album (*Avant Slant*, 1968) by a jazz composer whose influence can hardly be charted.[3] Or maybe it only makes sense. In the first chapter, I considered the notion of co-optation, which tells us that the surest way to defeat cultural radicalism is to permit it, but on compromised terms. If some piece of subversive culture is widely admired, we cannot be sure that it has not been co-opted in some way, all the better to foreclose the very subversion it appears to represent. Perhaps it would be better for it to remain underground, unseen and unheard except by the most dedicated and discriminating of cultural connoisseurs. Perhaps *Avant Slant*'s failure is its secret success.

This is most unlikely. Nothing can remain immune from the suspicion of co-optation when everyone wants in on the underground, and since hipness is only ever a positional good—as Carl Wilson writes, "for you to be cool requires someone else to be less cool"—the underground must always stay a step ahead of the mass of hip consumers.[4] As Joseph Heath and Andrew Potter write:

> what the rebel is looking for, in the end, is the unco-optable subculture. Like the gambler in the Leonard Cohen song, looking for the card so high and wild he'll never need to play another, the countercultural rebel is looking for a path that no one else will ever follow, a look so extreme it will never be mainstream.[5]

They go on to note, though, that there is something self-defeating about this. Making music that cannot be co-opted might simply mean making music that no one likes, which in turn might mean bad, unlistenable music. And even then, something intended to be bad and unlistenable, like Lou Reed's *Metal Machine Music,* might end up becoming a cult classic anyway.[6]

The latter is such an obvious and oft-repeated cavil about avant-garde art of any sort that it almost doesn't bear repeating; I bring it up only to say that it is not the point I wish to make.[7] Neither do I wish to say that *Avant Slant* is resistant to a cultural mainstream or that it serves as any kind of model for oppositional, anticonsumerist culture. I have argued throughout this book that the opposition between counterculture and consumer culture is an illusion, but even if it were not, *Avant Slant* would hardly stand as an example of principled anticommercialism. Brooks's initial motivation for creating it was to make enough money to cover his mother's medical bills and contribute something to his household economy. He hoped for the album's success and was disappointed by its failure—though Brooks, thoroughly modernist in his sensibility, did fret that he was conceding too much to popular taste. (He needn't have worried.)

Nor yet do I wish to say whether *Avant Slant* is good or bad or even successful on its own terms or anyone else's. Its success is entirely beside the point: it doesn't matter whether it is good or bad, whether we like it or understand it, or whether it even means anything to us at all. Of course, its meaning matters to *me*, but that doesn't matter much, either. In itself, the meaning of *Avant Slant* is only for its creator and the small circle of intimates and collaborators who participated in its creation. I have intruded myself into this circle, but my presence is not at all necessary. The public issue of *Avant Slant* was only a secondary aspect, a contingent manifestation, of Brooks's real work: a half-century-long practice of private musical, intellectual, and spiritual work, recorded in a vast series of notebooks. In this way *Avant Slant* is similar to Robert Irwin's late line paintings, whose "achievement . . . was in their making" and each of which can be seen as "an incidental relic, a fossil of that original process of discovery."[8] Lawrence Weschler suggests that such works are hardly works at all but relics of practice, and as such they present a strange and formidable barrier to interpretation: "not only do you have to be present before these paintings in order to experience them, it may be that you have to have made them as well."[9] Practice is a concept familiar to musicians, but one whose homey everydayness obscures its deeper implications. Ultimately, I will suggest, it is a way to step off the devil's staircase of the co-optation thesis and win something of the freedom the countercultural idea has always promised—though it is not quite the same freedom, and it is not won without cost.

Born in 1917, Brooks attended the New England Conservatory for a couple of years, studying piano and taking composition classes. Before a brief and unhappy stint of service in World War II he studied composition with Joseph Schillinger; in 1960, he took classes with John Cage at the New School.[10] In the 1940s he was a composer and arranger for several big jazz orchestras (particularly the Randy Brooks orchestra, of which he was a part-owner) and wrote a few hits.[11] A couple of Brooks's songs have become standards, and the royalties from "You Came a Long Way from St. Louis" alone helped bankroll his later periods of reclusive study. He was a brilliant autodidact and polymath, many of whose best friends were writers: Robert Graves, Harold Courlander, Seymour Krim, and John Clellon Holmes.[12] He knew almost everyone you've ever heard of in the postwar New York jazz scene while remaining relatively unknown himself. Hanging out in Gil Evans's apartment when the "birth of the cool" nonet with Miles Davis was taking shape, making the jazz-and-poetry scene with the Beats in the late 1950s, or sharing the same small corner of New York City with the emerging New York avant-garde in the early 1960s, Brooks had a Zelig-like habit of appearing off in the corner of now-legendary historical tableaux.[13] Don Heckman, who was Brooks's closest friend and collaborator in the early 1960s, recalls that although everyone was awed and intimidated by his intellect, they also found him enigmatic, out-there, a bit crazy. Heckman himself sees Brooks as "a Beat in his own way, but in the richest sense of the word, interested in finding the layers and levels of thinking."[14]

Figure 6.1 Lawrence N. Shustak, photo of John Benson Brooks at the *Alabama Concerto* sessions (1958). Image courtesy of Peggy Brooks.

Brooks created three LPs. The first was *Folk Jazz USA* (1956), which he conceived as the first step in a larger project to adapt folk forms and idioms within modern jazz.[15] The second was *The Alabama Concerto* (1958), which continued this project and is still honored as a small classic of 1950s modernist chamber jazz (Fig. 6.1). But after 1958, Brooks's work took an experimental and inward turn, and little was heard from him for ten years. Then in 1968, an audio collage called *Avant Slant* featuring the John Benson Brooks Trio (with Heckman on alto saxophone and Beat poet Howard Hart on drums) appeared on the Decca label. It made no impact whatsoever and Brooks never released another recording.

Remaindered LPs used to get a hole punched through a corner of their cardboard sleeves, just as the edges of remaindered books get marked with a sharpie; my copy has three holes punched through it, as if some record dealer had tried to drive a stake through its heart, exorcising its failure (Fig. 6.2). When *Avant Slant* came out in September 1968 it got few reviews, and what notices it did get were either respectful or dismissive but in any event puzzled. *Avant Slant* was the overcooked product of ten years' private study and musical experimentation, and there was no public context for it. *Avant Slant* was like an iceberg, the album being a slender visible peak supported by a great hidden bulk of Brooks's studies. In the ten years since *The Alabama Concerto*, Brooks had worked on a number of mostly private projects, two of which—a system of twelve-tone jazz improvisation and a kind of pop-art *musique concrète* he called DJology—formed the basis of *Avant Slant*. John Clellon Holmes did his best to explain the album's complicated gestation in his liner notes, writing that even though it had formed

Figure 6.2 Alex Steinweiss, cover art for *Avant Slant* (Decca, 1968).

out of two incongruous elements, "the same sensibility had shaped them both, and each described, from a different angle, a similar vision of the world."[16] But if this was true, then that vision had remained obscure. If there was a logic by which audio collage fitted together with twelve-tone jazz, it remained a cipher whose key had been lost.

But the best metaphor by which we might understand *Avant Slant* might be one of microcosm and macrocosm. The album stands in relation to its creator as its creator stood in relation to the wider world—the album a miniature picture of the man, the man a picture of the world, man and work both realizations of the axiom of Hermes Trismegistus, the legendary magician of antiquity: "as above, so below." Brooks's restless and relentless studies, recorded in tens of thousands of notebook pages, were Hermetic in both senses of the word. A disciple of Marc Edmund Jones, he was a serious and lifelong student of esoteric knowledge.[17] Withdrawing from social life as much as his successful and outgoing wife would tolerate, he spent up to sixteen hours in his study every day writing, composing, playing piano, practicing divination, working out music-theoretical systems, and reading widely from mathematics, linguistics, philosophy, logic, history, religion, mythology, art theory, media theory, etc. etc., seeing in every branch of human learning the possibility of a new signpost toward a final truth, some all-encompassing system of systems that would at last lay bare the human experience of the universe. He depended on logical procedures ("technics") to control the waywardness of chance and his own imagination, but he never doubted that chance and imagination were the paths to a hidden totality that eluded rational control—"the empire of souls and the empire of stars and spirits" (Nov. 21, 1968).[18] So his work lay in an unstable zone between rationality and mysticism, its ultimate aim the magical one of harmonizing the self and the cosmos. The magician sees the whole universe reflected in each of its parts—as above, so below. To Aleister Crowley, the magician's Great Work lay in overcoming all dualisms and in realizing the macrocosm within his own microcosm, the self raised "in perfect balance to the power of infinity."[19] Marc Edmund Jones, Brooks's teacher, called this the "Immortal Task":

> The universal integrity is knowable, consciously and in its entire or infinite implication, if man will continue to perfect himself sufficiently to become an adequate channel. Hence the initiatory processes are said to lead to ILLUMINATION, available to everyone with the will to make the transcendent state of understanding a personal achievement.[20]

To this end, Jones enjoined each student to "subject himself to a continual self-directed schooling, and to participate in whatever arcane discipline proves best suited to his own private needs."[21] This Brooks did, for half a century. Music in these terms is pure practice without goal or public issue; the Brooks archive is the physical trace of practice, the artifact of a vast project of illumination, a musical and magical Great Work. The songs and albums he composed are valuable in themselves and can be understood by means of the archive, but they are the contingent and limited expressions of his practice. Put another way, the archive does not merely explain Brooks's work; it *was* his work.

Brooks's Great Work grew out of a conviction that there is no such thing as coincidence, so it is probably fitting that my own path to his archive was one of lucky accident. I did not listen to *Avant Slant* because of its composer (I had never heard of him), but because Holmes had written its liner notes and its collage cover art caught my eye.[22] When I put *Avant Slant* on the turntable I was confounded by an assaultive mix of atonal jazz, Tin Pan Alley songs, poems, found sounds, and non sequitur lines read by ham actors; after about four minutes I turned it off and forgot about it. (In this respect my experience was probably fairly typical of those who bought the album in 1968.) A couple of years later, I was doing research at the Institute of Jazz Studies Archive at Rutgers-Newark and, while looking for something else, noticed a large collection of file boxes, one of which was marked "Avant Slant." Opening those boxes and discovering the notebooks, glimpsing the true extent of Brooks's archive, uncovering the entire process by which *Avant Slant* was conceived, nourished, born, and then swiftly killed by near-total indifference and incomprehension—this was the experience of a kind of archival sublime.

In one scene of the documentary *Scratch,* DJ Shadow walks through an enormous basement piled floor to ceiling with hundreds of thousands of old pop records, most of them forgotten:

> Just being in here is a humbling experience to me, because you're looking through all these records, and it's sort of like a big pile of broken dreams in a way. Almost none of these artists still have a career really, so you have to kind of respect that in a way. I mean, if you're making records and if you're a DJ and you're putting out new releases, whether it's mix tapes or whatever, you're sort of adding to this pile, whether you want to admit it or not.... Ten years down the line, you'll be in here. So keep that in mind when you start thinking, like, I'm invincible or I'm the world's best or whatever, because that's what all these cats thought.[23]

This scene shows something familiar to anyone who has spent time in sound archives: the experience of bewildering vastness. Walking through the archive, you might even amplify its immensity, projecting it from the visible bulk of the collection, itself overwhelming, to the far horizon, a vanishing point of near-infinity. What lies behind the manifested archive is an ideal Archive, the imagination of some vast Borgesian library comprising every recording ever made, all the records, CDs, acetates, tapes, cylinders, wire recordings, even home recordings, even recordings for which there are now no surviving copies, all the records you've never heard of and will never hear. Even if you played them all end to end in unbroken succession you could never live enough years to come to the end of it all...before this vastness we might feel an emotion akin to sublimity. As you browse the shelves of this imaginary Archive (or even a real one), you would see a thousand or maybe ten thousand unknown records for every one known, and you might begin to reflect on the processes by which the winners have become familiar to us. You might also reflect on how the losers lost.

A melancholy thought: each record had someone who loved it. Every recording has a story; recordings are snapshots of those stories, of the careers and lives of those who made them, frozen at a particular moment in time. Likewise they preserve the traces of those processes by which they have been remembered or forgotten. The sheer endless profusion of records throws those processes in doubt, suggests they are they merest happenstance, the lucky collision of variables that no person could ever have calculated or controlled. Within the Archive there is not one canon (the Dylans and Coltranes) but an infinity of possible canons. We might imagine that in some alternate universe every one of these unknown records could have been a hit. Every record represents a broken dream; every record also represents an alternate history, perhaps dreamed by the forgotten artist, in which they are the Dylans and Coltranes. And if every record represents a possible history, it also represents a different kind of listening within which it would not only make sense but maybe even become essential.

The reason to contemplate a minor album by a minor composer is not only to imagine such alternative histories and listening practices but thereby to question the history that is not alternative but given—in Deleuze and Guattari's terms, to use a minor language to "send the major language racing."[24] In Branden Joseph's handling of the concept, minor history effects a complex series of negations that displace our understandings of both well-known figures and their seeming opposites within the Archive's "pile of broken dreams." Writing minor history does not mean trying to make the minor figure into a new major one, though this is most often what scholars try to do when they exhume forgotten composers, often deploying what Jeffrey Magee has called the "trope of woeful neglect." At the same time, minor figures are not completely separate from major history; they are not the makers of naïve or outsider art. Minor figures appear in major contexts, though their work is "seemingly too prolix, too heterogeneous, too variable, too undeveloped for major histories to account for."[25] It is possible to assimilate the minor figure such as Brooks to a formation of major history—to think of him as a *kleinmeister* working within a field of midcentury American modernism defined by greater masters—but to do so obscures his real position. Brooks's work and career describes a line that runs at an oblique angle to the axis of major history.

"Minor" does not mean "mediocre." Against the major, the minor "is not the qualitatively or quantitatively inferior, but what is marked by an irreducible or uncontainable difference."[26] Brooks was in many ways a typical figure of midcentury modernism, not only in his use of modernist compositional idioms but also in his sensibility—a fierce and competitive intellectualism, an aspiration to genius and monumental works, and a romanticism about the individual creator who stands in lonely defiance of the mass-cultural tide. But in Brooks this orientation coexists with another one, an interpretive orientation that Christopher Lehrich has called "magical hermeneutics," which does not so much oppose a modernist orientation as lead off in another direction entirely.[27] Brooks's cultivation of magical hermeneutics within the modern gives his work its special character; it is an "irreducible difference" that prevents Brooks from being assimilated into any straightforward narrative of Cold War American modernism. At the same time, magical hermeneutics throws the problems of midcentury modernism into a new light and blurs its seemingly solid, square-shouldered contours.

To be sure, Brooks is hardly the only modernist artist to become interested in magical thought, and anthropologists have lately begun to question the assumption that modernity and magic are intrinsically opposed.[28] But then modernism was never a monolithic entity. Although it came to seem an oppressive cultural dominant during and after the 1960s, within modernism lie zones that simultaneously manifest a straitening cultural logic and the means by which that logic is undone. Sven Spieker has written that modernism is "a set of protocols that govern the production and transmission of culture from a place that is by definition not the place of the subject, not simply *our* place," and he defines the Archive as both the place those protocols take physical form and the point where they are undone.[29] Brooks's vast archival work was a means by which he could return to the place of the subject—or, in Michel Foucault's terms, it is a technology of the self—but one developed within, or around, or somehow through modernism, not simply in opposition to it.[30] The minor modernism that Brooks represents is something like Svetlana Boym's notion of the "off-modern," whose "adverb *off* confuses our sense of direction; it makes us explore sideshadows and back alleys rather than the straight road of progress; it allows us to take a detour from the deterministic narrative of twentieth-century history." *Off-* can mean "'aside' and 'off-stage,' 'extending and branching out from,' 'somewhat crazy and eccentric' (off-kilter), 'absent or away from work or duty,' 'off-key,' 'off-beat,' occasionally off-color but not offcast," any of which descriptions will work equally well for Brooks.[31] Brooks's minor or off-modernism (off-minor modernism?) matters in part because it marks a place within modernism from which we can survey the tensions between abstract logic and concrete experience, thinking and doing, works and practice.

Music of the Isms

This book has told the story of a vernacular sensibility that crystallizes in the early years of the Cold War and takes on something of that era's intellectual coloration: its dislike of the mass, its disaffiliative individualism, its modernist orientation toward intellectual challenge. As that sensibility becomes a mass phenomenon in the 1960s and drives the social changes of the eventful decade, it takes a participatory, populist turn, and its privileged musical form changes from jazz to rock. But this is a formidably abstract way of putting it, writing about such an amorphous entity as a sensibility as if it were a human character, able to change its mind and choose different kinds of music to suit its mood. Brooks's career in the 1960s shows us the large movements of intellectual and cultural history as they play out in the life of an individual. In Brooks we find an arch-modernist of a kind peculiar to the Cold War—someone who blended the hipster's stance of sullen disaffiliation from the cultural mainstream and the *Partisan Review*'s intellectual critique of mass culture and mass society. Yet in *Avant Slant* he envisioned the pop postmodernity that buried his native culture of Cold War modernism, and he tried, with mixed success, to represent it. *Avant Slant* wears the traces of this history like the beatniks of Ed Sanders's funny short story, "The Great Tomkins Park Beatnik-to-Hippie Conversion Ceremony," who retire their corduroy jackets and black sweaters for brocaded shirts and headbands, though not always comfortably.[32]

Avant Slant often gives the impression of a Cold War modernist trying (and failing) to loosen up and adapt to an emerging pop postmodernity, but it is more way-out than its 1968 listeners could have known. Brooks owed the entire project to divinatory magic, especially the *I Ching*, a very old Chinese system of bibliomancy in which the random throw of coins determines one of sixty-four hexagrams and a greater number of commentaries associated with the hexagrams' individual lines. "They [the hexagrams] are first to thank for the unique values of the thing," Brooks wrote (Oct. 13, 1967). Brooks had used other divination systems (especially astrology) in the 1940s and 1950s, but after studying with Cage the *I Ching* became his constant companion. He involved it in almost every aspect of his life, both trivial ("shall I purchase a Geiger counter?") and profound: he credited it with improving relationships with his wife, parents, and children, as well as opening up the experimental path he took after *The Alabama Concerto* (May 22, 1966). Divination was not simply one odd passion among many, but the central axis around which everything else turned—a practice by which Brooks harmonized the many disjunct pieces of his intellectual and creative world, and by which he harmonized his art and study to his life. One particularly clear expression of this practice was what Brooks called "*I Ching* piano": "an archetypal kinesics putting the Y CHING hexagrams on the three phalanges, hands, forearm and upper-arm"—the body mapped into six zones, each one governed by coin throws and constituting one line of a hexagram.[33] In other words, Brooks used his body as a medium for the forces of chance, and for Brooks chance was not random, but an upwelling of meaning from the hidden archetypal world. In this way Brooks aimed to make himself a transducer of cosmic force into sound and motion, inscribing the macrocosm onto his own flesh. William S. Burroughs, a lifelong practitioner of magic, was after something similar in his cut-ups, which were poems made by cutting found texts into strips and shuffling them; as his biographer Ted Morgan writes, Burroughs "came to believe that his accidental combinations of words were prophetic subliminal announcements, coming to him from a collective, extratemporal consciousness."[34]

The *I Ching* was what Brooks called an object-with-saturation-value, an informationally dense system from which a maximum of meaning could be derived.[35] This was very different from the Zen spirit with which Cage incorporated the *I Ching* into compositions such as *Music of Changes* (1951). For Cage, meaning is something we impose on the things of the world, so occluding them. In Cage's aesthetic, when we accept the meaninglessness of the chance event, we can perceive it without the interference of our grasping and tendentious minds and thus open ourselves to an experience of the world in its true suchness. In contrast to Cage, we might paraphrase a line from R. H. Blythe's *Zen in English*

Literature and Oriental Classics and say that for Brooks the fall of the coins is just as weighty a matter as the fall of Adam from Eden. As Blythe notes, this betrays a mysticism that lies close to Zen but is not quite the same thing: "Mysticism sees the infinite meaning in the 'apparently' trivial thing; Zen sees the thing, the fall of Adam, your own fall out the window, *and no more.* True, everything is in the thing, but it is not seen as everything, but as the thing."[36] Though Brooks's study with Cage completely transformed his work, his relationship to the older composer was agonistic, like Jacob wrestling with the angel, and Brooks sometimes grumbled that the Cagean avant-garde's handling of chance was an "empiricist Dadaism" inferior to the "humble & devout & contrite spirituality" that drove him[37] (May 22, 1965). In any event, he believed that chance composers were not really getting random results anyway but were simply ignorant of the metaphysical questions their work opened up. One of his few published articles, which appeared in the Beat little magazine *The Provincetown Review,* makes this point in Brooks's typically elliptical way:

> It seems these cats who figure composers are trespassing gentlemanly limits in using statistical sets for random numbers by which to order their pitches, should relax. That immaculate lady, Pure Chance is not so easily seduced. Quite the contrary it appears that composers along with other types are so loaded with determined characteristics they're lucky to even glimpse her in a dream. It's the mud of it all; the frustrating narrowness of being born an individual; you can't exist except by assuming certain characteristics out of all possible cosmic ones and it's always too late <u>now</u>.[38]

All the same, Brooks had a vexed relationship with chance and magic:

> Around the age of 18 a card reader told me the numbers of a sum on a check I'd receive within 2 weeks. I subsequently received a phone call offer for a job which I performed and received a check with the numbers on it as the card reader predicted—
>
> Since then I've read through, studied & practiced ancient methods of divination, games of chance & esoteric occult philosophies mythologies etc—I found that <u>I can do it too</u>, but also <u>that I don't like to</u> so it remains a skill I've never sharpened…I fear it. (Whatever that means) <u>Dread</u> reveals nothing? It is subtler than any of our sciences and an art of darkness [Dec. 31, 1964].

Clearly he *did* practice divination—almost every notebook entry records this work—but it is also clear that he did not always trust it. After a night of tormenting revelatory dreams, he wrote that that he "Tossed and turned till 7 am wondering about these fortune tellers and dreams in my life and how to pull it to pieces analytically to protect myself" (May 15, 1967). Brooks did work that threatened to dissolve the boundaries of his autonomous self, but having invested much in an autonomous self that applied artistic and intellectual force to the world around it, he did not feel he could give up this kind of control and relied on his analytical intellect to contain what he set loose. And yet for Brooks, revelation—an irruption of meaning from outside the ordinary channels of the rational mind—always remained possible. The contrary pull between occult gnosis and defensive rationalism gives Brooks's work its characteristic tension[39]: "I see no hope whatsoever (save revelation by visitation?) <u>except analytical ability to formalize logic & philosophy & then music, astrology, etc.</u>—**then** a real kind of composition can take place—if & only if (then & only then?)" (July 21, 1966).

As this notebook entry indicates, one of Brooks's goals was to formalize an unshakable foundation for his music, grounded in logic and philosophy. But this is a little too simple, for it suggests that he sought his foundations solely in the latter disciplines, whereas for Brooks the foundation might be found in any discipline, including music itself. Furthermore, the ends of his systematic inquiry were far more ambitious than music alone: he sought to explain his experience of reality—the individual consciousness within which music and everything else manifested—as well as reality itself. Ultimately, what he wanted was to understand the relationship between these two horizons of self and world, microcosm and macrocosm. (It was not for nothing that Gerry Mulligan called him "our dreamer of impossible dreams" and his old bandmates called him "cloud.")[40] And at times Brooks glimpses some startling depth at which even the dualism of self and other dissolves:

> There is no object for existence other than existence itself.
> This implies there are but subjects in existence?
> Identifications, by tooth and horn, lost...
> Transcendence seems <u>to go back to</u> an original being?
> Immanence seems <u>to come up to</u> this derived being? [Sep. 8, 1966]

But at such moments he invariably backs away from whatever place he has found himself and, taking up the weapons of analysis, begins to cut his insights into confetti.

In order to find a final unified theory of everything, Brooks moved restlessly from one intellectual discipline to another. Typically he would discover a book in some new area, buy as many related books as he could, and for a few weeks or months every fresh question or problem would be posed in the terms of the new idea. He would announce a breakthrough, everything explained at last, the corner finally turned. Yet at some point the new intellectual system would fail

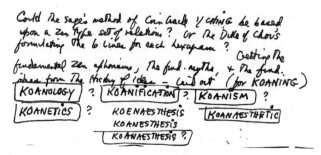

Figure 6.3 John Benson Brooks notebooks, July 3, 1966. Institute of Jazz Studies Archive, Rutgers University, Newark.

him, and he would turn to some other system to supplement the first one, and the process would repeat. With every new intellectual enthusiasm, Brooks would seek a higher synthesis with what had come before, but then the new synthesis would collapse in turn, pulled to pieces by Brooks's relentless combinatorial application of his "technics."

A straightforward example can be found in his notebook entry of July 3, 1966 (Fig. 6.3). Around this time he was reading about Zen Buddhism, and although Zen's radical questioning of language, logic, and the self would always remain a bit alien to him, the possibility that its very radicalism might short-cut to the answer he sought was enough to hook him, at least for a couple of days. He comes up with a relatively simple idea of applying the structure of the *I Ching* to Zen koans. On its own, this would have been an interesting thing to try out. But fastening on the word "koan," he starts appending suffixes to it, every combination generating another technic—koanology, koanetics, koanification, koanism, koanaesthesis—each one graced with a question mark. The question mark was Brooks's favorite mark of punctuation; they fend off closure, and like a dog chasing a car (what would he do if he caught it?) Brooks found fulfillment in the search for a final synthesis, perhaps more than in its reality, which remained elusive in any event.[41] The question mark suspends the hypothetical entities of thought in a half-formed state, pregnant with possibility; every question mark is another road not taken, a path down which Brooks's busy mind might scurry, or not. Meanwhile, the modest and practical idea with which he started is forgotten.

One of the small discoveries to be made in the Brooks notebooks is who had the best pot in New York. (Not surprisingly, it was the Beat writers.) Brooks found marijuana useful, but the characteristic involutional style of marijuana thinking—making links between everything without heed to which links really work—had its drawbacks. In 1958, when he was working on a jazz-and-poetry album he never finished, he wrote that he was giving up pot:

Too goddam many questions—throw em out and work on what will contribute to your [satisfaction] and achievement. But here you're like a horse that looks at several roads & can't choose & go—LP projects, poetry, songs, technics like punctuation—Pot enables you to go but on a wide swathe & there's the risks involved [May 18, 1958].

The resolution did not last; pot was congenial to a temperament that moved in wide swathes anyway. A jazz-and-poetry album could not be finished—indeed, could scarcely be attempted—until he had first built for it a foundation in linguistics...or logic...or linguistics and logic? Linguistics *as* logic? Linguistics and/or logic? Neither linguistics nor logic? Maybe phenomenology? The language of phenomenology? Phenomenological linguistics? This sort of thing will go on for pages, moments of brilliant insight struggling to the surface like a drowning man breaking the water and waving to shore, only to be dragged back under by a riptide of stoned involuted abstraction.

But Brooks was also unsparingly self-critical and self-aware; anything you can say about him he says himself. And he could see that he wasn't getting projects finished:

From math to logic & science to philosophy. Now you're less certain of any philosophies. But somewhat acquainted with the general subject matter, its beginnings & recent developments—re. the latter, the phenomenologist, existentialist thinkers also fail—THEY ALL FAIL, but why? [...] What do humans have that numbers, objects & words lack? [...]
So write music! <u>All representation</u> is false [...] [Feb. 25, 1965].

Yet music alone could never entirely satisfy him either. So finding a system of systems, an -ism to bracket all -isms, was his constant pursuit. And this became the basic idea of *Avant Slant*: finding a musical form to contain all the -isms he had incorporated into himself and making a play of them. But what form could that be? Not the traditional jazz forms, certainly:

The trad. jazz geniuses were mostly caught-up with virtuosi dance & minstrel patterns. As a result the present field is not equipped to sponsor artists involved with the general contemplative verities—their audiences run mostly to the vital dance & popular romance pursuits—so if your friends are Heraclitus, Pythagoras, Lao-tse, Husserl & Merleau Ponty, PD Ouspensky, Harold Courlander, Joseph Schillinger, Marc Jones, John Cage, Dave Lambert, Robert Graves, etc.—Where (how)/ does or can music **settle** over such a set of influence variables? [Jan. 11, 1965].

What was called for was a meta-music, a "jazz on jazz" that would assimilate the cultural items of Brooks's world in the same way that jazz signifies on musical materials.

A year later, the idea crystallized. On January 4, 1966, his mother's medical bills piling up, he starts puzzling out how he might make some money. As his thoughts drift, he thinks of Zen, which he associates with meta-things generally, and this leads him to the thought of a meta-music, music as a play of competing -isms, which leads him to the idea of embodying those -isms in audio clips and making an album out of them. This is what he calls DJology and what we would call sampling.

> The ZEN-ic of MUSIC?
>
> SONGS OF American ZEN? (use their written sayings)
>
> A COLLECTION OF SONGS about adventures with the contemporary ISMS
>
> **From** "SONGS OF THE ISMS"... **MUSIC OF THE ISMS**? American Dada
>
> **Sections** like [Wittgenstein Bible], American Zen, Fact, Indeterminacy, Serialism (German etc) a few songs in each section/ some for choir, solo, with instrumental accompaniment
>
> DJOLOGY as 'pop art'? [Jan. 4, 1966]

The idea of DJology as a "music of the isms" that works as both a self-portrait and a scale model of the cultural macrocosm ("the Cultural Village called Music USA/Western Community") is the fundamental idea behind *Avant Slant*.

DJology

The finished album ended up comprising three streams of music and sound: *The Twelves*, a twenty-minute suite of twelve-tone jazz pieces; six newly composed songs recorded for the album; and the DJology, which in turn is made up of a number of sources. There are sounds and voices taped from TV and radio broadcasts, pieces by other musicians, a conventional jazz piano quartet number by Brooks called "El Bluebirdo," poems read with or without music, and bits of text read by actors—short exchanges or single lines of dialogue, some of them impersonations of celebrities. David Toop, the only major critic to have taken *Avant Slant* seriously, writes that Brooks's DJology was prophetic, and perhaps it was more prophetic than Toop knew.[42] Brooks imagined not only creating his own album of sampled cultural associations but also the possibility that such sampling might become the basis of a new art form practiced by a nation of enthusiastic amateurs equipped with nothing more than a turntable, a recorder, and a good collection of records—"The vision of a nation of DJs each with a pop-art style of their own"[43] (Jan. 5, 1966).

The only major ingredient of the finished album missing from the January 4 notebook entry is *The Twelves*, which Brooks, Heckman, and Hart had performed and recorded in 1962. From 1958 to 1962, Brooks and his collaborators worked on his system of twelve-tone jazz improvisation. Gunther Schuller told Brooks that twelve-tone improvisation was impossible; when Brooks proved him wrong, Schuller made room for the Brooks Trio to appear in the International Jazz Festival in Washington, D.C., sandwiched between Sonny Rollins and Duke Ellington.

Brooks had spent four years to get twenty minutes of tape, a typical rate of return for Brooks's investment of time in his projects, but soon found he couldn't get anyone interested in releasing it. While working on *Avant Slant* he considered a number of theories of what cutting up *The Twelves* and splicing in unrelated sound clips might mean—what goes through the artist's mind as he improvises, the artist contending with what everyday life presents to him, or the art of jazz competing with everything else in Music USA—but more pragmatically it was one way to get *The Twelves* heard. His plan backfired, though: those who supported his experimental jazz work thought that *Avant Slant's* pop-culture DJology put *The Twelves* in low company. Martin Williams called the album's DJology "stilted unfunny verbal gaggery"; Gil Evans called it "entertainment," which for Brooks may have been even more wounding.[44]

Brooks knew that such reactions were predictable: this was the moment where jazz intellectuals could feel themselves being shoved aside by a new pop culture that did not share their modernist values. At the same time, Brooks could not bring himself to admit something about what came to be called postmodernism that the old guard of jazz modernists saw clearly: when you throw items from art and pop registers together in a collage, no privilege will attach to any of them. Brooks's insight was that camp issued from the collision of -isms—clashing and unintegrated worldviews from which every other would appear in the light of irony, diminished and absurd. But he held out the hope that somehow *The Twelves* would remain the authoritative voice in his virtual cultural village. This hope was a product of Brooks's belief in the power of the autonomous artist to determine meaning in the exchange between music and listeners—a bit of Cold War modernism that consorted strangely with the proto-postmodernism he was envisioning in *Avant Slant*.

In truth, Brooks did worry that he was selling out *The Twelves*; intercutting it with other things was mostly Milt Gabler's idea. I have been writing of *Avant Slant* as if Brooks were its sole creator, but actually this album was a collaboration between Brooks and Gabler, a legendary producer who was an A & R executive at Decca, the company that released *Avant Slant*.[45] Gabler's work on the album went well beyond executive oversight. He found most of the album's samples, wrote lyrics for five of its six new songs (the sixth, the beautiful "Mend Them Fences," featured a lyric by Robert Graves) and did most of the sequencing of the record's many parts.[46] The weakest aspect of the album—the quick lines and snatches of dialogue read by actors, camping shamelessly—was also Gabler's idea. From the beginning the problem was how to manage the cost of licensing all the audio clips Brooks wanted. Gabler kept costs down by re-recording all the clips they didn't want to pay for. Brooks's original concept of DJology was rather different, though.

For years Brooks had been fascinated by the possibilities of using the tape recorder as a musical instrument. He recalled first using a wire recorder in the late 1940s to capture moments that seemed like "emblems" of favorite jazz recordings and stringing them together with environmental sounds, which he treated as emblems of a wider experience. He writes that he didn't have a name for this kind of art until 1958, when he discovered Pierre Henry and learned it was called *musique concrète*. After studying with Cage, Brooks combined his old interest in *musique concrète* with chance procedures. He composed *Bird Meets Cage*, for which he made two tapes: one with clips of himself and Heckman playing atonal jazz duets and the other with clips from electronic music LPs he owned. Each tape had its own playback machine, and there was a third machine for recording. Brooks then created a deck of cards and lay out a spread.[47] Each card had an instruction for manipulating one or both of the playback machines, and the third machine recorded the subsequent performance. A few years later Brooks made a tape he called DJology as a Christmas present for Heckman and George Russell. This was the tape Brooks used as a demo when he first began approaching producers with the idea for the album that would become *Avant Slant*.

Brooks's homemade *musique concrète* sounds exactly like what it is: someone trying to do in his living room what composers were doing in the big state-subsidized electronic music studios of New York and Paris. The tapes are audibly homemade, with razored-out pieces of tape shouldering one another awkwardly; the sounds are minimally altered and placed in a series rather than layered. You might think that when Brooks later had Decca's resources at his disposal he would have taken the opportunity to do something more sophisticated, but as one recent critic points out the finished album suffers from the same limitation: "Despite four engineers and Gabler's editing supervision, the treatment of the material is often simply linear and consecutive. It never interacts, the way it might have if it were layered, but then again, the sequential presentation leaves [*The Twelves*] virtually intact."[48]

We might compare *Avant Slant* to the Columbia LP of *The Medium Is the Massage*, a pop-art audio collage version of Marshall McLuhan's most popular book. Brooks was annoyed when it appeared a year before his own album:

McLuhan's "The Medium is the Massage" on Col[umbia] LP—not bad, but not very good either. Music, comedy, electr. sounds, poetry, lecture on the age & history of the Mediums of communication—he beat us to the post though! Pain in the ass—(They'll now say I took his idea!) [July 13, 1967].

The McLuhan LP has many of the same kinds of sounds as *Avant Slant* and tiles them together in random-sounding arrangements. It even has a kind of conceptual *basso continuo*: recordings of McLuhan speaking the text aloud, which, like *The Twelves* in *Avant Slant,* provides a constant point of reference. But in contrast to *Avant Slant, The Medium Is the Massage* layers its audio elements much more densely, distorts its sounds, and foregrounds the materiality of its recording media. And the strata of sounds transform at different times and rates, avoiding the lockstep feeling of *Avant Slant,* which was easily mapped as a series of discrete segments in the producer's script (see Fig. 6.4)

John Simon, the producer of *The Medium Is the Massage,* clearly wanted his record to represent the subjective experience of human beings in the media age that McLuhan envisioned—a total immersion in discontinuous, simultaneous, and rapidly changing multisensory inputs. In this respect, Simon's and Brooks's albums overlapped. Multimedia collage was the style of the time; as Brooks wrote, people wanted "multi-media representation to describe their subjectivity" (May 4, 1967). In his discussion of *Avant Slant,* Toop notes how widespread mass-media collage was in the 1960s:

> The influence of mass media was affecting all innovative artists of the period, and comparisons could be made with the assemblages, prints, sculptures, films and paintings of Robert Rauschenberg, Jasper Johns, Richard Hamilton, Jeff Keen and Eduardo Paolozzi, or film maker Kenneth Anger's strategic use of pop songs in *Scorpio Rising.* Since the advent of radio, music could always be heard in contiguous sequences, interspersed with chatter—inane, informative or inspired—of the disc jockey, so the accepted presence and mediation of the voice adds a specific history to audio cut-ups and break-ins.[49]

Life itself seemed saturated in randomness and discontinuity; the representational paradigm for a subjectivity thus saturated was the radio or TV, channels constantly changing. Spin the dial and get a bit of a song, a bit of laughter, a senseless fragment of a sentence spoken angrily, a man swimming, something blowing up. This was realism for a new televisual age. The interweaving of sounds could represent traces from the trajectories of different lives, or the sum of such mediated traces experienced within a life, and this could be a powerful way to represent postmodern life itself.

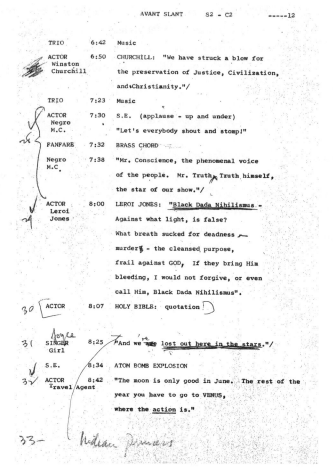

Figure 6.4 Producer's script for *Avant Slant*, end of side 2. Institute of Jazz Studies Archive, Rutgers University, Newark.

McLuhan excited and unsettled Brooks. He knew McLuhan was onto something that everyone else had missed, and the notion that "the content or message of any particular medium has about as much importance as the stenciling on the casing of an atomic bomb" satisfied his yearning for insights radical enough to knock the pins out from under all previous interpretations.[50] But the same idea went against Brooks's conviction that the artist is the guarantor of meaning. Brooks could never assent to the random semiosis that McLuhan's theories seemed to imply—that whatever a composer might intend would become just another blip in a high-velocity barrage of audiovisual information whose shape no one could intend or control.

For McLuhan, the new media age was doing away with linear sequence; for Brooks, meaning depended on linear sequence. Brooks's hope of reserving a place of cultural authority for *The Twelves* within his DJology was anchored in the hope that "the meaning of any clip can be discovered if you check its possible relations"—meaning logical relations that could be stated in operators (not, and, or) between items in sequence. Brooks tried fitfully to create a language of clip relations that could amount to a formal syntax, so that the relations between, say, a clip of Kirsten Flagstad followed by a clip of Louis Armstrong would have a definite, semiotic meaning to an audience, which the composer could manipulate in the same rational way as a series of tonal chords. He had trouble imagining how to map simultaneous relations, so he didn't bother with them much. Linear relations, on the other hand, could allow one to "travel" from one frame of reference to another, and this analog to real-world processes might offer a basis for a meaningful technic of sound juxtaposition. Early on he imagined his as-yet unrealized album as a narrative of literal travel, or in other narrative ways, for example as an "LP pop opera" with Louis Armstrong as father, Kirsten Flagstad as mother, Ray Charles as son, and so on.[51] But in the end he never found a single consistent technic for ordering his clips.

Cipher

All the same, the finished work retains Brooks's fundamental orientation toward linear sequencing. Brooks intended specific meanings in the serial juxtaposition of *Avant Slant*'s audio elements, and even though he failed in his ambition to create a language of clip relations by which those intentions could be shared with an audience, some meanings are still recoverable through study of Brooks's archive, which provides the missing key to what ended up a private cipher. Consider the first six things we hear on the album—the first half-minute of *The Twelves,* followed by the first song, "Gods On High," which segues without pause into another song, "Pie in the Sky." Then we hear the sound of a rocket, another thirty-eight seconds of *The Twelves,* and then an actress (Joyce Todd) mimicking a child whining "Mommy, mommy, can I have a drink of water?" accompanied by Webernian string quartet music. However random this sounds, there are specific reasons behind this particular sequence of audio elements, and a network of connections that binds them together.

The Twelves, which applied serial procedures to improvisation, was naturally a skein of motivic interconnections. For example, after all three musicians play an opening fanfare, Brooks plays a seven-note segment (A#–B–D#–F#–G#–C#–G) that generates many subsequent details. Now, Brooks worked out a system whereby his musicians could jump from any segment of the row to any other.[52] This allows them to use parts of the row to generate motivic units and chords that can retain modal jazz connotations while functioning in a nontonal environment. The first four notes of the seven-tone segment (itself a part of a larger twelve-note row) can be understood, in tonal terms, as a B major triad inflected by a leading-tone, or an arpeggiated Bmaj[7] chord; the D$^#$–F$^#$–G$^#$ trichord can be mapped onto the pentatonic blues scale and used to articulate a motion toward a local tonic by way of the flattened seventh scale degree; the F$^#$–G$^#$–C$^#$–G segment could sound like something in F sharp offset by a boppish downward tritone flip. These and other motivic units reappear throughout *The Twelves*, of course, but some of them also appear in the new songs that Brooks wrote with Gabler.

From early on, Brooks envisioned writing a song that would appear at the beginning of the album and frame everything that followed—a song that would establish a god's-eye view of the doings of those who populated his "Cultural Village USA." As we have seen, Brooks conceived *Avant Slant* as a way of establishing an encompassing perspective on his various musical and intellectual influences, and in any event his cognitive style was geared toward solving a given problem by viewing it from a position of greater abstraction. His habitual style of interacting with the world was one of irony, in the sense of Kenneth Burke's "perspective of perspectives." Even in social life (which he mostly felt to be a burden and a chore) he habitually retreated to metaperspectives as a kind of self-defense: "Since it becomes necessary to be with people more you must be able to exercise sufficient control of their language implications by your metalanguage" (Dec. 17, 1965). When he first conceived the idea for *Avant Slant*, Brooks was reading Edward T. Hall's *The Silent Language* and was impressed by Hall's idea of "culture as communication," which allowed him an analytical perspective on his own culture, but from the high and removed vantage point he sought.[53] Just as the hipster's perspective is *in* but not *of* his society, Brooks sought to see the workings of his culture as if through binoculars, his perspective disembedded from the objects of his scrutiny. In Brooks's thought, though, this by-now-familiar schema of asymmetrical consciousness is placed in an occult register: "Culture as communication expresses the will of the gods. 'That' lives in a constellation, solar system (of planets) & earth place but appears/exercises itself in the primary message systems of cultural life. To use the will of the gods? To play along—man's existence" (Jan. 18, 1966).

This passage betrays the occultist conviction that cosmic forces beyond human perception and understanding manifest themselves in human lives— as above, so below. Brooks suggests that Hall's matrix of cultural communication is the medium within which these forces manifest. "Man's existence" is a process of playing the game that the gods have imposed on him. One has no choice but to play along, and most of the time one has no idea one is playing a game, either. But the occultist, like the hipster, knows the game for what it is, accepts its terms, and finds liberation in his secret knowledge. The artist, inspired by this knowledge, harnesses the hidden forces ("to use the will of the gods") and makes them the materials of his art. Brooks eventually lost interest in Hall, but he held on to the idea that *Avant Slant* would picture culture as a totality and would open with a song that establishes the lofty vantage point from which the follies and compulsions of its inhabitants would appear *sub specie aeternitatis.*

Gabler responded by writing the lyric for "Gods on High," in which indifferent gods idly play with the fortunes of human beings. For the music, Gabler wanted a "Rodgers or Kern style" while Brooks wanted something twelve-tone (May 22, 1967). Brooks compromised: the finished song is tonal (though harmonically complicated) until the end, where the singer (Judy Scott) sings an unaccompanied atonal line that suggests that the "gods" may be only a computer. This line is a transposition of the seven-note row segment that Brooks plays at the opening of *The Twelves.* Less obviously, an earlier, tonal part of the song recontextualizes the same sequence of pitches: it was doubtless one of Brooks's private jokes that the row, an absent presence that acts on music in much the same way that gods are envisioned acting on human beings, should manifest itself at Gabler's line "they set the rules for men and then you'lls [*you alls*]." Brooks was proud of his ability to weave twelve-tone materials into something resembling a Tin Pan Alley framework and celebrated his accomplishment with another private joke, this one at Gabler's expense: fuming about having to compromise his idea of a twelve-tone song, he positioned a "laugh-in-the-music by interpolating a hymn cadence on the line 'and if you don't play the game their way, then you don't play at all'" (May 27, 1967).

Once "Gods on High" has established a metaperspective from which human beings appear small and deluded, "Pie in the Sky" mocks their pitiable goals and desires. "Pie in the Sky" represents Brooks's attempt to write a song in the rock idiom; with his typical thoroughness, he carefully researched hippie youth culture, listening to dozens of rock albums and subscribing to the *Underground Digest,* a periodical compilation of articles from the underground press. Brooks, then about fifty years old, viewed the new counterculture sympathetically and a little enviously, though from a distance: in a letter to Gabler, he describes an essay on Drop City's postscarcity utopianism and analyzes its writing style, confessing "It's terrible man; youth has it (how long since I wrote a song with that full open vonce?)."[54] And yet, even though "Pie in the Sky" was idiomatically performed by a decent rock band that Decca had recently signed, the song itself sounds very much like the work of a middle-aged composer who believed he could write a rock song by analyzing its musical idiom and deducing its cultural assumptions.[55] Gabler's lyrics did the song no favors, sounding less like an Olympian meditation on human vanity than a Nixon voter's grouse about lazy, feckless hippies, and in idioms that would have sounded corny in *West Side Story.* The lyric lurches into an ostentatiously hippified last line that sounds both like a non sequitur and a pandering bid for the hoped-for "love generation" audience:

Pie in the sky
Is what most men dream of
A handout for putting their foot in the ring
Step over the line knock the chip from my shoulder
Don't touch me or you'll dirty my glove
The shortest distance between two points of view is love.

The song itself is a rock waltz with country vocal harmonizing—Brooks called it a "hillbilly waltz"—which even he suspected was not quite what the kids were into in 1968 but which he wanted for the album anyway, for complicated reasons. He had been listening carefully to *Rubber Soul, Revolver,* and *Sgt. Pepper* and was particularly struck by the Beatles' use of music-hall style. In glum moments, Brooks felt oppressed by a spirit of one-upping criticism that could be visited on anyone naïvely trying to accomplish some large goal for idealistic reasons. (At one point he compared his attempts to sell *The Twelves* to the white activists who had been expelled from SNCC.) Anyone could be put down: black activists put down white activists, jazz musicians put one another down, rock musicians put jazz down, and even rock bands were being put down by hippies. Was no one safe? As always, Brooks sought a permanent higher ground, and he believed that the Beatles had found it: "The only ploy is a Beatles music-hall approach—broad pop song with rhythm a part only—and not a major part in the production" (July 31, 1967). The Beatles' strategic deployment of knowing corniness, corniness that advertises its own ironies without assuming any set and definable point of view on them, defuses any possible objection that the music is, in fact, corny.[56] Brooks's "hillbilly waltz" was an attempt to do the same thing.

The "drink of water" bit that breaks up the following excerpt of *The Twelves* is set to a registrally disjunct, Webernian R-5 version of the same seven-note segment that has already appeared in several guises. As for what the point might have been in having this music accompany the voice of a small child calling for a drink of water, one can only speculate, but this was one of the bits Brooks wrote for the album, and given his annoyance at how his own children's demands had distracted him from his studies in earlier years, it seems possible that a whining child was meant to symbolize one of the things the artist (himself symbolized by *The Twelves*) was forced to put up with. Brooks had two daughters by his first wife and later looked back on his life as paterfamilias with a shudder of horror:

That fathers should do things with mother & children for "fun & togetherness" is strictly from Dagwood & the propaganda of feminists and Lesbian school teachers....I almost was "drowned" in the social quicksands of 20th century USA by ignorant if well-meaning parents, teachers, etc.... This hedonistic mass of ignoramuses & half-baked assortment of idea-men with their sub-esthetic sensibilities was almost enough to ruin me [May 14, 1958].

At times, Brooks's self-image was that of the critical outsider whose mind and sensibilities occupied a plane higher than that of the dullards around him—a self-image cultivated equally in the circles of hip culture and mandarin high modernism, with which Brooks identified in equal measure. This pose can be theatrically misogynistic, enacting the drama of the misunderstood hipster/artist as a spectacle of domestic misery, with the demands of family standing in for the oppression and incomprehension of the square world at large. Brooks's knowing deployment of yet another row permutation at this point would seem to enact this self-understanding: the row does its work unheeded by both whining child and album-buying public alike, its creator "working like Noah to build a boat nobody could care less about" and secretly gratifying himself with the knowledge that he, at least, is hip (Sep. 8, 1966).

Now consider the end of the album: an actor reads a quotation from Thomas Jefferson ("The tree of liberty must be refreshed from time to time with the blood of patriots and tyrants") accompanied by Brooks's string quartet arrangement of "America," and then we hear the Brooks trio playing the end of *The Twelves* and a showbiz MC introducing LeRoi Jones's poem "Black Dada Nihilismus." With the frenzied end of *The Twelves*, the twin stabs of massed brass that set off the MC's introduction, and the impressive *basso profundo* of the actor reading the first few lines of Jones's poem (far more impressive than Jones's own reedy tenor, heard on his recording with the New York Art Quartet), "Black Dada Nihilismus" sounds a rare note of gravity. After all the goofing around that has come before, *this* feels like the culmination of something; *this* feels serious. It sounds like the end, but is not: immediately after "Black Dada Nihilismus," we hear a drawn-out and wide-spaced dissonant string quartet chord, followed by Joyce Todd intoning "then this beautiful Indian princess comes out and says [in cigar-store Indian voice, with added reverb] 'we no lost, Big Dipper lost.'" Then we hear the sound of an atom bomb explosion, and then the smarmy voice of a travel agent saying "the moon is only good in June. The rest of the year, you have to go to Venus, where the action is." And that's it—record over.

What could anyone possibly have made of this? This deflated finale sounds aggressively, annoyingly random, like the frugging Indian paratroopers at the end of *Casino Royale* (1967), the sort of thing that led an apoplectic *Coda* reviewer to call *Avant Slant*'s DJology "ultra-hip, pretentious, money-grubbing, and several other things the editor would not be allowed to print."[57] (Clearly the reviewer did not mean "ultra-hip" in a good way.) But again, Brooks had his reasons.

"Black Dada Nihilismus" marked Jones's shift to an increasingly militant stance in his writing.[58] It was taken as a fantasy of bloody vengeance against the white race and in retrospect can be seen as the cultural expression of an emerging black nationalism. It also strikes an oddly magical tone: the name of Hermes Trismegistus glitters out of its verbal shards, and the poem concludes with the invocation of a Voodoo *loa*: "may a lost god damballah, rest or save us / against the murders we intend / against his lost white children / black dada nihilismus."[59] Brooks thought this was "poisonous rot" when he first heard Jones's recording, and from the moment he began planning *Avant Slant* he plotted how to deflate the poem through camp juxtaposition (Sep. 14, 1965). But at the same time he believed that its cruelty was in some way necessary, that local injustices done to whites were needed to establish a larger pattern of justice within the United States:

> For the White Americans [Black Power] is a necessary good; though killings and trouble are evil, if white America doesn't face up to its obligations historically it seems to me they deserve to be pressured—i.e.: for the sake of **America as a whole**...Personally I can't stand Leroy [sic] Jones any more than I can stand the average white racist but this is a phenomenon larger than personal, it is social on an international scale [July 24, 1966].

Brooks's interpretation of "Black Dada Nihilismus" had the same dialectical double thrust as Jefferson's "tree of liberty" remark, and the clip in *Avant Slant*—both Jefferson's words and their accompaniment—functions as a proleptic ironic gloss on the fragment of "Black Dada Nihilismus" that appears a minute later. So there is a connection between the "tree of liberty" and "Black Dada Nihilismus" clips—a specific connection that lay in Brooks's own mind and that is recoverable through examination of his archive. And perhaps a more low-res connection could have been forged in a casual listener's mind as well. Someone buying *Avant Slant* in 1968 might at least have understood that both clips were in some way political, that they had something to do with the revolutionary mood of the times—an interpretation that would have been strengthened by the preceding clips of machine gun fire, George Wallace, and protesters intoning "We Shall Overcome" and "Black Power!" But a record buyer might still have been left wondering what this political context could have to do with the album's concluding reference to interplanetary travel.

Avant Slant's running theme of extraterrestrial travel appears to have come from Brooks's belief, common to Theosophists and other esoteric groups, that humans are approaching a point in their evolution where they will leave the planet and take their place in the stars.[60] So at the end of this album political and occult subtexts come together, a cosmic solution for political crisis, or crisis the necessary stage prior to specieswide initiation. The magical undertone of "Black Dada Nihilismus" itself suggests the connection, and in any event something of the same sort of idea was latent in the pop millenarianism of the "age of Aquarius."[61] But if this connection between occult and political contexts was something that Brooks shared with the late-1960s counterculture, Brooks's way of making this connection was typically oblique and left too many links hidden.

This is the main problem with *Avant Slant*. Without knowing Brooks's own intricate theories and personal history, listeners will likely understand little of this. The relationships between the clips that constitute Brooks's DJology, between the DJology and Brooks's own life, between the musical style of the songs and late-1960s culture, between Brooks and the wider world—the harmonizing of microcosm and macrocosm that Brooks worked out so carefully over two and a half years—are intentions without a matching horizon of intersubjective meaning. Brooks intended his hillbilly waltz to be a complicated ironic bracketing of corniness, but if you don't know his culture-critical intentions, it just sounds corny. At about the same time, Frank Zappa was playing similar games of Brechtian alienation with American pop styles in songs like "Bow Tie Daddy" and "Fountain of Love," but Zappa had a caustic celebrity persona, and anyone following the rock press could scarcely have mistaken his intentions. Likewise, Brooks's uses of hidden tone-row segments were not particularly novel; any art-music composer at that time might have done the same. But composers in the Western art music tradition are supported by the institutional and social norms of that tradition. A new serialist work would be accompanied by a published score, and the score would be available to those interested in understanding it. A composer's manipulations of the row might be difficult to hear, but, given a trip to the university music library, relatively easy to figure out. And from a certain point of view, figuring them out is the point of the exercise: Carolyn Abbate has argued that music functions in academia as a set of puzzles whose expressive end is a "cryptographic sublime."[62] In short, the aesthetics of serial music assumed a certain set of institutional arrangements. Brooks tried to write the same kind of music without their support, so what would have been an ordinary array of meanings within the institutions of art music were, on a pop record, marooned without any hope of rescue.

To some extent, Brooks's difficulty in communicating his vision is the characteristic problem of modernism. A wholly autonomous, artist-created system of meaning excludes audiences from the process by which it is made, and this in turn excludes the audience from meaning itself—unless, of course, a key is available. A score is one kind of key; celebrity is another. The point of *The Medium Is the Massage* could have been grasped by anyone who had read McLuhan, which in the late 1960s meant almost everyone. To grasp the point of *Avant Slant* would have meant living in Brooks's head and working through the maze of personal associations for which these clips stood as tokens. And it never occurred to Brooks that this could be a problem.

Magical Hermeneutics

Soon after their first meeting, Brooks recalled that Gabler had asked him to think of the album as "an experience of my musical self" (May 22, 1966). What Gabler meant by a "musical self" was probably the sum of all the ways in which Brooks had intersected with the public history of postwar music: swing and Tin Pan Alley, bebop, the folk music revival, Third Stream, serialism, free jazz, chance music, and now pop art. This way, Brooks could be positioned as an artist worth hearing, a major though unaccountably neglected talent whose full dimensions Decca could at last reveal to the public, just as Atlantic had rolled out Ornette Coleman. (Decca certainly took Brooks seriously: they gave him a $5,000 advance, which would be about $37,000 in 2013.[63]) Brooks's reaction to Gabler's pitch is telling, though. He didn't think of this album as a bid for a place in history; rather, his instinct was to go inward, to take "an experience of my musical self" literally and start taping all the sounds of his immediate environment, like the garbage truck he heard every week from his Greenwich Village townhouse.

This was not what Gabler had in mind. From a marketing point of view it would have been useful for Brooks to fashion a unified identity for his music to go with a readily comprehensible artistic persona, some -ism that Brooks could embody. But for Brooks, identity was an -ism of -isms, the self he carefully built, day by day, out of the materials of his Great Work, and his experience of his self, musical or otherwise, was irreducibly plural and ever-changing. Decca wanted to establish Brooks as an artist worth hearing, and if I were to resort to the trope of woeful neglect I should do something similar and argue that Brooks deserves the place of honor reserved for better-known creators such as Milton Babbitt and Coleman. But Brooks is stubbornly hard to assimilate to the major narratives of history that we might want to claim for him. To Brooks, what made someone worth hearing was the shape of his or her whole life, as an exchange from an interview with Julian Barber suggests:

JB: Is there anything really new, or do we just give it a different label, a different name?

JBB: Let's say that we're new, every minute.

JB: [long pause] Well your music, your sounds, reflect that. What would you call your sound if you had to give a one-syllable name? It's not scat, it's not bop...what is it?

JBB: [laughing] Boy, if I, if I could be able to answer that one I should win a big prize!

When Barber asks if anything is really new, he means to challenge the typical warrant for modernist experimentalism: that for something to be valuable it must make a claim of significant newness. But Brooks simply sidesteps that assumption. He cared much less that his art was new, and would be understood as such by a public, than that he himself was new, that *we* are new, every minute, and that each of us can use art to experience our newness or evolution or—to use a word that Brooks favored—*initiation* from moment to moment. Brooks was not completely indifferent to the modernist "rush to the patent office," but what made art important to him was ultimately spiritual.[64] *Avant Slant,* and the vast archive out of which it emerges, is an art with no audience, but only initiates.

To think of art as initiation is to think magically. In the narrow sense, the word *initiation* refers to the grades of attainment that the adepts of occult or esoteric orders must earn. In a larger sense, though, it is the process by which initiates are progressively enriched by the "arcane unfoldment" of the meaning they seek.[65] Occultists have almost always believed that there is some master meaning to be sought, some final, eternal, and universal truth that is the goal and fulfillment of all the contingent meanings that unfold in their experience.[66] The medium through which meaning manifests is the entire phenomenal world, even as the meaning itself pertains to both the phenomenal world and an absolute world that both includes and transcends it. For example, in Aleister Crowley's system, initiates must "cross the abyss" between phenomenal and absolute realms and for this purpose vow, "I will interpret every phenomenon as a particular dealing of God with my soul."[67] To initiates, the meanings that result from taking this vow are infinitely variable and contingent on their own private experience, even though the abyss, and the Absolute that lies beyond it, is not. A high initiate could then see something as insignificant as a garden slug and ask, "What is the purpose of this message from the Unseen? How shall I interpret this Word of God Most High?"[68] The experience of daily life is thus endowed with an ineffable private significance that points toward a more general and symbolized meaning shared within an esoteric group or tradition.

Charging everyday things with occult significance is universal within esoteric and magical practice: as Marc Edmund Jones writes, "No assurance of truth is ever possible without a definite present experience of the reality in which it is grounded, and so all arcane instruction is directed to the discovery and validation of the real in a very personal fashion."[69] Crowley's insistence on treating the entire phenomenal universe as the stage for revelation is not peculiar to his system but is basic to what Susan Greenwood calls "magical consciousness."[70] Other twentieth-century occultists have developed their own versions of this style of thought. The science fiction novelist Robert Anton Wilson attributed to Crowley his own belief that "beyond a certain point, the whole Universe becomes a continuous Initiation."[71] The English magician and theorist Ramsey Dukes considers magic a mode of thought whose most characteristic method is to treat all phenomena as conscious entities.[72] Jason Louv, a younger American occultist, has defined magic as "a way of living that involves interacting with the universe *as if it were alive and intelligent*."[73] Though Brooks was unconnected to these figures, his own practice was conducted in the same spirit: not only books, music, and the *I Ching* allowed the Unseen to manifest, but potentially every person and thing he encountered. In his *Provincetown Review* essay, he defended chance composers (i.e., himself) from the charge of nihilism by arguing that such "nihilists" are the ones who find the most meaning in the world:

> At most, nihilism asserts accident. But nihilists (and atheists) are more religious than many churchgoers, for to divine accident is to put it to work in a way which inescapably, one's own. They use The Unborn which is assumed as not yet become, not created, nor formed. Any choice of an-object-with-saturation-value becomes then a <u>way</u>, and since the faith of the individual is his way, how else to proceed? (man just give me something I dig, an object-with-saturation-value like the mating rates of salmon, unemployment statistics, economic resource percentages, horoscopes, rorschacts [sic], cards, dice, chapter numbers from the Bible, Y King, or girls I didn't dare kiss and I'll convert em to my own sounds-noise version of Finnegan's Worth!)[74]

An interpreter can use any object-with-saturation-value to generate meaning, and it becomes a *way* when the meanings attain a certain density and cohere into a pattern, a feeling of where to take the next step, an orientation of the self in space and time such that every moment is imbued with a feeling of direction and significance that welds past, present, and future together into a single structure.[75] The occult experience of truth is a feeling that disparate things and events fit together by means of a vast acausal and nonlinear network of relationships; the words "fate," "prophecy," and "revelation" all pertain to this feeling. *Faith* in Brooks's sense is the enabling assumption that meaning hides in everything that presents itself to the senses. With one's interpretive faculties primed by this faith, one goes forward with an eye for correspondences and portents, small coincidences and larger patterns. William S. Burroughs describes how writers can use this interpretive orientation to create and inhabit a magical reality:

> Writers operate in the magical universe and you will find the magical law that like attracts like often provides a key note. The sinister clown in *Death in Venice*. The stories of John Cheever abound in such warnings of misfortune and death ignored by his compulsively extroverted and spiritually underprivileged Wasps.
>
> I gave my writing students various exercises designed to show how one incident produces a similar incident or encounter. You can call this process synchronicity and you can observe it in action.

Take a walk around the block. Come back and write down precisely what happened with particular attention to what you were thinking when you noticed a street sign, a passing car or stranger or whatever caught your attention. You will observe that what you were thinking just *before* you saw the sign relates to the sign. The sign may even complete a sentence in your mind. You are getting messages. Everything is talking to you. You start seeing the same person over and over. Are you being followed? At this point some students become paranoid. I tell them that of course they are getting messages. Your surroundings are *your* surroundings. They relate to *you*.[76]

As this passage suggests, magical thought relies on pattern recognition. *I Ching* divination obviously does, but any other practice of magical interpretation could serve equally well as an example. Christopher Lehrich notes how the practice of descrying ley lines—straight tracks or "lines of force" that are said to connect ancient monuments—are the product of ley hunters' ability to find patterns within the myriad data points generated by a cluttered landscape. In ley hunting as in divination, though, it is difficult to argue that these patterns are really there, instead of being mere statistical apparitions of an information-ally dense field.[77] For professional archeologists, ley lines do not have a verifi-able and independent existence in the world but exist only for the ley hunters themselves. A skeptic, standing outside the interpretive practice in which ley hunters participate, might say that they have not found any meaningful pattern, but only what seems to be such. An occultist, however, might retort that "there is no 'seems' in an experience, paranormal or otherwise. I can only experience seeing a ghost; I can't experience 'seeming' to see one."[78] It is the ley hunters' experience that they have found ley lines, and it is that experience that vouch-safes their reality. If your commitment to your own experience of reality lies prior to any commitment to intersubjective reality, then the matter of what is "really" true is beside the point. Reality is no longer singular, but plural, and the job of magical consciousness is to investigate an immediate and experienced reality, not an abstract, objective, and transcendental one.[79] To say that a ley line is "really" there is to speculate about something that lies beyond the physical and temporal horizon of immediate experience. The magical, "neo-medieval" conception of reality that Norman Mailer claimed for the hipster is unmoved by this "really":

...it is as if the universe which has usually existed conceptually as a Fact...which it was the aim of all science and philosophy to reveal, becomes instead a changing reality whose laws are remade at each instant by everything living, but most particularly man, man raised to a neo-medieval summit where the truth is not what one has felt yesterday or what one expects to feel tomorrow but rather truth is no more nor less than what one feels at each instant in the perpetual climax of the present.[80]

I have argued elsewhere that exotica pop demands a controlled credulity, in which listeners permit themselves to believe seemingly ridiculous or impossible things by living out their belief; acting on a belief makes it true at the moment of the action and places one's unbelief in a kind of blind trust.[81] The same mental operations of managing belief and unbelief are essential for those who would seek to cultivate magical consciousness in the modern West and against the overwhelmingly pervasive background assumptions of scientific rationalism. Such operations allow a modern-day magician to believe that a magical act has the same meaning as its intended result: "the act is the experience of the belief. The act makes the belief true."[82] This is similar to the thesis of William James's *Pragmatism:* "Truth *happens* to an idea. It *becomes* true, is *made* true by events. Its verity is in fact an event, a process."[83]

For the ley hunter or tarot reader, interpretation is an action taken on a belief; interpretative meaning and experience become one. In divination, the experience is the moment of revelation in which a meaning is disclosed. In that moment, the truth, a universal structure that is always already in place, breaks through the world of mundane appearance that hides it, and the timeless emerges within profane time. Lehrich argues that the perennial truth that "the occult mind" seeks to recover is *illud tempus*, a time-out-of-time in which "the secrets of the cosmos were known to priests and magicians, who manipulated spiritual powers to achieve mighty ends."[84] Lehrich uses Mircea Eliade's notion of "reactualization" (the power of ritual to make *illud tempus* available as real presence) to argue that ley hunters "perceive time as distance from illud tempus...and thus the historical mapping procedure of rediscovery becomes reactualization with a messianic tinge...reading the ley of the land entails the possibility of renewal."[85] Ley hunting is a practice of magical hermeneutics, "a way to read the landscape" with the aim of reactualizing a lost or hidden wisdom, though it is worth remembering that ley hunting is just an example and the landscape can be anything: the *I Ching*, a city block, twelve-tone rows, mating rates of salmon, or any other "object with saturation value."

The embodied, here-and-now experience of truth that magical hermeneutics entails is not at all the same as the transtemporal and intersubjective experience of truth that rational thinking demands. Magical meaning is always *meaning for* a particular person and is inseparable from that person's experience. Even when it is mapped within some initiatory system, one person's experience is never exchangeable with anyone else's because initiatory meaning applies only to an individual human life, and no one can live your life for you. As Brooks writes, "to divine accident is to put it to work in a way which is inescapably one's own." Magical hermeneutics is a technology for experiencing your own experience.

Magic in this sense lies close to the subject of this book: the intellectual culture of those postwar artists and writers who valued sound as the means of reconnecting with the lived actuality of their own experience. All of them would have agreed with Austin Osman Spare that "knowledge is but the excrement of experience."[86] All were engaged in a critique of something much larger than any mere arrangement of politics or culture: from within hip culture arises a critique of our habitual ways of deriving meaning from the world, and what it seeks is not just another new doctrine but rather a faculty that moves beyond the making of doctrines. Stanley Tambiah has argued that there are "at least two orientations to our cosmos, two orderings of reality that woman and man everywhere are capable of experiencing." The first is causality, which is "quintessentially represented by the categories, rules and methodology of positive science and discursive mathematico-logical reason."[87] This ordering of reality, along with its associated cultural ills, was what hip intellectuals sought to dethrone. What they sought in its stead was what Tambiah, following Lucien Lévy-Bruhl, calls participation. Participation in Lévy-Bruhl's sense means a consubstantial rather than causal relationship between one thing and what might be taken as its representation—for example, between an epidemic and a portrait of Queen Victoria that New Guinea natives blamed for it. What Lévy-Bruhl called the "law of participation" was his answer to the question asked by every anthropologist who has thought seriously about magic: How can any reasonable person find a meaningful relationship between such causally unrelated things?

> Why, for example, should a picture or portrait be to the primitive mind something quite different from what it is to ours? Whence comes that attributing of mystic properties to it, of which we have just had an instance? Evidently from the fact that every picture, every reproduction "participates" in the nature, properties, life of that of which it is the image. This participation is not to be understood as a share—as if the portrait, for example, involved a fraction of the whole of the properties or the life which the model possesses. Primitive mentality sees no difficulty in the belief that such life and properties exist in the original and in its reproduction *at one and the same time*. By virtue of the mystic bond between them, a bond represented by the law of participation, the reproduction *is* the original.... Therefore one may obtain from the one what one gets from the other; one may influence the second by influencing the first.[88]

To Lévy-Bruhl and Tambiah, participation is the mainspring of magical consciousness. It is the noetic mode that allows an experience of truth, however strange and nonconsensual, to *become* truth. It allows people to feel connections between disparate things and events, between themselves and the world, despite all appearances of separation and whatever causal logic might have to say about it. Tambiah's contrastive definitions of causality and participation will be strangely familiar to readers of this study:

Causality

Ego against the world. Egocentricity. Atomistic individualism. The language of distancing and neutrality of action and reaction. The paradigm of evolution in space and time. Instrumental action that changes matter and the causal efficacy of technical acts. The successive fragmentation of phenomena, and their atomization, in the construction of scientific knowledge. The language of "dimensional" classification (Piaget). Science and experimentation. The doctrine of "representation" (Foucault). "Explanation" (Wittgenstein). "Natural scientific objectification and explanation of events" (K. Apel).

Participation

Ego/person with the world, a product of the world. Sociocentrism. The language of solidarity, unity, holism, and continuity in space and time. Expressive action that is manifest through conventional intersubjective understandings, the telling of myths and the enactment of rituals. The performative efficacy of communicative acts. Pattern recognition, and the totalization of phenomena. The sense of encompassing cosmic oneness. The language of "complexive" classification (Piaget) dictated by contiguity relations and the logic of interaction. The doctrine of "resemblance" (Foucault). "Form of life" (Wittgenstein) and the totality of experience associated with it.[89]

To the intellectual concepts that Tambiah associated with each of these noetic orderings we might add a few of the distinctions Mailer draws in his famous list:

Hip	*Square*
body	mind
associative	sequential
alchemists	chemists
instinct	logic
the present	the past and/or the planned future
to seduce by touch	to seduce by reasoned argument
nuance	fact
to listen to the sound of the voice and take one's meaning from there	to listen for the meaning of the words and obey no other meaning[90]

The experiential wholeness and interdependence of mind and phenomena that Mailer took as the essence of hip is also what McLuhan meant when he wrote that "youth...lives mythically and in-depth."[91] For Chester Anderson, it was "group participation, total experience, complete involvement" (Chapter 4). For Jack Kerouac, it was "the IT," the "big moment of rapport all around" (Chapter 3).[92] For Timothy Leary (Chapter 4), it was "the terrestrial conspiracy of dna. The plot of earth. The love-freedom network. The process."[93] When Mailer insisted that the hipster is really a mystic, or when Kerouac tells us of his "vision of the word Beat as being to mean beatific," maybe we should believe them.[94] The late-1950s enthusiasm for Zen (see Chapter 1) may have been a fad, but it was no fluke: to Gary Snyder and his friends, Zen was a revelation because it seemed to crystallize a new, holistic way of experiencing and understanding the world that had been hinted at by the writings of the Transcendentalists, the poetry of Ezra Pound, and the social vision of pacifist anarchism. In every case, "the emphasis on personal direct experience seemed to lead in the same direction."[95]

Technologies of Experience

It is unsurprising, then, that there would also be a connection between hip culture and magic: not only Brooks, Burroughs, Mailer, and Wilson, but Harry Smith, Wallace Berman, Kenneth Anger, Paul Bowles, Carolyn Cassady, Timothy Leary, Philip K. Dick, Diane di Prima, Patti Smith, Jimmy Page, and Mick Jagger (among others) were fascinated by magic and the occult, and after an English translation of *The Morning of the Magicians* appeared in 1964, magic became a serious preoccupation of the counterculture.[96] The depth of this engagement can be gauged by looking at the *Whole Earth Catalog,* which had an extensive list of magical books and lobbied as hard for Carlos Castaneda as for Buckminster Fuller and Marshall McLuhan.[97] The *Whole Earth Catalog* epitomized a techno-utopian register that was much taken with the idea of a convergence between scientific and magical modes of thought—a collision of the modern and the archaic that appealed to the countercultural appetite for exotica.[98] Gene Youngblood appealed to *Morning of the Magicians* to argue that this convergence was vital to countercultural and avant-garde experiments in film and multimedia:

> At their present limits astrophysics, biochemistry, and conceptual mathematics move into metaphysical territory. Mysticism is upon us: it arrives simultaneously from science and psilocybin. Pauwels: "Modern science, once freed from conformism, is seen to have ideas to exchange with the magicians, alchemists and wonder-workers of antiquity. A revolution is taking place before our eyes—the unexpected remarriage of reason and intuition."[99]

Some precincts of the post-Cage musical avant-garde, too, strongly suggest magical thought. In some music, the connection is overt: Jerry Hunt's *Sur (Doctor) John Dee* creates a musical analog to the sigils that Dee devised in order to speak to angels; Frederic Rzewski's *Plan for Spacecraft* describes a process in which a group of improvisers attempt to make music out of chaos by means of either "magic" or "work"; some of Pauline Oliveros's *Sonic Meditations* ask participants to develop a telepathic connection with one another. In other pieces the connection to magic is more indirect. The Rzewski and Oliveros pieces are event scores, and although an event score does not always ask its performers to do anything explicitly magical, it will always ask them to participate in an experience, the contours of which shape their apprehension of reality at the moment in which the piece is acted out. Event scores, too, are technologies for experiencing experience.

Event scores are text instructions for processes (which may or may not involve music in a conventional sense) that one or several persons execute, with or without an audience.[100] La Monte Young's *Composition 1960 # 10 (to Bob Morris)*, for example, is a single sentence: "Draw a straight line and follow it."[101] We can imagine some people carrying out this instruction, in a studio or rehearsal space or black-box theater, with chalk and plumb line, maybe, clambering over the piano, pushing aside chairs and onlookers, their passage making sounds of scrapes and rustles while others murmur and laugh and walk around. What happens is an actual event within the lives of those gathered in that space, rather than a representation of an event—a Happening, in Allan Kaprow's terms, or as Richard Schechner put it, an "Actual."[102] By contrast, a traditional theatrical work like *Die Walküre* is understood to represent actions, not present them (nobody calls the police when Hunding kills Siegmund). And a work like *Die Walküre* is representational in other ways: it is understood that both performance and score represent the work, insofar as both performances and scores are understood as instantiations of something that exists outside of the places and occasions that those scores and performances occupy. Yet in a piece like *Composition 1960 # 10*, the work is the performance is the experience: nothing is *representing* anything. The words on the page describe what performers must do in order to have a certain kind of experience, but those words in no way represent the experience itself, and the experience is really what matters. And if the work and the performance are the same thing, a performance of an event score is not a representation of a work, as we would feel a performance of *Die Walküre* is. We might then ask what kind of thing an event score text represents. This is always ambiguous: it is a script, perhaps, or something like the instructions from a grimoire or a liturgical handbook. Or maybe the text is a parallel creation, like a poem, which needs no realization outside the act of reading. (Young's *Piano Piece for David Tudor #3* suggests this possibility: "most of them were very old grasshoppers.") In any event, as distinctions of score, work, performance, life, and representation collapse, we find ourselves in a space defined by a logic of participation, not causality. It is not only that the performance is the work; the performers are the work as well. The work is in them, not in the score or even in the sounds they happen to create. Even saying that the work is "in them" is a bit too dualistic. It might be better to say that performers participate in the work, in the sense of Lévy-Bruhl's "law of participation": they are consubstantial with it; who they are and what they do share in the same essence. Event scores are performative, in J. L. Austin's sense—utterance is identical to action—and aim at the integration and holism that is the hallmark of participation rather than the representational mode of causality.[103]

A near relative of the event score, the Happening was a product of the early-1960s New York avant-garde of Kaprow, Young, Jack Smith, Andy Warhol, and the Fluxus group—a cultural assemblage that substantially overlapped the later Beats as well.[104] As the hip sensibility made its breakthrough into mass awareness after 1965, the Happening moved out of its exclusively avant-garde precincts and into public life, and by the late 1960s all sorts of ordinary events were routinely called Happenings.[105] The 1967 San Francisco "Human Be-In" popularized the idea of reframing a concert or arts festival as a Happening, and Michael Wadleigh's film *Woodstock* (1970) bronzed this social image in myth, memorializing the Woodstock music festival as a freeform work of life-as-art collectively created by the half-million people who showed up. The limits of this utopian notion are demonstrated in *Woodstock*'s evil twin, the Rolling Stones documentary *Gimme Shelter* (1970), in which a cynical hippie concert organizer decides to reimagine the Altamont festival's parking debacle as experimental theater.

Other forms of experimental theater aimed even more directly at cultural revolution.[106] The Living Theatre's *Paradise Now* (1968) represents the quintessential fusion of avant-garde aesthetics with revolutionary activism, heavily dosed with magic. *Paradise Now* attempted not merely to represent nonviolent anarchist revolution but to enact it here and now. The play was structured as a ladder, each rung consisting of rituals and actions designed to trigger political, psychological, social, and spiritual transformations among performers and spectators. The means of these transformations are magical in both form and style: every rung is associated with a chakra, a kabbalistic sephira, and three hexagrams from the *I Ching,* and each collective movement from one rung to the next is an initiation that culminates in a miraculous act of transcendence, called a "flashout." This is the point at which "the actor by the force of his art approaches a transcendent moment in which he is released from all the hangups of the present situation."[107] Thus the first rung ("The Rung of Good and Evil") inhabits the sephira of Malkuth, "the Kingdom," the realm of earth and earthly power. Transcending this realm means destroying the inhibiting values of the old culture, and so it begins with the actors strolling among the audience and repeating (with ever-greater urgency) five statements of those values: "I am not allowed to travel without a passport," "I don't know how to stop the wars," "you can't live if you don't have money," "I'm not allowed to smoke marijuana," and "I'm not allowed to take my clothes off." In the "vision" that is enacted next, the performers "smoke the pipe of peace until they become Indians."[108] This is the first flashout: the performers do not *represent* Indians, they become Indians. The Indians are then ritually slaughtered and reborn as hippies, the Natural Man, at which point the audience, too, is transformed: "The Natural Man confronts the spectator. The Natural Man knows he can travel without a passport, that he can smoke marijuana, that he can find ways to live without money, that he can take off his clothes. He knows how to stop the wars. That's the flashout."[109] Hardheaded revolutionaries were unmoved—how was this really going to stop the war?—but for those who threw themselves into *Paradise Now,* the war *was* over.[110] This was the truth they experienced, acted on, participated in, and made real through their action. Now it was up to everyone else to experience the same thing. For that brief time in the late 1960s when mass consciousness seemed on the point of evolutionary breakthrough, this did not seem so impossible.

Some event scores demand a process of magical hermeneutics remarkably similar to Brooks's own. Cornelius Cardew's *Draft Constitution* contains instructions for a "Research Project" that might as well be an account of Brooks's working method, and the insistence that "the results of your research are in you, not in the book" draws attention to the element of participation inherent in such a method:

> *Conduct of Research*: Research should be through direct experience rather than academic; neglect no channels. The aim is: by direct contact, imagination, identification and study to get as close as possible to the object of your research. Avoid the mechanical accumulation of data; be constantly awake to the possibility of inventing new research techniques. The record in the Scratchbook should be a record of your activity rather than an accumulation of data. That means: the results of your research are in you, not in the book.[111]

Walter de Maria's COLUMN *with a* BALL *on* TOP suggests another aspect of Brooks's work, which Dick Higgins called "private art"—a notion of creative acts whose existence is known only to the creator.[112] "I have built a box eight feet high. On top place a small gold ball. Of course no one will be able to see the ball sitting way up there on the box. I will just know it is there."[113]

I have suggested at the beginning of this chapter that the life's work of John Benson Brooks is better understood as a certain kind of musical process than as a collection of discrete musical products. From this point of view, it would be fairly easy to imagine the event score for which Brooks's life is the realization:

The Great Work: The player is to create a Great Work. To this end, he subjects himself to a "continual self-directed schooling," here called practice. The player is to interpret his experience in the spirit of initiation: everything that manifests within practice will take a place within a progressive revelation of meaning. The player is to record the unfolding of this revelation in notebooks every day. Performances, publications, and recordings may occur at intervals and should be considered a part of the Work as well. Ultimately, everything is part of the Work, musical or not.

Practice will comprise piano playing, composition, research, and divination. The player will start out playing and composing in a traditional jazz idiom but may branch out to modernist and avant-garde Western art music if he wishes. His compositional studies may be formal or informal, but he should not associate exclusively with any one style of music or intellectual camp. Neither should he limit his interests to music: the player will take an interest in any intellectual discipline that seems to further the aims of the Work. Once an intellectual interest is acquired, the player should buy as many books on the topic as he can, until either he runs out of money or no longer finds the topic serviceable to the Work.

The player may work with one or several kinds of divination. Whichever divinatory tool is preferred, it is to be used to guide all areas of the Work; it is in this way that the Work becomes revelation. In fact, it is by means of divination that the Work ceases to be bounded as a separate activity within the player's life and becomes identical (or nearly so) with it. Once the player's life and Work have merged completely, the performance is over.[114]

Practice

Avant Slant is a work of magical hermeneutics. Jammed with the revelations of John Benson Brooks's own life, it is saturated in meaning, albeit a meaning that existed for and in Brooks himself and only incidentally and at second hand for anyone else who might have stumbled upon it. I have been able to recover a handful of those meanings, but most of them are gone, just as Brooks himself is gone, because they were meanings for him and in him. Even the archive he left— a uniquely comprehensive record of a jazz composer's creative process—can never fully be opened to me or anyone else.

Imagine that Brooks throws three coins six times, finds the corresponding *I Ching* hexagram, and maps it onto his piano-playing body. In his notebook he records the process and perhaps some thoughts on the result, but what he cannot record is revelation, his embodied experience of a truth emerging from a hidden realm. If I seek to reproduce the result recorded on this notebook page and map the same hexagram onto my own body, I will not have experienced Brooks's meaning as a meaning for me, a "message from the Unseen" breaking through into my own life. Even if I did experience such a revelation, its meaning is then *for me*, not anyone else. So when Brooks's entire life lies spread out before me on the tables at the Institute of Jazz Studies, I cannot fully experience the Great Work of John Benson Brooks, because I am not John Benson Brooks—his Great Work was his life as it was illuminated by his artistic practice, and I cannot live his life for him. Being John Benson Brooks is the necessary condition for fully appreciating the kind of art he made. And this makes his music radical in ways that no one else in this book is. You might say you would rather listen to John Coltrane or Bob Dylan, but even if every single reader of this book felt this way it still wouldn't matter. *Avant Slant* wasn't for you in the first place. You and I are only interlopers. Whatever I've managed to explain in this chapter and whatever purpose it might serve for my larger argument changes nothing; the reader and the writer remain uninitiated. Academic explication is as irrelevant to the aims of initiation as magical hermeneutics is to the interpretive practices of the academy.

And this brings up an unavoidable question: What is magical hermeneutics good for? The answer is dispiriting. It is good for nothing but itself, which for the purposes of the academy means it is good for nothing at all. It represents the vanishing point of culture, the point at which cultural forms no longer find a place in a public conversation. In the academic discourse of the humanities, interpretation is the coin of the realm, but wherever magical hermeneutics appears, it is treated as debased or counterfeit currency, because its meanings are not fungible. Magical hermeneutics undermines the near-universal assumption of academic discourse that an interpretation has value only when it is verifiably intersubjective. Interpretations must extend from my own observation to the shared intersubjective world, and their terms must designate something definite and verifiable in your world as well as mine. The voice of observation must be third-person, not first-person.[115] If this condition is not met, we cannot exchange our interpretations in the "marketplace of ideas," an idiom that is a cliché precisely because it is so apt—academic interpretation is a fundamentally economic enterprise.

So when Gary Tomlinson considered the various approaches to Renaissance music and magic with which his own study might profitably engage, he ruled out the work of those, like Joscelyn Godwin, who are practitioners as well as scholars of the occult, because their interpretations designate truths that demand a buy-in of faith and can be arrived at only through initiatory experience:

> In his [Godwin's] quest for "intrinsic truth," which he opposes to the "academic approach which regards its subject as historically instructive,"

Godwin rejects the contextual negotiation of meaning and allows such out-of-control juxtapositions as those on pages 60–61, where Andean Indians, the Greek historian Strabo, the Talmud, Ravel, and Chekhov are all called upon to testify to the sounds made by the sun. To the occultist—or for that matter to any believer in the possibility of transcendent (i.e. noncontingent) meaning—the far-flung sources of such testimonies must confirm their contact with universal truths. But to the historian or anthropologist their uprootedness from the situations that engendered them renders them meaningless, or at best narrowly reflective of their interpreter's own expectations. Godwin's book, and the modern-day occultists' approach in general, promotes solipsistic transcendentalism rather than dialogue.[116]

Godwin, in weaving disparate cultural sources into a single interpretive structure, has breached the usual boundaries by which scholars make sense of culture and entered the space of magical hermeneutics, in which everything becomes a part of a vast acausal system of correspondences and by which the world bristles with significances, deeply felt, vouchsafed by perennial wisdom, but always just beyond the reach of third-person demonstration. Tomlinson finds Godwin's perennialism solipsistic, because what matters to Godwin is his own experience of correspondences and an initiatory system within which they make sense, not what any skeptical colleague might be able to say about any of it. To Tomlinson, this offers no medium of exchange, no ground for dialogue. To Godwin, perhaps, what Tomlinson calls dialogue is but a narrow aim, hedged in by the strictures of materialist rationality. An occultist is after something fundamentally different: not only the "academic approach which regards its subject as historically instructive" but "intrinsic truth;" not only knowledge, but spiritual transformation.[117]

The uselessness of magical hermeneutics to professionalized interpretation is also a problem for any interpretive practice founded in experience rather than verbalized, scriptable meaning. Carolyn Abbate's article "Music—Drastic or Gnostic?" is perhaps the most widely read challenge to the academic habit of mistaking "music" for the symbolic abstractions by which we handle it in our classrooms. "Real music," for Abbate, means performances that make sound present in real bodies at real times and places, and it is invisible to musicological interpretation, which generally proceeds from a notion of works that are ontologically prior to their performances. Confronted with the challenge of "real music," academic interpreters respond with indifference, scorn, or paralysis. And indeed some responses to Abbate's article have borne out her argument. Asks Michael Puri, "If the experience of performed music is, in fact, 'drastic' and 'ineffable,' as Abbate claims, how could any discourse about music (other than a nihilistic, self-abasing one) ever develop from it?"[118] And if Puri's reaction seems a bit vehement (nihilistic and self-abasing? really?), it is not very different from some reactions to Wayne Koestenbaum's *The Queen's Throat*, which goes much further than Abbate's essay in actually envisioning and articulating a realm of private, embodied musical experiences. As Kevin Kopelson writes, the book's detractors "tend to see Koestenbaum as narcissistic—to think: He's interested in himself, but not in *me*."[119] And to professional interpreters, this is disturbing.

In response to Abbate, Karol Berger asks why this should be so and suggests that it is "the professional deformation of the clerk: Meaning, not experience, is the academy's favorite coin."[120] It is not enough for me to say that "Melancholy Baby" makes me sad because when I was dating my ex-girlfriend it was "our song." That only tells you something about me, not about "Melancholy Baby." An interpretation of the song itself must be based on something that you can examine as easily as I—chord changes, a quote from a published source, anything that can be written down, anything that can be footnoted. Like scientists, we should be able to check one another's work, and the form of our conversation supplies the form of our interpretations. An appeal to my experience with my ex counts for nothing, because even if you experienced something like it, what happened to me was not what happened to you, and without that shared experience, you would have to take my word for it that it happened the way I said it did. And yet this kind of musical meaning—conjunctions between music and ex-lovers, lovers, weddings, children, deaths, God or the gods, and the presence of sounded music at the lived moment of those conjunctions— this is what music means to almost everybody, almost all the time. This is the dark matter of the musical universe, which is to say, it constitutes the vast bulk of it and yet remains invisible to the most sensitive instruments of objective analysis. To the hipsters and avant-gardists who have peopled this book, the idea of an academic discipline of music that would systematically exclude and erase such human experience from its interpretations and permit only those meanings that can be written down and exchanged would have seemed like the *reductio ad absurdum* of the technocratic and capitalistic culture of abstraction they were united in fighting.

In *Real Presences*, George Steiner asks us to imagine a society in which all arts are practiced as they are now but all secondary interpretations are banned. The only permitted commentary on a composition, then, would be another composition (or a performance, poem, dance, etc.).[121] In asking us to imagine such a society, Steiner wishes to argue that the vast, potentially limitless body of written and professionalized meaning that grows within artistic creation is entirely parasitic, unnecessary to the health of the host and even harmful to it. The experience of artistic presence is not the same as the things we can say about it, and indeed our infatuation with our words might tempt us to substitute our interpretations for the artworks, to take a secondary abstraction for the primary encounter. No one would call Steiner a hipster, but the target of his critique is another aspect of the abstraction that hip culture has always opposed.

Now imagine a slightly more radical version of the same society, in which there is no such thing as a "public" for art. A society without a musical public would be a society without capitalism, and indeed the vision of such a society impelled many in the avant-garde to create event scores and Happenings, which leave no material traces once they are completed, no objects to buy or sell. But these pieces *did* leave traces. If their public was not constituted by record or ticket sales, they still had a public—those who read about them in *Source: Music of the Avant Garde,* or who attended new music festivals and art galleries, read about the artists' aesthetic theories in academic journals, or studied composition in university music departments. The avant-gardists plied their trade within the command economy of arts and educational institutions rather than the capitalist economy of pop records and concert halls, but they still worked within a "marketplace of ideas." What I am asking you to imagine is a society in which there is not only no published discourse on the arts but no real way to experience art without making it yourself, and no way to take credit for the art you make any more than taking credit for frying eggs in the morning. (Your spouse might thank you for cooking breakfast, but you won't get famous for it.) This is hard to picture, but what is certain is that all at once the tensions with which this book has been concerned—the tension between authentic and co-opted art, experience and abstraction, reality and representation—would simply not exist. You can't sell out when no one can buy in.

Music within such a regime is music as *practice.* When we conceive of music entirely as practice, it takes on the same properties as our lives. On a given day, practice takes place at particular times and in particular spaces, but practice itself is not bound by place and occasion. A performance makes a sound, but practice itself doesn't sound like anything. Likewise it makes no sense to talk about what a life looks like or sounds like, except metaphorically. As John Cage wrote,

> Everybody has a song
> which is no song at all:
> it is a process of singing,
> and when you sing,
> you are where you are.

"Practice makes perfect": this truism suggests that practice is only the means to successful musical performance. And yet whatever it is that practice *makes* (performances, scores, recordings), practice itself cannot be measured at all. In itself, practice can be neither successful nor unsuccessful, any more than our living is successful. We might say that a life is successful, but this is not quite the same thing: "a life" is the process of living completed and viewed in hindsight, or an ongoing process viewed from the outside as a completed or perfected unity, and this is not what we mean by *living*. Those philosophers who have attempted to understand the world in light of participation rather than causality—Heraclitus, Nietzsche, Whitehead, Heidegger, Dewey, Deleuze and Guattari, and the religious mystics of various traditions—challenge us to see the world not as a collection of perfected things but as becomings. This has also been a central preoccupation of the hip sensibility, and the reason for sound's perennial place of honor within it. Sound is itself always in a state of becoming, and shapes made in sound model a reality made up of actions rather than objects, of human subjects defined entirely by the processes that constitute them and not fixed in any stable identity. Music as practice—pure practice, autotelic and without reference to any fungible musical object, product, or commodity—is music conceived entirely within the world of becomings.[122]

John Benson Brooks's life was, like every human life, darkened by disappointment, failure, futility, and loss. His Great Work ended with a sour irony: the man who had counted on his analytical mind to divine the secrets of the cosmos developed Alzheimer's Disease, and at the end of his life he could not remember his half-century-long intellectual adventure and had no idea where the notebooks that jammed his shelves had come from.[123] Questioning what Brooks really had to show for his practice, Gunther Schuller has mourned the tragedy of a vast intellect and musical talent wasted on a life full of false starts and blind alleys.[124] Perhaps. I would not want to live in a world without musical products, and I would give a great deal to have a few more albums like *The Alabama Concerto* and a few more songs like "Mend Them Fences," of which a sad little fragment appears in *Avant Slant*. But even so, I believe that what John Benson Brooks's life teaches us is that practice itself, practice without perfection, offers a real freedom in the moment it is realized. True, Brooks's practice left few traces, either on the historical record or even, by the end of his life, on his own memory. Brooks's life, reified and seen as a completed process, has less to show for itself than those of the major figures with whom he shared the New York City jazz and arts scene in the 1940s, 1950s, and 1960s. But his practice did not pertain to "a life"; it pertained to living, right now, every minute, and it is in this "right now" that the freedom of practice lies; perhaps this is what Brooks meant when he said "let's say that we're new, every minute." Practice is how we participate in our experience and thereby create little realities, refractory to and yet also containing our lives, as well as the lives of our friends, collaborators, and loved ones. The little realities constituted in practice can never be co-opted. In fact, the freedom that practice represents is more total than can be suggested by saying it can never be co-opted; putting it in Deleuze and Guattari's terms, we might say that practice deterritorializes the entire terrain that co-optation and transgression constitutes. It does not contest this terrain, but forms a different geometry entirely, a smooth space that is always accessible in the interstices of the grid mapped out by capitalism and its odd twin, counterculture.

Nothing comes for free, though. The freedom that practice offers comes at a cost that few are willing to bear: the renunciation of art that the avant-garde always promised and could never quite bring itself to deliver. The problem was, it was artists who promised the end of art; there was a conflict of interest. Avant-gardists argued for the end of art but not the end of their own careers—their ability to imagine anti-art artworks, communicate them to a public, and take credit for them. To take practice seriously is to contemplate a different ending: the end of art careers, arts publics, art reputations, art institutions, art markets, art scholarship, but not the end of art itself. To take practice seriously—to take John Benson Brooks seriously—is to remember that these are not the same thing.

Practice is hard, dull work, and we never feel like doing it. Like magical hermeneutics, practice as such makes nothing but itself, gives us little to show for it.[125] At least if you go to the gym every day you might look sexier; to get to the point of being able to stumble through a Bach minuet takes even more work, and it probably won't get you laid. However much they affect to reject commercialism and mass conformity, most hipsters do not have the heart for Brooks's more radical disaffiliation.[126] If hipness really is defined by how thoroughly you reject the mass-culture scene, then the hippest thing you could do would be to throw out your TV, stop going to movies and concerts, hole up in your study and play Bach on the piano, and read Dante in facing-page translation. But then this isn't what anyone thinks of as hip transgression, because it isn't something you can do with your friends on TV. The countercultural idea is an ideology of radical individualism, but the mechanism by which things become hip is inescapably social and collective. If, as John Leland says, hipness is a game, it's a game you play with a million of your closest friends.[127]

In the first chapter of this book I argued that the theory of co-optation grows organically from the countercultural idea, and that this theory is a dismal way of viewing the world. And yet some readers may ask what alternative we have. Stupid crap is daily borne in upon us like a tide of dirty floodwater—horrible art and horrible ideas manufactured by people for whom art and thought exist only to make money, who are trying to monetize every last item of our life and consciousness, who would print ads on our children's skin if they could, for whom "art" is merely another way to hustle more of their stupid crap. They have taken all the real art and turned it into another part of this trap they have made, this fiendish contraption from which there is no escape, except only those escapes that are (surprise!) just more things they are trying to sell you. Bill Hicks's sublime rage aria against marketers paints this picture as darkly as anything by Adorno:

> You are the ruiner of all things good. No this is not a joke, you're going, "there's going to be a joke coming," there's no fucking joke coming. You

are Satan's spawn filling the world with bile and garbage. . . . I know what all the marketing people are thinking right now, too: "Oh, you know what Bill's doing, he's going for that anti-marketing dollar. That's a good market, he's very smart." Oh man, I am not doing that. You fucking evil scumbags. "Ooh, you know what Bill's doing now, he's going for the righteous indignation dollar. That's a big dollar. A lot of people are feeling that indignation. We've done research—huge market. He's doing a good thing." Goddamn it, I'm not doing that, you scumbags! Quit putting a goddamn dollar sign on every fucking thing on this planet! "Ooh, the anger dollar. Huge. Huge in times of recession. Giant market, Bill's very bright to do that." God, I'm just caught in a fucking web. "Ooh the trapped dollar, big dollar, huge dollar. Good market— look at our research. We see that many people feel trapped. If we play to that and then separate them into the trapped dollar. . . ."[128]

Following the example of Richard Leppert and James Currie, I will end this book with hope—suggesting, like them, that in music, even very bad music, simply by virtue of *being* music, there is always something that cannot be caught, tamed, assimilated, or used.[129] Against the almighty machinery of commodification, you might ask, what can I do? What can one person do? You can do what one person can do. Buy a musical instrument and learn how to play it. If you can't afford a piano, buy a cheap guitar; if you can't afford a cheap guitar, sing. Make music with others. Of course, your music may not be very good in any objective sense, but who cares? Practice, magical or musical, is entirely indifferent to "objective sense"; experience is the gold standard of practice. Ramsey Dukes points out that the magician is not at all interested in whether he "really" summoned a demon or not, let alone whether he "really believes" that he has: "'really' and 'believe' are not words that go happily together in magical thought."[130] The magician has experienced it; this is enough. So magical hermeneutics is good for something after all: considered as a disposition of mind rather than as a set of practices, it provides a model for how to value an experience in itself rather than in terms of some external standard, and this in turn suggests a new way of approaching musical amateurism. Amateurism has fallen into disrepute as music performance is caught between regimes of professionalization and specialization, on the one hand, and commodification, on the other—the former owed largely to the sacralization of art, the latter to sacralization's apparent enemy, the capitalist marketplace.[131] Whatever their other differences, free-market absolutists and high-art Brahmins alike believe there is a standard of musical excellence realized in commodities, in the concerts and recordings of musical professionals, and there is little value in any musical experience that fails to measure up to it. And this belief has become unquestioned common sense: it is now difficult for most music lovers to imagine why they should listen to an amateur saw through a Brahms cello sonata when they can hear many better performances of the same music, either live or on record. However, Wayne Booth, an eminent English professor who played cello for a half-century (by his account quite badly), suggests that the value of amateur musical practice lies not in whatever might be judged by an audience, but in the musician's experience of self-transcendence in the unequal struggle with a vastly complicated skill, and in the way friends and family are drawn into the charmed circle of his practice.[132]

By way of an example, if I were to hear Wayne Booth (whom I do not know) play a Brahms sonata, I would probably be bored, mentally contrasting his scratchy and out-of-tune playing unfavorably with the recording of Jacqueline du Pré I have at home. Booth would not be bored, though, and while he would doubtless know the distance between his own efforts and du Pré's recording, the latter would remain, in the moment of his own performance, an ideal with (at best) only a faint and abstract claim on him. (The same is doubtless true for garage-band guitarists, who might daydream of jamming with Jack White but whose musical satisfaction has nothing to do with whether that dream is ever realized.) In short, Booth's performance would have a meaning for him it would not have for me. But if Booth were my friend—if he and I had played together for many years; if we had weathered the hardships of Brahms's tricky ensemble writing; if we knew one another's musical struggles and triumphs as only friends and collaborators can—I would be completely uninterested in how his performance measures up to any "objective" standard. His performance would be rich in meaning for me—for me but not you. Likewise, if I go to hear my child play violin in one of those marathon end-of-term concerts where thirty kids get up and play one Suzuki solo after another, my experience will be a single interval in which my attention is galvanized, as if on a performance by Heifetz, surrounded on either side by a vast Sahara of boredom. And every other parent will have the same experience, the only difference being the interval of their acute attention. What kind of asshole would complain that his child's performance wasn't "really" any good?[133]

The social sphere of practice is the private circle rather than the public audience; the latter demands an impersonal kind of sociability depending not on intimacy but renown. The potential social force of practice cannot be measured against that of a celebrated art. Music for a public has influence; it offers itself up not only for sale, but for writing and thus history. A history of practice music can scarcely be imagined.[134] But practice does have a social force, because it forges living connections to other human beings, and in this way it is inescapably social, though on an intimate scale. To Kalle Lasn or Naomi Klein, whose quarrel over the proper strategy against capitalist co-optation we encountered in Chapter 1, nothing I have suggested would effect change on the mass scale against which they measure their own activism. But throughout this book we have seen how such activism does not and cannot work as advertised. The countercultural ideology that drives it is incoherent: as the subtitle of *The Rebel Sell* puts it, culture can't be jammed. There cannot be a stable realm of counterculture that is not or does not become, somehow, the culture itself. Hip intellectuals and artists were right to think that our problem is the abstraction of human life into frozen meanings, into *things*. But if we sense there is something wrong with an abstracted and reified life, we still end up going back to old habits and looking for yet another *thing* that might deliver us from the tyranny of *things*. Perhaps the hipsters are right and music is not the re-presentation of experience but its direct presentation, its making-present; perhaps, then, of all art forms it is music that resists the reifications of our capitalist society. But even if this is true, for the most part hipsters have still fallen back on the assumption that to have music we must have musical *things* that can be bought or sold or otherwise exchanged within the impersonal economy of the public. However, the Great Work of John Benson Brooks suggests an alternative.

So that's it? Playing Brahms badly or making a baffling and solipsistic jazz record—*that's* the grand new principle of intellectual and existential liberation to be recuperated from the hip sensibility? To advocate practice, as well as the hermeneutic style that sustains it, seems deflatingly trivial. Practice will not give us a new, radical, unco-optable subculture; it merely gives us back our own lives, in all their smallness and unimportance. It will not give us a new kind of criticism we can mine for articles and books; it leads us only outside critical discourse entirely and into the uncritical business of playing music for our own satisfaction. Since the 1960s, scholars working within the cultural-studies idiom of the humanities have taken up the counterculture's great overriding problematic: the possibilities and limits of cultural freedom within a liberal capitalist order. This vast literature above all seeks transcendence, a way out. But almost always this is a "vertical" transcendence, in Mark Johnson's terms, an attempt to get free of the here-and-now, to "rise above and shed our finite human form" with all its "limitation, weakness, dependence, alienation, loss of meaning, absence of love, and anxiety over sickness and death."[135] The great projects of vertical transcendence in the West have been inspired by the visions of eternal afterlife in Abrahamic religion or those of a future utopia in Marxism.[136] That which leaves us right here and now, in the mire of our human contingency, seems small and unimportant by contrast. But what is here and now is all there is and all there will ever be; transcendence, if it can be found anywhere, can only be found here, in small and unimportant things. Such is the view of what Johnson calls horizontal transcendence, which

> recognizes the inescapability of human finitude and is compatible with the embodiment of meaning, mind, and personal identity. From this human perspective, transcendence consists in our happy ability to some-times "go beyond" our present situation in transformative acts that

change both the world and ourselves. This is tied to a sense of ourselves as part of a broader human and more-than-human ongoing process in which change, creativity, and growth of meaning are possible.... Hope is commitment to the possibility of realizing some of this growth—not in some final eschatological transformation of the world, but rather *locally*, in our day-to-day struggles and joys.[137]

The intellectual demands vertical transcendence through some formidable and abstract system of cultural resistance; the musician finds horizontal transcendence through the strings, wood, brass, and flesh of her daily practice. The intellectual will always win the argument, since arguments are not won with strings, wood, brass, and flesh. But the musician can always say, as Dave Hickey does in defense of his own practice, 'tis a small thing, but mine own.[138]

To have a practice does not mean having Brooks's practice. I do not suggest that my readers become occultists; magical hermeneutics is only the ideal-typical form of a much more general way of experiencing the world, in which we make a play of everything we encounter, and in which this play constitutes the shifting tissue of our identity. Seen from this point of view, we are all doing magic, whether or not we are aware of it. *Let's say that we're new, every minute.* To understand Brooks's practice is to see culture in a new way, not as the sum of things to be collected and exchanged, but as the processes we can enact on all the information we receive. As Michel de Certeau writes, "By itself, culture is not information, but its treatment by a series of operations as a function of objectives and social relations," and this conception of culture has not only aesthetic and political dimensions but ethical ones as well:

> The first aspect of these operations is *aesthetic:* an everyday practice opens up a unique space within an imposed order, as does the poetic gesture that bends the use of common language to its own desire in a transforming reuse. The second aspect is *polemical:* the everyday practice is relative to the power relations that structure the social field as well as the field of knowledge. To appropriate information for oneself, to put it in a series, and to bend its montage to one's own taste is to take power over a certain knowledge and thereby overturn the imposing power of the ready-made and preorganized. It is, with barely visible or nameable operations, to trace one's own path through the resisting social system. The last aspect is *ethical:* everyday practice patiently and tenaciously restores a space for play, an interval of freedom, a resistance to what is imposed (from a model, a system or an order). To be able to do something is to establish distance, to defend the autonomy of what comes from one's own personality.[139]

The practice that inspires De Certeau's thoughts is cooking, not music or magic, but it makes no difference. The deep features of practice remain consistent, as do its rewards—a "space for play" and an "interval of freedom" that opens up within the ruled bounds of everyday life. One generation of hipsters after another has sought to find these little somewheres within the vast nowhere. To discover these spaces for ourselves, without also having to shoulder the illusions and follies of the hip sensibility, is the great task that hip culture still leaves to us.

Endnotes

Introduction

1. Del Close and John Brent, "Basic Hip," from *How to Speak Hip*, LP, Mercury Records OCM 2205, 1959.
2. Julian "Cannonball" Adderley, "Introduction," from *The Cannonball Adderley Sextet in New York*, LP, Riverside RLP 9404, 1962.
3. LeRoi Jones, "Milneburg Joys (or, Against 'Hipness' As Such)," *Kulchur* 3 (1961), 41; Amiri Baraka, *The Autobiography of LeRoi Jones* (Chicago: Lawrence Hill Books, 1997), 261–62.
4. Quoted in Nat Shapiro and Nat Hentoff, eds., *Hear Me Talkin' to Ya: The Story of Jazz As Told by the Men Who Made It* (New York: Holt, Rinehart and Winston, 1955; repr. New York: Dover, 1966), 405.
5. This figure was first introduced to a wide public in Malcolm Gladwell, "The Coolhunt," *New Yorker*, Mar. 17, 1997, 78–88. Lee Konstantinou devotes a chapter to the coolhunter in *After Irony: Countercultural Fictions from Hipster to Coolhunter* (Cambridge: Harvard University Press, forthcoming).
6. This dynamic is elaborated in Sarah Thornton, *Club Cultures: Music, Media, and Subcultural Capital* (Hanover, NH: Wesleyan University Press, 1996).
7. The conceptual category of "sensibility," which I use throughout this book, was suggested to me by Susan Sontag's essays, especially "Notes on Camp," in *Against Interpretation, and Other Essays* (New York: Farrar, Straus and Giroux, 1966), 275–92. Sontag's use of "sensibility" suggests a capacious and broadly useful term in cultural history, somethings that "lets us dig beneath the social actions and apparent content of sources to the ground upon which those sources stand: the emotional, intellectual, aesthetic, and moral dispositions of the persons who created them." Daniel Wickberg, "What Is the History of Sensibilities? On Cultural Histories, New and Old," *American Historical Review* 112, no. 3 (June 2007), 669.
8. This was the central image of Paul Goodman's discussion of the "organized system" in his chapter "An Apparently Closed Room," in *Growing Up Absurd: Problems of Youth in the Organized System* (New York: Random House, 1960), 159–69. Though hugely influential on the 1960s Movement, Goodman kept his distance from hip critique, and his understanding of the rat-in-a-maze metaphor differs a little from the hipster's. To Goodman, the square is fully aware of the construct in which he is trapped but feels powerless to do anything about it and tries to fit in as well as he can. For a fictional representation of this type, see Sloan Wilson, *The Man in the Gray Flannel Suit* (Simon and Schuster, 1955). Richard Yates, *Revolutionary Road* (New York: Little, Brown, 1962), refines the portrait by making his protagonist, Frank Wheeler, a failed literary intellectual who knows that complaining about conformity and suburbia has become a middlebrow cliché but all the same finds himself trapped in a conformist suburban life.

9. This is the "construct," the hyperreal counterfeit of reality, pictured in Philip K. Dick's novel *Time Out of Joint* (1959) and the film *The Matrix* (1999). As Joshua Clover notes, the aim of such fictions is to represent the "edge of the construct," the point at which the construct becomes visible as such; see Joshua Clover, *The Matrix*, BFI Film Classics (London: British Film Institute, 2004). Since the hipster is the one gifted with the ability to see through the construct's systematic deceptions, the "edge of the construct" constitutes a trope of representation in hip culture; see Phil Ford, "Music at the Edge of the Construct," *Journal of Musicology* 26, no. 2 (2009), 240–73.

10. Readers will doubtless note the preponderance of masculine pronouns, here and elsewhere, especially when I am writing not about hipsters but "the hipster." In life, hipsters have always been male and female alike, but as a mythic abstraction "the hipster" was always masculine, at least in the era under discussion in this study. Barbara Ehrenreich in particular has considered how "the hipster" was fashioned as a masculine myth intended to free men from feminine claims and domestic responsibilities: Barbara Ehrenreich, *The Hearts of Men: American Dreams and the Flight from Commitment* (Garden City, NY: Anchor Press, 1984).

11. From a post-1960s perspective, it is intuitively obvious to extrapolate the hip stance of disaffiliation to a more general principle of cultural separatism, so it is worth noting that the term "counterculture" did not come into use until 1969, when Theodore Roszak used it in his influential *The Making of a Counter-Culture: Reflections on the Technocratic Society and Its Youthful Opposition* (New York: Doubleday, 1969).

12. Scott Saul, *Freedom Is, Freedom Ain't: Jazz and the Making of the Sixties* (Cambridge: Harvard University Press, 2003).

13. Seymour Krim, "What's This Cat's Story?" in *Views of a Nearsighted Cannoneer* (New York: Excelsior, 1961), 12. For a good musicological account of the Cold War narrative of political disillusionment, see Martin Brody, "Music for the Masses: Milton Babbitt's Cold War Music Theory," *Musical Quarterly* 77, no. 2 (Summer 1993), 161–92.

14. The well-worn (and often misunderstood) phrase "the end of ideology" is owed to Daniel Bell, *The End of Ideology: On The Exhaustion of Political Ideas in the Fifties* (Glencoe, IL: Free Press, 1960). Used to typify a collective mood among postwar intellectuals, the phrase denotes less a coherent point of view than a discontented and homeless attitude borne of its multiple rejections of Communism, anti-Americanism, pro-American nationalism, or indeed any single definable tendency.

15. The classic study of this dynamic is Andrew Ross, "Hip, and the Long Front of Color," in *No Respect: Intellectuals and Popular Culture* (London: Routledge, 1989), 65–101. Though excellent, it has largely been superseded by two outstanding studies that treat hipness and the symbolic politics of race: Scott Saul, *Freedom Is, Freedom Ain't*; and Michael Szalay, *Hip Figures: A Literary History of the Democratic Party* (Stanford: Stanford University Press, 2012).

16. Daniel Bell, "The Mood of Three Generations: *Dissent* in the Fifties," in *The End of Ideology*, 298.

17. Donald Allen, *The New American Poetry* (New York: Grove Press, 1960).

18. Gregory Corso to LeRoi and Hettie Jones, Feb. 4, 1960, folder marked correspondence 1960, Jan.–Apr., LeRoi Jones Collection, Lilly Library, Indiana University.

19. John Benson Brooks, notebook entry, Aug. 23, 1967, John Benson Brooks Collection, Institute of Jazz Studies Archives, Rutgers University at Newark.

20. The latter phrase is owed to Susan Sontag, "The Image-World," in *On Photography* (New York: Farrar, Straus and Giroux, 1977), 154. Sontag's subject is photography, but her meditations on it apply also to sound; see Chapter 3.

21. Marshall McLuhan, "Introduction," in *Explorations in Communication: An Anthology*, ed. Marshall McLuhan and Edmund Carpenter (Boston: Beacon Press, 1960), xi.

22. McLuhan's principle works are *The Gutenberg Galaxy* (Toronto: University of Toronto Press, 1961), and *Understanding Media* (New York: McGraw Hill, 1964). A collaboration with designer Quentin Fiore, *The Medium Is the Massage: An Inventory of Effects* (New York: Bantam, 1967), popularized the thought of these earlier books for a countercultural mass audience.

23. Secondary orality is an orality newly enabled by electronic communications technology and supported by and nested within a literate culture. Walter Ong, "Literate Orality of Popular Culture," in *Rhetoric, Romance, and Technology: Studies in the Interaction of Expression and* Culture (Ithaca and London: Cornell University Press, 1971), 284–303. The standard work on this subject is Walter Ong, *Orality and Literacy: The Technologizing of the Word* (London: Methuen, 1982; repr. New York and London: Routledge, 2002).

24. Daniel Belgrad, *The Culture of Spontaneity: Improvisation and the Arts in Postwar America* (Chicago: University of Chicago Press, 1998).

25. As Mark Johnson and others have argued, this commonsense understanding of meaning as something essentially propositional and cognized is based on the persistent philosophical error of mind-body dualism. Johnson argues for a more expansive understanding of meaning that comprises a sense of our embodied relation to environment. Mark Johnson, *The Meaning of the Body: Aesthetics of Human Understanding* (Chicago: University of Chicago Press, 2007). The English language itself makes it difficult to discriminate between narrower and broader notions of meaning; there is no single word that one can use consistently to mark the distinction. I want to make it clear that that my opposition of meaning and experience here is a crude heuristic to which the following chapters are intended to supply necessary subtleties.

26. The hip conception of sound as the other of cognized and verbalized meaning is a chapter in a broader narrative of sound as the irrational other of a rationalist modernity. This narrative is challenged and rewritten in Veit Erlmann's brilliant work *Reason and Resonance: A History of Modern Aurality* (New York: Zone, 2010).

27. Anatole Broyard, *Kafka Was the Rage* (New York: Carol Southern Books, 1993), 29–30.

28. Carl Solomon to Allen Ginsberg, undated note, folder 29, box 5, series 1 (correspondence 1942–1994), Allen Ginsberg Papers, Stanford University Special Collections. "The Remo" was the San Remo bar, which was (along with the White Horse Tavern) the best-known Village literary-hipster hangout in the early 1950s; Anatole Broyard memorialized it in "Village Cafe," *Partisan Review* 17, no. 5 (1950), 524–28. Almost all firsthand accounts of New York intellectual life in this period spend much of their time in bars; Dan Wakefield, *New York in the 50s* (New York: Houghton Mifflin, 1992), and Ronald Sukenick, *Down and In: Life in the Underground* (New York: Beech Tree Books, 1987), are both personal memoirs and good historical accounts of the time; see also Lewis MacAdams, *Birth of the Cool: Beat, Bebop, and the American Avant-Garde* (New York: Free Press, 2001).

29. Fran Landesman, Jay Landesman, and Tommy Wolf, "Man, We're Beat," on The Nervous Set, LP, Columbia OL 5430, 1959. It was Jay Landesman who founded *Neurotica*, the first little magazine to filter society and culture through a recognizably countercultural perspective, as later publications such as *The Evergreen Review* did more idiomatically and without *Neurotica's* heavy Freudian overlay. For an account of *Neurotica's* genesis, see Jay Landesman, *Rebel without Applause* (Sag Harbor, NY: Permanent Press, 1987).

30. Norman Podhoretz, "The Know-Nothing Bohemians," *Partisan Review* 25, no. 2 (Spring 1958), 305–18; Hilton Kramer, "Susan Sontag: The Pasionaria of Style," in *Twilight of the Intellectuals* (Chicago: Ivan R. Dee, 1999), 225.

31. By the time Malcolm X wrote his autobiography he had left his hipster youth far behind him and come to see his earlier hustling self as a figure of self-abasement. Alex Haley and Malcolm X, *The Autobiography of Malcolm X* (New York: Grove Press, 1965). Robin D. G. Kelley challenges Malcolm X's repudiation of his own earlier style of transgression; see Kelley, "The Riddle of the Zoot: Malcolm Little and Black Cultural Politics During World War II," in *Race Rebels: Culture, Politics, and the Black Working Class* (New York: Free Press, 1994). Manning Marable's excellent biography observes how Malcolm X dramatized and shaded his portrait of himself as a young hipster to suit his later purposes. More generally, Marable understands Malcolm X's successive reinventions in ways that parallel my own understanding of hipster self-invention. Manning Marable, *Malcolm X: A Life of Reinvention* (New York: Viking, 2011).

32. Joel Dinerstein has written a fine study of "cool," arguing that Lester Young pre-eminently embodied (but did not explicitly articulate) this emerging stance of African American resistance; Dinerstein, "Lester Young and the Birth of Cool," in *Signifyin(g), Sanctifyin', and Slam Dunking: A Reader in African American Expressive Culture*, ed. Gena Dagel Caponi (Amherst: University of Massachusetts Press, 1999), 239–76.

33. Norman Mailer and Richard G. Stern, "Hip, Hell, and the Navigator," in *Advertisements for Myself* (New York: Putnam, 1959; Cambridge: Harvard University Press, 1992), 379.

34. Milton (Mezz) Mezzrow and Bernard Wolfe, *Really the Blues* (New York: Random House, 1946).

35. Bernard Wolfe, *The Magic of Their Singing* (New York: Scribner, 1961), 246.

36. Ross Russell to Harlan Ellison, July 5, 1961, folder 7, box 8, "Correspondence 1960–1961, other than Dutton," Ross Russell Papers, Harry Ransom Center at the University of Texas at Austin.

37. Joseph Heath and Andrew Potter, *Nation of Rebels: How Counterculture Became Consumer Culture* (New York: HarperCollins, HarperBusiness, 2004), 16.

38. See, for example, my own public dispute with Robert Christgau: Phil Ford, "*I* Own the Sixties, Dammit," *Dial 'M' for Musicology*, posted May 9, 2008, accessed May 3, 2013, http://musicology.typepad.com/dialm/2008/05/i-own-the-sixti.html. This kind of resistance to the historicization of "resistance" is particularly pronounced in the study of the 1960s. See Peter Braunstein and Michael William Doyle, "Historicizing the American Counterculture of the 1960s and 70s," in *Imagine Nation: The American Counterculture of the 1960s and 70s* (New York: Routledge, 2002), 5–14.

39. François Furet, *Interpreting the French Revolution*, trans. Elborg Forster (Cambridge: Cambridge University Press, 1981), 1.

40. Stuart Hampshire, "Self-Consciousness and Society," in *Power and Consciousness*, ed. Conor Cruise O'Brien and William Dean Vanech (London: University of London Press, 1969), 231.

41. Like many men of the 1960s counterculture, Sinclair assumed a casual misogyny that quickly became unacceptable within Movement circles after a largely unanswerable feminist critique of it emerged, seemingly overnight, from the Women's Liberation Movement. See especially Robin Morgan's 1970 broadside "Goodbye to All That," reprinted in *Dear Sisters: Dispatches from the Women's Liberation Movement*, ed. Rosalyn Fraad Baxandall and Linda Gordon (New York: Basic Books, 2001), 53–57, which calls Sinclair out by name. When he had the opportunity to reprint his 1960s writings in 1972, Sinclair took care to edit out both the sexism and the " 'Off the Pig' and similarly 'heavy' radical bullshit" of his earlier positions: John Sinclair, *Guitar Army: Street Writings/Prison Writings* (New York: Douglas Book Corporation, 1972), 58–59.

42. The tendency to find "transgression" and "resistance" in popular music is particularly pronounced in the first generation of musicological writing in the cultural-studies idiom, for example in the work of Susan McClary and Robert Walser. This tendency now seems increasingly old-fashioned, but it is still pronounced in certain academic subdisciplines (for example in studies of hip-hop) and in pop music journalism. Recent academic studies that continue to deploy counterculture as an analytical category are more ambivalent, seeking to sustain an opposition between counterculture and mainstream in the face of recent skepticism. Nadya Zimmerman, *Counterculture Kaleidoscope* (Ann Arbor: University of Michigan Press, 2008), argues that counterculture never sought to fight against the mainstream but only to exist apart from it, though this leaves open the question of whether mainstreams and countercultures can remain distinct, regardless of how their opposition is construed; R. A Lawson, *Jim Crow's Counterculture: The Blues and Black Southerners 1890–1945* (Baton Rouge: Louisiana State University Press, 2010), splits the difference, maintaining that the blues constituted a counterculture that at once subverted and accommodated white supremacy.

43. Dick Hebdige, *Subculture: The Meaning of Style* (London: Methuen, 1979). For Hebdige and the school of thought he has helped define, hip style is interesting less for its autonomous formal features than for how it articulates strategies of resistance against a "power-bloc" whose existence is assumed from the outset and whose formulation is integral to Hebdige's project of Marxist critique. The term "power-bloc" was coined by Stuart Hall, one of Hebdige's teachers at the Birmingham Centre for Contemporary Cultural Studies, in order to denote an elastic, Gramscian conception of hegemony. This formulation was extremely influential in the cultural studies of the 1980s and 1990s. Stuart Hall, "Notes on

Deconstructing the Popular," in *People's History and Socialist Theory* (London: Routledge, 1981).

44. Furthermore, Frank's writing on counterculture did not quite follow the logic of his own theory of "hip consumerism": he derides the radical pretenses of 1960s counterculture but suggested that punk (or at least his favorite bands) represents a real radicalism. While this is sometimes problematic in *The Conquest of Cool,* it is most obvious in Frank's contributions to his 'zine *The Baffler.* See Thomas Frank and Matt Weiland, eds., *Commodify Your Dissent: Salvos from the Baffler* (New York: Norton, 1997).

45. One very notable exception is J. Hoberman, *The Dream Life: Movies, Media, and the Mythology of the Sixties* (New York and London: New Press, 2003), which considers the interpenetration of politics and representation more sensitively than any book that touches on the subject of my own work. In both the title of his book and in his approach, Hoberman is clearly indebted to Norman Mailer's work, as indeed am I.

46. LeRoi Jones, *Blues People* (New York: Morrow, 1963), 219.

47. Hans-Ulrich Gumbrecht, *The Production of Presence: What Meaning Cannot Convey* (Stanford: Stanford University Press, 2003).

48. Frank O'Hara, "Personism: A Manifesto," in *Selected Poems,* ed. Mark Ford (New York: Knopf, 2008), 247–48.

49. Norman Mailer, *The Presidential Papers* (New York: Putnam, 1963), 38.

50. The rhizome-root distinction is owed to Gilles Deleuze and Félix Guattari, *A Thousand Plateaus: Capitalism and Schizophrenia,* trans. Brian Massumi (Minneapolis: University of Minnesota Press, 1987).

51. "It is self-evident that under these circumstances no other advice can be given as to how one may enter into the thought explained in this work than to read the book twice, and the first time with great patience, a patience which is only to be derived from the belief, voluntarily accorded, that the beginning presupposes the end almost as much as the end presupposes the beginning, and that all the earlier parts presuppose the later almost as much as the later presuppose the earlier." Arthur Schopenhauer, *The World as Will and Idea [Die Welt als Wille und Vorstellung],* trans. R. B. Haldane and J. Kemp (London: Kegan Paul, 1909), viii.

Chapter 1

1. Benedict Anderson, *Imagined Communities* (London: Verso, 1983, 2006), 6.

2. Diane di Prima, *Recollections of My Life as a Woman* (New York: Viking, 2001), 202–03.

3. Tower of Power, "What Is Hip," from *Tower of Power,* LP, Warner Brothers BS 2681, 1973.

4. David W. Maurer, "Phrase Origins: Get Hep," *American Mercury* (May 1947), 548.

5. Ned Polsky, "The Village Beat Scene: Summer 1960," in *Hustlers, Beats, and Others* (Chicago: Aldine, 1967), 151.

6. Robert S. Gold, *A Jazz Lexicon* (New York: Knopf, 1964), 145.

7. David Dalby, "Americanisms That May Once Have Been Africanisms," *Times* (London), July 19, 1969, 9; repr. in *Mother Wit from the Laughing Barrel: Readings in the Interpretation of Afro-American Folklore,* ed. Alan Dundes (Englewood Cliffs: Prentice-Hall, 1973; repr. Jackson: University of Mississippi Press, 1990), 136–40; J. L. Dillard, *Black English* (New York: Random House, 1972), 119; cited in John Birks "Dizzy" Gillespie, *To Be Or Not . . . to Bop* (Garden City, NY: Doubleday, 1979), 297; Greil Marcus, "Birth of the Cool," *Speak* (Fall 1999), 16–25; John Leland, *Hip: The History* (New York: Ecco, imprint of HarperCollins, 2004), 5–6. This etymology has lately been questioned by Jesse Sheidlower, an OED lexicographer, in "Crying Wolof: Does the Word *Hip* Really Hail from a West African Language?" *Slate,* Dec. 8, 2004, accessed May 3, 2013, http://www.slate.com/id/2110811.

8. Norman Mailer, "The White Negro: Superficial Reflections on the Hipster," in *Advertisements for Myself* (New York: Putnam, 1959), 337–58. "The White Negro" was originally published in *Dissent* 4, no. 3 (1957), 276–93.

9. McLuhan first called the radio a "tribal drum": he considered it a medium with the "power to turn the psyche and society into a single echo chamber" and to reverse Western individualism into collectivism. However, he continued to use the "tribal drum" metaphor more

generally to describe all electronic communications media. Marshall McLuhan, *Understanding Media: The Extensions of Man* (New York: McGraw-Hill, 1964; repr. Corte Madera, CA: Gingko Press, 2003), 401.

10. Edward Binns, Ernest Pintoff, and Guy Fraumeni, *This Is Marshall McLuhan: The Medium Is the Massage*, film (New York: NBC, McGraw-Hill Films, 1967). This was a one-hour NBC television documentary explaining McLuhan's ideas to a youth audience in psychedelic style. McLuhan was annoyed by its vulgarization of his ideas, but it remains a valuable document of the unlikely spectacle of mass-media intellectual celebrity. Philip Marchand, *Marshall McLuhan: The Medium and the Messenger* (New York: Ticknor and Fields, 1989; repr. Cambridge: MIT Press, 1998), 203.

11. Leland, *Hip: The History,* 13.

12. Greil Marcus, "Time Is Longer than Rope," in *The Old, Weird America: The World of Bob Dylan's Basement Tapes* (New York: Picador, 2001), 42–66.

13. R. U. Sirius [Ken Goffman] and Dan Joy, *Counterculture Through the Ages: From Abraham to Acid House* (New York: Random House, 2005).

14. Timothy Leary's eight-circuit model of consciousness is an odd scientific/mystic hybrid theory that proposes four levels of "higher consciousness" in exactly this manner. Timothy Leary, *Neurologic* (Los Angeles: Starseed, 1973), *Exo-Psychology* (Los Angeles: Starseed, 1977). Robert Anton Wilson's treatment of Leary's eight-circuit model is better known than Leary's own in latter-day countercultural circles; see Robert Anton Wilson, *Prometheus Rising* (Tempe, AZ: New Falcon Press, 1983).

15. The mutability of human subjectivity, the incommensurabilities of its various epistemes within "the West," and the ideological operations of this seemingly monolithic latter category make up one of the great themes of the postmodern humanities. Its literature is correspondingly large, but its great originating work is of course Michel Foucault, *The Order of Things: An Archaeology of the Human Sciences* (New York: Pantheon, 1971).

16. Jeffrey Kripal, *The Serpent's Gift: Gnostic Reflections on the Study of Religion* (Chicago: University of Chicago Press, 2007) represents a new kind of comparative religious studies that tries to find a balance point between postmodernism's refusal of universalization and the tendency of mystical traditions to converge on a common and changeless human experience. From this point of view, then, the durable and changeless tropes of a tantric mysticism can enter specific societies with all the infinite contingency that human culture can introduce. Thus Kripal can write that the "enlightenment of the body"—an understanding of matter and spirit, body and mind, as aspects of a single indissoluble substance—is the definitive new force in a twentieth-century American spirituality that had not previously entertained such notions. Jeffrey Kripal, *Esalen: America and the Religion of No Religion* (Chicago: University of Chicago Press, 2007). Kripal's notion of the "enlightenment of the body" has obvious parallels with my own focus on the postwar American interest in holism, presence, and participation.

17. Marcus's general intellectual project is one of mapping possible secret histories—underground streams by which the inner life of one cultural domain is mysteriously transmitted to its kindred in other times, places, and cultural registers. See especially Marcus's *Lipstick Traces: A Secret History of the Twentieth Century* (Cambridge: Harvard University Press, 1989), which connects punk rock to the Dadaists and Situationists. Here, as elsewhere, the causality of this underground transmission is never made clear; John Lydon (Johnny Rotten of the Sex Pistols) once remarked that this "secret history" of punk "was so secret that nobody told us." John Lydon, quoted in *Punk Rock: So What? The Cultural Legacy of Punk,* ed. Roger Sabin (London: Routledge, 1999), 4.

18. Robin D. G. Kelley, "The Riddle of the Zoot," 169. Manning Marable, *Malcolm X* (New York: Viking, 2011) fleshes out Malcolm X's process of self-invention considerably.

19. Farah Jasmine Griffin, *"Who Set You Flowin'?" The African American Migration Narrative* (New York: Oxford University Press, 1995), 102.

20. Guthrie P. Ramsay, Jr., "'We Called Ourselves Modern': Race Music and the Politics and Practice of Afro-Modernism at Midcentury," in *Race Music: Black Cultures from Bebop to Hip-Hop* (Berkeley: University of California Press, 2003), 96–130. Ramsay's is the most

important study of Afro-modernism in musicology; in literature, the concept was first developed by Houston Baker. See Houston A. Baker, Jr., *Blues, Ideology, and Afro-American Literature: A Vernacular Theory* (Chicago: University of Chicago Press, 1984); Houston A. Baker, Jr., *Modernism and the Harlem Renaissance* (Chicago: University of Chicago Press, 1987).

21. Marshall Berman, *All That Is Solid Melts into Air: The Experience of Modernity* (New York: Simon and Schuster, 1982; repr. New York: Penguin, 1988), 345–46.

22. There are several good studies on bohemians in the nineteenth and early twentieth centuries: for specifically American contexts, see especially Joanna Levin, *Bohemia in America, 1858–1920* (Stanford: Stanford University Press, 2009); Christine Stansell, *American Moderns: Bohemian New York and the Creation of a New Century* (New York: Metropolitan, 2000); for a study of Paris bohemia, see Jerrold Seigel, *Bohemian Paris: Culture, Politics, and the Boundaries of Bourgeois Life, 1830–1930* (New York: Viking, 1986).

23. Ludwig Wittgenstein, *Philosophical Investigations*, trans. G. E. M. Anscombe (Oxford: Blackwell, 1997), 32^e.

24. Ibid.

25. The list of possible examples is seemingly inexhaustible. The word "Zen" has been used to sell beauty products, an MP3 player, a putative aphrodisiac, vegetarian burgers, a wine, chewing gum, a sex toy, various bands and albums (not least Hüsker Dü's classic album *Zen Arcade*), various books whose titles reprise Robert Pirsig's mis-hearing of Eugen Herrigel's *Zen in the Art of Archery*—"Zen and the Art of" writing, producing, running, knitting, stand-up comedy, faking it, etc.—Zen knives, Zen sneakers, Zen perfume, and so on, to say nothing of Jon Stewart's daily "moment of Zen." The best source for tracking Western cultural appropriations of Zen (and Buddhism more generally) is a blog called The Worst Horse (http://theworsthorse.com/).

26. When Hans Ulrich Gumbrecht mentions Zen in passing as he considers presence in terms of the Buddhist idea of emptiness, his squirm of embarrassment is an acknowledgment of the cliché: "there is nothing more intellectually kitsch than the enthusiasm for Zen Buddhism among Western intellectuals who (like myself) do not know a single Asian language and have, at best, a touristic knowledge of one or other Asian Culture." Hans-Ulrich Gumbrecht, *The Production of Presence: What Meaning Cannot Convey* (Stanford: Stanford University Press, 2003), 149.

27. Jack Kerouac, "239th Chorus," *Mexico City Blues* (New York: Grove Press, 1959), 241.

28. James Baldwin, "The Black Boy Looks at the White Negro," in *Price of the Ticket: Collected Nonfiction, 1948–1985* (New York: St. Martin's Press, 1985), 296. The reference is to D. T. Suzuki, the most influential writer on Zen in English at midcentury and a powerful influence on John Cage, Erich Fromm, the Beats, and other midcentury intellectuals.

29. Alan Watts, "Beat Zen, Square Zen, and Zen," *Chicago Review* 12, no. 2 (Summer 1958), 3–11. This was a special issue of *Chicago Review* devoted to Zen, and it was an important early point of dissemination of these ideas among American intellectuals: in addition to Watts's now-classic essay, it included writings by Kerouac, Philip Whalen, D. T. Suzuki, and Ruth Fuller Sasaki. Lawrence Coupe discusses Watts's critique of Kerouac at length in "This Is IT: Alan Watts and the Visionary Tradition," in *Beat Sound, Beat Vision: The Beat Spirit and Popular Song* (Manchester: Manchester University Press, 2007), 22–55.

30. The heart of Kerouac's engagement with Buddhism is the voluminous notebook of his studies, *Some of the Dharma*, which he considered one of his most important achievements but for which he could not find a publisher. Among other things, it contains lists of books that Kerouac read and is useful for tracing the sources of his understanding of Buddhism. Jack Kerouac, *Some of the Dharma* (New York: Viking, 1997).

31. Gary Snyder, "On the Road with D. T. Suzuki," in *A Zen Life: D. T. Suzuki Remembered*, ed. Masao Abe (New York: Weatherhill, 1986), 207–8.

32. Harold Rosenberg, "The American Action Painters," *Art News* 51, no. 8 (December 1952), 22–23, 48–50.

33. Jack Kerouac, "Belief and Technique for Modern Prose" *Evergreen Review* 2, no. 8 (Spring 1959): 57.

34. Ernest Fenollosa and Ezra Pound, *The Chinese Written Character as a Medium for Poetry*, ed. Haun Saussy, Jonathan Stalling, and Lucas Klein (New York: Fordham University Press, 2008), 46. Saussy notes that Fenollosa was heavily influenced by Nagarjuna's teachings on emptiness by way of Tendai Buddhism, though Pound knew nothing about this influence.

35. R. Buckminster Fuller, Jerome Agel, and Quentin Fiore, *I Seem to Be a Verb* (New York: Bantam, 1970).

36. Friedrich Nietzsche is a notable exception. He traced what he felt was the great fundamental error of Western philosophy—the prior assumption of stable identities—back to Socrates and looked to the pre-Socratics for an alternative. "With the highest respect, I except the name of Heraclitus. When the rest of the philosophical folk rejected the testimony of the senses because they showed multiplicity and change, he rejected their testimony because they showed things as if they had permanence and unity." Friedrich Nietzsche, *Twilight of the Idols*, in Walter Kaufmann, ed., *The Portable Nietzsche* (New York: Penguin, 1954), 480. For an extraordinary study of how Nietzsche's writing embodied his ethical notion of a self constituted in multiplicity and change, see Alexander Nehamas, *Nietzsche: Life as Literature* (Cambridge: Harvard University Press, 1987).

37. Bernard Faure has argued that D. T. Suzuki's writing on Zen exploited this sense of strangeness, gratifying a Western sentiment of "reverse orientalism" that held Asians to be naturally conversant with mystical truths denied to Westerners. Bernard Faure, *Chan Insights and Oversights: An Epistemological Critique of the Chan Tradition* (Princeton: Princeton University Press, 1993), 52–88. Jung, for example, wrote that Westerners could never really accommodate themselves to something so alien as Zen. Carl Jung, foreword to D. T. Suzuki, *An Introduction to Zen Buddhism* (New York: Philosophical Library, 1949).

38. Theodore Roszak, *The Making of a Counter Culture: Reflections on the Technocratic Society and Its Youthful Opposition* (Garden City, NY: Anchor Books, 1969), 134.

39. Ibid., 134–35.

40. Robert Fink, *Repeating Ourselves: American Minimal Music as Cultural Practice* (Berkeley: University of California Press, 2005), 228.

41. Daniel J. Bronstein, "Search for Inner Truth," *Saturday Review*, Nov. 16, 1957, 22–23. These arguments are made at greater length in Erich Fromm's and D. T. Suzuki's contributions to *Zen Buddhism and Psychoanalysis*, ed. Erich Fromm (New York: Harper & Brothers, 1960).

42. Brian Daizen Victoria's *Zen at War* (New York: Weatherhill, 1997) offers a sobering portrait of how Zen institutions conformed themselves to the political demands of Japanese imperialism.

43. Gary Snyder, "Buddhist Anarchism," *Journal for the Protection of All Beings* 1 (1961): 12.

44. Fran Kelley, liner notes for Fred Katz, *Zen: The Music of Fred Katz*, LP, Pacific Jazz PJ-1231, 1957.

45. Kenneth Rexroth, letter to Lawrence Lipton, Lawrence Lipton Collection Box 2, F7, sheet 21, University of California Los Angeles. Quoted in Melissa Dawn Goldsmith, "Kindred Riffs, Rival Banter: Kenneth Rexroth's and Lawrence Lipton's Jazz and Poetry Experiments," unpublished paper presented at the Seventy-Eighth Annual Meeting of the American Musicological Society (New Orleans, 2012).

46. Jonathan Lethem, "Collapsing Distance: The Love-Song of the Wanna-Be, or, Fannish Auteur," keynote address to the 2007 Experience Music Project Pop Conference, Seattle WA, Apr. 19, 2007.

47. Brian Eno, "Pretension," in *A Year with Swollen Appendices* (London: Faber, 1996), 381.

48. For an overview of the history of Buddhism in the United States, see Rick Fields, *How the Swans Came to the Lake: A Narrative History of Buddhism in America*, 3rd ed. (Boston: Shambhala, 1992).

49. Friedrich Nietzsche, *On the Genealogy of Morals*, trans. Douglas Smith (New York: Oxford University Press, 1996), 60.

50. Leland, *Hip: The History*, 10–11.

51. Rod McKuen, Buddy Collette, and Paul Gray, *Beatsville*, LP, High Fidelity R419, 1959; Tony Scott, Shin'ichi Yuize, and Hozan Yamamoto, *Music for Zen Meditation and Other Joys*, LP, Verve V-8634, 1964.

52. Gerald Graff, "Co-optation," in *The New Historicisms*, ed. H. Aram Veeser (London: Routledge, 1989), 168–69.

53. Ibid., 170.

54. See, for example, Hugh Barker and Yuval Taylor, *Faking It: The Quest for Authenticity in Popular Music* (New York: Norton, 2007). The bibliography for this concept is too large to summarize—a keyword search on RILM turns up hundreds of relevant items—but suffice it to say, once someone has written a guide for "crafting and implementing business strategies for rendering authenticity," it must be generally understood that the game is up: James H. Gilmore and B. Joseph Pine, *Authenticity: What Consumers Really Want* (Cambridge: Harvard Business Press, 2007). The idea of authenticity has come to be used as a basic analytical category in dozens of studies in the popular music of every genre and region of the world. For the most part, such studies seek to understand how various audiences and musicians construct an authentic subjectivity or use authenticity as a basis for negotiating musical meaning, an approach at once granting that authenticity is always contingent and ideological in character while stopping short of denying its validity altogether.

55. Bernard Wolfe, *The Magic of Their Singing* (New York: Scribner, 1960), 118.

56. This was the black nationalist mood of the early 1970s that Francis Davis remembered expressed in impromptu between-set lectures, "the confusing gist of which was likely to be that only blacks were culturally equipped to understand jazz and white people ought to be ashamed of themselves for not supporting it in greater numbers." Francis Davis, "The 1970s, Religious and Circus," in *Like Young: Jazz and Pop, Youth and Middle Age* (New York: Da Capo Press, 2001), 142–43.

57. Anatole Broyard, "Portrait of the Hipster," *Partisan Review* 15, no. 6 (1948), 727.

58. Wolfe, *The Magic of Their Singing*, 119.

59. Francis J. Rigney and L. Douglas Smith, *The Real Bohemia* (New York: Basic Books, 1961).

60. joy [pseud.], "(to sociologists & publicists of the beat generation)," *Beatitude* 8 (Aug. 15, 1959), last page.

61. Joseph Heath and Andrew Potter, *Nation of Rebels: How Counterculture Became Consumer Culture* (New York: HarperCollins, HarperBusiness, 2004), 34–35.

62. Ibid., 2.

63. Julian Sanchez, "Anti-Consumerist Capitalism," *Reason* 35, no. 6 (November 2003), 11.

64. *Adbusters* 64, "Spiritual Pollution" (March/April 2006), unpaginated.

65. David Brooks, *Bobos in Paradise* (New York: Simon and Schuster, 2000), 92.

66. The best and most comprehensive study of the Blue Note design aesthetic is Alisa White, "'No Room for Squares': The Hip and Modern Image of Blue Note Records, 1954–1967" (Ph.D. diss., Indiana University, 2011). For the covers themselves, see Graham Marsh, Felix Cromey, and Glyn Callingham, eds., *Blue Note: The Album Cover Art* (San Francisco: Chronicle Books, 1991); Graham Marsh and Glyn Callingham, eds., *Blue Note 2* (San Francisco: Chronicle Books, 1997).

67. The distinction between sincerity and authenticity is best expressed in Lionel Trilling, *Sincerity and Authenticity* (Cambridge, MA: Harvard University Press, 1972). Trilling locates a decisive shift in modern consciousness in the emergence of authenticity as the axial concept by which individuals interpret their relationship to society. If sincerity is a harmonization of feeling and action, authenticity consists in the deeper process of ascertaining what one's own "true" feelings are. When authenticity becomes the individual's paramount value, "mere" sincerity comes to be seen as a form of inauthenticity.

68. I hardly know where to begin in documenting this; those who are interested can simply Google "I hate hipsters" or "hipster douchebag" and form their own conclusions. Just as everyone professes no illusions about the concept of authenticity while tacitly continuing to rely on those same illusions, no one wants to be called a hipster, least of all those who are obvious, indisputable hipsters: see "Two Hipsters Angrily Call Each Other 'Hipster,'" *The Onion*, Mar. 29, 2006, accessed May 3, 2013, http://www.theonion.com/articles/two-hipsters-angrily-call-each-other-hipster,5230.

69. Max Black makes this point in "The Prevalence of Humbug," in *The Prevalence of Humbug, and Other Essays* (Ithaca, NY: Cornell University Press, 1983).

70. I make both these arguments at length in "Taboo: Time and Belief in Exotica," *Representations* 103 (2008), 107–35.
71. Wilson, *Prometheus Rising,* 166.
72. Alfred North Whitehead, *Process and Reality: An Essay in Cosmology,* ed. David Ray Griffin and Donald W. Sherburne (New York: Free Press, 1929, 1979), 23.
73. The relationship between Whitehead and the postwar arts scene is described in Daniel Belgrad, *The Culture of Spontaneity: Improvisation and the Arts in Postwar America* (Chicago: University of Chicago Press, 1998), 120–41.

Chapter 2

1. Anatole Broyard, "Portrait of the Hipster," *Partisan Review* 15, no. 6 (1948), 722.
2. Ned Polsky, "The Village Beat Scene: Summer 1960," in *Hustlers, Beats, and Others* (Chicago: Aldine, 1967), 153.
3. Ibid., 175.
4. Kenneth B. Clark and James Barker, "The Zoot Effect in Personality: A Race Riot Participant," *Journal of Abnormal and Social Psychology* 40, no. 2 (April 1945), 143–48.
5. In the black press, Dan Burley's column in the *New York Amsterdam News,* Billy Rowe's column in *The Pittsburgh Courier,* and "Home Boy Says," a *People's Voice* column that featured stories told in jive (sometimes with a translation provided) were notable early forums for hipster anecdotes and jive glossaries. The earliest journalistic treatment of hipsters emphasized their impenetrable slang, and the first books that dealt with hipsters were glossaries: Dan Burley, *Dan Burley's Original Handbook of Harlem Jive* (New York, 1941, 1944); Cab Calloway, *The New Cab Calloway's Cat-ologue* (1938) and *The New Cab Calloway's Hepsters Dictionary* (1944). David Maurer and other linguists studied the slang of various underworld subcultures, some of which (especially drug users) overlapped hip subcultures; David Maurer, "The Argot of the Underworld Narcotic Addict," *American Speech* 11, no. 2 (April 1936), 116–27; see also William C. De Lannoy and Elizabeth Masterson, "Teen-Age Hophead Jargon," *American Speech* 27, no. 1 (February 1952), 23–31. Sociological studies in the "sociology of deviance"—one of the few discourses within which midcentury academia could find a place for the hipster—include Clark and Barker, "The Zoot Effect in Personality"; Harold Finestone, "Cats, Kicks, and Color," *Social Problems* 5, no. 1 (1957), 2–13; Howard Becker, "The Professional Dance Musician and His Audience," *American Journal of Sociology* 57, no. 2 (1951), 136–44.
6. In 1957, Robert Reisner could compile a fairly long list of "hip authors" (including Anatole Broyard, Nelson Algren, John Clellon Holmes, Norman Mailer, Chandler Brossard, Jack Kerouac, and Norman Mailer) and publish it in what was widely understood to be a hip newspaper. Robert Reisner, "The Hip Ones," *Village Voice,* Sep. 18, 1957, 6. In 1960, *Swank*—a nudie magazine that had started publishing literary fiction and poetry—advertised itself as "the best in hip writing," taking for granted that in 1960 there *was* such a thing as "hip writing." *Evergreen Review* 4, no. 15 (1960), 8. None of this would have made any sense in the early 1940s.
7. One well-known example is "Zombies Put Kiss of Death on 52nd St. Jazz," *Down Beat,* Feb. 25, 1946, 3. This piece is typical in expressing the jazz fan's resentment of hipsters as the *nouveaux riches* of subcultural capital—phonies whose musical enthusiasms are shallow and contrived. An even better example is Barry Ulanov, "Morality and Maturity," part 14, *Metronome* (June 1954), 17, a piece of concentrated jazz-critical snobbery against the "non-playing, non-writing, non-managing" hanger-on. On the other hand, the black jazz magazine *The Music Dial* was more easygoing. Its writers make free use of hip slang, assuming that the audience will get the humor of a heading like "That Hep Stoky Digs Gabe" (about Leopold Stokowski dropping in on an Erskine Hawkins show at the 20th Century Gabriel); *The Music Dial* 1, no. 2 (May 1944), 7. On the same page there is a firmly integrationist and progressive agenda (union politics and demands to take an equal part in the war effort) suggestive of the same kind of Popular Front leftism as *PM. The Music Dial* accepts hipness as part of the scenery, but nowhere does it suggest that hipness could

or should set the tone of any more serious social commitment. Again, such notions belonged to a later, post-1948 hip discourse.

8. Joel Dinerstein has gathered a good amount of anecdotal and biographical material in support of his contention that Lester Young was the first real hipster artist. Joel Dinerstein, "Lester Young and the Birth of Cool," in *Signifyin(g), Sanctifyin', and Slam Dunking: A Reader in African American Expressive Culture,* ed. Gena Dagel Caponi (Amherst: University of Massachusetts Press, 1999), 239–76.

9. Scott Saul, "Birth of the Cool: The Early Career of the Hipster," in *Freedom Is, Freedom Ain't: Jazz and the Making of the Sixties* (Cambridge, MA: Harvard University Press, 2003), 29–60. This chapter is the outstanding and indispensable study of hipness in this early period. Saul ties Calloway to a line of entertainers who, like Calloway, made hipness a showbiz gimmick; these include the boogie-woogie pianist Harry "the Hipster" Gibson, guitarist Slim Gailliard, and DJs Al "Jazzbo" Collins, Albert "Dr. Hepcat" Durst, and Holmes "Daddy-O" Daylie.

10. Jack Kerouac, "The Origins of the Beat Generation." *Playboy* 6, no. 6 (June 1959), 41–43.

11. John Leland, "The Tricksters," in *Hip: The History* (New York: Ecco, imprint of HarperCollins, 2004), 162–63.

12. This was how the network announcer introduced each program. *Quizzicale* in Cleveland, Feb. 25, 1942; *Quizzicale* in Detroit, Mar. 4, 1942, Doug and Hazel Anderson Storer Collection, 1920s–2003, in the Southern Historical Collection at the Louis Round Wilson Special Collections Library, University of North Carolina.

13. Percival L. Prattis, "Hi-de-ho King Plays Villainous Role in Radio *Quizzicale,*" *Pittsburgh Courier,* Sep. 20, 1941, 13.

14. Henry Louis Gates, *The Signifying Monkey: A Theory of Afro-American Literary Criticism* (New York: Oxford University Press, 1988), 58.

15. *Quizzicale* in Cleveland, Feb. 25, 1942.

16. Jacob Brackman, *The Put-On: Modern Fooling and Modern Mistrust* (Chicago: Regnery, 1971), 90. *Don't Look Back* (Docurama, 1967), D. A. Pennebaker's documentary of Bob Dylan's 1964 British tour, is a master class in the art of the put-on and offers several examples of "relentless agreement," among other modes. More recently, this is the strategy theorized by Slavoj Žižek as "overidentification" in *The Plague of Fantasies* (London: Verso, 1997) and used most often by political satirist Stephen Colbert.

17. *Quizzicale* in Detroit, Mar. 4, 1942.

18. Ibid.

19. Daniel Goldmark discusses how classical music is represented in this and other cartoons of the same period; Daniel Goldmark, *Tunes for 'Toons: Music and the Hollywood Cartoon* (Berkeley: University of California Press, 2005).

20. Leland, *Hip,* 86, 163.

21. Gates, *Signifying Monkey,* 52.

22. Bruce Tyler, "Zoot-Suit Culture and the Black Press," *Journal of American Culture* 17 (Summer 1994), 21–33.

23. See Malcolm X and Alex Haley, *The Autobiography of Malcolm X* (New York: Grove Press, 1965; Ballantine, 1992), 40 *passim.* LeRoi Jones's classic study of jazz and its culture, *Blues People* (New York: Morrow, 1963), is in part an extended critique of the black middle class along these lines. More recent scholarly work has challenged any such simple opposition of black hipsters and black middle classes; see Maureen Mahon, *Right to Rock: The Black Rock Coalition and the Cultural Politics of Race* (Durham, NC: Duke University Press, 2004), a study of the Black Rock Coalition that understands its members as "young, well-educated, middle class, bohemian" musicians who do not fit into standard narratives of race and authenticity.

24. Dan Burley, "In Which We Introduce the 'Back Door Man' to Harlem," *New York Amsterdam News,* Dec. 11, 1937, 15.

25. Milton "Mezz" Mezzrow and Bernard Wolfe, *Really the Blues* (New York: Random House, 1946), 220. Emphasis in the original.

26. Dan Burley, "At This Time We'll Wax a Bit Scholarly," *New York Amsterdam News,* Dec. 18, 1937, 12.

27. Dan Burley, "One, Two, Three: You Drop Your Finger Down, Then Strut Around the Town!" *New York Amsterdam News*, Feb. 25, 1939, 17.

28. Broyard, "Portrait of the Hipster," 726.

29. Dan Burley, "Life and Letters of a Back Door Man," *New York Amsterdam News*, Apr. 17, 1943, 13, letter from a reader.

30. Dan Burley, "In Which a Hipcat is Studied by Experts," *New York Amsterdam News*, Apr. 24, 1943, 11.

31. Mezzrow and Wolfe, *Really the Blues*, 222–23.

32. Chicago Sunday Tribune (Nov. 3, 1946), part 4, 9. See Gayle Wald, "Mezz Mezzrow and the Voluntary Negro Blues," in *Race and the Subject of Masculinities*, ed. Harry Stecopoulos and Michael Uebel (Durham, NC: Duke University Press, 1997), 116–37.

33. Norman Mailer, "The White Negro: Superficial Reflections on the Hipster," in *Advertisements for Myself* (New York: Putnam, 1959), 340.

34. The classic work on this topic is, of course, Eric Lott, *Love and Theft: Blackface Minstrelsy and the American Working Class* (New York: Oxford, 1993).

35. LeRoi Jones, *Blues People*, 219.

36. One representative example of the moral panic story is "Jive Called Marihuana Traffic Aid," *Washington Post*, July 12, 1943, B1. For an article on teen "jive," see Maureen Daly, "Jive," *Chicago Daily Tribune*, Dec. 26, 1943, F7.

37. See Michael Rogin, *Blackface, White Noise: Jewish Immigrants in the Hollywood Melting Pot* (Berkeley: University of California Press, 1996), and particularly its title essay on Al Jolson, which meditates on the uses of blackface for reframing the possibilities of white (and specifically Jewish) identity. The theatrical practice of blackface must be understood here as a figure for a larger pattern of imposture; as Eric Lott writes, "every time you hear an expansive white man drop into his version of black English, you are in the presence of blackface's unconscious return." Lott, *Love and Theft*, 5.

38. I discuss the entertainment logic of black representation—and its attendant foreshortening of character—in Phil Ford, "Ellington the Entertainer: Prophetic History on Film," in *Ellington Studies*, ed. John Howland (Cambridge: Cambridge University Press, forthcoming).

39. Jane Feuer terms this the "opera vs. swing narrative" of the American film musical; see Jane Feuer, *The Hollywood Musical*, 2nd ed. (Bloomington: Indiana University Press, 1993), 54.

40. Mezzrow and Wolfe, *Really the Blues*, 3. Scott Saul argues that this book's strident note of criminality was probably Wolfe's contribution, and it was certainly something Random House was happy to use to sell the book. Scott Saul, *Freedom Is, Freedom Ain't*, 48, 30n.

41. These would include *The Autobiography of Malcolm X*, John Birks "Dizzy" Gillespie, *To Be or Not…to Bop* (Garden City, NY: Doubleday, 1979); Miles Davis and Quincy Troupe, *Miles: The Autobiography* (New York: Simon and Schuster, 1989); and Art Pepper, *Straight Life* (New York: Da Capo, 1994).

42. John Clellon Holmes, "The Name of the Game," in *Passionate Opinions* (Fayetteville: University of Arkansas Press, 1988), 54–55.

43. Malcolm X and Haley, *Autobiography of Malcolm X*, 55.

44. R. Lincoln Keiser, *The Vice Lords, Warriors of the Streets* (New York: Holt, Rinehart and Winston, 1969). See also Julius Hudson, "The Hustling Ethic," in *Rappin' and Stylin' Out: Communication in Urban Black America*, ed. Thomas Kochman (Urbana: Illinois University Press, 1972), 410–24.

45. Finestone, "Cats, Kicks, and Color," 4.

46. Sudhir Venkatesh, *Gang Leader for a Day: A Rogue Sociologist Takes to the Streets* (New York: Penguin, 2008), offers an account of his years of fieldwork in the Robert Taylor Homes, studying the hustling culture of a Chicago gang and RTH residents during the height of the crack trade. This book is a more personal account of the underground economy Venkatesh chronicled in *Off the Books: The Underground Economy of the Urban Poor* (Cambridge: Harvard University Press, 2006); most interestingly, it offers a shrewd understanding of his own sociological research as a kind of hustle structured along the lines I have laid out here.

47. Julius Hudson, "Hustling Ethic," 413.
48. Jack Gelber, *The Connection*, film directed by Shirley Clarke (New York: Mystic Fire Video, 1960, 1983).
49. This is also the understanding of society that emerges in film noir and roman noir; see Phil Ford, "Jazz Exotica and the Naked City," *Journal of Musicological Research* 27, no. 2 (2008), 113–33.
50. Robin D. G. Kelley, "The Riddle of the Zoot: Malcolm Little and Black Cultural Politics During World War II," in *Race Rebels: Culture, Politics, and the Black Working Class* (New York: Free Press, 1994), 177.
51. The systemic inequalities suffered by the residents of black ghettoes in the 1960s and 1970s, and the hustling styles adapted to deal with them, are illustrated in Bettylou Valentine, *Hustling and Other Hard Work: Life Styles in the Ghetto* (New York: Free Press, 1977).
52. Gelber, *The Connection*.
53. Lionel Trilling, *Sincerity and Authenticity* (Cambridge, MA: Harvard University Press, 1972), 11.
54. Charles Taylor, *The Ethics of Authenticity* (Cambridge, MA: Harvard University Press, 1992), 65.
55. "The Voutians," *Life*, May 6, 1947, 129–35.
56. "Bebop Fashions," *Ebony* 4, no. 2 (December 1948), 31; see also "How to Make a Pork-Pie Hat," *Ebony* 4, no. 10 (August 1949), 43.
57. "How Deaf Can You Get?" *Time*, May 17, 1948, 74. For more on this ideological framing of bebop, see Ron Radano, *New Musical Figurations: Anthony Braxton's Cultural Critique* (Chicago: University of Chicago Press, 1993), 16.
58. Dr. Utopia resembles Prince Chawmin', the zoot-suited cad in the 1943 Warner short *Coal Black and de Sebben Dwarves*. The problem with Prince Chawmin' is not that he's politically suspect, though, but that he's a coward. Daniel Goldmark discusses *Coal Black* in the context of wartime and midcentury cartoon representations of jazz and race in "Jungle Jive: Animation, Jazz Music, and Swing Culture," in *Tunes for 'Toons: Music and the Hollywood Cartoon*, 77–106; see also Leland, "Hip Has Three Fingers," in *Hip: The History*, 186–201.
59. *Neurotica* 1, no. 1 (Spring 48), 3.
60. John Clellon Holmes, "Crazy Days, Numinous Nights: 1948–1950" [journal excerpts], *the unspeakable visions of the individual*, vol. 12, ed. Arthur and Kit Knight (California, PA, 1982), 113.
61. Allen Ginsberg, "Bop Lyrics" (1949), in *Collected Poems 1947–1997* (New York: Harper Collins, 2006), 50. In one of the few journalistic articles that tried to sort out the various strains of hipness in the 1940s, Jim Burns also insists that 1948 is the year that intellectual hipsterism came into its own: Jim Burns, "The Hipster," *Jazz Journal* 21, no. 7 (July 1968), 2–3.
62. "Glorified jazz" is John Howland's term for a kind of classicized jazz motivated by middlebrow notions of uplift; John Howland, *Ellington Uptown: Duke Ellington, James P. Johnson, and the Birth of Concert Jazz* (Ann Arbor: University of Michigan Press, 2009). Conversely, Edmund Wilson's unfinished novel *The Higher Jazz*, ed. Neale Reinitz (Iowa City: University of Iowa Press, 1998), is a document of how white intellectuals in the 1920s found in jazz a principle by which European art traditions could be renewed. Composers took part in this project of transatlantic rapprochement: as Carol Oja has written, "any gangplank interview with European luminaries visiting the United States in the 1920s, whether with Stravinsky, Bartók, or Ravel, revealed, sometimes painfully, that American jazz, not concert music, was what interested them." Carol Oja, "Gershwin and American Modernists of the 1920s," *Musical Quarterly* 78, no. 4 (Winter 1994), 650.
63. Eithne Wilkins, "Jazz, Surrealism, and the Doctor," *Jazz Forum* 1 (1946), 10. A similar sentiment can be found in *Angry Penguins*, an Australian literary journal from the same time; see "Riff in the Blue," *Angry Penguins* (1945), 109.
64. John Clellon Holmes, "Crazy Days, Numinous Nights," 113.
65. Responding to Holmes's jazz writing, Orrin Keepnews grumpily remarks that "jazz, being practically by definition a part of the non-conformist world, is forever being adopted as a

sort of tag-along side-issue by one cult or another (from the Jazz Age speakeasy crowd, through the American Communist Party, on down to the Beat generation)." Orrin Keepnews, review of *The Horn*, by John Clellon Holmes, *Jazz Review* 1, no. 1 (1958), 42–43.

66. Undated postcard, folder 16, box 2 series 1 (correspondence 1942–1994), Allen Ginsberg Papers, Stanford University Special Collections.

67. Anyone who has seen *A Christmas Story* knows this tale. Shepherd told it several times, once in a very rare jazz-and-spoken-word LP where it is backed by blues harpsichord music composed by a pair of Paul Hindemith's Yale students. Jean Shepherd, Mitch Leigh, and Art Harris, *Jean Shepherd: Into the Unknown with Jazz Music*, LP (Abbott Records 5003, 1955).

68. Carl Wilson, *Let's Talk About Love: A Journey to the End of Taste* (New York: Continuum, 2007), 92.

69. James Baldwin, "The Black Boy Looks at the White Negro," in *Price of the Ticket: Collected Nonfiction, 1948–1985* (New York: St. Martin's Press, 1985), 292.

70. Carl Rollyson, *The Lives of Norman Mailer: A Biography* (New York: Paragon House, 1991), 110. Mailer's tone-deafness is attested in Adele Morales Mailer's memoir *The Last Party: Scenes from My Life with Norman Mailer* (New York: Barricade, 1997) and was informally mentioned to me in a conversation with J. Michael Lennon. Neil Cassady made a similarly inconclusive experiment with a C-melody saxophone: Neal Cassady to Jack Kerouac, Dec. 30, 1950, folder 2, box 1, Jack Kerouac Papers (1948–1982), Harry Ransom Center, University of Texas at Austin.

71. Abbie Hoffman, *Woodstock Nation: A Talk-Rock Album* (New York: Vintage, 1969), 10–13.

72. For a consideration of the former question, see Nat Hentoff, "A Brief Note on the Romance of the 'White Negro,'" in *The Jazz Life* (New York: Dial Press, 1961), 138–42; for the latter question, see Steve Shoemaker, "Norman Mailer's 'White Negro': Historical Myth or Mythical History?" *Twentieth Century Literature* 37 (1991), 343–60.

73. The notion of the "ideal type" originates with the sociologist Max Weber and in musicology is most closely associated with Carl Dahlhaus, who defined it as "a hypothetical construction in which a historian assembles a number of phenomena which in historical reality are observed haphazardly and always in different combinations, and relates and compares them to each other in order to bring out the connection between them." Carl Dahlhaus, *Realism in Nineteenth-Century Music*, trans. Mary Whittall (Cambridge: Cambridge University Press, 1982), 121. Philip Gossett notes that the "ideal type" is really a heuristic device historians construct in order to make sense of the profusion of historical details at their disposal. Philip Gossett, "Carl Dahlhaus and the 'Ideal Type,'" *Nineteenth-Century Music* 13, no. 1 (1989), 51.

74. Broyard, "Portrait of the Hipster," 723.

75. John Gilmore makes a similar point in his memoir of life in the 1950s and 1960s Los Angeles actors' subculture. This was a bohemia characterized by the same kinds of "deviant" behavior that marked the hip subcultures of eastern cities: sexual adventurism, drug use, vagabondage, and occasional crime. Yet, though a few actors, such as Dennis Hopper, sought a philosophical rationale that could lend coherence to their actions and integrate them into a hipster persona, most simply accepted Hollywood "decadence" as a by-product of their work. "What's been called 'subterranean Hollywood' by some writers hardly presents a whole or accurate picture . . . nor was there any kind of allegiance to a sociological sweep or a countercultural movement such as the Beats; all that mattered was who was working and who wasn't." John Gilmore, *Laid Bare: A Memoir of Wrecked Lives and the Hollywood Death Trip* (Los Angeles: Amok Books, 1997), 95.

76. Chandler Brossard, *Who Walk in Darkness* (New York: New Directions, 1952), 73. Two of the characters in Brossard's novel were based on members of his circle: Broyard himself, who was cast as the caddish Henry Porter; and Milton Klonsky, who became Max Glazer, a pot-smoking Jewish poet whose liberation from all forms of bourgeois morality makes him the only ideal-typical hipster in the book. Brossard appears never to have commented publicly on the identities of his characters; they were "unmasked" in print after Broyard and Klonsky had died. See Henry Louis Gates, "White Like Me," *New Yorker* 72, no. 16

(June 17, 1996), 69; Mark Shechner, "Introduction," in Milton Klonsky, *A Discourse on Hip* (Detroit: Wayne State University Press, 1991), 27.

77. Chandler Brossard, "Tentative Visits to the Cemetery: Reflections on *My* Beat Generation," *Review of Contemporary Fiction* 7, no. 1 (1987), 7. This circle has been best chronicled in the autobiographical writings of its members: see Jay Landesman, *Rebel without Applause* (Sag Harbor, NY: Permanent Press, 1987); Anatole Broyard, *Kafka Was the Rage* (New York: Carol Southern Books, 1993); Klonsky, *A Discourse on Hip*; Delmore Schwartz, *The Journals and Notes of Delmore Schwartz*, ed. Elizabeth Pollet (New York: Farrar, Straus, and Giroux, 1986); and of course in Brossard's *roman à clef*. One can experience something of the intellectual flavor of this group in an anthology of the group's essays: Chandler Brossard, ed., *The Scene Before You: A New Approach to American Culture* (New York: Rinehart, 1955).

78. John Clellon Holmes, "The Pop Imagination," in *Nothing More to Declare* (New York: Dutton, 1967), 39, 12.

79. Marshall McLuhan, "The Psychopathology of Time and Life," *Neurotica* 5 (Fall 1949).

80. Shechner, "Introduction," in Klonsky, *A Discourse on Hip*, 9–10. The bibliography on the New York Intellectuals is quite large: the standard books are Richard Pells, *Liberal Mind in a Conservative Age: American Intellectuals in the 1940s and 1950s* (New York: Harper and Row, 1985); and Harvey Teres, *Renewing the Left: Politics, Imagination, and the New York Intellectuals* (New York: Oxford, 1996). But there are many more studies on specific topics either directly or indirectly associated with the figures of this circle. In music history, see David Paul, *Charles Ives in the Mirror: American Histories of an Iconic Composer* (Champaign: University of Illinois Press, 2013), which places the reception of Charles Ives within Cold War intellectual currents; see also Martin Brody, "Music for the Masses: Milton Babbitt's Cold War Music Theory," *Musical Quarterly* 77, no. 2 (Summer 1993), 161–92, which views Babbitt's generational experience and musical metatheory in parallel to the lives and works of the New York Intellectuals.

81. Although the earliest issues of *Partisan Review* are fairly typical products of the 1930s Communist intelligentsia, its editors soon broke with the Communist party over the question of artistic autonomy, namely the autonomy of radical literature from the CPUSA. The magazine suspended publication briefly in 1937 and then returned with a new editorial mission. "Any magazine, we believe, that aspires to the vanguard of literature today, will be revolutionary in tendency; but we are also convinced that any such magazine will also be unequivocally independent.... Indeed we think that the cause of revolutionary literature is best served by a policy of no commitments to any political party." Philip Rahv and William Philips, "Editorial Statement," *Partisan Review* 4, no. 1 (1937), 3. Thomas Schaub has written of the "liberal narrative" of anti-Communist apostasy the New York Intellectuals developed in reaction to their experiences in the 1930s. The liberal narrative is a story of youthful illusion giving way to a darker realism about the human condition: scarred by the horrors of totalitarianism and disillusioned by the intellectual compromises of its apologists, the intellectual arrives at a mature understanding of the ironies, ambiguities, and limitations of political life. Thomas H. Schaub, *American Fiction in the Cold War* (Madison: University of Wisconsin Press, 1991).

82. The memoirs of the New York Intellectuals are studded with memories of friendships ended for recherché intellectual reasons; the crude, second-time-as-farce degeneration of the genre is a memoir by Norman Podhoretz, *Ex-Friends: Falling Out with Allen Ginsberg, Lionel and Diana Trilling, Lillian Hellman, Hannah Arendt, and Norman Mailer* (New York: Free Press, 1999). A more comprehensive biographical treatment of the New York Intellectuals may be found in David Laskin, *Partisans: Marriage, Politics, and Betrayal Among the New York Intellectuals* (Chicago: University of Chicago Press, 2001).

83. George Lewis, *A Power Stronger Than Itself: The AACM and American Experimental Music* (Chicago: University of Chicago Press, 2008), 31. In his memoirs, Broyard recalls his discomfort at "being typecast as an aficionado of the primitive" by his *Partisan Review* elders, who translated African American vernacular culture into the terms ("Picasso, D. H. Lawrence, and Hemingway; bullfighting and boxing") most familiar in their modernist milieu. Broyard, *Kafka Was the Rage*, 110. Hans Ulrich Gumbrecht, *In 1926: Living at the*

Edge of Time (Cambridge: Harvard University Press, 1997) evokes the dream logic by which these items were connected in the modernist imagination. If one were to choose a single figure to represent the complex interfaces between modernism and Africanist primitivism, it would doubtless be Josephine Baker; for a brilliant study of such interfaces in Baker's person, see Anne Anlin Cheng, *Second Skin: Josephine Baker and the Modern Surface* (New York: Oxford, 2011).

84. Broyard, *Kafka Was the Rage*, 111.

85. Seymour Krim, "What's *This* Cat's Story?" in *Views of a Nearsighted Cannoneer* (New York: Excelsior, 1961), 12.

86. Seymour Krim, review of "The Holy Barbarians," by Lawrence Lipton, *Evergreen Review* 3, no. 9 (1959), 211.

87. Broyard, *Kafka Was the Rage*, 29.

88. Gates, "White Like Me," 66–81. Broyard's daughter has published a memoir of her family: Bliss Broyard, *One Drop: My Father's Hidden Life—A Story of Race and Family Secrets* (New York: Little, Brown, 2007).

89. Bernard Wolfe, *Memoirs of a Not Altogether Shy Pornographer* (New York: Doubleday, 1972), 148.

90. The model for Broyard's "Portrait" was Jarvis Braun, a freeloader who lived on the couches of his literary friends and inspired a young Jack Kerouac to extemporize the unpreserved poem "Jack Braun, Don't Come to Florida." Dan Wakefield, *New York in the 50s* (New York: Houghton Mifflin, 1992), 171.

91. These include Broyard's "Portrait of the Hipster," his memoir *Kafka Was the Rage,* and his sketch of the Bistro, a Village bar and hipster hangout: Anatole Broyard, "Village Cafe," *Partisan Review* 17, no. 5 (1950), 524–28. Broyard also wrote several other pieces on the *demimonde* of nightclubs and dancehalls he visited. Most directly relevant to the interests of this chapter are two essays Broyard contributed to *Neurotica* on dance gestures and their sociosexual implications: Anatole Broyard, "Mambo," *Neurotica* 6 (1950), 29–30; Anatole Broyard, "American Sexual Imperialism," *Neurotica* 7 (1950), 36–40. Broyard also wrote two essays on African American social personae for *Commentary*: Anatole Broyard, "Keep Cool, Man," *Commentary* 11, no. 4 (1951), 359–62; Anatole Broyard, "Portrait of the Inauthentic Negro," *Commentary* 10, no. 1 (1950), 56–64.

92. Broyard, "Portrait of the Hipster," 722. This gesture appears in fictional representations of hip milieux: see Douglass Wallop, *Night Light* (New York: Norton, 1953), 199–200; "The Crisis Today: The Delinquent, the Hipster, and the Square," *Look Up and Live* (CBS-TV series), produced by Jack Kuney, aired Jan. 4, 1959.

93. Michael Cherlin, *Schoenberg's Musical Imagination* (Cambridge: Cambridge University Press, 2007), 6.

94. Broyard, "Portrait of the Hipster," 722.

95. Ibid., 721.

96. Kenneth Burke, "Four Master Tropes," *A Grammar of Motives* (New York: Prentice-Hall, 1945), 503–15.

97. I owe the term "deformation" to James Hepokoski and Warren Darcy, who have adopted it from Russian formalist criticism and applied it to the study of sonata form. A deformation is an expressive departure from a generic model and, consequently, from the expectations a competent audience derives from those models. James Hepokoski and Warren Darcy, *Elements of Sonata Form* (New York: Oxford University Press, 2006).

98. Mezzrow and Wolfe, *Really the Blues*, 227.

99. I prefer to use George Lewis's useful terms "Afrological" and "Eurological" to characterize the cultural influences bearing on hipness for the same reason Lewis uses them to discuss improvisation: the qualities they designate are "historically emergent rather than ethnically essential, thereby accounting for the reality of transcultural and transracial communication." George Lewis, "Improvised Music after 1950: Afrological and Eurological Perspectives," *Black Music Research Journal* 16, no. 1 (Spring 1996), 93.

100. Cleanth Brooks, "Irony as a Principle of Structure," in *Literary Opinion in America*, rev. ed., ed. Morton D. Zabel (New York: Harper, 1951).

101. Michael Denning, *The Cultural Front: The Laboring of American Culture in the Twentieth Century* (London: Verso, 1997), reclaims Burke for the Popular Front; Elizabeth Crist, *Music for the Common Man: Aaron Copland During the Depression and War* (New York and Oxford: Oxford University Press, 2005), offers a fine discussion of Burke's role in the Popular Front aesthetics that inform Aaron Copland's music from the 1930s and 1940s.

102. Lee Konstantinou, "The Hipster," in *After Irony: Countercultural Fictions from Hipster to Coolhunter* (Cambridge: Harvard University Press, forthcoming).

103. Quoted in Konstantinou, *After Irony.*

104. Broyard, "Portrait of the Hipster," 722.

105. Ibid.

106. Herbert Gold, "The Beat Mystique," in *The Beats,* ed. Seymour Krim (Greenwich, CT: Gold Medal Books, 1960), 158.

107. Robert S. Gold, *A Jazz Lexicon* (New York: Knopf, 1964), 23, 281, 99.

108. A "horizon of expectations" is a set of generic expectations that a public shares and with which a work of art engages in order to make its effects. "A literary work, even when it appears to be new, does not present itself as something absolutely new in an informational vacuum, but predisposes its audience to a very specific kind of reception by announcements, overt and covert signals, familiar characteristics, or implicit allusions. It awakens memories of that which was already read, brings the reader to a specific emotional attitude, and with its beginning arouses expectations for the 'middle and end,' which can then be maintained intact or altered, reoriented, or even fulfilled ironically in the course of the reading according to specific rules of the genre or type of text." Hans Robert Jauss, *Toward an Aesthetic of Reception,* trans. Timothy Bahti (Minneapolis: University of Minnesota Press, 1982), 23.

109. These forms and their narrative implications in American popular song are discussed in Graham Wood, "The Development of Song Forms in the Broadway and Hollywood Musicals of Richard Rodgers, 1919–1943" (Ph.D. diss., University of Minnesota, 1999).

110. Wood, "Song Forms," 136.

111. For an analytical template of lyric binary form and a bibliography on its use in nineteenth-century Italian opera, see James Hepokoski, "*Ottocento* Opera as Cultural Drama: Generic Mixtures in *Il Trovatore,*" in *Verdi's Middle Period, 1849–1859: Source Studies, Analysis, and Performance Practice,* ed. Martin Chusid (Chicago: University of Chicago Press, 1997), 147–96. For a discussion of this form's early adaptation from folk to Austrian art music repertories, see Dénes Bartha, "Song Form and the Concept of 'Quatrain,'" in *Haydn Studies: Proceedings of the International Haydn Conference, Washington, D.C., 1975,* ed. Jens Peter Larsen, Howard Serwer, and James Webster (New York: Norton, 1981), 353–55.

112. Herbie Nichols, "Step Tempest," on vol. 1 of *The Prophetic Herbie Nichols,* 10-inch LP, Blue Note BLP 5068, 1955; Herbie Nichols, "Chit Chatting," on *The Herbie Nichols Trio,* LP, Blue Note 1519, 1956.

113. Miles Davis, "So What," on *Kind of Blue,* Columbia CS 8163, 1959, LP.

114. Ashley Kahn, *Kind of Blue* (New York: Da Capo Press, 2000), 17.

115. Thelonious Monk, "Misterioso," on disc 2 of *Thelonious Monk: The Complete Blue Note Recordings,* CD, Blue Note 30363, 1994.

116. Thelonious Monk, "Off Minor," on *Thelonious Monk with John Coltrane,* CD, Riverside/ Original Jazz Classics OJCCD-039-2, 1987; Thelonious Monk, "Well, You Needn't," on *Monk's Music,* LP, Riverside RLP 12-9242, 1957.

117. André Hodeir, *Towards Jazz,* trans. Noel Burch (New York: Grove Press, 1962), 166.

118. In analyzing this passage, I pulled the root of each chord in the changes out of the sounded chord and placed it on the bottom, and then placed the remaining notes in their most compact arrangement above. The resulting chords can be mapped with pitch-class notation, which reveals the fundamental identity of measure 38 <0, 1, 4, 9, 10>, measures 39 and 44 <0, 1, 4, 6, 9, 10>, measure 46 <0, 1, 4, 6, 10>, and measure 47 <0, 1, 4, 6, 7, 10>.

119. Thelonious Monk, "I Should Care," on disc 2 of *Thelonious Monk: The Complete Blue Note Recordings,* CD, Blue Note 30363, 1994.

120. Monk evidently worked this introduction out in advance. It reappears in modified form as the introduction to the alternate take, and in the codas to his recordings of the same tune on *Solo Monk* and *Thelonious Himself*. Thelonious Monk, "I Should Care, alternate take," on disc 2 of *Thelonious Monk: The Complete Blue Note Recordings*, CD, Blue Note 30363, 1994; Thelonious Monk, "I Should Care," *Solo Monk*, CD, Columbia/Legacy CK 47854, 1992; Thelonious Monk, "I Should Care," *Thelonious Himself*, CD, Riverside/Original Jazz Classics 254, 1987.

121. Laurent de Wilde, *Monk*, trans. Jonathan Dickinson (New York: Marlow, 1997), 60–61.

122. These artistic qualities, as much as Monk's personal eccentricities, were responsible for Monk's reputation as the "mad monk" or the "high priest of bebop"—a weirdness so profound it could be expressed only in sacerdotal terms. Monk had already won this reputation by the time the 1948 Blue Note sessions were being released. For an early mass-media portrait of Monk along these lines, see Richard O. Boyer, "Bop," *New Yorker* 24 (July 3, 1948), 30–31. See also Dan Morgenstern, "An Evening with Monk," in *Reading Jazz*, ed. Robert Gottlieb (New York: Vintage, 1996), 608. For more on the various public meanings that attached to Monk's pianism, see Ben Givan, "Thelonious Monk's Pianism," *Journal of Musicology* 26, no. 3 (Summer 2009), 404–42. Robin D. G. Kelley's biography of Monk supersedes all previous understandings of Monk's inner life: see Kelley, *Thelonious Monk: The Life and Times of an American Original* (New York: Free Press, 2009).

123. Marshall McLuhan, Eric McLuhan, and David Carson, *The Book of Probes* (Corte Madera, CA: Gingko Press, 2003), 350.

124. John Covach has likewise contextualized Schoenberg's musical thought in the turn-of-the-century occultism of Rudolph Steiner and the Swedenborgians; John Covach, "Schoenberg and the Occult: Some Reflections on the Musical Idea," *Theory and Practice* 17, 103–18.

125. Broyard, "Portrait of the Hipster," 724.

126. This is a version of the punch line to a story in which an elderly woman asked Fats Waller to define jazz ("If you don't know by now, don't mess with it"). Marshall W. Stearns, *The Story of Jazz* (New York: Oxford University Press, 1956), 3. In an alternate version of this story, it is Louis Armstrong who replies, "If you still have to ask…shame on you." Max Jones, "Seventy Years on the Throne," in *Salute to Satchmo* (London: IPC Specialist and Professional Press, 1970), 25.

127. LeRoi Jones, "Milneburg Joys (or, Against 'Hipness' As Such)," *Kulchur* 3 (1961), 41.

128. Gillespie, *To Be or Not…to Bop*, 297.

129. Frank's quick sketch of the countercultural idea forms a background to his more fully worked-out idea of "hip consumerism," an ideology by which people resist what they perceive as personal inauthenticity by constructing images of their authentic selves through the products they purchase and appropriate. Thomas Frank, *The Conquest of Cool* (Chicago: University of Chicago Press, 1997).

130. *Neurotica* 1, no. 1 (Spring 48), 3.

131. See especially Jerrold Seigel, *Bohemian Paris: Culture, Politics, and the Boundaries of Bourgeois Life, 1830–1930* (New York; Viking, 1986). Seigel's use of the term "bohemia" is grounded in geographical and spatial metaphors; he conceives bohemia primarily as an anteroom for young bourgeois awaiting their entry into bourgeois society and as a place where the limits of permissible social identity are tested. Thus Seigel's bohemia is a site that originates a loose collection of antinomian ideas rather than a generative idea, image, or narrative. Firsthand accounts of contemporary American bohemia deal with countercultural art and thought primarily in terms of subcultural social groups; for example, see Ronald Sukenick, *Down and In: Life in the Underground* (New York: Beech Tree Books, 1987); Ann Powers, *Weird Like Us: My Bohemian America* (New York: Simon and Schuster, 2000); Herbert Gold, *Bohemia: Where Art, Angst, Love, and Strong Coffee Meet* (New York: Simon and Schuster, 1993).

132. Thomas Frank, "Why Johnny Can't Dissent," in Thomas Frank and Matt Weiland, eds., *Commodify Your Dissent: Salvos from the Baffler* (New York: Norton, 1997), 31–32.

133. Mailer, "The White Negro," 339.

134. LeRoi Jones, *Blues People*, 219.

135. Michael Szalay, *Hip Figures: A Literary History of the Democratic Party* (Stanford: Stanford University Press, 2012), 280.

136. Yet another interesting artifact from 1948 is an English translation of Marx's recently discovered "Alienation and Labor," published in the spring 1948 issue of *Twelfth Street*, a little magazine published by New School for Social Research. The New School was the "University in Exile" that sheltered many displaced German thinkers, including figures from the Frankfurt School whose thinking would influence countercultural radicals in the 1960s. Erich Fromm, for example, was heavily influenced by Marx's early "humanistic" writings, with their vision of people overcoming the fragmentation of their labor and personalities and achieving wholeness of community and self, and this vision in turn would become the structural footing on which the 1960s Movement bridged Marxism to their countercultural sensibility. Some of the intellectual appropriation of jazz in the 1940s had a Marxist cast; see Sidney Finkelstein, *Jazz: A People's Music* (New York; Citadel, 1948). Unlike the later jazz writing of Frank Kofsky, though, this kind of socialism has an old-fashioned Popular Front flavor in which the focus on individual freedom and a specifically cultural liberation is conspicuous by its absence.

137. Barbara Ehrenreich, *The Hearts of Men: American Dreams and the Flight from Commitment* (Garden City, NY: Anchor Press, 1984), 61.

138. These include David Riesman and Nathan Glazer, *The Lonely Crowd* (New Haven: Yale University Press, 1950); William Whyte, *The Organization Man* (New York: Simon and Schuster, 1956); John Kenneth Galbraith, *The Affluent Society* (Boston: Houghton Mifflin, 1958); C. Wright Mills, *The Power Elites* (New York: Oxford University Press, 1956); C. Wright Mills, *White Collar* (New York: Oxford University Press, 1951); Vance Packard, *The Hidden Persuaders* (New York: D. McKay, 1957). Three examples of the "middlebrow" discourse of conformity are Ardis Whitman, "The Danger of Being Too Well-Adjusted," *Reader's Digest* (December 1958), 43–45; Caroline Bird, "Born 1930: The Unlost Generation," *Harper's Bazaar* 2943 (February 1957), 104–7, 174–75; Paul O'Neil, "The 'Clan' Is the Most," *Life*, Dec. 22, 1958, 116, 122. The ironies of a mass discourse of nonconformity are pitilessly exposed in Richard Yates's novel *Revolutionary Road* (Boston: Little, Brown, 1961). As Daniel Bell noted at the time, "no-one in the United States defends conformity. Everyone is against it, and probably everyone always was." Daniel Bell, "America as a Mass Society: A Critique," in *The End of Ideology: On the Exhaustion of Political Ideas in the Fifties* (New York: Free Press, 1960), 35. For a more thorough consideration of the cultural and historiographical consequences of this insight, see Phil Ford, "Music at the Edge of the Construct," *Journal of Musicology* 26, no. 2 (2008), 240–73.

139. Quoted in Joseph Satin, *1950s: America's "Placid" Decade* (Boston: Houghton Mifflin, 1960), 166.

140. Writes Maritain, "I do not forget that the cultivated American—perhaps because he feels a particular urge to cast a critical eye in a national environment he considers uncritical—is as anxious to have America criticized as to have her loved. As a result, any writer who bitterly denounces the vices of this country is listened to with special care and sorrowful appreciation . . . The love of Americans for their country is not an indulgent, it is an exciting and chastening love; they cannot tolerate its defects." Jacques Maritain, *Reflections on America* (New York: Scribner, 1958), 43–44.

141. Saul, *Freedom Is, Freedom Ain't*, 33–34.

142. Milton Klonsky, "A Discourse on Hip," in *A Discourse on Hip*, 135–36.

143. Frank, *The Conquest of Cool*, 18–20.

144. Other writers on bohemian and avant-garde movements have repeatedly said much the same thing: Seigel, *Bohemian Paris*; Daniel Bell, *The Cultural Contradictions of Capitalism* (New York: Basic Books, 1996); Joseph A. Schumpeter, *Capitalism, Socialism, and Democracy* (New York: Harper & Brothers, 1942), 81–86, 139–55; Marshall Berman, *All That Is Solid Melts into Air: The Experience of Modernity* (New York: Simon and Schuster, 1982; repr. New York: Penguin, 1988).

145. Lionel Trilling, in Edward Grossman, Cynthia Ozick, Hilton Kramer, Norman Podhoretz, Lionel Trilling, Michael Novak, and Jack Richardson, "Culture and the Present Moment," *Commentary* 58, no. 6 (1974), 34.

146. Karl Marx and Friedrich Engels, *The Communist Manifesto,* ed. and trans. David McLellan (New York: Oxford University Press, 1992), 6.

147. George Orwell, review of *Stendhal,* by F. C. Green, in *Complete Works of George Orwell,* ed. Peter Davison, vol. 11 (London: Secker and Warburg, 1998), 379. Amiri Baraka makes a similar connection between bohemianism and the black middle class throughout his auto-biography: see especially Amiri Baraka, *The Autobiography of LeRoi Jones* (Chicago: Lawrence Hill Books, 1997), 342, 436 *passim.*

148. This trope of social criticism, though venerable, was most influentially articulated in Tom Wolfe's famous takedown of Leonard Bernstein, "Radical Chic: That Party at Lenny's," *New York,* June 8, 1970, 26–56. Although such arguments tend to degenerate into *ressentiment,* David Brooks's work of "comic sociology" on the confluence of bohemian and bourgeois styles and values is a suave modern performance: David Brooks, *Bobos in Paradise* (New York: Simon and Schuster, 2000).

149. Michael Azerrad, "Nirvana," *Rolling Stone,* Apr. 16, 1992, cover. Joseph Heath uses the same example to make a similar point in his gloss on Frank's theory of hip consumerism: "Is it possible to interpret [Cobain's appearance on the cover of *Rolling Stone*] as evidence that 'the system' is able to co-opt dissent? No. What it really shows is just that dissent *is* the system. Capitalism does not require hierarchy or cultural hegemony in order to function smoothly." Joseph Heath, "The Structure of Hip Consumerism," *Philosophy and Social Criticism* 27, no. 6 (2001), 16.

150. Rick Perlstein, "Who Owns the Sixties?" *Lingua Franca* 6 (May/June 1996), 32. Although nearly every sympathetic account of the 1960s tells this story, its best and fullest expres-sion is found in Todd Gitlin, *The Sixties: Years of Hope, Days of Rage* (New York: Bantam, 1987). Hostile accounts of the 1960s usually tell roughly the same story, only with an inversion of the value placed on each decade: the narrative of repression followed by liberation is transformed into one in which social harmony is destroyed by pointless agitation.

151. Morris Dickstein, "Cold War Blues: Notes on the Culture of the Fifties," *Partisan Review* 41, no. 1 (1974), 31; Gitlin, *The Sixties,* 12.

Chapter 3

1. Jack Kerouac, *Visions of Cody* (New York: McGraw-Hill, 1972; repr. New York: Penguin, 1993), 156.

2. Marshall McLuhan, Eric McLuhan, and David Carson, *The Book of Probes* (Corte Madera: Gingko Press, 2003), 350.

3. Miles Davis and Quincy Troupe, *Miles: The Autobiography* (New York: Simon and Schuster, 1989), 89. As Arnold Schoenberg's increasingly paranoid correspondence with Russell shows, some of the artists Russell recorded assumed he was getting rich at their expense. However, Russell never seems to have made much money with Dial, which eventually went bankrupt. Arnold Schoenberg, correspondence with Ross Russell, folder 14, box 19, Ross Russell Papers, Harry Ransom Center at the University of Texas at Austin. See David H. Smyth, "Schoenberg and Dial Records: The Composer's Correspondence with Ross Russell," *Journal of the Arnold Schoenberg Institute* 12 (1989), 68–90.

4. This novel has been both praised and damned for its lurid evocation of the hip underworld that surrounded Parker. For an account of this novel's reception, as well as the only full scholarly treatment of Russell, see John Gennari, "Race-ing the Bird: Ross Russell's Obsessive Pursuit of Charlie Parker," in *Blowin' Hot and Cool: Jazz and Its Critics* (Chicago: University of Chicago Press, 2006), 299–338.

5. In his 1949 and 1950 diaries alone, he records his encounters with Truman Capote, Igor Stravinsky, Robert Craft, Rene Kolisch, Rene Liebowitz, John Cage, Dizzy Gillespie, Bud Powell, Charlie Parker, Leonard Bernstein, Edgard Varèse, David Diamond, Dan Burley,

Howard McGhee, Edward Steuermann, Dylan Thomas, John Lewis, and Art Tatum, among others. Ross Russell, unpublished diaries (1949–1950), folders 1 and 2, box 55, Ross Russell Papers, Harry Ransom Center at the University of Texas at Austin.

6. This line was jotted down in a series of broad statements that Russell intended to use in his press interviews for *The Sound*. Royal composition notebook titled "Novel—The Sound/ New York May 1961," entry titled "General Points for Discussion/Social Aspects," folder box 56, "New York Notebooks: The Sound" (1960, 1961), Ross Russell Papers, Harry Ransom Center at the University of Texas at Austin.

7. Ross Russell, *The Sound* (New York: Dutton, 1961), 26.

8. Ross Russell, entry dated Jan. 11–12 1949, unpublished diaries (1949–1950), folders 1 and 2, box 55, Ross Russell Papers, Harry Ransom Center at the University of Texas at Austin.

9. John Clellon Holmes, *Go* (New York: Charles Scribner's Sons, 1952; repr. New York: Thunder's Mouth Press, 1988), 36. Holmes's line in *Go* apparently originated in a private remark Kerouac made to Holmes about theirs being a "generation of furtives." John Clellon Holmes, "Crazy Days, Numinous Nights: 1948–1950" [journal excerpts], *the unspeakable visions of the individual,* vol. 12, ed. Arthur and Kit Knight (California, PA: 1982), 113. This kind of talk, in turn, informed Holmes's famous public introduction of the "Beat generation": Holmes, "This is the Beat Generation," *New York Times Magazine*, Nov. 16, 1952, 10, 19–21. In a journal entry from around this time, Kerouac meditates on the connection between bebop and "our Reichians, our Orgonists, who mostly all smoke marijuana, listen to frantic 'bop' jazz, believe in homosexuality…and are beginning to recognize the beginning of an 'atomic disease' of sorts…There is definitely something afoot, a madness, not unlike the late Roman cult-madnesses." Jack Kerouac, *Windblown World: The Journals of Jack Kerouac 1947–1954,* ed. Douglas Brinkley (New York: Viking Penguin, 2004), 141–42.

10. Allen Ginsberg, "On Huncke's Book," *the unspeakable visions of the individual,* vol. 3, nos. 1–2, ed. Arthur and Kit Knight (California, PA: 1973), 21.

11. Neal Cassady to Jack Kerouac, July 16, 1949, in *Collected Letters 1944–1967*, ed. Dave Moore (New York: Penguin, 2004), 120.

12. Ernest Van den Haag, "Conspicuous Consumption of Self," *National Review*, Apr. 11, 1959, 656–58.

13. Ibid., 658.

14. Diane di Prima, *Recollections of My Life as a Woman* (New York: Viking, 2001), 202.

15. Lucien Lévy-Bruhl, *How Natives Think (Les Fonctions Mentales dans les Sociétés Inférieures),* trans. Lilian A. Clare (London: George Allen and Unwin, 1926).

16. Riley's poem is preserved in the clippings files at the Institute of Jazz Studies at Rutgers University, in a folder marked "jazz poetry." The only information I have been able to find about Riley is a short newspaper article: Don Safran, "Life of Riley in Beat Tempo," *Dallas Times Herald*, July 19, 1959.

17. Russell, entry dated Monday July 11 1949, unpublished diaries (1949–1950), folders 1 and 2, box 55, Ross Russell Papers, Harry Ransom Center at the University of Texas at Austin.

18. Roger-Pol Droit, *Astonish Yourself! 101 Experiments in the Philosophy of Everyday Life*, trans. Stephen Romer (New York: Penguin Compass, 2003), 197–98.

19. Robert Reisner wrote that the Beat, lacking "the fundamental intellectual honesty of the hipster," merely imitated his manner; Herbert Gold believed that the Beat was "the Hipster parodied and packaged as a commercial product." On either account, the Beats were pretending to be a more authentic kind of person. Van Den Haag, on the other hand, argues that they were pretending to a more authentic experience. Robert George Reisner, "The Parlance of Hip," in *The Jazz Titans* (New York: Da Capo Press, 1977), 149; Herbert Gold, "How to Tell the Beatniks from the Hipsters," *The Noble Savage* 1 (1960), 138.

20. Alan Watts, *Beat Zen, Square Zen, and Zen* (San Francisco: City Lights Books, 1959), 9–10.

21. Thomas Cleary, trans., Case 75, "Ruiyan's 'Constant Principle,'" *The Book of Serenity* (Boston: Shambhala, 1998), 316.

22. Svetlana Boym, *The Future of Nostalgia* (New York: Basic Books, 2001), xv. See also Benedict Taylor, "Nostalgia and Cultural Memory in Barber's *Knoxville: Summer of 1915,*" *Journal of Musicology* 25, no. 3 (2008), 211–29; Michael Long, "The Fantastic, the Picturesque, and the Dimensions of Nostalgia," in *Beautiful Monsters: Imagining the Classic in Musical Media* (Berkeley: University of California Press, 2008), 121–56.

23. John Clellon Holmes, *Nothing More to Declare* (New York: Dutton, 1967), 68.

24. Kerouac, *Visions of Cody,* 24.

25. "Das Firmament blaut ewig, und die Erde/Wird lange fest steh'n und aufblüh'n im Lenz/ Du aber, Mensch, wie lange lebst denn du?/Nicht hundert Jahre darfst du dich ergötzen/ An all dem morschen Tande dieser Erde!" Text by Hans Bethge and Gustav Mahler, *Lied von der Erde* (Vienna and Leipzig: Universal, 1911).

26. The phrase "nostalgia for the present" is Frederic Jameson's, from the ninth chapter of *Postmodernism, or, the Cultural Logic of Late Capitalism* (Durham, NC: Duke University Press, 1991).

27. Sevil Duvarci and Karim Nader, "Characterization of Fear Memory Reconsolidation," *Journal of Neuroscience* 24, no. 42 (Oct. 10, 2004), 9269–75.

28. Jonah Lehrer, *Proust Was a Neuroscientist* (New York: Houghton Mifflin Harcourt, 2007), 85.

29. The term "spontaneous bop prosody" was coined by Allen Ginsberg: Allen Ginsberg, *Howl and Other Poems* (San Francisco: City Lights, 1956), 3.

30. Allen Ginsberg, "Visions of the Great Rememberer," in Jack Kerouac, *Visions of Cody*, 409.

31. Ibid.

32. Ibid., 410.

33. Erik Mortenson writes that this gap is a central problematic in the Beats' engagement with presence, and that they "do not passively suffer such gaps; on the contrary, they theorize, inhabit, and produce them." Mortenson discusses the gap in terms of Ginsberg's photographs and the captions he wrote to accompany them; Mortenson, "Recording the Moment: The Role of the Photograph in Beat Representation," in *Capturing the Beat Moment: Cultural Politics and the Poetics of Presence* (Carbondale: Southern Illinois University Press, 2011), 121–54.

34. Ginsberg, Visions of the Great Rememberer," 410.

35. John Shapcott, "'I Didn't Punctuate It': Locating the Tape and Text of Jack Kerouac's *Visions of Cody* and *Dr. Sax,*" *Journal of American Studies* 36 (August 2002), 237.

36. Preston Whaley, *Blows Like a Horn: Beat Writing, Jazz, Style, and Markets in the Transformation of U.S. Culture* (Cambridge: Harvard University Press, 2004).

37. Greil Marcus, *The Old, Weird America: The World of Bob Dylan's Basement Tapes* (New York: Picador, 2001), 81.

38. John Clellon Holmes Recordings 1949–1951, 1968, Kent State University Libraries, Special Collections and Archives.

39. John Clellon Holmes, bibliographic note on the acetates, in Ann Charters, *A Bibliography of Works by Jack Kerouac* (New York: Phoenix Book Shop, 1967), 109–110.

40. The 1949 date is recorded by Kerouac in his journal; Kerouac, *Windblown World*, 237; the date of March 30, 1951 is indicated in acetate 4, which captures Symphony Sid announcing a live broadcast "next Friday April the sixth." (There was a Friday, April 6, in 1951 but not in neighboring years.) Confusingly, Holmes labeled acetate 15 "March 30 1951," but this contains Kerouac's "boyishly sad Hamlet soliloquies," which Kerouac notes in his 1949 journal entry. The two firm boundary dates of October 1949 and March 1951 do not exclude the possibility that some recordings were made earlier or later, though Holmes remembered having the acetate recorder for only a few months before his brother-in-law reclaimed it.

41. Along with canonic Kerouac biographies by Ann Charters, Gerald Nicosia, and Barry Miles, much of the biographical context for this chapter (particularly the party scene at Holmes's Lexington Avenue apartment) can be supplied by Ann and Samuel Charters, *Brother-Soul: John Clellon Holmes, Jack Kerouac, and the Beat Generation* (Jackson: University of Mississippi Press, 2010), a chronicle of Holmes's and Kerouac's friendship.

42. The details of Ginsberg's life at this time are told in Bill Morgan, *I Celebrate Myself: The Somewhat Private Life of Allen Ginsberg* (New York: Viking, 2006), one of the very best and most even-handed Beat biographies.

43. The scroll has been published as a separate edition: Jack Kerouac, *On the Road: The Original Scroll* (New York: Viking, 2007).

44. R. Murray Schafer, "The Music of the Environment," in *Audio Culture: Readings in Modern Music*, ed. Christoph Cox and Daniel Warner (New York and London: Continuum, 2004), 32–33. These ideas were developed at greater length in R. Murray Schafer, *The Tuning of the World* (New York: Knopf, 1977).

45. Allen Ginsberg, "A Mad Gleam," from *Holy Soul Jelly Roll*, Rhino Word Beat R2 71693, 1994, CD. Some excerpts of the Holmes acetates, notably Kerouac reading excepts from *The Town and the City*, have appeared on bootlegs.

46. Allen Ginsberg, "Fie My Fum," John Clellon Holmes Recordings 1949–1951, side 9a, Kent State University Libraries, Special Collections and Archives; Allen Ginsberg, "Fie My Fum," *Collected Poems 1947–1997* (New York: HarperCollins, 2006), 31. Aside from a couple of erotic new lines (Lick my peak/Pull my soul), the acetate version differs from the *Collected Poems* edition in the ordering of lines. If each consecutive line of the canonical version were assigned a number and each new line assigned an asterisk, the acetate version could be mapped 1, 2, 3, 4, 5, 6, 19, 20, *, *, 7, 8, and so on.

47. John Clellon Holmes to Allen Ginsberg, July 28, 1949; Ginsberg to Holmes, mid-July 1949, folder 32, box 1 (1940–1949), series 1 (correspondence 1942–1994), Allen Ginsberg Papers, Stanford University Special Collections.

48. Allen Ginsberg, liner notes for *Holy Soul Jelly Roll*.

49. John Clellon Holmes, "Fragment of Attila," John Clellon Holmes Recordings 1949–1951, side 12a.

50. Jack Kerouac, selection from *The Town and the City*, John Clellon Holmes Recordings 1949–1951, side 11a.

51. Shapcott, "'I Didn't Punctuate It,'" 236.

52. This field originated in Schafer's *The Tuning of the World* and Jacques Attali's *Noise: The Political Economy of Music*, trans. Brian Massumi (Minneapolis: University of Minnesota Press, 1985). While small, this field has sustained a literature too large and interesting for quick summary; the studies most relevant to this book are Jonathan Sterne, *The Audible Past: Cultural Origins of Sound Reproduction* (Durham, NC: Duke University Press, 2003); Douglas Kahn, Noise Water Meat: *A History of Sound in the Arts* (Cambridge: MIT Press, 2001); Viet Erlmann, *Reason and Resonance: A History of Modern Aurality* (New York: Zone Books, 2010).

53. Allen Ginsberg and Jack Kerouac, conversation, John Clellon Holmes Recordings 1949–1951, side 11a.

54. Friedrich Kittler, *Gramophone, Film, Typewriter*, trans. Geoffrey Winthrop-Young and Michael Wutz (Stanford: Stanford University Press, 1999), 51–68; Jonathan Sterne, "A Resonant Tomb," in *The Audible Past*, 287–333.

55. Stan Getz, "Running Water," John Clellon Holmes Recordings 1949–1951, side 13b.

56. Perhaps the earliest sustained example of this is Warren Tallman, "Kerouac's Sound," *Evergreen Review* 4, no. 11 (1960), 153–69. A shorter but more successful attempt is Clark Coolidge, "Kerouac's Sound," in *Beats at Naropa: An Anthology*, ed. Anne Waldman and Laura Wrights (Minneapolis: Coffee House Press, 2009), 19–23. Gerald Nicosia writes a few suggestive (though brief) comments on the cadence of Kerouac's prose in *Memory Babe: A Critical Biography of Jack Kerouac* (New York: Grove Press, 1983), 305–8.

57. Jon Panish, *The Color of Jazz: Race and Representation in Postwar American Culture* (Jackson: University of Mississippi Press, 1997), 138. See also Regina Weinreich, *The Spontaneous Poetics of Jack Kerouac: A Study of the Fiction* (Carbondale: Southern Illinois University Press, 1987); W. T. Lhamon, *Deliberate Speed: The Origins of a Cultural Style in the American 1950s* (Washington: Smithsonian Institution Press, 1990).

58. Panish, *The Color of Jazz*, 139.

59. Jack Kerouac and Seymour Wyse, "Hot House," by Dizzy Gillespie, John Clellon Holmes Recordings 1949–1951, side 20a.

60. It is probably truest to say that Kerouac's use of jazz "lies in the music's ideological, behavioral, and semiotic implications—in particular their roots in African American culture—rather than in direct application of its formal rules." Douglas Malcolm, "'Jazz America': Jazz and African American Culture in Jack Kerouac's *On The Road*," *Contemporary Literature* 40, no. 1 (Spring 1999), 85.

61. Kerouac makes a similar point with some asperity in a letter to Neal Cassady a few months after these recordings were made. Jack Kerouac, *Selected Letters 1940–1956*, ed. Ann Charters (New York: Viking, 1995), 231–32. The acetates include transcriptions of Stravinsky's Firebird and several other classical pieces that Holmes made for his own use. Kerouac lost enthusiasm for Tristano because it seemed too intellectual, too cool: "I agree with the hot. *Play some music.* An art which expresses the mind of the mind, and not the mind of life (the idea of mortal life on earth), is a dead art." Jack Kerouac, *Windblown World*, 267.

62. John Clellon Holmes, Jack Kerouac, and Seymour Wyse, "Logic" and "The Absolute," John Clellon Holmes Recordings 1949–1951, sides 13b, 15a.

63. Eunmi Shim, *Lennie Tristano: His Life in Music* (Ann Arbor: University of Michigan Press, 2007) provides an analysis and historical overview of these recordings. Preston Whaley writes a lengthy, impressionistic evocation of "Intuition" in the manner of Greil Marcus and considers this piece as a parallel to Kerouac's "Frisco Tape," apparently without being aware of Holmes's earlier home recordings. See Whaley, *Blows Like a Horn*, 133–38.

64. Holmes, in Charters, *Bibliography*, 109–10.

65. Jack Kerouac, *Windblown World*, 237.

66. Jack Kerouac to Allen Ginsberg, Jan. 2, 1948, in *Selected Letters 1940–1956*, 141.

67. Lee, "While You Are Gone," John Clellon Holmes Recordings 1949–1951, side 7b. The identity of "Lee," who is addressed as such on the acetates, is one of the most interesting puzzles in these acetates. Could it be Alene Lee? It is universally agreed that Kerouac and Alene Lee did not meet until 1953, and Holmes remembers his brother-in-law taking back his acetate cutter earlier. And yet "Lee," like Alene Lee's character in *The Subterraneans*, "can freely and with great pleasure vocally improvise on the music," unlike everyone else captured on the Holmes acetates. Whaley, *Blows Like a Horn*, 89. Is it possible that Alene Lee was one of the many anonymous hipsters who drifted through Holmes's apartment in those hard-partying years? Is it possible that Kerouac met her without really registering who she was until two years later? Who knows. This is yet another example of how these acetates raise questions they cannot answer.

68. Simon Frith, "What Is Bad Music?" in *Bad Music: The Music We Love to Hate* (New York and London: Routledge, 2004), 18.

69. Sasha Frere-Jones, "Screen Shot," *New Yorker*, Feb. 6, 2012.

70. Jack Kerouac, "Belief and Technique for Modern Prose," *Evergreen Review* 2, no. 8 (Spring 1959), 57.

71. Eduard Hanslick, *On the Musically Beautiful: A Contribution Towards the Revision of the Aesthetics of Music*, trans. Geoffrey Payzant (Indianapolis: Hackett, 1986), 29.

72. Daniel Albright, *Modernism and Music: An Anthology of Sources* (Chicago: University of Chicago Press, 2004), 270.

73. Kerouac, "Belief and Technique for Modern Prose," 57.

74. Allen Ginsberg, letter to John Clellon Holmes, mid-July 1949, folder 32, box 1 (1940–1949), series 1 (correspondence 1942–1994), Allen Ginsberg Papers.

75. Ibid.

76. Kerouac, *Visions of Cody*, 351.

77. By extraordinary coincidence (or maybe not?), this exact moment, minus the rest of the number, appears on the B side of acetate 15, immediately after Kerouac's Hamlet soliloquies. Side A of this record features "The Three Men of Music" (Wyse, Kerouac, and Holmes again) performing another Tristano imitation, "The Absolute."

78. Scott DeVeaux, *The Birth of Bebop: A Social and Musical History* (Berkeley: University of California Press, 1997), 220.

79. Thomas Frank, "Why Johnny Can't Dissent," in *Commodify Your Dissent: Salvos from the Baffler*, ed. Thomas Frank and Matt Weiland (New York: Norton, 1997), 33.

80. Susan Sontag, "The Image-World," in *On Photography* (New York: Farrar, Straus and Giroux, 1977), 154.

81. The term "magical consciousness" is owed to Susan Greenwood, *The Anthropology of Magic* (Oxford: Berg, 2009), 63–73.

82. William S. Burroughs, a lifelong practitioner of magic, treated recordings in exactly this way, for example cursing a café owner by surreptitiously recording several hours of the café's soundscape and playing it back at subliminal volumes, in order to reflect "the target's own base shittiness" back at him. Cabell McLean, "Playback: My Personal Experience of Chaos Magic with William S. Burroughs, Sr.," *Ashé: The Journal of Experimental Spirituality* 2, no. 3, 21–29. Recordings were an important part of Burroughs's magical/artistic praxis: see Melissa Dawn Goldsmith, "'Star Me Kitten': William S. Burroughs' Musical Recordings, Marlene Dietrich, and the Aesthetics of his Dark Americana," unpublished paper presented at the seventy-fifth Annual Meeting of the American Musicological Society (Philadelphia, 2009).

83. Wayne Koestenbaum, *The Queen's Throat: Opera, Homosexuality, and the Mystery of Desire* (New York: Poseidon Press, 1993; New York: Da Capo, 2001), 53.

84. Ibid., 56.

85. Allen Ginsberg to John Clellon Holmes, mid-July 1949, folder 32, box 1 (1940–1949), series 1 (correspondence 1942–1994), Allen Ginsberg Papers, Stanford University Special Collections.

86. The unromantic story of how this film was made is told in Blaine Allen, "The Making (and Unmaking) of *Pull My Daisy*," *Film History* 2, no. 3 (1988), 185–205. An entertaining and more romantic account may be found in David Amram, *Offbeat: Collaborating with Kerouac* (Boulder: Paradigm, 2008). The myth of spontaneity that instantly attached itself to this film had much to do with Jonas Mekas's advocacy: see Jonas Mekas, "*Pull My Daisy* and the Truth of Cinema," in *Movie Journal: The Rise of the New American Cinema, 1959–1971* (New York: Collier, 1972), 5–6. For an early dissenting view, see Parker Tyler, "For *Shadows*, Against *Pull My Daisy*," in *Film Culture Reader*, ed. P. Adams Sitney (New York: Praeger, 1970), 108–17.

87. Jack Kerouac to Carolyn Cassady, June 23, 1961, in *Dear Carolyn: Letters to Carolyn Cassady, the unspeakable visions of the individual*, vol. 13, ed. Arthur and Kit Knight (California, PA: 1983), 24.

88. Jack Kerouac to Carolyn Cassady, Oct. 21, 1962, in *Dear Carolyn*, 31.

89. Kerouac was not the only writer of his cohort to express alarm at what they saw as the coarsening of their literary hip sensibility. See also Paul Goodman, *New Reformation: Notes of a Neolithic Conservative* (New York: Random House, 1970); John Clellon Holmes, "The Game of the Name," in *Passionate Opinions: The Cultural Essays* (Fayetteville: University of Arkansas Press, 1993); Gershon Legman, *The Fake Revolt* (New York: Breaking Point, 1967); Michael Harrington, "We Few, We Happy Few, We Bohemians," *Esquire*, August 1972, 99–103, 162–64.

Chapter 4

1. Milt Gabler and John Benson Brooks, "What's a Square?" from *Avant Slant (One Plus 1 = II?): A Twelve Tone Collage*, LP, Decca DL 75018, 1968.

2. Marshall McLuhan, *Culture Is Our Business* (New York: Ballantine, 1970), 192.

3. "The Inner Sleeve," a promotional publication of CBS records, ed. Mort Goode, possibly attached to CBS C 2908. For Horowitz, a sidebar titled "Pure Brilliance!"

4. Thomas Frank, *The Conquest of Cool: Business Culture, Counterculture, and the Rise of Hip Consumerism* (Chicago: University of Chicago Press, 1997), 238.

5. For more on the representational conventions of the too-normal, see Phil Ford, "Music at the Edge of the Construct," *Journal of Musicology* 26, no. 2 (Summer 2009), 240–73. The

television series *Mad Men* puts the structural absence of hipness at the center of its drama. The show's depiction of America in the early 1960s depends on our knowledge of how quickly the certainties of an America Before Hipness would soon disappear—a knowledge that the show's characters necessarily do not share.

6. A fine dissertation traces the phenomenon of beat tourism: Clinton Robert Starr, "The Beat Generation and Urban Countercultures in the United States During the Late 1950s and Early 1960s" (Ph.D. diss., University of Texas, 2005).

7. Diane di Prima, *Recollections of My Life as a Woman* (New York: Viking, 2001), 202.

8. The term "presence culture," along with its opposite, "meaning culture," is from Hans-Ulrich Gumbrecht, *The Production of Presence: What Meaning Cannot Convey* (Stanford: Stanford University Press, 2003).

9. Hannah Higgins, *Fluxus Experience* (Berkeley: University of California Press, 2002), 36.

10. Eric Hobsbawm, "Jazz Since 1960," in *Uncommon People* (London: Weidenfeld and Nicolson, 1998), 281.

11. Billy Taylor, "Jazz in the Contemporary Marketplace: Professional and Third-Sector Strategies for the Balance of the Century," in *New Perspectives on Jazz* (Washington, DC: Smithsonian Institution Press, 1990), 89–98.

12. Philip Larkin, "Jazz as a Way of Life," in *All What Jazz: A Record Diary 1961–68* (London: Faber and Faber, 1970), 62.

13. The literature on the American New Left is huge. The classic study of the Students for a Democratic Society, the flagship organization of the student New Left, is Kirkpatrick Sale, *SDS* (New York: Random House, 1973). There have been excellent studies that place the SDS in the context of liberal Christianity, the burgeoning New Right, the counterculture, and society at large. See Douglas Rossinow, *The Politics of Authenticity: Liberalism, Christianity, and the New Left in America* (New York: Columbia University Press, 1998); Rebecca E. Klatch, *A Generation Divided: The New Left, the New Right, and the 1960s* (Berkeley: University of California Press, 1999); and David Farber, *Chicago '68* (Chicago: University of Chicago Press, 1988). The best general histories of the New Left are probably Todd Gitlin, *The Sixties: Years of Hope, Days of Rage* (New York: Bantam, 1987; repr. 1993), and James Miller, *Democracy Is in the Streets* (New York: Simon and Schuster, 1987).

14. Industrial Workers of the World, "Resurgent Youth Movement," pamphlet, Mar. 12, 1967, box 34, New Left Collection, Hoover Institution Library and Archives, Stanford University. The tension between the New Left and countercultural ends of the Movement spectrum can be traced through successive issues of *Ramparts,* one of the most important publications of the New Left. See, for example, Joan Holden and R. G. Davis, "Living," *Ramparts* 8, no. 2 (August 1969), 63; Joan Holden, "The Wild West Rock Show: Shooting Up a Rock Bonanza," *Ramparts* 8, no. 6 (December 1969), 70–76; Ed Leimbacher, "The Crash of the Jefferson Airplane," *Ramparts* 8, no. 7 (January 1970), 14–16.

15. See, for example, *Rolling Stone*'s front-page polemic against the Yippies and their attempt to recruit rock musicians to their 1968 action in Chicago. Jann Wenner, "Musicians Reject Political Exploiters," *Rolling Stone*, May 11, 1968, 1, 22.

16. Nelson Barr, "A Bouquet of Fuck Yous," *Fuck You: A Magazine of the Arts* 5, no. 4 (1963), unpaginated. A good overview of this topic is Doug Rossinow, "The Revolution Is About Our Lives: The New Left's Counterculture," in *Imagine Nation: The American Counterculture of the 1960s and 70s,* eds. Peter Braunstein and Michael William Doyle (New York: Routledge, 2002), 99–124.

17. Laurence Leamer, *The Paper Revolutionaries: The Rise of the Underground Press* (New York: Simon and Schuster, 1972), 13. See also Terry H. Anderson, *The Movement and the Sixties* (New York: Oxford University Press, 1995).

18. Chandler Brossard, *Who Walk in Darkness* (New York: New Directions, 1952), 54.

19. Ned Polsky, "The Village Beat Scene: Summer 1960," in *Hustlers, Beats, and Others* (Chicago: Aldine, 1967), 163. Dave Van Ronk recalled that "the real Beats liked cool jazz, beebop, and hard drugs, and the folkniks would sit around on the floor and sing songs of the oppressed masses." Robbie Woliver, *Bringing it All Back Home: Twenty-Five Years of American Music at Folk City* (New York: Pantheon, 1986), 11–12. See also Ronald Sukenick, *Down*

and In: Life in the Underground (New York: Beech Tree Books, 1987), 13. The contrasting cultural politics of bebop and folk music are illustrated in a print exchange between the *Village Voice*'s jazz critic and a folk musician named Piute Pete. Robert Reisner, "Folk Jazz, U.S.A." *Village Voice*, Apr. 3, 1957, 8; Piute Pete, letter to the editors, *Village Voice*, Apr. 17, 1957, 4. As always, there were those who bridged the gaps between adjacent social and artistic circles; among these Ronald Cohen lists John Cohen, the Clancy brothers, Mary Travers, Harry Smith, Izzy Young, and David Amram. Ronald Cohen, *Rainbow Quest: The Folk Music Revival and American Society, 1940–1970* (Amherst: University of Massachusetts Press, 2002), 108. And throughout the 1950s, John Benson Brooks devoted himself to creating a fusion of jazz and folk music; see Chapter 6. Brooks's album *Folk Jazz USA* (Vik LX-1083, 1956) and Fred Katz's *Folk Songs for Far-Out Folks* (Warner Brothers 1277, 1959) both attempt this fusion.

20. Suzanne Kiplinger, "This Hip-Historian Knows a Man's Pad Is His Castle," *Village Voice*, June 24, 1959, 7. Examples of this criticism from the conservative (or at least "consensus liberal") point of view are legion; two examples from the Left are David McReynolds, "Youth 'Disaffiliated' from a Phony World," *Village Voice*, Mar. 11, 1959, 5; and Nicholas Brownrigg's response to LeRoi Jones's writing on Cuba, "Cuba Libre," *Evergreen Review* 17 (1961), 126–27.

21. For a study of music in the French student protests of May 1968, see Eric Drott, *Music and the Elusive Revolution: Cultural Politics and Political Culture in France, 1968–1981* (Berkeley: University of California Press, 2011).

22. Hobsbawm, "Jazz Since 1960," 284–85.

23. A good introduction to Sinclair may be found in Jeff A. Hale, "The White Panthers' 'Total Assault on the Culture,'" in *Imagine Nation*, 125–56.

24. John Sinclair, "We Are a People," in *Guitar Army: Street Writings/Prison Writings* (New York: Douglas Book, 1972), 223. This theory was arrived at only after tortuous wrangling among the central committee of the White Panther Party, some of which is captured in an unpublished audiotape, "White Panther Party Meeting and Criticism," unit 1, no. 1, Box 30, John and Leni Sinclair Papers 1957–2003, Bentley Historical Library, University of Michigan at Ann Arbor.

25. Tom Hayden, Stew Albert, Judy Clavir, et al., "Berkeley Liberation Program," leaflet, box 63, folder "Leaflets 1969," Hardin B. Jones Archive, Hoover Institution Library and Archives, Stanford University. The Berkeley Liberation Program was first issued in the *Berkeley Barb*, May 30, 1969, shortly after the People's Park demonstrations in Berkeley. The ideological significance of this imagery is similar to that of the anarchist, socialist, and countercultural signs fitted together into the "Yippie flag" that Abbie Hoffman presumptuously called the "generally agreed upon flag of our nation." The flag was designed as a red five-pointed star and marijuana leaf on a black background. Abbie Hoffman, *Steal This Book* (New York: Pirate Editions, Grove Press, 1971), 37.

26. Hunter S. Thompson, *Fear and Loathing in Las Vegas: A Savage Journey to the Heart of the American Dream* (New York: Random House, 1976), 68.

27. Ibid.

28. Norman Mailer, "The White Negro: Superficial Reflections on the Hipster," in *Advertisements for Myself* (New York: Putnam, 1959), 339.

29. Norman Mailer, "The Hip and the Square," in *Advertisements for Myself*, 424–25.

30. Elizabeth Hardwick, "The American Woman as Snow-Queen: Our Self-Contemptuous Acceptance of Europe's Myth," *Commentary* 12, no. 6 (December 1951), 546–50.

31. Greil Marcus, *The Old, Weird America: The World of Bob Dylan's Basement Tapes* (New York: Picador, 2001), 8.

32. Bob Dylan, "Ballad of a Thin Man," on *Highway 61 Revisited*, LP, Columbia CS 9189, 1965.

33. John Sinclair modified this interpretation and suggested that Mr. Jones represents someone addicted to "death drugs" (heroin and amphetamines) and mistakenly thinking that he or she is hip. John Sinclair, *Guitar Army*, 306.

34. Bobby Seale recounts the story of Newton's passionate exegesis of this song in *Seize the Time: The Story of the Black Panther Party and Huey P. Newton* (New York: Random House,

1970), 183–87. The extraordinary Dylan biopic *I'm Not There* contains a brief scene drawn from this account.

35. Nat Hentoff, "Something's Happening and You Don't Know What It Is Do You, Mr. Jones?" *Evergreen Review* 10, no. 4 (1966), 54.

36. Pauline Kael felt that this dual consciousness was the source of Dylan's sense of humor: "The Bob Dylan [his fans] responded to was a put-on artist. He was derisive, and even sneering, but in the Sixties that was felt to be a way of freaking out those who weren't worthy of being talked to straight. Implicit in the put-on was the idea that the Establishment was so fundamentally dishonest that dialogue with any of its representatives (roughly, anyone who wore a tie) was debased from the start. And Dylan was a Counterculture hero partly because of the speed and humor of his repartee." Pauline Kael, "The Calvary Gig," *New Yorker*, Feb. 13, 1978, 107–11. Compare this with Jacob Brackman's discussion of put-on humor later in this chapter.

37. Yale '54 [pseud.], letter to "Saloon Society," *Village Voice*, Mar. 11, 1959, 12. Jules Feiffer commented on this kind of quasi-anthropological (and sexual) tourism, as he did on almost every other aspect of Village life and its culture. See Jules Feiffer, "Sick, Sick, Sick," cartoon, *Village Voice*, Jan. 21, 1959, 4.

38. Brossard, *Who Walk in Darkness*, 65.

39. Jay Landesman, *Rebel Without Applause* (Sag Harbor, NY: Permanent Press, 1987), 86. Broyard's role in Brossard's novel is discussed in Henry Louis Gates, Jr., "White Like Me," *New Yorker*, June 17, 1996, 60.

40. Kenneth Burke, "Four Master Tropes," in *A Grammar of Motives* (New York: Prentice-Hall, 1945), 503–15.

41. John Clellon Holmes, "The Name of the Game," in *Passionate Opinions: The Cultural Essays* (Fayetteville: University of Arkansas Press, 1988), 54–55.

42. Anatole Broyard, "Portrait of the Hipster," *Partisan Review* 15, no. 6 (1948), 724.

43. Charlie Parker, "Ornithology," Dial 1002, 1946, 78 rpm recording, reissued on disc 1 of Charlie Parker, *The Complete Savoy and Dial Master Takes*, CD, Savoy SVY 17149, 2002.

44. André Hodeir, *Towards Jazz*, trans. Noel Burch (New York: Grove Press, 1962), 181.

45. Jay-Z, *Decoded* (New York: Spiegel and Grau, 2011), 12. This kind of friction between flow and beat is a formal or aesthetic point hip-hop and bebop have in common; for an analysis of Blackalicious's "Paragraph President" along similar lines, see Philip Ford, "American Popular Music in the Cold War: The Hip Aesthetic and the Countercultural Idea" (Ph.D. diss., University of Minnesota, 2003), 307–9.

46. Broyard, "Portrait of the Hipster," 724. Emphasis in the original.

47. An episode from Ralph Ellison's novel *Invisible Man* muses on this complex perceptual operation: the protagonist describes listening to Louis Armstrong after smoking a reefer and sensing time differently, becoming aware not only of the succession of perceptual moments as they appear to him but of the spaces between them. Stoned, "you slip into the breaks and look around." Ellison, *Invisible Man* (New York: Random House, 1952; New York: Vintage, 1995), 8.

48. Ross Russell, "Bird and Sartre" manuscript (n.d.), Ross Russell Papers, folder 3, box 13, Harry Ransom Center at the University of Texas at Austin.

49. Louis Gottlieb, "Why So Sad, Pres?" in *The Lester Young Reader*, ed. Lewis Porter (Washington: Smithsonian Institution Press, 1991), 215–16. Gottlieb, like Fred Katz, was a minor figure who appears everywhere in hip culture. Gottlieb had a Ph.D. in musicology from Berkeley, edited the little magazine *Jazz: A Quarterly of American Music*, was a comedian and folksinger with the Limeliters, and was the moving spirit behind the Digger commune Morningstar.

50. Peter Tamony, "Bessie: Vocumentary," *Jazz: A Quarterly Review of American Music* (Fall 1959), 284.

51. Philip H. Ennis, *The Seventh Stream: The Emergence of Rocknroll in American Popular Music* (Hanover, NH: Wesleyan University Press, University Press of New England, 1992), 86.

52. Thomas Pynchon, "Entropy," in *Slow Learner* (Boston: Little, Brown, 1984), 94–95.

53. John Mehegan, letter to the editors, *Down Beat*, June 13, 1956, 4.

54. Erle Irons, letter to the editors, *Down Beat*, Jan. 7, 1960, 8.

55. Ross Russell, "The Benedetti Tapes," typescript, folder 6, box 13 ("Yardbird in Lotusland"), Ross Russell Papers, Harry Ransom Center at the University of Texas at Austin. This article has been published in French as Ross Russell, "Yardbird in Lotusland: Les Souvenirs de Ross Russell sur Charlie Parker," *Jazz Hot* 255 (November 1969), 22–25. I have used Russell's original typescript as the source for my quotations.

56. Charlie Parker, *Bird on 52nd Street*, LP, Jazz Workshop JWS-501, 1958.

57. Russell, "Benedetti Tapes," 13–14.

58. Ross Russell, *The Sound* (New York: Dutton, 1961), 165.

59. Nat Hentoff was particularly vocal about finding a place for jazz in mainstream intellectual life: see Nat Hentoff, "Jazz and the Intellectuals: Somebody Goofed," *Chicago Review* 9, no. 3 (1955), 110–21; Hentoff, "Whose Art Form? Jazz at Midcentury," in *Jazz: New Perspectives on the History of Jazz by Twelve of the World's Foremost Jazz Critics and Scholars*, ed. Nat Hentoff and Albert J. McCarthy (New York: Rinehart, 1959).

60. Nat Hentoff, "Lennie Tristano: Multitaping Doesn't Make Me a Phony," *Down Beat*, May 16, 1956, 11.

61. William Bruce Cameron, "Sociological Notes on the Jam Session," *Social Forces* 33, no. 1 (December 1954), 177–82; Alan P. Merriam and Raymond W. Mack, "The Jazz Community," *Social Forces* 38, no. 3 (1960), 211–22; and Howard Becker, "The Professional Dance Musician and His Audience," *American Journal of Sociology* 57, no. 2 (1951), 136–44. This last article was republished, in slightly different form, as Howard Becker, "The Culture of a Deviant Group: The Dance Musician," in *Outsiders: Studies in the Sociology of Deviance* (New York: Free Press, 1963), 79–100.

62. Stephen Kercher, *Revel with a Cause: Liberal Satire in Postwar America* (Chicago: University of Chicago Press, 2006), 78.

63. The topic of sick humor and "sickniks" (sick-joking hipsters) was a journalistic fad of the late 1950s and early 1960s—the same years as the parallel fad for Beatnik stories. See "The Sickniks," *Time*, July 13, 1959, 42; Robert Ruark, "Lets Nix the Sickniks," *Saturday Evening Post*, June 29–July 6, 1963, 338–39; "Bloody Mary, Anyone?" *Time*, Oct. 21, 1957, 27; Gerald Walker, "Sick Jokes," *Esquire*, December 1957, 151–53; and Gilbert Millstein, "The New Sick and/or Well Comic," *New York Times Magazine*, Aug. 7, 1960, 36.

64. Jonathan Miller, "The Sick White Negro," *Partisan Review* 30, no. 1 (1963), 151.

65. Benjamin DeMott, "The New Irony: Sickniks and Others," *American Scholar* 31 (Winter 1961–62), 108–19. See also Donald Phelps, "The Muck School," *Kulchur* 1, no. 1 (Spring 1960), 11–17.

66. Individual exceptions notwithstanding, there is a good deal of sociological evidence that suggests Movement participants were not rebelling against their parents' politics. Many of them were "red-diaper babies" who sought to honor their parent's radicalism by reinventing it. Rebecca Klatch points out that this is equally true of the young activists in the 1960s New Right: "Rather than a rejection of the older generation, the involvement of the majority of activists of both the left and the right represents an *extension of parental beliefs*." Klatch, *A Generation Divided*, 43. See also Richard Flacks, "The Liberated Generation: An Exploration of the Roots of Student Protest," *Journal of Social Issues* 23, no. 3 (1967), 52–75; Steven H. Lewis and Robert E. Kraut, "Correlates of Student Political Activism and Ideology," *Journal of Social Issues* 28, no. 4 (1972), 131–49; and James Donovan and Morton Shaevitz, "Student Political Activists: A Typology," *Youth and Society* 4, no. 4 (June 1973), 379–411. More generally, the model of generational conflict has proved inadequate to explain the differences in attitude between young people as a whole (not only the radicals) and their parents. See Kent Jennings and Richard Niemi, "Continuity and Change in Political Orientations: A Longitudinal Study of Two Generations," *American Political Science Review* 69 (1975), 1316–55.

67. Jacob Brackman, *The Put-On: Modern Fooling and Modern Mistrust* (Chicago: Regnery, 1971), 90.

68. Ibid., 91.

69. Leslie A. Fiedler, "The New Mutants," *Partisan Review* 32, no. 4 (1965), 505–25. For an example of this sort of writing from a slightly later time, see *Kaiser Aluminum News* 27,

no. 1 (May 1969), a graphically sophisticated publication devoted to analyzing the dawning awareness of the "children of change." In this context, it is worth noting science fiction's influence on the 1960s counterculture; see especially Theodore Sturgeon, *More Than Human* (New York: Farrar, Straus and Young, 1953), whose notion of a "homo gestalt"—a mutation that fuses a generation of young people into a collective higher consciousness—was particularly influential.

70. Jean Shepherd's monologues provide particularly clear examples of this. See especially Jean Shepherd, "The Night People vs. Creeping Meatballism," *Mad* 32 (March–April 1957).

71. Those within the 1960s counterculture often contrasted the new rock to older forms of American popular music in such terms; for example, "white American music, in finally discarding its phony tin-pan alley plastic-sugar trip, has exposed the poverty of sensitivity that characterizes this culture." "Indo-Rock," *P.O. Frisco*, Sep. 3, 1966, 8.

72. Irving Howe, "Mass Society and Post-Modern Fiction," *Partisan Review* 26, no. 3 (1959), 426.

73. Marcuse's writing at times showed the influence of the counterculture: "Liberation from the Affluent Society" in *To Free a Generation! The Dialectics of Liberation*, ed. David Cooper (London: Penguin, 1968) was his contribution to a symposium whose participants included R. D. Laing, Gregory Bateson, Paul Goodman, and Stokely Carmichael. A range of New Left opinion on Marcuse can be sampled in *Critical Interruptions: New Left Perspectives on Herbert Marcuse*, ed. Paul Breines (New York: Herder and Herder, 1970).

74. Although the New Left was originally conceived in reaction to the doctrinaire Marxism of the Popular Front Left, when talk of revolution spread in the late 1960s "no other coherent, integrative, and explicit philosophy of revolution" could be found, and orthodox Marxism made a comeback. Carl Oglesby, "Notes on a Decade Ready for the Dustbin," *Liberation* (August–September 1969), 6.

75. Even those who did not quite like or understand the new music could sense that bebop demanded understanding as an urgent expression of its times. A cartoon parody of the new bebop hipsters in a 1948 issue of *Down Beat* makes a joke out of the modernist critical language that works this trope: a rube listens with slack-jawed credulity at a bebopper's put-on, a torrent of modernist clichés ("What's bebop?? Why, man, it's the inevitable! It's a classic protest against the chaos, the desolation, the abject melancholia of our times," etc.) J. Lee Anderson, "What's Bebop?" cartoon, *Down Beat*, Apr. 21, 1948, 3. The outstanding discussion of modernism's temporal paradoxes is Matei Calinescu, *The Five Faces of Modernity: Modernism, Avant-Garde, Decadence, Kitsch, Postmodernism* (Durham, NC: Duke University Press, 1987).

76. The best-known example of this kind of writing is Gunther Schuller, "Sonny Rollins and the Challenge of Thematic Improvisation," *Jazz Review* 1, no. 1 (November 1958), 6–9, 21–22; Sidney Finkelstein, "Inner and Outer Jazz" *Jazz Review* 2, no. 8 (September 1959), 19–22 considers jazz in terms of Béla Bartók's distinction between *parlando-rubato* and *tempo giusto*; George Russell and Martin Williams muse on the parallels between Arnold Schoenberg's break with tonality and Ornette Coleman's free jazz in "Ornette Coleman and Tonality," *Jazz Review* 3, no. 5 (June 1960), 7–10; John Benson Brooks (see Chapter 6) contributed a typically gnomic and theoretically dense piece on George Russell's Lydian chromatic concept in *Jazz Review* 3, no. 2 (February 1960), 38; and these are only four of many possible examples.

77. An example of the latter is the television series *Jazz Scene U.S.A.*, in which the hip patter of host Oscar Brown Jr. (notable, among other things, for the genuinely funny hipster spoof "But I Was Cool") periodically stiffens around Leonard Feather's and John Tynan's didactic scripts. For a study of the role that *Jazz Review* and similar publications played in jazz's critical discourse, see John Gennari, *Blowin' Hot and Cool: Jazz and Its Critics* (Chicago: University of Chicago Press, 2006).

78. The most crystalline and epigrammatic expression of this thought may be found in Theodor Adorno, "Finale," in *Minima Moralia*, trans. E. F. N. Jephcott (London: Verso, 1978), 247.

79. Leszek Kolakowski, *The Breakdown*, vol. 3 of *Main Currents of Marxism: Its Origin, Growth, and Dissolution*, trans. P. S. Falla (New York: Oxford University Press, 1978), 489.

80. This analysis, though implied or assumed in a wide variety of late-1960s Movement writings, appears to have crystallized within the New York anarchist group Up Against The Wall Motherfucker. See especially "Up Against the Wall Mother Fucker," in Ron Hahne, Ben Morea, et al., *Black Mask and Up Against the Wall/Motherfucker: The Incomplete Works of Ron Hahne, Ben Morea and the Black Mask Group* (London: Unpopular Books and Sabotage Editions, 1993), 97–107. A more systematic exposition of these ideas may be found in Murray Bookchin, *Post-Scarcity Anarchism* (Berkeley, CA: Ramparts Press, 1971). Again, there is a fine line between science fiction and social theory: see Samuel R. Delany's *Dhalgren* (New York: Bantam, 1975), in which the anarchic labyrinth city of Bellona offers a thrilling and dangerous post-scarcity landscape to those brave or crazy enough to make it their home.

81. Jon Weiner, *Come Together: John Lennon in His Time* (New York: Random House, 1984), 107–9.

82. Julian Beck, "The Seven Lamps of Architecture," in *The Life of the Theater* (San Francisco: City Lights Books, 1972), essay no. 71 (unpaginated).

83. Bill Gottlieb, "Six Arrangers Examine Modern Art," *Down Beat*, Mar. 26, 1947, 2.

84. *Dough for the Do-Do* is a remake of *Porky in Wackyland* (1938), which likewise associated modernist imagery with jazz but in an earlier idiom.

85. LeRoi Jones, *Blues People: Negro Music in White America* (New York: Morrow, 1963), 207.

86. Ed Bland's film *The Cry of Jazz* (1959) makes a similarly Adornian argument: the social limitations placed on African Americans are intimately linked to jazz's musical organization (the chorus form and the changes), while resistance against limitation, "the Negro's eternal recreation of the present," is likewise manifest in improvisation, swing, and sound. See also Ed Bland, "On 'The Cry of Jazz,'" *Film Culture* 21 (Summer 1960), 28–32.

87. Jones, *Blues People*, 200.

88. He may have had a point. Some early rock writing suggested that rock released white youth from its dependency on black music; Ralph Gleason, for one, gloated that white people no longer needed black music to be hip. Ralph Gleason, "Like a Rolling Stone," *American Scholar* 36, no. 4 (Autumn 1967), 555–63. Jones, writing as Amiri Baraka, outlined this critique in his one-act play "Rockgroup," a grotesque parody of the Beatles (renamed "The Crackers"). Amiri Baraka, "Rockgroup," *The Cricket* 1 (1969), 41–43.

89. Beck, "Seven Lamps of Architecture."

90. Morton Feldman, "Mr. Schuller's History Lesson," review of *Twentieth Century Innovations: Prime Movers*, by Gunther Schuller, *Kulchur* 3, no. 9 (1963), 88. A rather more sympathetic (and fascinatingly detailed) document of this concert is Martin Williams, "Rehearsal Diary," *Evergreen Review* 31 (October–November 1963), 115–27.

91. The literary journal *Tri-Quarterly* published a special issue on little magazines that contains a great deal of information on the interlocking hip literary circles that created *Kulchur* and other similar publications; see especially Lita Hornick, "*Kulchur*: A Memoir," *Tri-Quarterly* 43 (Fall 1978), 281–97; and Gilbert Sorrentino, "*Neon, Kulchur, etc.*," *Tri-Quarterly* 43 (Fall 1978), 299–316.

92. Ben Morea, "Culture and Revolution," *Black Mask* no. 8 (October/November 1967), reprinted in *Black Mask and Up Against the Wall/Motherfucker,* 50. Avant-garde composer Henry Flynt held a similar view; see Ben Piekut, "Demolish Serious Culture! Henry Flynt Meets the New York Avant-Garde," in *Experimentalism Otherwise: The New York Avant Garde and Its Limits* (Berkeley: University of California Press, 2011), 65–101.

93. Hilton Kramer, "Modernism and Its Enemies," *New Criterion* 4, no. 7 (March 1986), 7.

94. Thomas Albright, "Visuals," *Rolling Stone*, Apr. 27, 1968, 14.

95. Ibid., 17.

96. Ronald Sukenick, *Down and In*, 221.

97. Sinclair's changing opinions can be gauged from reading through successive issues of the underground newspapers that published his columns: *Fifth Estate, Guerilla,* and the *Ann Arbor Sun*. In 1966 he still championed Archie Shepp and Sun Ra over rock. In one column by another music critic, Rob Tyner of the MC5 responded to Sinclair in one-upping, asym-

metrical-consciousness terms: Franklin Bach, "Bach on Rock," *Fifth Estate* Oct. 16–31, 1966, p. 12. Sinclair later pinned his hopes for rock revolution on the MC5; the story of Sinclair's relationship with the MC5 is told in David A. Carson, *Grit, Noise, and Revolution: The Birth of Detroit Rock'n'Roll* (Ann Arbor: University of Michigan Press, 2005).

98. Greil Marcus, "Who Put the Bomp in the Bomp De-bomp De-bomp"? in *Rock and Roll Will Stand* (Boston: Beacon Press, 1969), 8.

99. This question remains unanswered in broader debates about postmodernism's relationship to its modernism more generally. The literature on this topic is large. Perhaps the best is Frederic Jameson, *Postmodernism, or, the Cultural Logic of Late Capitalism* (Durham, NC: Duke University Press, 1991). Other influential studies include Jürgen Habermas, *The Philosophical Discourse of Modernity: Twelve Lectures,* trans. Frederick Lawrence (Cambridge, MA: MIT Press, 1987); Andreas Huyssen, *After the Great Divide: Modernism, Mass Culture, Postmodernism* (Bloomington: Indiana University Press, 1986); and Calinescu, *The Five Faces of Modernity.* An illuminating primary document of the moment that "postmodernism" began appearing in musicological discussion is the debate between Gary Tomlinson and Lawrence Kramer, which circled around issues of how residues of modernism could be found in apparently postmodernist music scholarship: Gary Tomlinson, "Musical Pasts and Postmodern Musicologies: A Response to Lawrence Kramer," *Current Musicology* 53 (1993), 18–24; Lawrence Kramer, "Music Criticism and the Postmodernist Turn: In Contrary Motion with Gary Tomlinson," *Current Musicology* 53 (1993), 25–35; and Gary Tomlinson, response to Lawrence Kramer, *Current Musicology* 53 (1993), 36–40. A good anthology on music and postmodernism is Joseph Auner and Judith Lochhead, eds., *Postmodern Music/Postmodern Thought* (London: Routledge, 2002).

100. Daniel Bell's writing on 1960s aesthetics defined the first of these positions; intellectual rock critics like Richard Meltzer and Greil Marcus have tended toward the latter ones. See Daniel Bell, *The Cultural Contradictions of Capitalism* (New York: Basic Books, 1976; repr. 1996), 120–45; Richard Meltzer, *The Aesthetics of Rock* (New York: Something Else Press, 1970); Greil Marcus, *Lipstick Traces: A Secret History of the Twentieth Century* (Cambridge, MA: Harvard University Press, 1989). Bernard Gendron offers a solid overview of how critics positioned the Beatles within the discourse of modernism; see Bernard Gendron, *Between Montmartre and the Mudd Club: Popular Music and the Avant-Garde* (Chicago: University of Chicago Press, 2002), 161–224.

101. Evan Ziporyn, "Who Listens If You Care," *New Observations* 86 (1991), 25–28; reprinted in Oliver Strunk, ed., *The Twentieth Century,* vol. 7 of *Source Readings in Music History,* ed. Robert P. Morgan (New York: Norton, 1998), 43. This was an insight with wide application. Glenn Gould was interested in how the world archive of recordings spanned not only space but time; modern performers, challenged by a vastly expanded repertory, were in a position to incorporate the insights afforded by a number of musical eras into a mosaic kind of performance practice (though Gould did not quite put it this way). Glenn Gould, "The Prospects of Recording," *High Fidelity* 16, no. 4 (April 1966), 46–63, reprinted in *The Glenn Gould Reader,* ed. Tim Page (Toronto: Lester, Orpyn and Dennys, 1984).

102. Theodore Gracyk, *Rhythm and Noise: An Aesthetics of Rock* (Durham, NC: Duke University Press, 1996).

103. Chester Anderson, "Notes for the New Geology," *San Francisco Oracle* 6 (February 1967), 2.

104. Louis Forsdale, "Marshall McLuhan and the Rules of the Game," in *Marshall McLuhan: The Man and His Message,* ed. George Sanderson and Frank MacDonald (Golden, CO: Fulcrum, 1989), 170.

105. Anderson, "Notes for the New Geology," 23. One small example of McLuhan's pervasive influence will have to stand in for a comprehensive account, which demands a book of its own. In 1967, McLuhan and graphic designer Quentin Fiore created a radically mosaic *précis* of his ideas, in which words and images shared a fluid space unbound by the traditional design grammar of the printed book. Marshall McLuhan and Quentin Fiore, *The Medium Is the Massage: An Inventory of Effects* (New York: Bantam, 1967). This book inspired an entire subgenre of books that sought to capture something of the dynamic flux

of the electronic media environment. Examples include Jerry Rubin, *Do It: Scenarios of the Revolution* (New York: Simon and Schuster, 1970); Abbie Hoffman, *Woodstock Nation: A Talk-Rock Album* (New York: Vintage, 1969); R. Buckminster Fuller, *I Seem to Be a Verb* (New York: Bantam, 1970). Inevitably, there were also books that sought to capture the mosaic quality of rock in the mosaic form of the McLuhanesque experimental book: John Sinclair, *Guitar Army*; and Jamake Hightower, *Rock and Other Four Letter Words: Music of the Electric Generation* (New York: Bantam, 1968). An excellent study of this phenomenon is Jeffrey T. Schnapp and Adam Michaels, *The Electric Information Age Book: McLuhan/Agel/ Fiore and the Experimental Paperback* (New York: Princeton Architectural Press, 2012).

106.   McLuhan's notions of secondary orality, even in Walter Ong and Eric Havelock's more respectable formulations, are far from uncontroversial. Jonathan Sterne suggests that Ong and McLuhan, both of whom were staunchly Catholic, privileged auditory over visual perception for religious reasons: both imagined a community of faith renewed through the intimacies of sound. Jonathan Sterne, *The Audible Past: Cultural Origins of Sound Reproduction* (Durham, NC: Duke University Press, 2003), 15–16. Stephen Feld has argued that orality does not determine consciousness; Steven Feld, "Orality and Consciousness," in *The Oral and the Literate in Music*, ed. Yosihiko Tokumaru and Osamu Yamaguti (Tokyo: Academia Music, 1986), 18–28. McLuhan's notions of "eye dominance" or "ear dominance" have long persisted in sound studies but are felt to be less and less useful: see Veit Erlmann, "But What of the Ethnographic Ear? Anthropology, Sound, and the Senses," in *Hearing Cultures*, ed. Veit Erlmann (Oxford: Berg, 2004), 1–20.

107.   The story of how French critical theory grew out of an academic-countercultural milieu is ably told in François Cusset, *French Theory: How Foucault, Derrida, Deleuze, & Co. Transformed the Intellectual Life of the United States*, trans. Jeff Fort (Minneapolis: University of Minnesota Press 2008).

108.   This is a simplified and condensed version of Ihab Hassan's table of oppositions in the widely read postscript to *The Dismemberment of Orpheus*, 2nd ed. (Madison: University of Wisconsin Press, 1982), 267–68.

109.   Anderson, "Notes for the New Geology," 2.

110.   Ibid., 23.

111.   Ibid., 2.

112.   Norman Mailer, "Reflections on Hip," correspondence between Mailer Ned Polsky, in *Advertisements for Myself*, 369–71.

113.   Lawrence Lipton, *The Holy Barbarians* (New York: Julian Messner, 1959), 213.

114.   Seymour Krim thought that, except for the "tooting of his own uncool horn," Lipton was true to the Beat outlook; if anything, Krim faults the book for failing to convey the urgency of Beat rebellion. Seymour Krim, review of "The Holy Barbarians," by Lawrence Lipton, *Evergreen Review* 3, no. 9 (1960), 208–9. According to Ginsberg, though, Kerouac hated the book's quasi-Marxist notion of hip rebellion: Sukenick, *Down and In*, 114.

115.   Allen Ginsberg, unpublished notebook 50-01 (c. 1950–1952), box 4, series 2, Allen Ginsberg Papers, Stanford University Special Collections, 129.

116.   See, for example, Orrin Keepnews, review of *The Horn*, by John Clellon Holmes, *Jazz Review* 1, no 1 (1958), 42–43. Some poets made similar complaints; Kenneth Rexroth, one of the first to read his poems to jazz, complained that the Beats saw jazz only as "savage jungle drums and horns blowing up a storm around the flickering fire while the missionary soup comes to a boil." Kenneth Rexroth, "Revolt: True and False," *Nation*, Apr. 26, 1958, 378.

117.   Morris Dickstein, *Leopards in the Temple: The Transformation of American Fiction, 1945– 1970* (Cambridge, MA: Harvard University Press, 2002), 86–87; W. T. Lhamon, Jr., *Deliberate Speed: The Origins of a Cultural Style in the American 1950s* (Washington, DC: Smithsonian Institution Press, 1990); Daniel Belgrad, *The Culture of Spontaneity: Improvisation and the Arts in Postwar America* (Chicago: University of Chicago Press, 1998); and Lewis MacAdams, *Birth of the Cool: Beat, Bebop, and the American Avant-Garde* (New York: Free Press, 2001).

118. Scott DeVeaux, *The Birth of Bebop: A Social and Musical History* (Berkeley: University of California Press, 1997), 26.

119. Elizabeth Von Vogt, *681 Lexington Avenue: A Beat Education in New York City 1947–1954* (Wooster, OH: Ten O'Clock Press, 2008), 22.

120. Ellison argues that no performer can escape entertainment's imperative to self-creation: "Whatever his style, the performing artist remains an entertainer, even as Heifetz, Rubinstein or young Glenn Gould." Ralph Ellison, "On Bird, Bird-Watching and Jazz," *The Collected Essays of Ralph Ellison*, ed. John F. Callahan (New York: Modern Library, 2003), 260. I discuss this idea at greater length in "Ellington the Entertainer: Prophetic History on Film," in *Ellington Studies*, ed. John Howland (Cambridge: Cambridge University Press, forthcoming).

121. Michael Szalay, *Hip Figures: A Literary History of the Democratic Party* (Stanford: Stanford University Press, 2012), 8.

122. For an example of the view of hipness as mere fashion, see Barry Ulanov, "Morality and Maturity" part 2, *Metronome* (June 1953), 20.

123. Kenneth Burke, "Four Master Tropes," *A Grammar of Motives* (New York: Prentice-Hall, 1945), 513.

124. Ken Nordine, Fred Katz, and Jim Cunningham, *Word Jazz*, LP, Dot DLP 3075, 1957.

125. The best single document of Dylan's mastery of the art of the put-on is D. A. Pennebaker's documentary *Don't Look Back* (1967), and particularly the painful and protracted scene in which Dylan deploys his well-honed rhetoric of asymmetrical consciousness to eviscerate a "science student" (Terry Ellis).

126. Fred Katz, liner notes for *Word Jazz*.

127. Bob Rolontz, "Whatever Became of Jazz and Poetry?," *Jazz Review* 2, no. 2 (February 1959), 27; Don Gold, review of a live Word Jazz performance with Ken Nordine, Bob Gibson, and Dick Campbell, *Down Beat*, 31 October 1957, 37–38.

128. See Kevin Holm-Hudson, ed., *Progressive Rock Reconsidered* (New York: Routledge, 2002); Edward Macan, *Rocking the Classics: English Progressive Rock and the Counterculture* (New York: Oxford University Press, 1997); Paul Stump, *The Music's All That Matters: A History of Progressive Rock* (London: Quartet Books, 1997); individual essays in *Expression in Pop-Rock Music*, ed. Walter Everett (New York: Garland, 2000); and *Understanding Rock: Essays in Musical Analysis*, eds. John Covach and Graeme M. Boone (New York: Oxford University Press, 1997).

129. Lester Bangs, "Of Pop and Pies and Fun," *Psychotic Reactions and Carburetor Dung*, ed. Greil Marcus (New York: Knopf, 1987), 43.

130. Dave Hickey, "The Delicacy of Rock-and-Roll," in *Air Guitar: Essays on Art and Democracy* (Los Angeles: Art Issues Press, 1997), 101.

131. See Richard Middleton, "Rock Singing," in *The Cambridge Companion to Singing*, ed. John Potter (Cambridge: Cambridge University Press, 2000), 28–41.

132. Gary Snyder at the 1967 Human Be-In, quoted in Allen J. Matusow, *The Unraveling of America: A History of Liberalism in the 1960s* (New York: Harper and Row, 1984), 276.

133. I use the capitalized Word to distinguish the concept of the embodied word of oral communication from the typographic word. This distinction is suggested in Leo Treitler's interpretation of the first Book of John: "In the beginning was the Word...And the Word was with God...And the Word <u>was</u> God...And the Word was made flesh." Treitler notes that "the beginning of any meditation on the conception behind these mysterious phrases must be the recognition that they reflect the thought of an oral culture, a culture in which the word can <u>only</u> be embodied, i.e. through sound, where, therefore it must be far more natural to think of an identity between the word and a human <u>being</u>, than in our culture, where the word can be fixed on the page or computer monitor and possessed by making a Xerox copy of it or covering it with a yellow marker." Leo Treitler, "Orality and Literacy in the Music of the European Middle Ages," in *The Oral and the Literate in Music*, 38.

134. Simon Frith, "Why Do Songs Have Words?" in *Music for Pleasure: Essays in the Sociology of Pop* (Cambridge: Polity Press, 1988), 120.

135. Gitlin, *The Sixties*, 201.

136. Douglas Kahn, "Introduction: Histories of Sound Once Removed," in *Wireless Imagination: Sound, Radio, and the Avant-Garde,* ed. Douglas Kahn and Gregory Whitehead (Cambridge, MA: MIT Press, 1992), 5.

137. Eric Havelock, "Radio and the Rediscovery of Rhetoric," in *The Muse Learns to Write: Reflections on Orality and Literacy from Antiquity to the Present* (New Haven, CT: Yale University Press, 1986), 31.

138. The classic study of the Chicago protests is David Farber, *Chicago '68* (Chicago: University of Chicago Press, 1988), a work that does justice to the idea of participation peculiar to Movement politics.

139. Timothy Leary, "How Merry Jerry's Yip Stopped the War," *Berkeley Barb,* May 31–June 6, 1968, 17.

140. As Eric Hobsbawm notes, one of the truly remarkable things about the new countercultural style of the 1960s was its self-conscious internationalism. Eric Hobsbawm, *The Age of Extremes: A History of the World, 1914–1991* (New York: Pantheon, 1994), 326–27.

141. John Benson Brooks, notebook entry Feb. 17, 1967, John Benson Brooks Collection, Institute of Jazz Studies Archive, Rutgers University at Newark.

Chapter 5

1. Norman Mailer, *An American Dream* (New York: Dial, 1965; repr. New York: Vintage, 1999; originally serialized in *Esquire,* 1964), 2.

2. Allen Ginsberg, "When the Mode of the Music Changes, the Walls of the City Shake," *Second Coming* 1, no. 2 (July 1961), 2, 40–42. Here "participation" should be understood in Lucien Lévy-Bruhl's sense, discussed in Chapters 3 and 6.

3. As Joe Boyd has written, this line was quoted everywhere in the 1960s counterculture, including on the masthead of the *International Times*; see Barry Miles, *Hippie* (London: Cassell, 2003), 174.

4. Marsilio Ficino, *Three Books on Life,* trans. Carol V. Kaske and John R. Clark (Binghamton: Center for Medieval and Early Renaissance Studies, State University of New York at Binghamton, 1989), 359.

5. It is beyond the scope of this book to explain why such ideas lay dormant throughout the seventeenth, eighteenth, and much of the nineteenth centuries, or to account for their varied reappearances among modernist composers of the Western art tradition, including Claude Debussy, Ferruccio Busoni, Charles Ives, Alexander Scriabin, Dane Rudhyar, Edgard Varèse, and above all Harry Partch, whose distinction between "corporeal" and "abstract" music is particularly relevant to this chapter. See especially Harry Partch, "From Emperor Chun to the Vacant Lot," *The Genesis of a Music,* 2nd ed. (Madison: University of Wisconsin Press, 1949; repr. New York: Da Capo, 1974), 3–47.

6. Antonin Artaud, "No More Masterpieces," in *Theater and its Double,* trans. Mary Caroline Richards (New York: Grove Press, 1958), 81. As noted below, this book was a powerful influence on literary hip culture, and its translator was tightly enmeshed in hip culture's network of creative figures in the 1950s and 1960s. Richards was a poet, painter, ceramics artist, and theorist of alternative education who participated in John Cage's *Theater Piece no. 1* at Black Mountain College, which is generally considered the first Happening. Richards also passed on an early version of Marshall McLuhan's *Understanding Media* to Gerd Stern, a multimedia artist who founded USCO and helped establish McLuhan as a countercultural guru in the mid-1960s. Gerd Stern, *From Beat Scene Poet to Psychedelic Multimedia Artist in San Francisco and Beyond, 1948–1978,* oral history conducted in 1996 by Victoria Morris Byerly (Berkeley: Regional Oral History Office, the Bancroft Library, University of California, Berkeley, 2001), http://archive.org/details/beatscenepoet00gerdrich (accessed May 3, 2013). Richards's exploration of artistic practices of presence in *Centering in Pottery, Poetry, and the Person,* 2nd ed. (Middletown, CT: Wesleyan University Press, 1989) parallels my discussion of John Benson Brooks's practice in Chapter 6.

7. Artaud, *No More Masterpieces,* 81.

8. Ernest Fenollosa and Ezra Pound, "The Chinese Written Character as a Medium for Poetry," *Little Review* 6, nos. 5, 6, 7 (1919); Ezra Pound, *Instigations of Ezra Pound, Together with an Essay on the Chinese Written Character* (New York: Boni and Liveright, 1920). The essay's postwar publication as a pamphlet from City Lights Books (San Francisco, 1964) suggests its later importance to the Beats and their successors.

9. The last, never-completed project of folk singer Richard Dyer-Bennet was to return Homer's *Odyssey* to the world of primary orality—to appear before his listeners not as a performer reading a text aloud but as a rhapsode in whom the Muse speaks and through whom the ancient tale is created anew with each performance. Dyer-Bennet's speech-song delivery, preserved in a filmed performance at the Village Vanguard, is a beautiful and stirring realization of integrated and musicalized Word. Richard Dyer-Bennet and Susan Fanshel, *The Odyssey Tapes* (New York: Museum of Modern Art, 1980).

10. Dewey's is only one energy-field theory to be considered in the twentieth-century art-world, though it is particularly distinguished and influential; Wilhelm Reich's orgone theory is particularly relevant to this chapter. The entire second part of Daniel Belgrad, *The Culture of Spontaneity: Improvisation and the Arts in Postwar America* (Chicago: University of Chicago Press, 1998), is devoted to energy-field theory in the postwar avant-garde.

11. John Dewey, *Art as Experience* (New York: Perigee, 1934, 2005), 245.

12. Ibid., 247.

13. Walter Ong, *Orality and Literacy: The Technologizing of the Word* (London: Methuen, 1982; repr. New York and London: Routledge, 2002), 32.

14. Ibid, 31.

15. Lawrence Lipton, "Poetry and Jazz: Love Match or Shotgun Wedding?" in *The Holy Barbarians* (New York: Julian Messner, 1959), 224. Lipton sought to legitimize his "jazz canto" by appealing to a tradition of the oral lyric that originated in ancient Greece and subsequently manifested in the *commedia dell'arte,* Schoenberg's *sprechtstimme,* and the African American talking blues. Lawrence Lipton, liner notes for *Jazz Canto,* LP, World Pacific Records PJ-1244, 1958.

16. Lawrence Lipton, undated draft notes, folder 16, box 4, Lawrence Lipton Papers 1940–1965, University of Southern California Rare Books and Manuscripts.

17. Seymour Krim, review of "The Holy Barbarians," by Lawrence Lipton, *Evergreen Review* 3, no. 9 (1959), 212.

18. Stuart Z. Perkoff, "Round About Midnite," in *Voices of the Lady,* ed. Gerald T. Perkoff (Orono, ME: National Poetry Foundation, 1998), 232.

19. Charles Olson, "Projective Verse," in *Collected Prose,* ed. Don Allen and Benjamin Friedlander (Berkeley: University of California Press, 1997), 242.

20. Charles Olson, "Against Wisdom as Such," *Black Mountain Review* 1, no. 1 (Spring 1954), 36.

21. John Sinclair, "Artists' Worksheet 1965," in *The Collected Artists' Worksheet 1965* (Detroit: Artists' Workshop Press, 1967).

22. Walter Kaufmann's *Existentialism from Dostoevsky to Sartre,* one of the books every Beat seemed to have at hand in the late 1950s, made connections between Existentialism and Buddhism: in both, "man stands alone in the universe, responsible for his condition, likely to remain in a lowly state, but free to reach above the stars." Kaufmann, *Existentialism from Dostoevsky to Sartre* (New York: Meridian Books, 1956), 47. This is a rather tendentious interpretation of Buddhism, though, and as Belgrad points out, Zen aimed to overcome a subject-object dualism that Existentialism tended to monumentalize; Belgrad, *Culture of Spontaneity,* 167. For a comprehensive study of Existentialism in postwar America, see George Cotkin, *Existential America* (Baltimore: Johns Hopkins University Press, 2003).

23. Belgrad, *The Culture of Spontaneity,* 107.

24. Harold Rosenberg, "The American Action Painters," *Art News* 51, no. 8 (December 1952), 22.

25. Out of all the many things written about 4'33", two recent pieces of scholarship are especially noteworthy: Philip Gentry, "The Age of Anxiety: Music, Politics, and McCarthyism (1948–1954)" (Ph.D. diss., UCLA, 2008); and Liz Kotz, "Proliferating Scores and the

Autonomy of Writing," in *Words to Be Looked At: Language in 1960s Art* (Cambridge: MIT Press, 2007), 13–58. Kyle Gann, *No Such Thing as Silence: John Cage's 4'33"* (New Haven: Yale University Press, 2010) is a lucid general survey of the piece's performance history and reception. In the 1950s the lines between hip culture and the avant-garde were blurred; the *Village Voice* encouraged its hip readers to dig John Cage, "music that is some few light-years 'farther out' than, say, Thelonius [sic] Monk...[it] does not swing but is guaranteed to send you if you can get with it." Kolya Tcherny, "For Adventurous Ears," *Village Voice*, Apr., 17, 1957, 4.

26. Artaud's theories were implicit in the way *The Connection* implicated the audience in its action. The audience was led to believe that it was watching real junkies loafing on stage, goaded by an obnoxious avant-garde director to live their lives out as theatrical spectacle. The junkies convince the director to shoot heroin, and the play ends when he passes out and they flee. The director remains onstage, motionless, with no curtain or curtain call, leaving the audience wondering if it had witnessed a representation of a deadly overdose or the real thing, and contemplating the possibility of its complicity in a man's death. See Nat Hentoff, "Who Else Can Make So Much out of Passing Out? The Surprising Survival of an Anti-play," *Evergreen Review* 4, no. 11 (1960), 170–77.

27. Havelock offers some tentative hypotheses of why so many books on aspects of orality should appear in the years after World War II: see Eric Havelock, *The Muse Learns to Write: Reflections on Orality and Literacy from Antiquity to Present* (New Haven: Yale University Press, 1986), especially pp. 24–62.

28. See for example Michael McClure, "Drug Notes," *Evergreen Review* 25 (1962), 103–17. Aldous Huxley, *The Doors of Perception* (New York: Harper and Row, 1954); and Alan Watts, *The Joyous Cosmology: Adventures in the Chemistry of Consciousness* (New York: Pantheon, 1962), are the major works to mention in this context; both suggested that drugs permit easy and general access to the paradoxical unitive states formerly available only to yogis undergoing years of arduous meditation. Through the writings of Timothy Leary and Baba Ram Dass (Richard Alpert), this idea would become very widespread in the later 1960s. Drug psychedelia in the 1960s is an enormous and difficult topic that deserves an entire study of its own. A good overview of the nexus of drugs and religion in the 1960s counter-culture may be found in Jeffrey Kripal, "Mind Manifest: Psychedelia at Early Esalen and Beyond," in *Esalen: America and the Religion of No Religion* (Chicago: University of Chicago Press, 2007), 112–34.

29. Linda Sargent Wood, *A More Perfect Union: Holistic Worldviews and the Transformation of American Culture After World War II* (New York: Oxford, 2010).

30. George Steiner, *Real Presences* (Chicago: University of Chicago Press, 1991), 20.

31. Jorge Luis Borges, "On Exactitude in Science," in *Collected Fictions*, trans. Andrew Hurley (New York: Penguin, 1999), 325.

32. Alfred Korzybski, *Science and Sanity: An Introduction to Non-Aristotelian Systems and General Semantics* (Lancaster, PA: Science Press, 1933), 750; Gregory Bateson, *Mind and Nature: A Necessary Unity* (New York: Dutton, 1979). This phrase (along with variants, like "the menu is not the meal") pops up in various contexts united by a common concern with the problem of meaning and experience—for example in Neuro-Linguistic Programming manuals and in the occult writings of Robert Anton Wilson. The menu/meal metaphor is anticipated in the conclusion of William James's *The Varieties of Religious Experience*, where James argues that the materialist idea of religion as a mere survival of primitive supersti-tion cannot negate subjective accounts of religious experience: "A bill of fare with one real raisin on it instead of the word 'raisin,' with one real egg instead of the word 'egg,' might be an inadequate meal, but it would at least be a commencement of reality. The contention of the survival-theory that we ought to stick to non-personal elements exclusively seems like saying that we ought to be satisfied forever with reading the naked bill of fare." William James, *The Varieties of Religious Experience*, in *William James: Writings 1902–1910* (New York: Library of America, 1988), 447–48.

33. Mark Johnson, *The Meaning of the Body: Aesthetics of Human Understanding* (Chicago: University of Chicago Press, 2007), 89.

34. Hannah Arendt, *Eichmann in Jerusalem: A Report on the Banality of Evil* (New York: Viking, 1963).

35. Thomas Merton, "Chant to Be Used in Processions Around a Site with Furnaces," *Journal for the Protection of All Beings* 1 (San Francisco: City Lights Books, 1961), 5–7.

36. The clearest and most influential articulation of the connection between calculative abstraction and social alienation is Erich Fromm, *The Sane Society* (New York: Rinehart, 1955), 110–20; see also Erich Kahler, *The Tower and the Abyss: An Inquiry into the Transformation of the Individual* (New York: Braziller, 1957).

37. Albert Votaw, "Toward a Personalist Socialist Philosophy," *politics* (January 1946), 16.

38. C. Wright Mills, "The Powerless People: The Role of the Intellectual in Society," *politics* (April 1944): 69.

39. Dwight Macdonald, "The Bomb," in *Memoirs of a Revolutionist* (New York: Farrar, Straus and Cudahy, 1957); revised edition, *Politics Past: Essays in Political Criticism* (New York: Viking Press, 1970), 175.

40. Erich Fromm, "Psychoanalysis and Zen Buddhism," in *Zen Buddhism and Psychoanalysis* (New York: Harper and Brothers, 1960), 78–79.

41. I owe this image to Grant Morrison's comics series *The Invisibles*, which makes the counter-cultural critique of Enlightenment in a postmodern popcult (and occult) register. Grant Morrison, *Say You Want a Revolution*, vol. 1 of *The Invisibles* (New York: DC Comics, 1996), 190–91. The strange-bedfellows connections within hip culture are nowhere better illustrated by the fact that the critique embodied by *The Invisibles* derives from that of Theodor Adorno and Max Horkheimer, in *Dialectic of Enlightenment*, trans. John Cumming (New York: Herder and Herder, 1972)—a work that influenced the 1960s counterculture by way of Herbert Marcuse (see Chapter 4).

42. For C. Wright Mills, the irony of the intellectual's situation is that although he is rendered just as powerless by this abstraction as anyone else, he is still able to understand the situation for what it is and thus is conscious above all of his own powerlessness. Mills, "The Powerless People: The Role of the Intellectual in Society," *politics* (April 1944).

43. Irving Howe, *Politics and the Novel* (New York: Horizon, 1957), 160.

44. Phil Ford, "Music at the Edge of the Construct," *Journal of Musicology* 26, no. 2 (2009), 240–73.

45. Norman Mailer, "The White Negro: Superficial Reflections on the Hipster," *Dissent* 4, no. 3 (1957), 276–93; reprinted in *Advertisements for Myself* (New York: Putnam, 1959; repr. Cambridge, MA: Harvard University Press, 1992), 338.

46. In response to Jean Malaquais's claim that hipsters were counterrevolutionary *lumpen*, Mailer wrote that they served a very different revolution. Socialist revolutions had failed to realize their aims, and the rational materialism that drove them had shown itself to be totalitarian in any event. Hip promised a "second revolution moving not forward toward action and more rational equitable distribution, but backward toward being and the secrets of human energy." Such a revolution was "admittedly impossible to conceive even in its outlines," since its entire point would be to undo the tyrannical rationality by which all known ideologies are conceived and executed. Norman Mailer, reply to Jean Malaquais, in *Advertisements for Myself*, 363.

47. Milton "Mezz" Mezzrow and Bernard Wolfe, *Really the Blues* (New York: Random House, 1946), 223.

48. Mailer, "The White Negro," 356.

49. Eldridge Cleaver, "Notes on a Native Son," in *Soul on Ice* (New York: Delta, 1968), 97–111.

50. Cornel West, "Black Sexuality: The Taboo Subject," in *Race Matters* (Boston: Beacon Press, 1993, repr. 2001), 88.

51. Roland Barthes, *Mythologies*, trans. Annette Lavers (New York: Hill and Wang, 1972), 137–42. George Lewis has made the most productive use of this concept in music-historical scholarship: see George Lewis, "Improvised Music After 1950: Afrological and Eurological Perspectives," *Black Music Research Journal* 16, no. 1 (Spring 1996), 91–122, which uses the idea of exnomination to understand the dynamic by which the Eurological avant-garde has defined jazz improvisation against its own presumed universality.

52. Richard Dyer, *White* (New York: Routledge, 1997), 38; David Lloyd, "Race Under Representation," *Oxford Literary Review* 13 (1991), 62–94.

53. Thus Ned Polsky wrote that "the white Negro accepts the real Negro not as a human being in his totality, but as the bringer of a highly specified and restricted 'cultural dowry,' to use Mailer's phrase. In so doing he creates an inverted form of keeping the nigger in his place." Ned Polsky, "Reflections on Hip," in *Advertisements for Myself*, 368–69.

54. Leonard Bernstein, "Life Is Juicy," *Neurotica* 1 (Spring 1948), 40. This poem contrasts life's filth with death's cleanliness in terms that evoke the technologized mass extinction discussed above.

55. Norman Mailer, "An Open Letter to Fidel Castro," in *The Time of Our Time* (New York: Modern Library, 1999), 387.

56. Norman Mailer, "The Hip and the Square," in *Advertisements for Myself*, 425.

57. The best discussion of Reich's influence on Mailer is Robert Solotaroff's chapter on "The White Negro" in *Down Mailer's Way* (Urbana: University of Illinois Press, 1974), 82–123.

58. John Dewey, *Art as Experience*, 245.

59. Norman Mailer, *The Spooky Art: Thoughts on Writing* (New York: Random House, 2004), 76. Mailer outlines a few suggestive notions of the sounding dimension of language in Mailer and Michael Lennon, *On God: An Uncommon Conversation* (New York: Random House, 2007), 139–40.

60. Carl Rollyson, *The Lives of Norman Mailer: A Biography* (New York: Paragon House, 1991), 112.

61. Gregory Corso to LeRoi and Hettie Jones (n.d.), folder marked "Correspondence 1960, Jan.–Apr.", LeRoi Jones Mss., Lilly Library, Indiana University Bloomington.

62. Mailer, "The White Negro," 349.

63. Mailer did not write enough about music to settle the question of his musical tastes. Some of his friends remember him as "tone-deaf" (see Chapter 2, note 70). However, Joel Dinerstein has uncovered new evidence of Mailer's enthusiasm for jazz and habits of music listening. Joel Dinerstein, *The Origins of Cool: Jazz, Film Noir, and Existentialism in Postwar America* (Chicago: University of Chicago Press, forthcoming).

64. Norman Mailer, draft 1 manuscript of "The White Negro" ("Dialectic of the American Existentialist"), 11 verso, drafts and notes for "The White Negro," folder 8, box 30, Norman Mailer Papers, Harry Ransom Center, University of Texas at Austin. There are four main drafts in this folder: a complete handwritten draft of "Dialectic of the American Existentialist" (draft 1); a typescript substantially the same as draft 1 but with small changes throughout and three passages either reworked or added (draft 2); a carbon of draft 2 with Mailer's editorial markings, along with two loose pages, on which the title "The White Negro" appears for the first time, that rework the troublesome first page (draft 3); and an incomplete near-final typescript draft with only minor editorial marks (draft 4). In its final form, "The White Negro" is divided into six numbered sections; Mailer appears to have become aware that something was missing from his argument as he was writing draft 2, as he marks the place for section 4 but continues without break to section 5. This missing section 4 has its own series of manuscript and typescript drafts and became the final essay's section 3—the notorious section on the psychopath, in which Mailer glorified crime and asserted the impotence of psychoanalysis. There are also several single pages and short draft sequences in manuscript that either add ideas to draft 4 or work through difficult passages (notably the opening), as well as a few miscellaneous notes. These materials are hopelessly jumbled; I am greatly indebted to Carolyn Carrier McClimon for her work in sorting them into a coherent draft history.

65. Mailer, "The White Negro," 348–49.

66. Ibid., 350.

67. The hipster's interlocutor speaks of "other-direction," a term drawn from David Riesman's intellectual blockbuster, *The Lonely Crowd: A Study of the Changing American Character* (New Haven: Yale University Press, 1950), which was then obligatory reading in New York intellectual circles and which Mailer loathed; the earlier drafts of "The White Negro" name it as a symptom of intellectual malaise.

68. The phrase "existential errands" is borrowed from the title of one of Mailer's own collections, *Existential Errands* (Boston: Little, Brown, 1972).

69. Laura Adams and Norman Mailer, "Existential Aesthetics: An Interview with Norman Mailer," *Partisan Review* 42 (Summer 1975), 202. When Colin Wilson asked Mailer what he meant by "existentialism," he "waved his hand vaguely" and replied "Oh, kinda playing things by ear." Colin Wilson, *Dreaming to Some Purpose* (London: Century, 2004), 244.

70. Norman Podhoretz claimed that frank admission of a desire to make it was the only real taboo of his intellectual circle, and he made a literary performance of his own hip-to-be-square reverse transgression in *Making It* (New York: Random House, 1967). Some years earlier, Seymour Krim had written an essay with the same title, arguing, contrarily, that the only real taboo among the hip intelligentsia was failing to make it: Seymour Krim, "Making It," in *Views of a Nearsighted Cannoneer* (New York: Excelsior Press, 1961), 32–38.

71. Philip Whalen to Lawrence Lipton, Oct. 10, 1957, box 5, Lawrence Lipton Papers 1940–1965, University of Southern California Rare Books and Manuscripts.

72. Solotaroff, *Down Mailer's Way*, 60.

73. Morris Dickstein, *Leopards in the Temple: The Transformation of American Fiction, 1945–1970* (Cambridge: Harvard University Press, 2002), 156.

74. Mailer, "The White Negro," 352.

75. Steve Shoemaker, "Norman Mailer's 'White Negro:' Historical Myth or Mythical History?" *Twentieth Century Literature* 37 (1991), 345.

76. Michael Szalay writes about Mailer's later novel *Why Are We in Vietnam?* (1968) from a similar point of view, as a musical and political fiction in which Mailer's writing can be "a phallus and an instrument of the human voice, a primitive totem and an up-to the minute piece of broadcast technology." Szalay, *Hip Figures: A Literary History of the Democratic Party* (Stanford: Stanford University Press, 2012), 221.

77. Norman Mailer, *The Armies of the Night: History as a Novel, the Novel as History* (New York: New American Library, 1968; Penguin Plume, 1994), 28.

78. Mailer, "Advertisement for Some Political Articles," in *Advertisements for Myself*, 186.

79. Mailer, draft 1 manuscript of "The White Negro" ("Dialectic of the American Existentialist), 1 recto.

80. Mailer, "The White Negro," 357–58.

81. Mailer, "Advertisement for Some Political Articles," 186.

82. To be sure, not all of Mailer's serpentine sentences were hammered together in such a deliberate way. The 208-word second sentence appears to have been written in a single burst, and its earliest draft versions are much the same as the final version, with only minor corrections. Even so, even the smallest changes reflect a general commitment to creating "a more limber style, less self-consciously literary, more like a man who had to admit he was improvising as he went along." Rollyson, *The Lives of Norman Mailer*, 102.

83. Mailer, manuscript notes for "The White Negro," unpaginated.

84. Mailer, "The White Negro," 357.

85. Mailer, draft 3 of "The White Negro," 4.

86. Kate Millett's chapter on Mailer, in *Sexual Politics* (New York: Doubleday, 1970, 2000), 314–35, along with Mailer's response, *The Prisoner of Sex* (Boston: Little, Brown, 1971), constitutes a (even *the*) foundational moment of modern feminist literary criticism. D. A. Pennebaker's *Town Bloody Hall (A Dialogue on Women's Liberation)*, a documentary of Mailer's debate with Millett, Germaine Greer, and others, is a riotous document of this historical moment, in which mass-mediated politics and American intellectual life converged.

87. Mailer, "The White Negro," 349–50.

88. Mailer first articulated this theory in a companion piece to "The White Negro," an interview with Richard G. Stern titled "Hip, Hell, and the Navigator," in *Advertisements for Myself* (New York: Putnam, 1959; Cambridge, Harvard University Press, 1992), 376–86. Mailer's book of interviews with J. Michael Lennon, *On God: An Uncommon Conversation*, is the most extensive exposition of Mailer's theology. Mailer's interest in the occult can be gauged in the essay "The Occult," which appears in *The Spooky Art*, 230–48.

89. The singer, Cherry, was modeled on Mailer's then-girlfriend, the actress Beverly Bentley, who had been dating Miles Davis shortly before she met Mailer. Davis, the acme of hip and a skilled boxer, "had long impressed Norman as a symbol of black male supersexuality." Mary Dearborn, *Mailer: A Biography* (New York: Houghton Mifflin, 1999), 194. The hyper-competitive Mailer felt driven to best him and settled for beating up his fictional representation.

90. Philip Rahv, "Crime Without Punishment," *New York Review of Books,* Mar. 25, 1965, 1, 3, 4; Elizabeth Hardwick, "Bad Boy," *Partisan Review* 32 (Spring 1965), 291–94.

91. Norman Mailer, letter to Francis Irby Gwaltney, Dec. 20, 1963, in *Norman Mailer's Letters on An American Dream, 1963–1969*, ed. J. Michael Lennon (Shavertown, PA: Sligo Press, 2004), 36.

92. Solotaroff, *Down Mailer's Way,* 137.

93. The image is Mailer's, from *An American Dream,* 95.

94. Ibid., 98.

95. Ibid., 100.

96. Ibid., 101.

97. Adams and Mailer, "Existential Aesthetics," 201.

98. This notion was broadly appealing to Beat writers: for example, one issue of *Beatitude* (June 6, 1959) published a comparative translation of "Maple Bridge Night Mooring" by Chang Chih T'ang, with the original ideograms up top and variant readings in English running underneath, by John Kelly, Ruth Weiss, and John Chance.

99. *Neurotica* 1, no. 1 (Spring 1948), 3.

100. Belgrad, *The Culture of Spontaneity,* 114.

101. Viktor Shklovsky, *Theory of Prose,* trans. Benjamin Sher (Elmwood Park, IL: Dalkey Archive Press, 1990), 6.

102. The word was coined by Carl Jung: see Jung, *Psychological Types,* vol. 6 of *The Collected Works of C. G. Jung,* trans. H. G. Baynes (Princeton: Princeton University Press, 1971), 425–27.

103. Tower of Power, "What Is Hip," from *Tower of Power,* LP, Warner Brothers BS 2681, 1973.

104. Frederic Jameson, *Postmodernism, or, the Cultural Logic of Late Capitalism* (Durham, NC: Duke University Press, 1993), 69.

105. See Ramsey Dukes [Lionel Snell], *S.S.O.T.B.M.E.: An Essay on Magic, Its Foundations, Development and Place in Modern Life* (Redbourn, UK: The Mouse That Spins, 1975); revised edition, *S.S.O.T.B.M.E Revised: An Essay on Magic* (2001), 33–34.

Chapter 6

1. John Crowley, *Ægypt* (New York: Bantam, 1987), 286.

2. John Cage, "Lecture on Nothing," from *Silence* (Middletown, CT: Wesleyan University Press, 1961), 126.

3. Brooks was not without personal influence; he taught several musicians, notably Bill Dixon, and to Seymour Krim he was "Mr. Music in my dramatis personae." Seymour Krim to John Benson Brooks, Oct. 24, 1978, John Benson Brooks Collection, Institute of Jazz Studies Archive, Rutgers University, Newark. But this influence was exercised outside the circuits of public renown.

4. Carl Wilson, *Let's Talk About Love: A Journey to the End of Taste* (New York: Continuum, 2007), 92.

5. Joseph Heath and Andrew Potter, *The Rebel Sell: Why Culture Can't Be Jammed* (Chichester: Capstone, 2005), 150.

6. Ibid., 152.

7. Mort Sahl's quip about the Kenton band ("a waiter dropped a tray and three couples got up to dance") exemplifies the notion that fashionable moderns will enjoy any bizarre or random thing so long as they can convince themselves that it is art. Ted Gioia, *West Coast Jazz: Modern Jazz in California, 1945–1960* (Berkeley: University of California Press, 1998), 156.

8. Lawrence Weschler, *Seeing Is Forgetting the Name of the Thing One Sees: A Life of Contemporary Artist Robert Irwin* (Berkeley: University of California Press, 1982); expanded ed., *Seeing Is Forgetting the Name of the Thing One Sees: Over Thirty Years of Conversations with Robert Irwin* (2008), 80.

9. Ibid.

10. Schillinger is best known for giving George Gershwin composition lessons as he was working on *Porgy and Bess,* though there is some dispute over how much Schillinger influenced its composition. See Paul Nauert, "Theory and Practice in Porgy and Bess: The Gershwin-Schillinger Connection," *Musical Quarterly* 78, no. 1 (Spring 1994), 9–33. I have not seen Schillinger's unpublished notebooks, but Warren Brodsky's account of them suggests points of similarity with Brooks's notebook project. Both men had a streak of aggressive scientism, and both sought to create rational systems by which they could effect a union between music and other art forms, or, more generally, between the various sense faculties corresponding to those art forms. The brief published excerpts of Schillinger's notebooks are remarkably similar to Brooks's musing on abstract musical, aesthetic, and philosophical problems. Warren Brodsky, "Joseph Schillinger (1895–1943): Music Science Promethean," *American Music* 21, no. 1 (Spring 2003), 45–73.

11. Brooks worked primarily with Randy Brooks (no relation) but also wrote arrangements for Les Brown, Tommy Dorsey, Boyd Raeburn, Johnny Richards, Ina Rae Hutton, and Eddie DeLange. His best-known songs include "Just As Though You Were Here," "Ninety-Nine Years," "Saturday," "In Brooklyn," "99 Years in the Penitentiary," "Who Threw the Whiskey in the Well," "Over the Weekend," "This Is the House That Love Built," "Ain't Nothing Wrong with That," "Where Flamingos Fly," and especially "You Came a Long Way from St. Louis." Some of his best songs remain unpublished.

12. Seymour Krim introduced Brooks and his third wife, Peggy, and told the story in a reminiscence of his friendship with Joan Blondell; Seymour Krim, "Joan Blondell: The Last of the Great Troupers Teaches Sadness to the Literary Kid," in *What's This Cat's Story? The Best of Seymour Krim,"* ed. Peggy Brooks (New York; Paragon House, 1991), 134–35. Peggy Brooks was John Clellon Holmes's editor and introduced her husband to him, later suggesting Holmes write the liner notes to *Avant Slant.* Peggy Brooks, private communication with the author, Oct. 7, 2012.

13. Brooks's archive is studded with his candid and generally unimpressed portraits of the historical figures he encountered: during the period he was working on a jazz-and-poetry album and rubbing shoulders with the Beats, for example, he recounts meeting Kerouac and describes him as "so mixed-up and indiscriminately identified with his idealised image of himself you wonder if [it] won't take several lifetimes for him to get out of it"—a statement that is true not only for Kerouac but for anyone caught in the sway of the hip sensibility, including Brooks himself. John Benson Brooks, letter to his parents, undated, probably 1960.

14. Interview with the author, Sep. 16, 2010.

15. This album was a product of Brooks's friendship with Courlander, who had done anthropological fieldwork in the American south and collaborated with Brooks on a volume of transcribed folk songs. Harold Courlander and John Benson Brooks, *Negro Songs from Alabama,* 2nd ed. (New York: Oak Publications, 1963). Brooks used these folk materials in *The Alabama Concerto* in something of the same way that Stravinsky used Russian folk songs in *Sacre du Printemps,* paraphrasing their forms and abstracting their contours rather than quoting directly.

16. John Clellon Holmes, liner notes for Milt Gabler and John Benson Brooks, *Avant Slant (One Plus 1 = II?): A Twelve Tone Collage,* LP, Decca DL 75018, 1968.

17. Jones is primarily known as "the dean of American astrology," but his importance to American occultism rests on broader accomplishments. He began his career under the auspices of Manly P. Hall, whose *Secret Teachings of All Ages* is a foundational text of American occultism. Jones created the Sabian Assembly, an esoteric study group to which Brooks belonged, and later earned a Ph.D. (with a thesis on George Sylvester Morris) from Columbia University. In the earlier decades of the twentieth century, Jones (who lived for

almost a century) had connections to the theosophists among American ultramodern composers: Dane Rudhyar learned astrology from him and remained the most effective advocate of Jones's system of "Sabian symbols," and a letter from Brooks to Jones indicated that he also knew Henry Cowell. Brooks studied with Jones from 1943 onward but moved in Gurdjieff circles as well.

18. The dates that appear in parentheses throughout this chapter refer to the notebook entries from which the quotations cited here are recorded. Since the notebooks constitute the main source of Brooks's day-to-day thoughts, I have kept the dates in the main text in order to track the place of each quotation in the larger context of Brooks's unfolding life and practice.

19. Aleister Crowley, *Magick in Theory and Practice,* part 2 of *Magick Book 4 (Liber ABA),* 2nd revised ed., ed. Hymenaeus Beta (York Beach, ME: Red Wheel/Weiser, 1997), 139. Elsewhere Crowley defined the Great Work as "the uniting of opposites. It may mean the uniting of the soul with God, of the microcosm with the macrocosm, of the female with the male, of the ego with the non-ego—or what not." Aleister Crowley, *Magick Without Tears,* ed. Israel Regardie (Tempe: New Falcon, 1991), 7. The traditional Hermetic schema of microcosm and macrocosm can be understood as one expression of a goal shared by mystical traditions more generally—the overcoming of the limitations of the binary logic inherent in the workings of language and the human mind and the direct perception of the nondual relationship of the cosmos (however understood) and the individual.

20. Marc Edmund Jones, *Key Truths of Occult Philosophy, Completely Rewritten and Expanded* (Philadelphia: D. McKay, 1948); reprint, *Occult Philosophy: An Introduction, the Major Concepts, and a Glossary* (Boulder: Shambhala, 1977), 113.

21. Ibid., 114.

22. The cover was a late creation of Alex Steinweiss, who established the first art department for a recording company (Columbia Records) and pioneered the development of album cover stylistic conventions. For an overview and anthology of Steinweiss's work, see Jennifer McKnight-Trontz and Alex Steinweiss, *For the Record: The Life and Work of Alex Steinweiss* (New York: Princeton Architectural Press, 2000).

23. DJ Shadow (Josh Davis), quoted in *Scratch,* dir. Doug Pray, DVD, Palm 3046-2.

24. Gilles Deleuze and Félix Guattari, *A Thousand Plateaus: Capitalism and Schizophrenia,* trans. Brian Massumi (Minneapolis: University of Minnesota Press, 1987), 116.

25. Branden W. Joseph, *Beyond the Dream Syndicate: Tony Conrad and the Arts After Cage (A "Minor" History)* (New York: Zone Books, 2008), 52.

26. Ibid., 50.

27. Christopher I. Lehrich, *The Occult Mind: Magic in Theory and Practice* (Ithaca: Cornell University Press, 2007), 18–25.

28. As Richard Taruskin has noted, postwar modernism excised and suppressed a prewar strain of occult modernism represented by Scriabin, Ives, Schoenberg, and the American ultramoderns; Richard Taruskin, *The Early Twentieth Century,* vol. 4 of *The Oxford History of Western Music* (New York: Oxford University Press, 2005). Carol Oja has written about the influence of Theosophical mysticism on the ultramoderns, especially Henry Cowell, Ruth Crawford Seeger, and Dane Rudhyar; see *Making Music Modern: New York in the 1920s* (New York: Oxford University Press, 2000). For a parallel study of the visual arts in the same period, see Linda Henderson, *The Fourth Dimension and Non-Euclidian Geometry in Modern Art* (Princeton: Princeton University Press, 1983). The conventional opposition of magic and modernity comes mainly from James Frazer, whose *The Golden Bough* exerted a huge influence on twentieth-century anthropologists, artists, philosophers, and occultists. The most interesting writing on the continued relevance of magical thought within modernity has come from Michael Taussig; see especially *What Color Is the Sacred?* (Chicago: University of Chicago Press, 2009) and *The Magic of the State* (London: Routledge, 1997). See also Birgit Meyer and Peter Pels, eds., *Magic and Modernity: Interfaces of Revelation and Concealment* (Stanford: Stanford University Press, 2003).

29. Sven Spieker, *The Big Archive: Art from Bureaucracy* (Cambridge, MA: MIT Press, 2008), 4.

30. Michel Foucault, *Technologies of the Self: A Seminar with Michel Foucault*, ed. Luther H. Martin, Huck Gutman, and Patrick H. Hutton (Amherst: University of Massachusetts Press, 1988). This final direction in Foucault's thought owes much to Pierre Hadot, who argued that ancient philosophy was less a set of ideas than a system of "spiritual exercises" by which students might work toward a better and wiser life. It was the latter goal that Foucault refigured as "the care of the self." See especially Hadot, "Spiritual Exercises," in *Philosophy as a Way of Life: Spiritual Exercises from Socrates to Foucault*, trans. Michael Chase (New York: Blackwell, 1995), 81–125.

31. Svetlana Boym, *The Future of Nostalgia* (New York: Basic Books, 2001), xvi.

32. Ed Sanders, "The Great Tomkins Park Beatnik-to-Hippie Conversion Ceremony," in *Tales of Beatnik Glory* (New York: Thunder's Mouth Press, 2004), 451–60.

33. John Benson Brooks, letter to Marc Edmund Jones, Feb. 13, 1968, John Benson Brooks Collection, Institute of Jazz Studies Archive, Rutgers University, Newark.

34. Ted Morgan, *Literary Outlaw: The Life and Times of William S. Burroughs* (New York: Holt, 1988), 322–23.

35. John Benson Brooks, "The Noise of Freedom?," *Provincetown Review* 3 (1960), 68.

36. R. H. Blythe, *Zen in English Literature and Oriental Classics* (New York: Dutton, 1960), 224.

37. In a 1970 interview, Brooks admitted that he had "spent ten years trying to refute him . . . or not . . . completely unsuccessfully." Interview with David Reitman, "Journey to the End of the Night" (1970), WKCR.

38. Brooks, "The Noise of Freedom," 67.

39. Carl Jung's public explanation of his work was marked by a similar tension. For both Jung and Brooks, the teeming strangeness and variousness of their experience needed to be mastered by a firm controlling intellect. Of the visions he recorded in his *Red Book*, Jung wrote "My science was the only way I had of extricating myself from that chaos. Otherwise the material would have trapped me in its thicket, strangled me like jungle creepers. I took great care to understand every single image, every item of my psychic inventory, and to classify them scientifically—so far as this was possible—and, above all, to realize them in actual life." Carl Jung, *Memories, Dreams, and Reflections*, ed. Aniela Jaffé, trans. Richard and Clara Winston (London: Collins, Routledge and Kegan Paul, 1963), 184. Jeffrey Kripal recounts the story of an unnamed scholar for whom academic research and analytical thought serves as a "coping mechanism" that grounds the wild energies of mystical states: Jeffrey Kripal, *The Serpent's Gift: Gnostic Reflections on the Study of Religion* (Chicago: University of Chicago Press, 2007), 19.

40. Gerry Mulligan "Jeru: In the Words of Gerry Mulligan: An Oral Autobiography," interview with Ken Poston, published Apr. 12, 1992, Library of Congress. Transcript published at http://lcweb2.loc.gov/diglib/ihas/html/mulligan/gm-gil.html (accessed May 3, 2013); telephone interview with Peggy Brooks, Oct. 3, 2012.

41. Although the notebooks and in particular one letter to Marc Edmund Jones (Mar. 19, 1975) seem to hint at breakthroughs, Peggy Brooks writes "I don't think he ever found an 'ultimate insight.' He was resigned at the end of his life to how it had played out. The astrology helped him there." Private communication with the author, Oct. 4, 2012.

42. David Toop, *Haunted Weather: Music, Silence, and Memory* (London: Serpent's Tail, 2004), 155–56.

43. Although Brooks's DJology comes closest to later notions of sample-based music (notably hip-hop), the general idea of creating a kind of pop-art *musique concrète* from fragments of commercial broadcasts had occurred to other artists and even home-taping enthusiasts of around the same time. An article in a hobbyist magazine suggests that recording and cutting up broadcast ads ("tape-libbing") was to be a new fad, though this prediction does not seem to have come true: Arthur Meiselman, "Tape-Libbing," *Tape Recording* (October 1966), 28–31. I thank Karl Hagstrom Miller for this source.

44. Martin Williams, *Jazz Masters in Transition, 1957–69* (New York: Da Capo Press, 1980), 269. This review originally appeared as "New Jazz Big Band/But . . ." *Saturday Review*, Dec. 28, 1968, 56. Brooks records his conversation with Evans on Sep. 6, 1967; the next month Robert Graves offended him by calling *Avant Slant* "journalism."

45. With his Commodore record label, Gabler originated the concept of the third-party reissue; he has been honored by the Rock and Roll Hall of Fame as one of the midwives of rock and roll (he produced early rock hits by Louis Jordan and Bill Haley). His enormously influential role in entertainment through a half-century has been memorialized by his nephew, Billy Crystal, in a documentary titled *The Milt Gabler Story.*

46. Gabler viewed *Avant Slant* as his own creative work, and its failure wounded him as much as it did Brooks. In a letter to Peggy Brooks, a publishing executive at E. P. Dutton to whom he had proposed his memoirs, Gabler wrote: "Give my best to John and tell him every time I feel low I play some jazz and then wind up with AVANT SLANT and wonder how we ever completed the idea. It was fun and a challenge and something never attempted before or since. I guess we were the only ones who cared." Milt Gabler to Peggy Brooks, Mar. 15, 1976, John Benson Brooks collection, Institute of Jazz Studies (Rutgers-Newark).

47. In an undated letter to Marc Edmund Jones (probably 1960 or 1961), Brooks describes his creation of "the composer's astrological tarot" and briefly explains its structure; in another letter to Jones, dated Sep. 30, 1960, he describes using three decks—one for time, the second for pitch, and the third for instrumentation. It is not clear whether either of these resembles the cards he created for *Bird Meets Cage,* but in any event it is clear that at this time Brooks was interested in creating multiple methods by which music could harnessed to divinatory systems, of which the "*I Ching* body piano" was the most important.

48. Stuart Broomer, review of *Avant Slant, Paris Transatlantic* (January 2007).

49. David Toop, *Haunted Weather,* 155–56.

50. Marshall McLuhan and Eric Norden, "The Playboy Interview," in *The Essential McLuhan* (London: Routledge, 1997), 238.

51. Letter to Harold Courlander, Jan. 20, 1966, John Benson Brooks Collection, Institute of Jazz Studies Archive, Rutgers University, Newark.

52. Brooks organized the group's improvisations by breaking them into timed periods, each one generally less than a minute long and with an instruction that would affect timbre, texture, and activity—instructions such as "Don will play in altissimo register," "Howard will drop out," and so on. Within each timed period, the musicians had to follow its instruction but would be free to determine which row segments they wished to develop. Unlike the procedures Brooks devised for *Bird Meets Cage,* the order of these periods and their instructions were not arranged by chance. The years in which Brooks worked on *The Twelves* were a transitional time—he studied with Cage while he was still developing his system of twelve-tone improvisation, and at the time of the trio's 1962 performance he was still wrestling with the implications of Cage's chance procedures and was not yet prepared to use them. Interview with Don Heckman.

53. Brooks was especially excited by the "map of culture" that appeared in the book's appendix. Like Brooks's own technics, Hall's "map of culture" is a combinatorial system, a grid that explains all forms of human interaction by lining up two axes, each listing Hall's ten "Primary Message Systems": interaction, association, subsistence, bisexuality, territoriality, temporality, learning, play, defense, exploitation. So the combination of terms from the two axes might produce interaction/learning (the activity of teaching), play/learning (educational games), and so on. This grid maps what Hall called "the communication of culture," which is the totality of cultural transactions that take place both in and outside of language. Edward T. Hall, *The Silent Language* (Greenwich, CT: Fawcett, 1959). McLuhan was certainly influenced by this book, particularly Hall's definition of a medium as an extension of a sense.

54. John Benson Brooks, undated letter to Milt Gabler (c. 1967), box marked "Avant Slant," John Benson Brooks Collection, Institute of Jazz Studies Archive, Rutgers University, Newark. "Vonce" is a slightly obscure bit of jazz slang; according to Whitney Balliett, it is a euphemism for marijuana, though other uses suggest it is akin to sex, soul, and whatever else might be down-and-dirty. Whitney Balliett, *Collected Work: A Journal of Jazz, 1954–2001* (New York: St. Martin's, 2002), 458.

55. The band was called The Rites, a psychedelic-folk outfit that released only one 45 rpm single. It sold poorly and, like *Avant Slant,* ended up in the Archive's "pile of broken dreams." The Rites, "Hour Girl" and "Things" (Decca 32218, 1967), 45 rpm recording.

56. This is essentially Jacob Brackman's definition of the put-on, and his understanding of the put-on as a kind of defensive ju-jitsu aimed at making the artist unassailable by ordinary criticism is very much the same as Brooks's. Jacob Brackman, *The Put-On: Modern Fooling and Modern Mistrust* (Chicago: Regnery, 1971).

57. Review of *Avant Slant, Coda* 9, no. 2 (August 1969), 19.

58. LeRoi Jones, "Black Dada Nihilismus," *Evergreen Review* 29 (1963), 85–87.

59. John Szwed suggests that Sun Ra, who lent Jones books that claimed to reveal the secret wisdom of lost black civilizations, may have been the "silent partner" of Jones's new interest in occultism. John Szwed, *Space Is the Place: The Lives and Times of Sun Ra* (New York: Pantheon, 1997), 209. Sun Ra belongs to a tradition of African American folk magic and mysticism, some of which constituted an important early site of Afrocentric ideology: see especially Henri Gamache, *Mystery of the Long Lost 8th, 9th, and 10th Books of Moses* (Highland Falls, NY: Sheldon, 1948), which is both a grimoire and a quasi-historical treatise arguing that Moses was "the great voodoo man of the bible," an African man of power whose occult secrets are the birthright of his modern-day descendants.

60. Undated letter to parents, late 1950s, John Benson Brooks Collection, Institute of Jazz Studies Archive, Rutgers University, Newark.

61. The best single document of 1960s Aquarian millenarianism is the "Age of Aquarius" issue of the *San Francisco Oracle* (February 1967).

62. Carolyn Abbate, "Music—Drastic or Gnostic?" *Critical Inquiry* 30 (Spring 2004), 524.

63. More skeptically, *Avant Slant* was also a way for Milt Gabler to set himself up as a pop song lyricist. Peggy Brooks believes that Gabler's vanity was the main reason the record got made, and the improbable sum of money Decca paid Brooks for it does lend credence to her interpretation. Peggy Brooks, conversation with the author, Dec. 1, 2012.

64. The phrase is owed to Richard Taruskin, who uses it in "Extinguishing the Petty 'I' (Transcendentalism I)," in *The Oxford History of Western Music,* vol. 4, *The Early Twentieth Century.*

65. Jones, *Occult Philosophy,* 61.

66. Perennialism is one of the most readily distinguishing features of occultism, though it is not invariable. The postmodern schools of magic called "discordianism" (associated with Robert Anton Wilson) and "chaos magic" (with which William S. Burroughs was reputed to have been associated late in life) explicitly disavow belief in any one conception of truth. Indeed, belief itself is treated as a magical technology. On Burroughs's association with chaos magic, see Sven Davisson, ed., *Playback: The Magick of William S. Burroughs,* special issue of *Ashé: The Journal of Experimental Spirituality* 2, no. 3 (2009).

67. Aleister Crowley called this the "oath of the abyss;" Crowley, *Magick Book 4,* 68. It is first listed as the last of a series of vows Crowley called "the Great Obligation" in his account of his magical development; Aleister Crowley, "John St. John: The Record of the Magical Retirement of G. H. Frater, O . . . M . . . ," supplement to *Equinox* 1, no. 1 (1909), 11. This account is an especially detailed illustration of the process of magical hermeneutics, with which this section is primarily concerned.

68. Crowley, *Magick Book 4,* 68.

69. Jones, *Occult Philosophy,* 101.

70. Susan Greenwood, *The Anthropology of Magic* (Oxford: Berg, 2009), 63–73.

71. Wilson, *Cosmic Trigger I: Final Secret of the Illuminati* (Reno: New Falcon, 1977), 223.

72. Ramsey Dukes [Lionel Snell], *Uncle Ramsey's Little Book of Demons: The Positive Advantages of the Personification of Life's Problems* (London: Aeon, 2005). Dukes has pursued this idea throughout his other books as well, all of which develop ideas first presented in *S.S.O.T.B.M.E: An Essay on Magic, Its Foundations, Development and Place in Modern Life* (Redbourn, UK: The Mouse That Spins, 1975; revised edition, *S.S.O.T.B.M.E Revised: An Essay on Magic* (2001). This volume, a masterpiece of deft theorization grounded in practical experience, strongly informs my own understanding of magic. Academic readers can

find a good introduction to the basic idea of this book in Lionel Snell, "Four Glasses of Water," *Journal for the Academic Study of Magic* (2004), 177–205.

73. Jason Louv, "Introduction: Towards an Ultraculture," in *Generation Hex* (New York: Disinformation, 2006), 9. Emphasis in the original.

74. John Benson Brooks, "The Noise of Freedom?" 68.

75. As Susan Greenwood writes, "magical thought is essentially emotional—it is built upon affective relationships developed over time." Greenwood, *The Anthropology of Magic*, 71.

76. William S. Burroughs, "On Coincidence," in *The Adding Machine* (New York: Seaver, 1986), 103–4.

77. Lehrich, *The Occult Mind*, 18–25.

78. Duncan Barford, *Occult Experiments in the Home: Personal Exploration of Magick and the Paranormal* (London: Aeon, 2010), x.

79. Of course, magical practitioners would often say they are doing both—that their own reality, however contingent and specific to them, nevertheless points to a larger meaning that is universally true. But this universal truth is not generally conceived in scientific terms, as an "objective" truth susceptible to experimental verification and falsification. As Robert Anton Wilson wrote, the difficulty of understanding magic lies in the fact that we are conditioned (to some extent by language) to conceive of reality as "one block-like entity, sort of like a huge New York skyscraper, in which every part is just another 'room' within the same building." Robert Anton Wilson, *Cosmic Trigger*, iii. For a magician, the rooms matter more than the skyscraper.

80. Norman Mailer, "The White Negro; Superficial Reflections on the Hipster," in *Advertisements for Myself* (New York: Putnam, 1959), 354.

81. Phil Ford, "Taboo: Time and Belief in Exotica," *Representations* 103 (Summer 2008), 107–35.

82. Alan Chapman, *Advanced Magick for Beginners* (London: Aeon, 2008), 53.

83. William James *Pragmatism: A New Name for Some Old Ways of Thinking* (New York: Longmans, Green, 1907), 201.

84. Christopher I. Lehrich, *The Occult Mind: Magic in Theory and Practice* (Ithaca: Cornell University Press, 2007), 1.

85. Ibid., 25.

86. Austin Osman Spare, *The Book of Pleasure (Self-Love): The Psychology of Ecstasy* (London, 1913), 29. Though in his own time known mostly as an artist, Spare has become one of the most influential occultists of the twentieth century.

87. Stanley Jeyaraja Tambiah, *Magic, Science, Religion, and the Scope of Rationality* (Cambridge: Cambridge University Press, 1990), 105.

88. Lucien Lévy-Bruhl, *How Natives Think (Les Fonctions Mentales dans les Sociétés Inférieures)*, trans. Lilian A. Clare (London: George Allen and Unwin, 1926), 79–80.

89. Tambiah, *Magic, Science, Religion, and the Scope of Rationality*, 109.

90. Norman Mailer, "The Hip and the Square," in *Advertisements for Myself*, 424–25.

91. Marshall McLuhan and Quentin Fiore, *The Medium Is the Massage: An Inventory of Effects* (New York: Bantam, 1967), 9.

92. Jack Kerouac, *Visions of Cody* (New York: McGraw-Hill, 1972; repr. New York: Penguin, 1993), 351.

93. Timothy Leary, "How Merry Jerry's Yip Stopped the War," *Berkeley Barb*, May 31–June 6, 1968, 17.

94. Jack Kerouac, "The Origins of the Beat Generation," *Playboy*, June 1959, 42.

95. Gary Snyder, "On the Road with D. T. Suzuki," in *A Zen Life: D. T. Suzuki Remembered*, ed. Masao Abe (New York: Weatherhill, 1986), 207–8.

96. Louis Pauwels and Jacques Bergier, *The Morning of the Magicians*, trans. Rollo Myers (New York: Stein and Day, 1964). For a journalistic overview of the connection between hip culture and the occult, see Gary Lachman, *Turn Off Your Mind: The Mystic Sixties and the Dark Side of the Age of Aquarius* (New York: Disinformation, 2003).

97. Wrote Stewart Brand of Castaneda's *A Separate Reality*, "I don't have words for the importance I consider these books to carry." *The Whole Earth Catalog* no. 2 (Menlo Park, CA:

Portola Institute, 1970), 430. Some of the books advertised in this same issue include Carl Jung's *Man and His Symbols*, Arthur Koestler's *The Ghost in the Machine*, Evelyn Underhill's *Mysticism*, Joseph Campbell's *The Hero with a Thousand Faces*, a book of Gurdjieff exercises by A. R. Orage, a great deal on Eastern religion and mysticism, and a few magical books from the occult publisher Weiser (whose New York phone number Brooks had written down in several places in his private address book). This same issue of the *Whole Earth Catalog* also published a magical remedy for headaches by Chester Anderson, whom we have already met in Chapter 4.

 98. See Ford, "Taboo," 107–35. Fred Turner, *From Counterculture to Cyberculture: Stewart Brand, the Whole Earth Network, and the Rise of Digital Utopianism* (Chicago, 2006) is the foundational work on the *Whole Earth Catalog* and its characteristic intermingling of computer technology and neo-tribal archaism. See also Andrew G. Kirk, *Counterculture Green: The Whole Earth Catalog and American Environmentalism* (Lawrence: University Press of Kansas, 2007).

 99. Gene Youngblood, *Expanded Cinema* (New York: Dutton, 1970), 136.

100. The essential study of event scores is Liz Kotz, *Words to Be Looked At: Language in 1960s Art* (Cambridge, MA: MIT Press, 2007), a work whose argument—the linguistic turn in 1960s art was a response to the materiality of language revealed by electronic media—intersects with my own.

101. La Monte Young, ed., *An Anthology of Chance Operations* (Bronx, NY: La Monte Young & Jackson Mac Low, 1963). For a thorough and thoughtful consideration of the political critique embedded in *Composition 1960 # 10*, see Branden Joseph, "The Tower and the Line," in *Beyond the Dream Syndicate: Tony Conrad and the Arts After Cage* (New York: Zone Books, MIT, 2008), 109–51.

102. Richard Schechner, "Actuals," in *Essays in Performance Theory, 1970–1976* (New York: Drama Book Specialists, 1977).

103. J. L. Austin, "Performative Utterances," in *Philosophical Papers* (Oxford: Clarendon, 1961), 220–39. Stanley Tambiah has used Austin's conception of the "performative utterance" as a way of understanding magical and ritual participation; see Tambiah, "A Performative Approach to Ritual," in *Culture, Thought, and Social Action: An Anthropological Perspective* (Cambridge, MA: Harvard University Press, 1985), 123–66. Theorists of performance art, like Richard Schechner, have used Austin's insights to understand radical performance as well.

104. Sally Banes, *Greenwich Village 1963: Avant-Garde Performance in the Effervescent Body* (Durham, NC: Duke University Press, 1993). Diane di Prima's *Recollections of My Life as a Woman* (New York: Viking, 2001) is an outstanding personal document of this relationship.

105. Allan Kaprow gives a wry inventory of such appropriations of his famous coinage in "Pinpointing Happenings," in *Essays on the Blurring of Art and Life*, ed. Jeff Kelley (Berkeley: University of California Press, 1993, repr. 2003), 84–89.

106. See Stephen J. Bottoms, *Playing Underground: A Critical History of the 1960s Off-Off Broadway Movement* (Ann Arbor: University of Michigan Press, 2004).

107. Judith Malina and Julian Beck, eds., *Paradise Now: Collective Creation of the Living Theatre* (New York: Random House, 1971), 16.

108. Ibid., 20.

109. Ibid., 27.

110. For a skeptical critique of *Paradise Now* from the standpoint of the political (as opposed to cultural) left, see Joan Holden and R. G. Davis, "Living," *Ramparts* 8, no. 2 (August 1969), 63.

111. Cornelius Cardew, "Draft Constitution," section 5, "Research Project," *Musical Times* 110, no. 1516 (June 1969), repr. in Christoph Cox and Daniel Warner, eds., *Audio Culture: Readings in Modern Music* (London: Continuum, 2004), 234–38.

112. Dick Higgins, "Boredom and Danger," in *Source: Music of the Avant Garde, 1966–1973*, ed. Larry Austin and Douglas Kahn (Berkeley: University of California Press, 2011), 178–82.

113. Walter de Maria, *COLUMN with a BALL on TOP*, in *Anthology of Chance Operations*.

114. I have invented this event score, but there is at least one other—Boudewijn Huckinx's *The Sound Womb*—that consists of a set of instructions for living a musical life that is not very different from my imaginary one. Boudewijn Huckinx, "The Sound Womb," *Source: Music of the Avant Garde* 4, no. 1 (Issue 8, January 1970).

115. Francisco Varela and Jonathan Shear, eds., *The View from Within: First-Person Approaches to the Study of Consciousness* (Exeter: Imprint Academic 1999) is an outstanding anthology that tackles the limits of third-person work in cognitive science and suggests the possibilities and perils of first-person approaches; see also its sequel, *Ten Years of Viewing from Within*, ed. Claire Petitmengin (Exeter: Imprint Academic, 2009).

116. Gary Tomlinson, *Music in Renaissance Magic* (Chicago: University of Chicago Press, 1993), 14–15.

117. See Joscelyn Godwin, *The Golden Thread: The Ageless Wisdom of the Western Mystery Traditions* (Wheaton, IL: Quest Books, 2007).

118. Michael Puri, review of Berthold Hoeckner, *Programming the Absolute: Nineteenth-Century German Music and the Hermeneutics of the Moment*, *Journal of the American Musicological Society* 59, no. 2 (Summer 2006), 489.

119. Kevin Kopelson, "Tawdrily, I Adore Him," *19th-Century Music* 17, no. 3 (Spring 1994), 276.

120. Karol Berger, "Musicology According to Don Giovanni, or: Should we Get Drastic?" *Journal of Musicology* 22, no. 3 (2005), 496.

121. George Steiner, *Real Presences* (Chicago: University of Chicago Press, 1991), 4–7 *passim*.

122. For Mihaly Csikszentmihalyi, the autotelic nature of an activity is the *sine qua non* of the "flow state," a phenomenon that substantially overlaps that of practice. See Csikszentmihalyi, *Beyond Boredom and Anxiety* (San Francisco: Jossey-Bass, 1975); and the essays in *Optimal Experience: Psychological Studies of Flow in Consciousness*, ed. Mihaly and Isabella Csikszentmihalyi (Cambridge: Cambridge University Press, 1988).

123. Dan Morgenstern, Annie Kuebler, and Peggy Brooks, private communications.

124. Gunther Schuller, public remarks made at the Frederick Loewe Symposium in American Music (Mar. 10, 2011).

125. The distinction I am making here is the same that James Carse makes in distinguishing finite and infinite games. The point of the finite game—any activity bounded by specific place and occasion—is successful completion; the point of an infinite game is extending the play. Thus completed things can emerge from a practice that indefinitely defers completion, but the latter—infinite play—is not identical to the former. Practice might make concerts or recordings, but one cannot say that making concerts or recordings is one's practice. As Carse writes, "Finite games can be played within an infinite game, but an infinite game cannot be played within a finite game." James Carse, *Finite and Infinite Games* (New York: Ballantine, 1986), 8. Carse argues that "there is but one infinite game," which is life itself, but I believe that this too easily assumes a definition of artistic praxis as something essentially bound to place and occasion and embodied in completed actions and objects.

126. To be sure, there are other artistic *oeuvres* that, like Brooks's, are private labors of magical hermeneutics. After undergoing a series of mystical experiences, Philip K. Dick spent the last eight years of his life trying to figure them out in a private eight-thousand-page notebook project he called the *Exegesis*, a large portion of which has been published in an excellent annotated edition: Philip K. Dick, *The Exegesis of Philip K. Dick*, ed. Pamela Jackson and Jonathan Lethem (New York: Houghton Mifflin Harcourt, 2011). Like Dick, Beat artist Wallace Berman also created work intended to illuminate his own spiritual experiences and communicate them to an intimate circle of friends and family through an esoteric, self-created code. As Richard Candida Smith writes, "The works he created assumed their meaning through mingling two approaches to experience that did not usually intersect: a daily intercourse of friendship; an aesthetic sense of every manifestation as pointing to a deeper level of universal reality. This dualism shifted focus from the creative configuration to the self-revelatory act of refiguration.... Berman had arrived at an aesthetic where the object itself was far less important than the care it inspired." Richard Candida

Smith, *Utopia and Dissent: Art, Poetry, and Politics in California* (Berkeley: University of California Press, 1995), 231.

127. John Leland, *Hip: The History* (New York: Ecco, imprint of HarperCollins, 2004), 174.

128. Bill Hicks, "Revelations," from *Bill Hicks Live: Satirist, Social Critic, Stand-Up Comedian*, DVD, Rykodisc, 2004.

129. Richard Leppert, "Music 'Pushed to the Edge of Existence' (Adorno, Listening, and the Question of Hope)," *Cultural Critique* 60 (2005), 92–133; James Currie, "Music After All," *Journal of the American Musicological Society* 62, no. 1 (2009), 145–203.

130. Dukes, *S.S.O.T.B.M.E. Revised*, 96.

131. On "sacralization," see Lawrence Levine, "The Sacralization of Culture" in *Highbrow/Lowbrow: The Emergence of Cultural Hierarchy in America* (Cambridge, MA: Harvard University Press, 1988), 85–146.

132. Wayne Booth, *For the Love of It: Amateuring and Its Rivals* (Chicago: University of Chicago Press, 1999).

133. For an excellent study of assholes, see Aaron James, *Assholes: A Theory* (New York: Doubleday, 2012).

134. Jonathan Dunsby has pointed out that although music scholarship was belatedly starting to account for performance, there was still no "systematic place for the pragmatism of the rehearsal room or the teaching studio, in which aural and verbal tradition is the essential currency." Jonathan Dunsby, "Guest Editorial: Performance and Analysis of Music," *Music Analysis* 8, nos. 1–2 (1989), 7. The fact that this is still true more than two decades later indicates the high conceptual hurdle that still lies between history and musical practice.

135. Mark Johnson, *The Meaning of the Body: Aesthetics of Human Understanding* (Chicago: University of Chicago Press, 2007), 281.

136. Despite their historical antagonisms, these may not be so different after all: it is by no mere whim that Slavoj Žižek has lately sought a reconciliation of Christianity and Marxism. In "Brünnhilde's Act," *Opera Quarterly* 23, No. 2–3 (2008), 199–216, for example, Žižek criticizes the nominally Christian opera *Parsifal* for its paganism and praises the nominally pagan *Götterdämmerung* for its Christianity, finding in the latter a model for a community, united in *agape*, facing the Existential situation of its own future.

137. Mark Johnson, *The Meaning of the Body*, 281.

138. Dave Hickey, "Air Guitar," in *Air Guitar: Essays on Art and Democracy* (Los Angeles: Art Issues Press, 1997), 163–71.

139. Michel de Certeau and Luce Giard, "Envoi," in *Living and Cooking*, vol. 2 of *The Practice of Everyday Life*, trans. Timothy J. Tomasik (Minneapolis: University of Minnesota Press, 1998), 254–55.

Bibliography

I. Books, Periodicals

Abbate, Carolyn. "Music—Drastic or Gnostic?" *Critical Inquiry* 30 (Spring 2004), 505–36.

Albright, Daniel. *Modernism and Music: An Anthology of Sources*. Chicago: University of Chicago Press, 2004.

Albright, Thomas. "Visuals." *Rolling Stone*, Apr. 27, 1968, 14, 17.

Allen, Blaine. "The Making (and Unmaking) of *Pull My Daisy*." *Film History* 2, no. 3 (1988), 185–205.

Anderson, Chester. "Notes for the New Geology." *San Francisco Oracle*, Feb. 6, 1967, 2, 23.

Artaud, Antonin. *Theater and Its Double*. Translated by Mary Caroline Richards. New York: Grove Press, 1958.

Austin, J. L. *Philosophical Papers*. Oxford: Clarendon, 1961.

Bach, Franklin. "Bach on Rock." *The Fifth Estate*, Oct. 16, 1966, 12.

Baldwin, James. *Price of the Ticket: Collected Nonfiction, 1948–1985*. New York: St. Martin's Press, 1985.

Bangs, Lester. *Psychotic Reactions and Carburetor Dung*, edited by Greil Marcus. New York: Knopf, 1987.

Baraka, Amiri. *The Autobiography of LeRoi Jones*. Chicago: Lawrence Hill Books, 1997.

Barr, Nelson. "A Bouquet of Fuck Yous." *Fuck You: A Magazine of the Arts* 5, no. 4 (1963), unpaginated.

"Bebop Fashions." *Ebony* 4, no. 2 (December 1948), 31.

Beck, Julian. *The Life of the Theater*. San Francisco: City Lights Books, 1972.

Becker, Howard. "The Culture of a Deviant Group: The Dance Musician." In *Outsiders: Studies in the Sociology of Deviance*, 79–100. New York: Free Press, 1963.

Belgrad, Daniel. *The Culture of Spontaneity: Improvisation and the Arts in Postwar America*. Chicago: University of Chicago Press, 1998.

Bell, Daniel. *The Cultural Contradictions of Capitalism*. New York: Basic Books, 1976. Twentieth-anniversary ed., 1996.

———. *The End of Ideology: On the Exhaustion of Political Ideas in the Fifties*. Glencoe, IL: Free Press, 1960.

Berger, Karol. "Musicology According to Don Giovanni, or: Should We Get Drastic?" *Journal of Musicology* 22, no. 3 (2005), 490–501.

Berman, Marshall. *All That Is Solid Melts into Air: The Experience of Modernity*. New York: Simon and Schuster, 1982. Reprint, New York: Penguin, 1988.

Bernstein, Leonard. "Life Is Juicy." *Neurotica* 1 (Spring 1948), 40.

Bookchin, Murray. *Post-Scarcity Anarchism*. Berkeley, CA: Ramparts Press, 1971.

Booth, Wayne. *For the Love of It: Amateuring and Its Rivals*. Chicago: University of Chicago Press, 1999.

Borges, Jorge Luis. *Collected Fictions*. Translated by Andrew Hurley. New York: Penguin, 1999.

Boym, Svetlana. *The Future of Nostalgia*. New York: Basic Books, 2001.

Brackman, Jacob. *The Put-On: Modern Fooling and Modern Mistrust*. Chicago: Regnery, 1971.

Braunstein, Peter, and Michael William Doyle. *Imagine Nation: The American Counterculture of the 1960s and 70s*. New York: Routledge, 2002.

Brody, Martin. "Music for the Masses: Milton Babbitt's Cold War Music Theory." *Musical Quarterly* 77, no. 2 (Summer 1993), 161–92.

Brooks, Cleanth. "Irony as a Principle of Structure." In *Literary Opinion in America*, edited by Morton D. Zabel, 729–41. Rev. ed. New York: Harper, 1951.

Brooks, David. *Bobos in Paradise*. New York: Simon and Schuster, 2000.

Brooks, John Benson. "The Noise of Freedom?" *Provincetown Review* 3 (1960), 67–68.

Brossard, Chandler, ed. *The Scene Before You: A New Approach to American Culture*. New York: Rinehart, 1955.

Brossard, Chandler. "Tentative Visits to the Cemetery: Reflections on *My* Beat Generation." *Review of Contemporary Fiction* 7, no. 1 (1987), 7–27.

——— . *Who Walk in Darkness*. New York: New Directions, 1952.

Broyard, Anatole. *Kafka Was the Rage*. New York: Carol Southern Books, 1993.

——— . "Portrait of the Hipster." *Partisan Review* 15, no. 6 (1948), 721–27.

Burke, Kenneth. *A Grammar of Motives*. New York: Prentice-Hall, 1945.

Burley, Dan. "At This Time We'll Wax a Bit Scholarly." *New York Amsterdam News*, Dec. 18, 1937, 12.

——— . *Dan Burley's Original Handbook of Harlem Jive*. New York, 1941, 1944.

——— . "In Which a Hipcat Is Studied by Experts." *New York Amsterdam News*, Apr. 24, 1943, 11.

——— . "In Which We Introduce the 'Back Door Man' to Harlem." *New York Amsterdam News*, Dec. 11, 1937, 15.

——— . "Life and Letters of a Back Door Man." *New York Amsterdam News*, Apr. 17, 1943, 13.

——— . "One, Two, Three: You Drop Your Finger Down, Then Strut Around the Town!" *New York Amsterdam News*, Feb. 25, 1939, 17.

Burns, Jim. "The Hipster." *Jazz Journal* 7 (July 1968), 2–3.

Burroughs, William S. *The Adding Machine*. New York: Seaver, 1986.

Cage, John. "Lecture on Nothing." In *Silence*. Middletown, CT: Wesleyan University Press, 1961.

Calinescu, Matei. *The Five Faces of Modernity: Modernism, Avant-Garde, Decadence, Kitsch, Postmodernism*. Durham, NC: Duke University Press, 1987.

Calloway, Cab. *The New Cab Calloway's Cat-ologue*, 1938.

Cardew, Cornelius. "A Scratch Orchestra: Draft Constitution." *Musical Times* 110, no. 1516 (June 1969), 617, 619. Reprinted in *Audio Culture: Readings in Modern Music*, edited by Christoph Cox and Daniel Warner, 234–38. London: Continuum, 2004.

Cassady, Neal. *Collected Letters 1944–1967*. Edited by Dave Moore. New York: Penguin, 2004.

de Certeau, Michel, and Luce Giard. *Living and Cooking*. Translated by Timothy J. Tomasik. *The Practice of Everyday Life*, vol. 2. Minneapolis: University of Minnesota Press, 1998.

Charters, Ann. *A Bibliography of Works by Jack Kerouac*. New York: Phoenix Book Shop, 1967.

Cherlin, Michael. *Schoenberg's Musical Imagination*. Cambridge: Cambridge University Press, 2007.

Clark, Kenneth B., and James Barker. "The Zoot Effect in Personality: A Race Riot Participant." *Journal of Abnormal and Social Psychology* 40, no. 2 (April 1945), 143–48.

Cleaver, Eldridge. *Soul on Ice*. New York: Delta, 1968.

Covach, John. "Schoenberg and the Occult: Some Reflections on the Musical Idea." *Theory and Practice* 17 (1992), 103–18.

Crowley, Aleister. *Magick Book 4 (Liber ABA)*. Edited by Hymenaeus Beta. 2nd rev. ed. York Beach, ME: Red Wheel/Weiser, 1997.

Currie, James. "Music After All." *Journal of the American Musicological Society* 62, no. 1 (2009), 145–203.

Dalby, David. "Americanisms That May Once Have Been Africanisms." *The Times*. July 19, 1969, 9. Reprinted in *Mother Wit from the Laughing Barrel: Readings in the Interpretation of Afro-American Folklore*, edited by Alan Dundes, 136–40. Englewood Cliffs: Prentice Hall, 1973. Reprint, Jackson: University of Mississippi Press, 1990.

Davis, Francis. *Like Young: Jazz and Pop, Youth and Middle Age*. New York: Da Capo, 2001.

Davis, Miles, and Quincy Troupe. *Miles: The Autobiography*. New York: Simon and Schuster, 1989.

Deleuze, Gilles, and Félix Guattari. *A Thousand Plateaus: Capitalism and Schizophrenia*. Translated by Brian Massumi. Minneapolis: University of Minnesota Press, 1987.

DeMott, Benjamin. "The New Irony: Sickniks and Others." *American Scholar* 31 (Winter 1961–62), 108–19.

DeVeaux, Scott. *The Birth of Bebop: A Social and Musical History*. Berkeley: University of California Press, 1997.

Dewey, John. *Art as Experience*. New York: Perigree, 1934. Reprint, 2005.

Dickstein, Morris. "Cold War Blues: Notes on the Culture of the Fifties." *Partisan Review* 41, no. 1 (1974), 30–53.

———. *Leopards in the Temple: The Transformation of American Fiction, 1945–1970*. Cambridge, MA: Harvard University Press, 2002.

Dinerstein, Joel. "Lester Young and the Birth of Cool." In *Signifyin(g), Sanctifyin', and Slam Dunking: A Reader in African American Expressive Culture*, edited by Gena Dagel Caponi, 239–76. Amherst: University of Massachusetts Press, 1999.

———. *The Origins of Cool: Jazz, Film Noir, and Existentialism in Postwar America*. Chicago: University of Chicago Press, forthcoming.

Di Prima, Diane. *Recollections of My Life as a Woman*. New York: Viking, 2001.

Dukes, Ramsey [Lionel Snell]. *S.S.O.T.B.M.E.: An Essay on Magic, Its Foundations, Development and Place in Modern Life*. Redbourn, UK: The Mouse That Spins, 1975. Rev. ed., *S.S.O.T.B.M.E Revised: An Essay on Magic*, 2001.

Dunsby, Jonathan. "Guest Editorial: Performance and Analysis of Music." *Music Analysis* 8, no. 1–2 (1989), 5–20.

Dyer, Richard. *White*. New York: Routledge, 1997.

Ehrenreich, Barbara. *The Hearts of Men: American Dreams and the Flight from Commitment*. Garden City, NY: Anchor Press, 1984.

Ellison, Ralph. *The Collected Essays of Ralph Ellison*. Edited by John F. Callahan. New York: Modern Library, 2003.

———. *Invisible Man*. New York: Random House, 1952. 2nd ed. New York: Vintage, 1995.

Ennis, Philip H. *The Seventh Stream: The Emergence of Rocknroll in American Popular Music*. Hanover, NH: Wesleyan University Press, 1992.

Eno, Brian. *A Year with Swollen Appendices*. London: Faber, 1996.

Erlmann, Veit. "But What of the Ethnographic Ear? Anthropology, Sound, and the Senses." In *Hearing Cultures*, edited by Veit Erlmann, 1–20. Oxford: Berg, 2004.

Farber, David. *Chicago '68*. Chicago: University of Chicago Press, 1988.

Feldman, Morton. "Mr. Schuller's History Lesson," review of *Twentieth Century Innovations: Prime Movers*, by Gunther Schuller. *Kulchur* 3, no. 9 (1963), 88–89.

Fenollosa, Ernest, and Ezra Pound. "The Chinese Written Character as a Medium for Poetry." *Little Review* 6, no. 5, 6, 7 (1919).

Ficino, Marsilio. *Three Books on Life*. Translated by Carol V. Kaske and John R. Clark. Binghamton: Center for Medieval and Early Renaissance Studies, State University of New York at Binghamton, 1989.

Fiedler, Leslie A. "The New Mutants." *Partisan Review* 32, no. 4 (1965), 505–25.

Finestone, Harold. "Cats, Kicks, and Color." *Social Problems* 5, no. 1 (1957), 3–13.

Fink, Robert. *Repeating Ourselves: American Minimal Music as Cultural Practice*. Berkeley: University of California Press, 2005.

Ford, Phil. "Music at the Edge of the Construct." *Journal of Musicology* 26, no. 2 (Spring 2009), 240–73.

———. "Taboo: Time and Belief in Exotica." *Representations* 103 (Summer 2008), 107–35.

Foucault, Michel. *Technologies of the Self: A Seminar with Michel Foucault*. Edited by Luther H. Martin, Huck Gutman, and Patrick H. Hutton. Amherst: University of Massachusetts Press, 1988.

Frank, Thomas. *The Conquest of Cool: Business Culture, Counterculture, and the Rise of Hip Consumerism*. Chicago: University of Chicago Press, 1997.

———, and Matt Weiland, eds. *Commodify Your Dissent: Salvos from the Baffler*. New York: Norton, 1997.

Frith, Simon. *Music for Pleasure: Essays in the Sociology of Pop*. Cambridge: Polity Press, 1988.

———. "What Is Bad Music?" In *Bad Music: The Music We Love to Hate*. New York: Routledge, 2004.

Fromm, Erich, and D. T. Suzuki. *Zen Buddhism and Psychoanalysis*. New York: Harper & Brothers, 1960.

Fuller, Buckminster R., Jerome Agel, and Quentin Fiore. *I Seem to Be a Verb*. New York: Bantam, 1970.

Gates, Henry Louis. *The Signifying Monkey: A Theory of Afro-American Literary Criticism*. New York: Oxford University Press, 1988.

———. "White Like Me." *New Yorker*, June 17, 1996, 66–81.

Gennari, John. *Blowin' Hot and Cool: Jazz and Its Critics*. Chicago: University of Chicago Press, 2006.

Gillespie, John Birks "Dizzy". *To Be or Not … to Bop*. Garden City, NY: Doubleday, 1979.

Ginsberg, Allen. *Collected Poems 1947–1997*. New York: HarperCollins, 2006.

———. "On Huncke's Book." In a special issue dedicated to Herbert Huncke. the unspeakable visions of the individual, vol. 3, no. 1–2, edited by Arthur and Kit Knight, 20–23. California, PA: editors, 1973.

———. "When the Mode of the Music Changes, the Walls of the City Shake." *Second Coming* 1, no. 2 (July 1961), 2, 40–42.

Gitlin, Todd. *The Sixties: Years of Hope, Days of Rage*. New York: Bantam, 1987. Rev. ed., 1993.

Givan, Ben. "Thelonious Monk's Pianism." *Journal of Musicology* 26, no. 3 (Summer 2009), 404–42.

Gladwell, Malcolm. "The Coolhunt." *New Yorker*, Mar. 17, 1997, 78–88.

Gold, Herbert. "The Beat Mystique." In *The Beats*, edited by Seymour Krim, 154–64. Greenwich, CT: Gold Medal Books, 1960.

———. *Bohemia: Where Art, Angst, Love, and Strong Coffee Meet*. New York: Simon and Schuster, 1993.

———. "How to Tell the Beatniks from the Hipsters." *Noble Savage* 1 (1960), 132–39.

Gold, Robert S. *A Jazz Lexicon*. New York: Knopf, 1964.

Goldmark, Daniel. *Tunes for 'Toons: Music and the Hollywood Cartoon*. Berkeley: University of California Press, 2005.

Goldsmith, Melissa Dawn. "Kindred Riffs, Rival Banter: Kenneth Rexroth's and Lawrence Lipton's Jazz and Poetry Experiments." Paper presented at the seventy-eighth Annual Meeting of the American Musicological Society, New Orleans, 2012.

———. "'Star Me Kitten': William S. Burroughs' Musical Recordings, Marlene Dietrich, and the Aesthetics of His Dark Americana." Paper presented at the seventy-fifth Annual Meeting of the American Musicological Society, Philadelphia, 2009.

Goodman, Paul. *Growing Up Absurd: Problems of Youth in the Organized System*. New York: Random House, 1960.

Gottlieb, Louis. "Why So Sad, Pres?" In *A Lester Young Reader*, edited by Lewis Porter, 211–23. Washington, DC: Smithsonian Institution Press, 1991.

Gracyk, Theodore. *Rhythm and Noise: An Aesthetics of Rock*. Durham, NC: Duke University Press, 1996.

Graff, Gerald. "Co-optation." In *The New Historicisms*. Edited by H. Aram Veeser. London: Routledge, 1989.

Greenwood, Susan. *The Anthropology of Magic*. Oxford: Berg, 2009.

Griffin, Farah Jasmine. *"Who Set You Flowin'?" The African American Migration Narrative*. New York: Oxford University Press, 1995.

Gumbrecht, Hans-Ulrich. *The Production of Presence: What Meaning Cannot Convey*. Stanford: Stanford University Press, 2003.

Hahne, Ron, Ben Morea, et al. *Black Mask and Up Against the Wall/Motherfucker: The Incomplete Works of Ron Hahne, Ben Morea and the Black Mask Group*. London: Unpopular Books and Sabotage Editions, 1993.

Hampshire, Stuart. "Self-Consciousness and Society." In *Power and Consciousness*, edited by Conor Cruise O'Brien and William Dean Vanech. London: University of London Press, 1969.

Hardwick, Elizabeth. "The American Woman as Snow-Queen: Our Self-Contemptuous Acceptance of Europe's Myth." *Commentary* 12, no. 6 (December 1951), 546–50.

Harrington, Michael. "We Few, We Happy Few, We Bohemians." *Esquire*, August 1972, 99–103.

Hassan, Ihab. *The Dismemberment of Orpheus*. 2nd ed. Madison: University of Wisconsin Press, 1982.

Heath, Joseph, and Andrew Potter. *Nation of Rebels: How Counterculture Became Consumer Culture*. New York: HarperCollins, HarperBusiness, 2004.

Hebdige, Dick. *Subculture: The Meaning of Style*. London: Methuen, 1979.

Hentoff, Nat. "Something's Happening and You Don't Know What It Is Do You, Mr. Jones?" *Evergreen Review* 10, no. 4 (1966), 54–56.

Hickey, Dave. *Air Guitar: Essays on Art and Democracy*. Los Angeles: Art Issues Press, 1997.

Higgins, Hannah. *Fluxus Experience*. Berkeley: University of California Press, 2002.

Hoberman, J. *The Dream Life: Movies, Media, and the Mythology of the Sixties*. New York: New Press, 2003.

Hobsbawm, Eric. *Uncommon People*. London: Weidenfeld & Nicolson, 1998.

Hodeir, André. *Towards Jazz*. Translated by Noel Burch. New York: Grove Press, 1962.

Hoffman, Abbie. *Woodstock Nation: A Talk-Rock Album*. New York: Vintage, 1969.

Holmes, John Clellon. "Crazy Days, Numinous Nights: 1948–1950." In *Beat Angels*. the unspeakable visions of the individual, vol. 12, edited by Arthur and Kit Knight, 107–27. California, PA: editors, 1982.

———. *Go*. New York: Scribner, 1952. Reprint, New York: Thunder's Mouth Press, 1988.

———. Liner notes to Milt Gabler and John Benson Brooks. *Avant Slant (One Plus 1 = II?): A Twelve Tone Collage*. LP. Decca DL 75018, 1968.

———. *Nothing More to Declare*. New York: Dutton, 1967.

———. *Passionate Opinions: The Cultural Essays*. Fayetteville: University of Arkansas Press, 1988.

———. "This Is the Beat Generation." *New York Times Magazine*, Nov. 16, 1952, 10, 19–20, 22.

"How to Make a Pork-Pie Hat." *Ebony* 4, no. 10 (August 1949), 43.

Howe, Irving. "Mass Society and Post-Modern Fiction." *Partisan Review* 26, no. 3 (1959), 420–36.

———. *Politics and the Novel*. New York: Horizon, 1957.

Hudson, Julius. "The Hustling Ethic." In *Rappin' and Stylin' Out: Communication in Urban Black America*, edited by Thomas Kochman, 410–24. Urbana: University of Illinois Press, 1972.

James, William. *Pragmatism: A New Name for Some Old Ways of Thinking*. New York: Longmans, Green, 1907.

Jameson, Frederic. *Postmodernism, or, the Cultural Logic of Late Capitalism*. Durham, NC: Duke University Press, 1991.

Jauss, Hans Robert. *Toward an Aesthetic of Reception*. Translated by Timothy Bahti. Minneapolis: University of Minnesota Press, 1982.

Jay-Z. *Decoded*. New York: Spiegel & Grau, 2011.

Johnson, Mark. *The Meaning of the Body: Aesthetics of Human Understanding*. Chicago: University of Chicago Press, 2007.

Jones's, Amiri Baraka. "Black Dada Nihilismus." *Evergreen Review* 29 (1963), 85–87.

———. *Blues People: Negro Music in White America*. New York: William Morrow, 1963.

———. "Milneburg Joys (or, Against 'Hipness' As Such)." *Kulchur* 3 (1961), 41–43.

Jones, Marc Edmund. *Occult Philosophy: An Introduction, the Major Concepts, and a Glossary. Key Truths of Occult Philosophy, Completely Rewritten and Expanded*. Philadelphia: D. McKay, 1948. Reprint, *Occult Philosophy: An Introduction, the Major Concepts, and a Glossary*. Boulder: Shambhala, 1977.

Joseph, Branden W. *Beyond the Dream Syndicate: Tony Conrad and the Arts After Cage (A "Minor" History)*. New York: Zone Books, 2008.

Joy [pseud.]. "(to sociologists & publicists of the beat generation)." *Beatitude* 8 (Aug. 15, 1959), unpaginated.

Kahn, Ashley. *Kind of Blue*. New York: Da Capo Press, 2000.

Kahn, Douglas. "Introduction: Histories of Sound Once Removed." In *Wireless Imagination: Sound, Radio, and the Avant-Garde*, edited by Douglas Kahn and Gregory Whitehead, 1–19. Cambridge, MA: MIT Press, 1992.

Kaprow, Allan. *Essays on the Blurring of Art and Life*. Edited by Jeff Kelley. Berkeley: University of California Press, 1993. Expanded ed., 2003.

Keepnews, Orrin. "Review of *The Horn*, by John Clellon Holmes." *Jazz Review* 1, no. 1 (1958), 42–43.

Keiser, R. Lincoln. *The Vice Lords, Warriors of the Streets*. New York: Holt, Rinehart and Winston, 1969.

Kelley, Robin D. G. *Race Rebels: Culture, Politics, and the Black Working Class*. New York: Free Press, 1994.

———. *Thelonious Monk: The Life and Times of an American Original*. New York: Free Press, 2009.

Kercher, Stephen. *Revel with a Cause: Liberal Satire in Postwar America*. Chicago: University of Chicago Press, 2006.

Kerouac, Jack. "Belief and Technique for Modern Prose." *Evergreen Review* 2, no. 8 (Spring 1958), 57.

———. *Dear Carolyn: Letters to Carolyn Cassady*. the unspeakable visions of the individual, vol. 13, edited by Arthur and Kit Knight. California, PA: editors, 1983.

———. *Mexico City Blues*. New York: Grove Press, 1959.

———. *On the Road: The Original Scroll*. New York: Viking, 2007.

———. "The Origins of the Beat Generation." *Playboy* 6, no. 6 (June 1959), 31–32, 42, 79.

———. *Selected Letters 1940–1956*. Edited by Ann Charters. New York: Viking, 1995.

———. *Visions of Cody*. New York: McGraw Hill, 1972. Reprint, New York: Penguin, 1993.

———. *Windblown World: The Journals of Jack Kerouac 1947–1954*. Edited by Douglas Brinkley. New York: Viking Penguin, 2004.

Kittler, Friedrich. *Gramophone, Film, Typewriter*. Translated by Geoffrey Winthrop-Young and Michael Wutz. Stanford: Stanford University Press, 1999.

Klatch, Rebecca E. *A Generation Divided: The New Left, the New Right, and the 1960s*. Berkeley: University of California Press, 1999.

Klonsky, Milton. *A Discourse on Hip*. Detroit, MI: Wayne State University Press, 1991.

Koestenbaum, Wayne. *The Queen's Throat: Opera, Homosexuality, and the Mystery of Desire*. New York: Poseidon Press, 1993. New edition, New York: Da Capo, 2001.

Konstantinou, Lee. *After Irony: Countercultural Fictions from Hipster to Coolhunter*. Cambridge, MA: Harvard University Press, forthcoming.

Kramer, Hilton. "Modernism and Its Enemies." *New Criterion* 4, no. 7 (March 1986), 1–7.

Krim, Seymour. "Review of *The Holy Barbarians*, by Lawrence Lipton." *Evergreen Review* 3, no. 9 (1960), 208–14.

———. *Views of a Nearsighted Cannoneer*. New York: Excelsior Press, 1961.

———. *What's This Cat's Story? The Best of Seymour Krim*. Edited by Peggy Brooks. New York: Paragon House, 1991.

Kripal, Jeffrey. *Esalen: America and the Religion of No Religion*. Chicago: University of Chicago Press, 2007.

Landesman, Jay. *Rebel Without Applause*. Sag Harbor, NY: Permanent Press, 1987.

Larkin, Philip. *All What Jazz: A Record Diary 1961–68*. London: Faber and Faber, 1970.

Leamer, Laurence. *The Paper Revolutionaries: The Rise of the Underground Press*. New York: Simon and Schuster, 1972.

Leary, Timothy. "How Merry Jerry's Yip Stopped the War." *Berkeley Barb*, June 31, 1968, 12–13, 17.

Lehrich, Christopher I. *The Occult Mind: Magic in Theory and Practice*. Ithaca, NY: Cornell University Press, 2007.

Leland, John. *Hip: The History*. New York: Ecco, imprint of HarperCollins, 2004.

Leppert, Richard. "Music 'Pushed to the Edge of Existence' (Adorno, Listening, and the Question of Hope)." *Cultural Critique* 60 (2005), 92–133.

Lethem, Jonathan. "Collapsing Distance: The Love-Song of the Wanna-Be, or, Fannish Auteur." Keynote Address at the Experience Music Project Pop Conference, Seattle, April 2007.

Lévy-Bruhl, Lucien. *How Natives Think (Les Fonctions Mentales Dans Les Sociétés Inférieures)*. Translated by Lilian A. Clare. London: George Allen and Unwin, 1926.

Lewis, George. *A Power Stronger Than Itself: The AACM and American Experimental Music*. Chicago: University of Chicago Press, 2008.

——— . "Improvised Music After 1950: Afrological and Eurological Perspectives." *Black Music Research Journal* 16, no. 1 (Spring 1996), 91–122.

Lipton, Lawrence. *The Holy Barbarians*. New York: Julian Messner, 1959.

——— . Liner notes to *Jazz Canto*. LP. World Pacific Records PJ-1244, 1958.

Long, Michael. *Beautiful Monsters: Imagining the Classic in Musical Media*. Berkeley: University of California Press, 2008.

MacAdams, Lewis. *Birth of the Cool: Beat, Bebop, and the American Avant-Garde*. New York: Free Press, 2001.

Macdonald, Dwight. *Memoirs of a Revolutionist*. New York: Farrar, Straus and Cudahy, 1957. Rev. ed., *Politics Past: Essays in Political Criticism*. New York: Viking Press, 1970.

Mailer, Norman. *Advertisements for Myself*. New York: Putnam, 1959. Reprint, Cambridge, MA: Harvard University Press, 1992.

——— . *An American Dream*. New York: Dial, 1965. Reprint, New York: Vintage, 1999. Originally serialized in *Esquire*, 1964.

——— . *Armies of the Night: History as a Novel, the Novel as History*. New York: New American Library, 1968. Reprint, New York: Penguin Plume, 1994.

——— . *Norman Mailer's Letters on An American Dream, 1963–1969*. Edited by J. Michael Lennon. Shavertown, PA: Sligo Press, 2004.

——— . "An Open Letter to JFK and Castro." *Village Voice*, Apr. 27, 1961, 14–15.

———, and Laura Adams. "Existential Aesthetics: An Interview with Norman Mailer." *Partisan Review* 42 (Summer 1975), 197–214.

Malcolm X, and Alex Haley. *The Autobiography of Malcolm X*. New York: Grove Press, 1965. 2nd ed. New York: Ballantine, 1992.

Malina, Judith, and Julian Beck, eds. *Paradise Now: Collective Creation of the Living Theatre*. New York: Random House, 1971.

Marcus, Greil. "Birth of the Cool." *Speak* (Fall 1999), 16–25.

——— . *The Old, Weird America: The World of Bob Dylan's Basement Tapes*. New York: Picador, 2001.

——— . *Rock and Roll Will Stand*. Boston: Beacon Press, 1969.

Maurer, David W. "Phrase Origins: Get Hep." *American Mercury* (May 1947), 548.

McLuhan, Marshall. *Explorations in Communication: An Anthology*. Edited by Marshall McLuhan and Edmund Carpenter. Boston: Beacon Press, 1960.

——— . *The Gutenberg Galaxy*. Toronto: University of Toronto Press, 1961.

——— . *Understanding Media*. New York: McGraw Hill, 1964. Reprint, Corte Madera, CA: Gingko Press, 2003.

———, and Quentin Fiore. *The Medium Is the Massage: An Inventory of Effects*. New York: Bantam, 1967.

McLuhan, Marshall, Eric McLuhan, and David Carson. *The Book of Probes*. Corte Madera, CA: Gingko Press, 2003.

Mehegan, John. Letter to the editors. *Down Beat*, June 13, 1956, 4.

Merton, Thomas. "Chant to Be Used in Processions Around a Site with Furnaces." *Journal for the Protection of All Beings* 1 (1961), 5–7.

Mezzrow, Milton "Mezz," and Bernard Wolfe. *Really the Blues*. New York: Random House, 1946.

Middleton, Richard. "Rock Singing." In *The Cambridge Companion to Singing*, edited by John Potter, 28–41. Cambridge: Cambridge University Press, 2000.

Miller, Jonathan. "The Sick White Negro." *Partisan Review* 30, no. 1 (1963), 149–55.

Mills, C. Wright. "The Powerless People: The Role of the Intellectual in Society." *politics* (April 1944), 68–72.

Morgan, Robin. *Goodbye to All That*. Pittsburgh: Know, 1971. Reprinted in *Dear Sisters: Dispatches from the Women's Liberation Movement*, edited by Rosalyn Fraad Baxandall and Linda Gordon, 53–57. New York: Basic Books, 2001.

Morgan, Ted. *Literary Outlaw: The Life and Times of William S. Burroughs*. New York: Holt, 1988.

Nietzsche, Friedrich. *On the Genealogy of Morals*. Translated by Douglas Smith. New York: Oxford University Press, 1996.

O'Hara, Frank. "Personism: A Manifesto." In *Selected Poems*, edited by Mark Ford, 247–48. New York: Knopf, 2008.

Olson, Charles. "Against Wisdom as Such." *Black Mountain Review* 1, no. 1 (Spring 1954), 35–39.

———. "Projective Verse." In *Collected Prose*, edited by Don Allen and Benjamin Friedlander, 239–49. Berkeley: University of California Press, 1997.

Panish, Jon. *The Color of Jazz: Race and Representation in Postwar American Culture.* Jackson: University of Mississippi Press, 1997.

Pauwels, Louis, and Jacques Bergier. *The Morning of the Magicians.* Translated by Rollo Myers. New York: Stein and Day, 1964.

Perkoff, Stuart Z. "Round About Midnite." In *Voices of the Lady*, edited by Gerald T. Perkoff, 232. Orono, ME: National Poetry Foundation, 1998.

Podhoretz, Norman. "The Know-Nothing Bohemians." *Partisan Review* 25, no. 2 (Spring 1958), 305–18.

Polsky, Ned. *Hustlers, Beats, and Others.* Chicago: Aldine, 1967.

Prattis, Percival L. "Hi-de-ho King Plays Villainous Role in Radio *Quizzicale.*" *Pittsburgh Courier*, Sep. 20, 1941, 13.

Puri, Michael. Review of *Programming the Absolute: Nineteenth-Century German Music and the Hermeneutics of the Moment*, by Berthold Hoeckner. *Journal of the American Musicological Society* 59, no. 2 (Summer 2006), 488–501.

Ramsay, Guthrie P., Jr. *Race Music: Black Cultures from Bebop to Hip-Hop.* Berkeley: University of California Press, 2003.

Reisner, Robert. "The Hip Ones." *Village Voice*, Sep. 18, 1957, 6.

Rigney, Francis J., and L. Douglas Smith. *The Real Bohemia.* New York: Basic Books, 1961.

Rollyson, Carl. *The Lives of Norman Mailer: A Biography.* New York: Paragon House, 1991.

Rosenberg, Harold. "The American Action Painters." *Art News* 51, no. 8 (December 1952), 22–33, 48–50.

Ross, Andrew. "Hip, and the Long Front of Color." In *No Respect: Intellectuals and Popular Culture*, 65–101. London: Routledge, 1989.

Rossinow, Douglas. *The Politics of Authenticity: Liberalism, Christianity, and the New Left in America.* New York: Columbia University Press, 1998.

Roszak, Theodore. *The Making of a Counter-Culture: Reflections on the Technocratic Society and Its Youthful Opposition.* New York: Doubleday, 1969.

Russell, Ross. *The Sound.* New York: Dutton, 1961.

———. "Yardbird in Lotusland: Les Souvenirs de Ross Russell sur Charlie Parker." *Jazz Hot* 255 (November 1969), 22–25.

Sanders, Ed. *Tales of Beatnik Glory.* New York: Thunder's Mouth Press, 2004.

Sargent Wood, Linda. *A More Perfect Union: Holistic Worldviews and the Transformation of American Culture After World War II.* New York: Oxford University Press, 2010.

Saul, Scott. *Freedom Is, Freedom Ain't: Jazz and the Making of the Sixties.* Cambridge, MA: Harvard University Press, 2003.

Schafer, R. Murray. *The Tuning of the World.* New York: Knopf, 1977.

Schechner, Richard. *Essays in Performance Theory, 1970–1976.* New York: Drama Book Specialists, 1977.

Seale, Bobby. *Seize the Time: The Story of the Black Panther Party and Huey P. Newton.* New York: Random House, 1970.

Seigel, Jerrold. *Bohemian Paris: Culture, Politics, and the Boundaries of Bourgeois Life, 1830–1930.* New York: Viking, 1986.

Shapiro, Nat, and Nat Hentoff, eds. *Hear Me Talkin' to Ya: The Story of Jazz As Told by the Men Who Made It.* New York: Holt, Rinehart and Winston, 1955. Reprint, New York: Dover, 1966.

Shepherd, Jean. "The Night People Vs. Creeping Meatballism." *Mad* 32 (April 1957), unpaginated.

Shoemaker, Steve. "Norman Mailer's 'White Negro:' Historical Myth or Mythical History?" *Twentieth-Century Literature* 37 (1991), 343–60.

Sinclair, John. "Artists' Worksheet 1965." In *The Collected Artists' Worksheet 1965.* Detroit: Artists' Workshop Press, 1967.

———. *Guitar Army: Street Writings/Prison Writings.* New York: Douglas Book, 1972.

Smith, Richard Candida. *Utopia and Dissent: Art, Poetry, and Politics in California*. Berkeley: University of California Press, 1995.

Solotaroff, Robert. *Down Mailer's Way*. Urbana: University of Illinois Press, 1974.

Sontag, Susan. *Against Interpretation, and Other Essays*. New York: Farrar, Straus and Giroux, 1966.

——— . *On Photography*. New York: Farrar, Straus and Giroux, 1977.

Spare, Austin Osman. *The Book of Pleasure (Self-Love): The Psychology of Ecstasy*. London, 1913.

Spieker, Sven. *The Big Archive: Art from Bureaucracy*. Cambridge, MA: MIT Press, 2008.

Steiner, George. *Real Presences*. Chicago: University of Chicago Press, 1991.

Sterne, Jonathan. *The Audible Past: Cultural Origins of Sound Reproduction*. Durham, NC: Duke University Press, 2003.

Sukenick, Ronald. *Down and In: Life in the Underground*. New York: Beech Tree Books, 1987.

Snyder, Gary. "Buddhist Anarchism." *Journal for the Protection of All Beings* 1 (1961), 10–12.

——— . "On the Road with D. T. Suzuki." In *A Zen Life: D.T. Suzuki Remembered*, edited by Masao Abe, 207–9. New York: Weatherhill, 1986.

Szalay, Michael. *Hip Figures: A Literary History of the Democratic Party*. Stanford: Stanford University Press, 2012.

Tambiah, Stanley Jeyaraja. *Magic, Science, Religion, and the Scope of Rationality*. Cambridge: Cambridge University Press, 1990.

Taylor, Billy. "Jazz in the Contemporary Marketplace: Professional and Third-Sector Strategies for the Balance of the Century." In *New Perspectives on Jazz*, edited by David N. Baker, 89–98. Washington, DC: Smithsonian Institution Press, 1990.

Taylor, Charles. *The Ethics of Authenticity*. Cambridge, MA: Harvard University Press, 1992.

Thompson, Hunter S. *Fear and Loathing in Las Vegas: A Savage Journey to the Heart of the American Dream*. New York: Random House, 1976.

Thornton, Sarah. *Club Cultures: Music, Media, and Subcultural Capital*. Hanover, NH: Wesleyan University Press, University Press of New England, 1996.

Tomlinson, Gary. *Music in Renaissance Magic*. Chicago: University of Chicago Press, 1993.

Toop, David. *Haunted Weather: Music, Silence, and Memory*. London: Serpent's Tail, 2004.

Treitler, Leo. "Orality and Literacy in the Music of the European Middle Ages." In *The Oral and the Literate in Music*, edited by Yosihiko Tokumaru and Osamu Yamaguti, 38–56. Tokyo: Academia Music, 1986.

Turner, Fred. *From Counterculture to Cyberculture: Stewart Brand, the Whole Earth Network, and the Rise of Digital Utopianism*. Chicago: University of Chicago Press, 2006.

Tyler, Bruce. "Zoot-Suit Culture and the Black Press." *Journal of American Culture* 17 (Summer 1994), 21–33.

Ulanov, Barry. "Morality and Maturity." Part 2. *Metronome* (June 1953), 20.

——— . "Morality and Maturity." Part 14. *Metronome* (June 1954), 17.

Van den Haag, Ernest. "Conspicuous Consumption of Self." *National Review*, Apr. 11, 1959, 656–58.

Von Vogt, Elizabeth. *681 Lexington Avenue: A Beat Education in New York City 1947–1954*. Wooster, OH: Ten O'Clock Press, 2008.

Votaw, Albert. "Toward a Personalist Socialist Philosophy." *politics* (January 1946), 15–16.

"The Voutians." *Life*, May 6, 1947, 129–35.

Wakefield, Dan. *New York in the 50s*. New York: Houghton Mifflin, 1992.

Watts, Alan. *Beat Zen, Square Zen, and Zen*. San Francisco: City Lights Books, 1959.

Weschler, Lawrence. *Seeing Is Forgetting the Name of the Thing One Sees: A Life of Contemporary Artist Robert Irwin*. Berkeley: University of California Press, 1982. Expanded ed., *Seeing Is Forgetting the Name of the Thing One Sees: Over Thirty Years of Conversations with Robert Irwin*, 2008.

West, Cornel. "Black Sexuality: The Taboo Subject." In *Race Matters*. Boston: Beacon Press, 1993. Reprint, 2001.

Whaley, Preston. *Blows Like a Horn: Beat Writing, Jazz, Style, and Markets in the Transformation of U.S. Culture*. Cambridge, MA: Harvard University Press, 2004.

Whitehead, Alfred North. *Process and Reality: An Essay in Cosmology*. Edited by David Ray Griffin and Donald W. Sherburne. New York: Free Press, 1929. Corrected ed., 1979.

Wickberg, Daniel. "What Is the History of Sensibilities? On Cultural Histories, New and Old" *American Historical Review*. 112, no. 3 (June 2007), 661–84.

Wilkins, Eithne. "Jazz, Surrealism, and the Doctor." *Jazz Forum* 1 (1946), 10.

Williams, Martin. *Jazz Masters in Transition, 1957–69*. New York: Da Capo Press, 1980.

Wilson, Robert Anton. *Cosmic Trigger I: Final Secret of the Illuminati*. Reno: New Falcon, 1977.

Wolfe, Bernard. *The Magic of Their Singing*. New York: Scribner, 1961.

——. *Memoirs of a Not Altogether Shy Pornographer*. New York: Doubleday, 1972.

Wolfe, Tom. "Radical Chic: That Party at Lenny's." *New York*, June 1970, 27–56.

Yale '54 [pseud.]. Letter to "Saloon Society." *Village Voice*, Mar. 11, 1959, 12.

Young, La Monte, ed. *An Anthology of Chance Operations*. Bronx, NY: La Monte Young & Jackson Mac Low, 1963.

Youngblood, Gene. *Expanded Cinema*. New York: Dutton, 1970.

Ziporyn, Evan. "Who Listens If You Care." *New Observations* 86 (1991), 25–28.

"Zombies Put Kiss of Death on 52nd St. Jazz." *Down Beat*, Feb. 25, 1946, 3.

II. Discography/Videography

Adderley, Julian "Cannonball". *The Cannonball Adderley Sextet in New York*. LP. Riverside RLP 9404, 1962.

Binns, Edward, Guy Fraumeni, and Ernest Pintoff. "This Is Marshall McLuhan: The Medium Is the Massage." 16 mm film. New York: NBC, McGraw-Hill Films, 1967.

Brooks, John Benson. "Journey to the End of the Night." Interview with David Reitman. Radio broadcast. New York: WKCR, 1970.

Close, Del, and John Brent. *How to Speak Hip*. LP. Mercury Records OCM 2205, 1959.

Davis, Miles. *Kind of Blue*. LP. Columbia CS 8163, 1959.

Dylan, Bob. *Highway 61 Revisited*. LP. Columbia CS 9189, 1965.

Gabler, Milt, and John Benson Brooks. *Avant Slant (One Plus 1 = II?): A Twelve Tone Collage*. LP. Decca DL 75018, 1968.

Gelber, Jack. *The Connection*. Directed by Shirley Clarke. Videocassette. New York: Mystic Fire Video, 1961. Reissue, 1983.

Ginsberg, Allen. *Holy Soul Jelly Roll*. CD. Rhino Word Beat R2 71693, 1994.

Hicks, Bill. *Bill Hicks Live: Satirist, Social Critic, Stand-Up Comedian*. DVD. Rykodisc, 2004.

McKuen, Rod, Buddy Collette, and Paul Gray. *Beatsville*. LP. High Fidelity R419, 1959.

Monk, Thelonious. *Monk's Music*. LP. Riverside RLP 12-9242, 1957.

——. *Thelonious Monk: The Complete Blue Note Recordings*. CD. Blue Note 30363, 1994.

——. *Thelonious Monk with John Coltrane*. CD. Riverside/Original Jazz Classics OJCCD-039-2, 1987.

Nichols, Herbie. *The Herbie Nichols Trio*. LP. Blue Note 1519, 1956.

——. *The Prophetic Herbie Nichols*. Vol. 1. 10-inch LP. Blue Note BLP 5068, 1955.

Nordine, Ken, Fred Katz, and Jim Cunningham. *Word Jazz*. LP. Dot DLP 3075, 1957.

Parker, Charlie. "Ornithology." 78 rpm. Dial 1002, 1946. Reissue, Charlie Parker, *The Complete Savoy and Dial Master Takes*, vol. 1. CD. Savoy SVY 171149, 2002.

Pennebaker, D. A., dir. Film. *Don't Look Back*. Docurama, 1967.

Tower of Power. *Tower of Power*. LP. Warner Brothers BS 2681, 1973.

III. Archival Sources

Allen Ginsberg Papers. Special Collections. Stanford University.

Hardin B. Jones Archive. Hoover Institution Library and Archives. Stanford University.

Jack Kerouac Papers. Harry Ransom Center. University of Texas at Austin.

John and Leni Sinclair Papers, 1957–2003. Bentley Historical Library. University of Michigan, Ann Arbor.

John Benson Brooks Collection. Institute of Jazz Studies Archives. Rutgers University, Newark.

Lawrence Lipton Collection. University of California, Los Angeles.

Lawrence Lipton Papers, 1940–1965. University of Southern California Rare Books and Manuscripts. Los Angeles, CA.

LeRoi Jones Collection. Lilly Library. Indiana University, Bloomington.

New Left Collection. Hoover Institution Library and Archives. Stanford University.

Norman Mailer Papers. Harry Ransom Center. University of Texas at Austin.

Ross Russell Papers. Harry Ransom Center. University of Texas at Austin.

Southern Historical Collection. Louis Round Wilson Special Collections Library. University of North Carolina at Chapel Hill.

Index